C000252944

Clark Blaise

Essays on His Works

ESSENTIAL WRITERS SERIES 44

Canada Council **Conseil des Arts**
for the Arts **du Canada**

ONTARIO ARTS COUNCIL
CONSEIL DES ARTS DE L'ONTARIO

an Ontario government agency
un organisme du gouvernement de l'Ontario

Canadä

Guernica Editions Inc. acknowledges the support of the Canada Council
for the Arts and the Ontario Arts Council. The Ontario Arts Council
is an agency of the Government of Ontario.

We acknowledge the financial support of the Government of Canada.
Nous reconnaissons l'appui financier du gouvernement du Canada.

Clark Blaise

Essays on His Works

Edited by J.R. (Tim) Struthers

**GUERNICA
EDITIONS**
TORONTO · BUFFALO · LANCASTER (U.K.)
2016

Copyright © 2016, J.R. (Tim) Struthers,
the authors and Guernica Editions Inc.
All rights reserved. The use of any part of this publication,
reproduced, transmitted in any form or by any means, electronic,
mechanical, photocopying, recording or otherwise stored in a
retrieval system, without the prior consent of the publisher is an
infringement of the copyright law.

J.R. (Tim) Struthers, editor
Michael Mirolla, general editor
Joseph Pivato, series editor
Cover and interior design: David Moratto
Front cover image: Ron Shuebrook
Guernica Editions Inc.
1569 Heritage Way, Oakville, (ON), Canada L6M 2Z7
2250 Military Road, Tonawanda, N.Y. 14150-6000 U.S.A.
www.guernicaeditions.com

Distributors:
University of Toronto Press Distribution,
5201 Dufferin Street, Toronto (ON), Canada M3H 5T8
Gazelle Book Services, White Cross Mills,
High Town, Lancaster LA1 4XS U.K.

First edition.
Printed in Canada.

Legal Deposit — First Quarter
Library of Congress Catalog Card Number: 2015949363
Library and Archives Canada Cataloguing in Publication
Clark Blaise : essays on his work / edited by J.R. (Tim)
Struthers. -- First edition.

(Essential writers series ; 44)
Issued in print and electronic formats.
ISBN 978-1-77183-111-6 (paperback).--ISBN 978-1-77183-112-3
(epub).--ISBN 978-1-77183-113-0 (mobi)

1. Blaise, Clark, 1940- --Criticism and interpretation.
I. Struthers, J.R. (Tim), 1950-, editor II. Series: Writers series
(Toronto, Ont.) ; 44

PS8553.L34Z55 2016   C813'.54   C2015-905897-X   C2015-905898-8

The cover art for this volume is derived
from a drawing by Ron Shuebrook,
Site of Discourse #1 (2013),
inspired by table talk with Will Alsop,
designer of the Sharp Centre for Design
at OCAD University in Toronto

Clark Blaise: Essays on His Works
and
Clark Blaise: The Interviews
are dedicated with gratitude to
JOHN METCALF
for the more than fifty years
he has ardently spent
creating and defining and championing
the very best in Canadian writing

Contents

The View from Seventy-Five:
Autobiographical Annex 2002–2015

Clark Blaise

I could have started this "annex" at a much earlier date, back in 1989, say, when I became Director of the International Writing Program at the University of Iowa, and the world (literally) opened to me, hosting thirty-five authors from every corner of the globe in Iowa City for three months each fall, then embarking world-wide on fund-raising and author-recruitment for the rest of the year. That was also the year my wife, Bharati Mukherjee, was offered a stupendous position at Berkeley, thus opening up the west coast to us in ways we'd never anticipated. The nine years that I served as Director of the IWP left me little time for "creative" writing, but they honed my letter-writing and grant-proposing skills.

Nevertheless, the stories in *Man and His World* were published by The Porcupine's Quill in 1992. At that time I went on an investigative trip back to village Québec to write *I Had a Father: A Post-Modern Autobiography* (1993). And an invitation from Meiji University in Tokyo to be scholar-in-residence led to *Here, There and Everywhere* (1994), a set of three lectures on American fiction, Canadian and Australian fiction, and post-modern theory. *If I Were Me,* a short novel in story form, appeared with The Porcupine's Quill in 1997.

Then in 2000 The Porcupine's Quill (with a strong editorial push by John Metcalf) published *Southern Stories*, the first of four volumes of new and selected stories (followed at about two-year intervals by *Pittsburgh Stories*, *Montreal Stories*, and *World Body*). For the introductions to those volumes I was able to call in high-powered help: for *Southern Stories* my long-ago Iowa student, Fenton Johnson (a Southerner); my one-time colleague at Skidmore College (and founding editor of *Salmagundi*), Robert Boyers, for *Pittsburgh Stories*; my long-ago student at Concordia, Peter Behrens, for *Montreal Stories*, and one of my IWP authors, the German poet and broadcaster, Michael Augustin, for *World Body*.

Or, I could have started it in 1998, the year I resigned from that prestigious Iowa position to begin research on a book-idea that had seized my imagination, the story of Sir Sandford Fleming, the father of world-wide Standard Time. Like the IWP position, it too was a kind of awakening to the world, leading me back to the nineteenth-century leviathan of steam-driven technology, scientific breakthroughs (evolution and molecular theory of matter, the telegraph, the typewriter, incandescence), and newfound artistic impatience with the status quo, starting with painting but later extending into music and literature. And it brought me back to Canada, where I spent six months on daily research at the National Archives in Ottawa, reading (I like to think) everything ever written by that gifted and restless Scottish emigrant. The struggle of Fleming to find his voice, and allies, and leverage in the world of European and American hegemonic struggles came as no surprise to this child of Manitoba and Québec. The resulting book, *Time Lord*, was published in different editions in 2000 in Canada, the United States, and Britain, then in various translations in Germany, Italy, the Netherlands, as well as China and Korea.

Finally, I could have started it in 2002, when our New York-based older son, noticing a change in his gait and appearance, went to a neurologist and received a diagnosis of myotonic muscular dystrophy, at a "classic" level. This caused me (then in San Francisco) to climb the hill up to UCSF (the medical school) to be tested. I always knew I had "a dystrophy" but it merely kept me at the low-end of normal physical activity. The same cannot be said of our son, who is now wheelchair-bound, and in rapid decline. He and his family are living in Korea, where his wife teaches at a super-progressive English-language school that their adopted daughters attend (relieved to look like everyone else in the school and the city) and our son, though in a chair, finds himself in a totally new, totally accessible city.

**

Between 2000 and 2006, The Porcupine's Quill released my four-volume new and selected stories, finishing with *World Body*. Then in 2008, Biblioasis brought out my *Selected Essays*, edited by John Metcalf and J.R. (Tim) Struthers—the easiest book I'll ever write since I was called on to do nothing but approve or dispute the changes that had been proposed, sometimes in essays that were thirty years old and long out of my concern.

At this time I was tapped to contribute a short essay for Harvard University's 1,095-page revolutionary rethinking of American literature, culturally and politically, *A New Literary History of America* (2009), edited by Greil Marcus and Werner Sollors. My assignment was to revitalize Melville's first meeting with Hawthorne, a climb up Monument Mountain in western Massachusetts (Bharati and I climbed that mountain) and the ways in which Hawthorne introduced "the power of blackness" to Melville's "romance in progress," a would-be sequel to his popular South Seas adventures, *Typee* and *Omoo*, set on a whaler. No Moby-Dick, no Ahab, just a lad coming to age amidst an interesting set of tattooed crewmen. Hawthorne introduced the power of allegory to the younger Melville. It was a great learning experience for me, and a departure from anything I'd ever written.

My subsequent new project took me by surprise. In 2004, I had published a story, "Dear Abhi," in the San Francisco journal *Zoetrope*. The story was set in contemporary California, but narrated in an Indian voice, by an unemployed Silicon Valley executive, reliving his early Calcutta memories. Over the next few years I devoted myself to more such stories, which came fluidly, mostly invented, but with rich memories that I'd obviously been storing, or mulling over, for the forty-five, then fifty years of my marriage to India, and to my wife's family, her stories, and our friends here and over there. The resulting collection, *The Meagre Tarmac*, published by Biblioasis in 2011, received gratifying attention all over Canada, and was even reviewed by Margaret Atwood in *The New York Review of Books*. I've reviewed Peggy over the years, but never thought I'd receive such attention, and in such a prominent publication.

Generous recognition came in various forms. A special issue of the journal *Short Story*, released in 2008 under the editorship of J.R. (Tim) Struthers, featured new fiction by long-time supporters of mine Margaret Atwood, Leon Rooke, and Kent Thompson, a memoir-essay by my good friend and fellow Montreal Story Teller Ray Smith, along with assorted critical work including an interview with me by the editor. In particular, I should add an appreciative note to those two Montreal universities that figured so prominently in Bharati's and my early teaching careers, McGill and Concordia, which awarded me honorary doctorates in 2004 and 2013, and to the Prime Minister's Office, which made me an Officer of the Order of Canada in 2010.

***

This year, 2015, Biblioasis is re-issuing my first novel, *Lunar Attractions*, a work portraying the missteps and adventures and dream landscape of David Greenwood (Boisvert), a very strange and enchanted boy. In 2016 or perhaps 2017, Random House Canada expects to publish *The Cruelest Gift*, the result of my self-education in the world of genetics, and a memoir of my family's struggle with myotonic muscular dystrophy, considered a "French-Canadian" disease because of the prevalence of its appearance among French-descended North Americans. (Québec, especially in the Saguenay–Lac-Saint-Jean region, hosts a great many fatal neuromuscular diseases because of its restricted gene pool. Myotonic muscular dystrophy is twenty-four times more common in Québec than in the rest of the world. My working assumption is that my father was a pre-mutational "carrier" but it is the nature of the disease to present earlier, and more seriously, in each successive generation. Usually, it is a three-generation disease.)

My final book, in this unlikely cluster of my seventy-fifth year, is again a novel, made up of two novellas and three stories, narrated by Richard (Dickie) Fréchette, a Franco-American boy born some sixty-five years ago into a poor, French-speaking, intensely Catholic (hence intensely atheistic) family in Winooski, Vermont. His older brother, Paulie, wants to be the new Kerouac, but develops the ancestral disease; their father dies from mesothelioma, strongly represented in Québec on account of unregulated asbestos mining around the town of Asbestos; and Paulie has to drop out of high school and get a job. Dickie's lifelong quest is Betsy Robitaille, the parish superstar whose French mother takes her back to Strasbourg (after her father dies, at thirty-eight) to complete her education, but Betsy calls him over. A scholarship is arranged, and so at fourteen Richard Fréchette finds himself a European schoolboy, living in a house with the girl of his dreams.

If you haven't already guessed, be careful of what you dream.

With time, though, the old Vermont community of Québec immigrants begins to assimilate, standards change, and Dickie's life, I hope, will be seen as an embodiment of how a community dissolves, and re-converges.

The book is called *Entre-Nous*. It is a record of my own reconnection with my French origins, much in the way I connected with "my" Indian origins in *The Meagre Tarmac*.

New York City
February 10, 2015

Ariel or Caliban?

Margaret Atwood

The Meagre Tarmac (2011) is the latest work of fiction by veteran story writer, novelist, essayist, and nonfiction writer Clark Blaise. Blaise has been publishing books of stories since the early 1970s, beginning with *A North American Education* (1973), which was followed by nine other collections, several of them having place names — *Southern Stories* (2000), *Pittsburgh Stories* (2001), *Montreal Stories* (2003). *The Meagre Tarmac* is a place name too, though it might not seem so at first. It alludes to the landing strips at airports — those long, thin layers of asphalt that cannot be inhabited, but nonetheless are where a number of Blaise's characters in this book secretly feel they live, or indeed what they think they resemble: embodiments of promise, dedicated to fast motion and uprooting, stretched between here and there, prone to shimmering mirages.

The title of Blaise's third collection, *Resident Alien* (1986), is also pertinent, for it describes how Blaise himself has felt all his life. Both of his parents were Canadian. His mother was a Protestant from Winnipeg, upstanding and tight-lipped and a great reader. His father was a handsome and charming *bon vivant* from Quebec — a classic travelling salesman, complete with the dubious philandering and imbibing habits such salesmen display in the jokes made about them.

The unlikely conjunction of this badly suited pair produced Blaise himself. He was born in 1940, in Fargo, North Dakota — a suitable portmanteau birthplace name for someone who would spend so much of his life covering long distances. He grew up partly in the southern United States, where he sometimes felt at home and sometimes did not. Then he was shuffled here and there by his parents, ever on the run from the financial and personal debris created by his optimistic though feckless dad. These embarrassing but fascinating situations were later recreated by Blaise in various stories, and in his memoir, *I Had a Father* (1993).

It would be almost impossible for such an upbringing to result in a person with a firm sense of a place-linked identity and an aversion to the packing and unpacking of suitcases. Much of Blaise's work has circled around questions that were a little ahead of their time when he first began investigating them, but now seem highly contemporary: Who am I? Where am I? Where do I belong? Does nationality count for anything? Am I a part of all that I have met? What airport is this anyway? A couple of other Blaise titles act as compass needles here: *The Border as Fiction* (1990) and *If I Were Me* (1997).

During his frazzled childhood Blaise attended approximately twenty-five schools, which would certainly lead to quick-wittedness and a finely honed ability to spot and classify accents and social quirks and differences. His adolescence was spent in Pittsburgh, where he was bedevilled not only by high intelligence, but by what was at first called "double-jointedness" but is now known as myotonic muscular dystrophy — an altogether more serious business that can have lethal consequences. (His party trick as a child was a demonstration of literary bendiness: he would shape his rubbery fingers into the letters of the alphabet, to the applause of some of the watching adults and no doubt to the consternation of others.)

This genetic disorder provides a limited answer to at least one of the Blaisean questions, for — as Blaise later discovered through medical research and by tracing his own family tree — it is highly prevalent among a limited group of interrelated Québécois, having been introduced to the Lac-Saint-Jean region in the eighteenth century. You want to "belong"? Fate seems to have asked him. Try belonging to this.

***

Somehow young Blaise untangled himself from the family drama sufficiently to make his way to Denison University, and then to the Iowa Writers' Workshop at a time — the early 1960s — when it was almost the only such scribe-centred game in town. There he met and married Bharati Mukherjee, who was similarly in flight, in her case from the expectations an Indian girl of her class was expected to fulfill. Clark Blaise was so in awe of her aristocratic Anglo-Indian manner that he thought of her not as "Miss Mukherjee," but as "Miss Missmukherjee."

Then, as part of Blaise's ongoing attempt to connect with his admired but rascally and elusive father, they moved to Montreal, where Mukherjee — not yet the published author who would herald the arrival of a generation of ocean-crossing Indian writers such as Pankaj Mishra and Jhumpa Lahiri, but already armed with a Ph.D. — taught at McGill. Blaise — less well equipped with degrees — was at Sir George Williams (now part of Concordia), a downtown edifice with a block-like shape. At this period of his life Blaise was taking a shot at being

Canadian: his parents were, after all, and he'd had close encounters with both kinds of relatives, the restrained English-speaking Manitobans and the much more unbuttoned Québécois. (Mukherjee was not quite so eager: she identified Canada with the British Raj, that state of unfreedom for Indians, and wept when crossing the border.)

It was a time of considerable ferment for writers in Canada. Since there was a shortage of publishing houses in the country, some writers were inventing their own. Many were involved with literary magazines, and with various forms of cultural nationalism and postcolonial self-assertion, generated by the feelings of invisibility and inferiority that were widespread also in Australia and New Zealand, among other countries. It was difficult to get a novel published in Canada — where was the sufficient readership, the larger publishers wondered. (It was in this decade that a New York publisher said to me, "Canada is death down here.")

But there were a lot of visible poets — poetry was short, and you could crank out your own chapbooks in the cellar. And there was a market of sorts for stories, on the CBC radio program *Anthology*, in other anthologies such as the ones put together for Oxford University Press by Robert Weaver, in the literary journals, and even in the odd commercial magazine. A disproportionate number of Canadian writers — Alice Munro and Mavis Gallant foremost among them — have become well known primarily through short stories, and this is the fictional form most often chosen by Clark Blaise. In the early 1970s, when publishing in Canada was expanding at a rapid rate and public readings were exploding, Blaise joined with four other writers to form the Montreal Story Teller Fiction Performance Group. But he was born under a wandering star, and it wasn't long before he set up shop in Toronto, only to head south again—eventually to lead Iowa's International Writing Program.

It was during the earlier period—Montreal in the 1960s—that I myself met Clark Blaise, for I too was a rookie teacher at Sir George. At Sir George you taught the same courses at night that you taught in the daytime, but to adult students, much more eager to learn and also to dispute. I was twenty-seven, Clark was six months my junior, and during the winter of 1967-68 we hung out together in the cafeteria in the interludes between our daily and nightly stints. Even at that tender age, Clark Blaise already knew a lot. He was like that old song "I've Been Everywhere," because he had been everywhere, or almost. In his case the song could also have been called "I've Read Everything."

Luckily he was amusing, which can cover up for a certain amount of erudition. When prodded, he would give oral samples of the several languages he already spoke or was learning (including Russian, Bengali, German, and both kinds of French), while adjusting his face and body language appropriately. He would have made a good spy, or contortionist. Imitations can verge on parodies, and some of his did. It's a risk run by those aiming for national or gender portraits, but happily it's something Blaise manages to duck in *The Meagre Tarmac*.

Anyface is also No-face, and "Who am I really?" is a recurring Blaisean question, which may be the most obvious link between Blaise himself and his *Meagre Tarmac* characters. More than ever, Blaise is probing his core question: Is it better to be Caliban, of the earth, earthly, with deeply felt territorial passions, or Ariel, of the air and rootless? Can one be both?

***

The Meagre Tarmac is a collection of eleven smart, peculiar stories—I use "peculiar" in the sense of particular and distinguishing—that are linked through time, space, and the characters who weave themselves into one another's plots. Most surprisingly for those readers who have followed Blaise's writing to date, *The Meagre Tarmac* avoids any obvious marks of autobiography.

The stories are all told by people who—like Blaise's wife, through whom he has learned much about that other culture—are Indian in origin, in one way or another. All are also puddle-jumpers: they've immigrated, to America, to Canada, to Britain; they've done well, either in Silicon Valley or in Hollywood or New York; they've immigrated back again; and in one case—that of two American adolescents whose father intends to move the family to India—they are about to *be* immigrated, against their wills.

A couple of decades ago Blaise would doubtless have been accused of "voice appropriation" on half a dozen counts, for not only are the characters all not-Blaise, they are not remotely Blaise. They're various ages, from thirteen to eighty; they're various genders and inclinations—straight male and female, gay male, bisexual female; they're various religions—Hindu, Parsi, Goan Christian (more or less). Such multiple impersonations would seem both overly ambitious and dauntingly hard to pull off, but Blaise has always had an ear for accent and a grasp of social attitude, and these talents do not fail him here. Happily for him, "voice appropriation" has been downgraded on the list of knee-jerk literary sneers, and whether you've appropriated a voice is now of much less interest than whether you've done it well.

The Meagre Tarmac's first three stories concern the Waldekar family—Vivek the father, Krithika the mother,

Jay the teenaged son, Pramila the thirteen-year-old
daughter. Vivek narrates the first story, "The Sociology
of Love." He's middle-aged, he has "succeeded" in America
— though not as much as some of his early friends — but
his life is turning to ashes. This is made more apparent
to him by the appearance at his front door of a very tall
blond Russian beauty in a skimpy T-shirt that says "*All
This and Brains, Too.*" She claims to be conducting a sociology survey of Indian success stories like himself, but
really she wants to connect with Indians for consolation,
since a classmate of Vivek's son has just dumped her in
order to marry the family's wife-of-choice back in Mumbai. "'Please, take water,'" is about all Vivek can offer in
the face of her heartbroken sniffling, as he peers at her
large breasts with their butterfly tattoo.

Vivek's own marriage was similarly arranged, and —
disrupted by America and its sexual temptations, to
which he succumbed while his wife, Krithika, was still
back in India — it has not turned out well. Krithika is
cold and resentful, fixated on her kids and their progress.
As is Vivek; for, as he says, "What else is there on this
earth, I want to ask, than safeguarding the success of
one's children?"

The next narrator, Pramila, is one of those children,
but she is a girl child, and Vivek computes success differently for her, because "'Pride is not good in a girl'."
Pramila has not been squashed flat by her father, not yet:
she delivers herself of a spirited and engaging monologue
in a perfect story called "In Her Prime." Pramila is pre-
cociously bright, a mathematical genius; she is due to go
to Stanford the next year. She is also, as her mother puts
it, "'a champion figure skater'." But unbeknownst to the
Waldekars senior, Pramila's Russian skating coach is in
the habit of sleeping with his young pupils, one after

another, and right now it is Pramila's turn, though — as she has already been molested by her older brother — this is not her first sexual encounter; nor is she resentful, because at least Borya notices her as a person. Her younger fellow pupil, Tiffy Hu, guesses, and asks her what sex is like. What Pramila thinks is, "It's like a puppy of some rough, large breed that just keeps jumping up and licking your face." What she says is, "'It makes you sleepy'."

Pramila has already learned to keep a thick wall between what she thinks and what she says, for whatever freedom she enjoys depends on secrecy. She knows a lot more about her own family than anyone else in it knows, because she's a watcher and a listener. "Sometimes it's good to be a quiet, studious, Indian daughter," she thinks. "I'm just furniture." When her father makes it known that he's moving the family back to India to "protect" her, though in reality he's fleeing the possible reappearance of his lover of long ago, Pramila finally manages an outburst. "'If you try to make me go back to India and if you stop me from going to Stanford and you try to arrange a marriage with some dusty little file clerk, I'll kill myself'," she tells Vivek.

But evidently he doesn't take this in, because in the next story Vivek is back in India, possibly arranging for the move, although his wife doesn't think he will be able to manage it so easily, now that India is booming and a man returning from America no longer has the instant prestige or indeed the high rate of exchange he once would have enjoyed. While Vivek is away, Krithika, who has long felt like "furniture" herself, has a tiny fling of her own with a Muslim grocer, thus crossing multiple borders — race, class, religion — and revealing a part of herself no one in the family has suspected. She manages to elude even the watchful Pramila, who through the eyes of Krithika is less a precocious genius than a sulky adolescent girl. We do not find out what happens to Pramila, although we would very much like to: she's a wonderful creation, caught in a perfect story.

***

No one else in the book is as young as Pramila, though all of them look back on their earlier selves — the selves they were before their encounters with the West rewarded them materially and eroded them spiritually, and in some cases embittered them. Wonder, nostalgia, and regret are in ample supply, especially among the men. For America they feel some gratitude — they have, after all, "succeeded" — but also some contempt, because Americans don't understand complexity and have, in their view, such shallow interests and such low standards of public and sexual behaviour. Mr. Dasgupta, in "Isfahan," feels outrage when casual American racial profiling hits him at JFK airport and he's roughed up as a possible terrorist. It's the gap between the brutality of the treatment and who he knows he is — *"Forbes 500! Hell, Forbes 35!"* — that particularly galls him. Many of the characters share the divided emotions of the girl visiting the Dasgupta household: "One minute she's attacking everything about India, it's all corrupt, all rotten, and everything about America is great and good and even glorious, and the next, she's weepy with nostalgia for just about everything in India that even I find appalling," says Dasgupta, who nevertheless has decided to return to the motherland.

But the further a character departs from the Indian male ideal, the more likely he or she is to have found a viable niche in the Western world. Alok, for instance, is extremely handsome and also gay, and has become an actor, even though "The one profession never mentioned and never permitted for an Indian son is anything remotely approaching the arts." Connie da Cunha, from the once-Portuguese ex-colony of Goa, has become a much-respected lesbian editor in New York, though she is then brusquely ejected when her publishing house is taken over by bean-counters, much as Goa itself was taken over by India. Back in Goa, struggling to write — at last — her own book while wondering if it's even worth doing, she reflects: "The columns she'd filled in — editor, cosmopolitan — ... are the common baggage ... of the Third World Immigrant. ... The lives of people like her seemed the endless middle of an unticketed journey."

It is Connie, too, who reflects, "It is a tight, mysterious fraternity, those who grew up with unconsummated love or complicated hate for their colonial masters." In the midst of her story, the reader has some difficulty remembering who in fact wrote it — not a middle-aged gay female, London party girl, and erstwhile New Yorker, but one of those elderly white straight males such a person would once have made offhand, derogatory jokes about. Why, in *The Meagre Tarmac*, did Blaise decide to stray so far from his usual terrain?

But again, why not? It isn't as if he hasn't been on both the giving and the receiving end of such complex transcultural exchanges. Canada/America, South/North, Quebec/English Canada, India/North America — he's familiar with the osmosis, and the resentments. Perhaps India/ North America is yet another embodiment of the push-pull drama between mother and father he's enacted so often before, with the bright, observant child — himself or Pramila — stretched between them.

Or perhaps the elegant stories in *The Meagre Tarmac* constitute a warning of sorts. Once upon a time the "colonial masters" didn't much care what those they were mastering thought of them, but now the situation is different. As so many *Tarmac* characters discover, India is different now: it's a lot richer, it has power on the world stage. The old tables are turning. Maybe the attitudes explored by Blaise will soon be subject to anxious or calculating scrutiny. Why did Vivek Waldekar never feel at home in America? What did he fail to learn, and what has America failed to learn about him? Why doesn't he want his children to marry Americans, anyway? *The Meagre Tarmac* — deft, intricate, wickedly observant — may help us find out.

Subcontinental Drift

W.H. New

Talking

New Year's Day, 1977: Clark Blaise was living in New Delhi, and by chance my wife Peggy and I met him then for the first time, the morning of our first day in India, in the lobby of Claridge's Hotel, along with Eli and Ann Mandel, who had also recently arrived. Clark was candid, gregarious, welcoming, observant: I was overdressed for the January heat. I would need to change. Yes. I would not be the only one.

Alert to irony, Clark was also ready with laughter and quick invitations. His wife — the novelist Bharati Mukherjee — was Shastri Professor that year, teaching and writing in Delhi, and our unscheduled encounter at Claridge's led a few days later to us all meeting up at their home. Later still that January I would be speaking with Clark and Eli, and with Michael Ondaatje, in Jaipur and elsewhere. But first ...

In Delhi, on our own, Peggy and I set out to see some of the city's *exotic, ordinary* sights (Connaught Circle, the Red Fort, *pashmina* sellers, a dancing bear). Noticing difference set us adrift. Behind a screen at the Delhi zoo, white tigers. On the back of an elaborately decorated bus, a slogan for the day: WORK MORE, TALK LESS, SOUND HORN. Out in the open, wreaths of marigolds, the orange petals scattering, spelling *Welcome, may you be happy.* We lurched through traffic on three wheels — the two-stroke auto-rickshaws fuming and loud — narrowly missing cows, camels, bicycles, crowds. On foot, scuffing the edge of confusion, we visited a friend from graduate school days, stumbled through local custom, and lost ourselves in the maze of the Old City till an English-speaking boy of ten led us nimbly out to a taxi.

A few days on, we'd moved to the less grand Lodi Hotel where we would be meeting with an international gathering of writers and critics. To talk, and to listen. At one late-afternoon reception, several leading Indian writers — secular journalist Khushwant Singh and left-leaning novelist Mulk Raj Anand among them — vociferously argued the politics of Indira Gandhi's current *Emergency.* Rights had been withdrawn; trade between states had been eased; beggars had been rounded up and moved to city outskirts. "Too bad you're not going to see the Real India," we were told. Not for the first time. Nor for the last.

Following the reception, several of us were invited to a party at the Blaise-Mukherjee home. Our hosts moved smoothly through the rooms, connecting visitors with friends, raw newcomers with local dignitaries. Actors, young poets, their anonymous companions. Talk swirled. Satyajit Ray was there, film fans attentive around him. So were Michael and Kim Ondaatje, Michael revisiting the subcontinent after a long absence, weighing place and custom against memories of his childhood in Ceylon (now Sri Lanka): touching ground — cautiously, not sentimentally — as though it might give way. Though I did not notice, Eli later observed that Kim was uneasy, and Ann nervous at Delhi's unfamiliarity.[1] As for Eli, he had initially closed himself off from India's seeming con-

fusion, eating omelets safely in his hotel room; only slowly was he enticed to taste (and trust) the local cuisine. A
week later he would laughingly tell us he was thinking
of writing a suite of poems called "Chicken Biryani," but
on this night he was still holding back, wondering if talk
was ever useful, across borders.

Bharati's remarkable sister Ranu (a Bombay scholar)
watched from the margin, her eyes reading everyone in
the room, as though following tales being told by body
language, motley narratives threaded through the drift
of conversation. I wondered what she was thinking about.
Maybe the unimportance of those who were seeking to
impress. Maybe the comedy of those who were parrying
gaffes and advances. Maybe the fate in store for those
who were attempting invisibility.[2] To me she was carefully polite (deferring judgment, I thought). To Eli she
said, "You will return." "She means to India," Bharati added. "She knows these things."

After an informal lunch on another day, Clark took
Ann, Peggy, Eli, and me on a short meander into his clay-
coloured Delhi neighbourhood, where the Real India — or
another face of it — was being lived in front of us. A man
with elephantiasis leaning back against makeshift
crutches. A blue-saried woman picking lice from her
small son's head. A white-saried woman flattening dung
patties, setting them out in rows on a rooftop, to dry into
fuel. Goats, pigs, scrawny chickens, lean dogs, wandering
cows. Nothing was still.

Clark greeted every person we passed, including the
scatter of wide-eyed children who giggled at the floppy-
hatted strangers. He'd also met the dozen or so men who
worked in a tiny local garment factory — a hot roomful
of treadle sewing machines where the men sat in rows,
assembling souvenir T-shirts, all printed with the names

of American football teams. I remember the staccato pulse of machinery, the thin drift of air through the open windows: the textures of contradiction. Clark taking us along to meet these men, engaging with them in a mix of English, simple Hindi, and a practised shake of the head that meant *I understand*. This was no casual encounter. We were entering one of Clark's stories: the writer as guide, taking us into experience through the rhetoric of detail. Walking us over a threshold.

Then another, and another.

These early encounters with Clark — his engagement with his immediate world, his outgoing manner, his ready acceptance of difference — were already shaping possibilities for what might follow. Including our friendship: which has crossed decades and time zones and thousands of miles, and never lost its energy. Am I telling another story here? Sewing a T-shirt that says *Bengals*, *Bills*, or *Buccaneers*? Perhaps. Clark and I have talked about short stories since, and story-making, and sometimes about the countries where Clark's stories dwell — the one called mortality; the one called desire; quilled anger at the erratic cruelties of nature; wry wonderment at creativity: how it persists.

About Politics and Proofs

Eli, Michael, and I were among the many delegates who were attending the triennial Commonwealth Literature and Language conference at Jawaharlal Nehru University that month. The Department of External Affairs (responding, it appeared later, to recommendations from Clark and Bharati) had asked all three of us before we'd left Canada to extend our stay in order to visit universities in Jaipur, Bombay (now Mumbai), Bangalore, Mysore, and Calcutta, and lecture to their faculty and students on various aspects of Canadian literature.[3] Clark would join us in Jaipur, bringing to our discussions his unique cross-border experience (Canadian heritage, Southern upbringing, Iowa marriage, more). At the time, government support for the arts was increasing in Canada (following on the recommendations of the Massey Commission in the late 1950s and the grants made possible by the Killam Family Trusts). This development coincided with support for an independent and active Canadian role in international affairs.

Plainly, Canadian activity in the arts (literature included) expressed how Canadian artists saw the world: *the* world and *their* world. Or worlds. Finding uniformity was not the intent of art, nor was criticism legislating any strict form of cultural nationalism.[4] The value of the arts mattered, intrinsically and unambiguously, partly because, internationally, while societies may be known by their trade balance or the length of their border, they are mostly judged by the creativity and behaviour of their people. By their arts.[5]

International recognition of cultural practices in Canada, it was argued at the time — even of the *existence* of cultural practices in Canada — would reconfirm around the world Canada's presence. Such recognition would serve an ancillary purpose: to help others recognize Canada's characteristic values — its principles of ethics and social organization — rather than merely accept the snowdrift stereotypes of tourist brochures.[6] I associate Clark with this politics of borders — specifically with the personal journey that informs his entire body of work, and more generally with any leap of empathy and understanding that might be said to blur a borderline.[7]

At the end of the week-long conference, with Ann, Kim, and Peggy accompanying us, Eli, Michael, and I embarked on the circuit that would take us first by plane to Jaipur (Clark travelled by bus on this first leg because airline tickets had unaccountably not been reserved for him), and into the first of many stumbles. The organizers at Jaipur University, who knew we were coming, had not been told when, so on the day we did arrive, a rush audience was assembled for us. Courtesy prevailed. We spoke. The roomful of students, perhaps uncertain of their role, asked a few tentative questions. We answered as best we could, and then the Vice-Chancellor himself, I believe, stepped in to thank us. "We in India," he intoned, "are proud of our many centuries of history and culture, and we are glad to hear that in the future Canada will have a culture too." We appreciated the quiet applause, and talked with each other, later, about how we might re-think what we had to say, and regroup. Clark shook his head in agreement, possibly hearing what had been left unsaid and what he already knew: that learning India meant first having to unlearn our dependence on home.

We took side-trips away. Looking for the real — "Avoid imitation. Avoid chic" was Eli's motto (Mandel 99) — but inevitably running into 'exotic' images, as though India were an endless film set. An elephant ride in Amber. The Lake Palace in Udaipur, glittering with crystal. The walls of the pink harem wing of Jaipur's Palace of the Winds. All real. The unsettling extravagance of numbers, the constancy of contradiction, the small moments of casual dismissal: these, too, were real. But beyond what our senses told us, something else was happening. A different (and far more elusive) reality was modifying how we would subsequently see and be seen. When we took little notice of the flute-player in the garden of the Rambagh

Palace, he opened his basket and let three cobras slither unleashed across the lawn towards us. When we reached Bombay, our lecture was cancelled because of the wind (unaccountably we'd been scheduled for Kite Day, a holiday). Outsiders, we had our place — especially in the villages, as curiosities (the blue-eyed and fair-haired most of all) — but once identified, we were set aside. Daily life spiralled on, its script ungraspable. In one village, we saw huge vats, red with cochineal, where large lengths of fabric were being dyed, then spread out on drying racks, to be hand-stamped later with figurative designs. No litter anywhere. Everything recycled and renewed. And yet. Contradiction. Discrepancy. Excrement in the gutters. Transistor radios in the hands of the village workers. The culture (do I mean *cultures*, in the plural?) at once fixed and changing, poised between *back then* and *still to come*. At Udaipur, Michael and Kim left for home. Commitments pressing, so did Ann.

On the flight between Udaipur and Bombay, Clark and Eli sat across the aisle from Peggy and me. Airborne, Clark opened his satchel and took out the proofs of his section of *Days and Nights in Calcutta*, which Doubleday would publish later that year. The two sections of the book, which he and Bharati composed separately (each recording impressions and experiences of an earlier year spent in India, 1973-74), tell of family and community: Clark eager to engage with new relationships but tripping over his distance from the everyday, Bharati recording how well she still understands such customs and also how far she has travelled from them. Each will talk about the other, reading difference: he observing an ease of recognition, she a failure to understand.

As he finished each page of proofs, Clark handed it to Eli. Eli read and passed it to me; I read next, passing pages to Peggy—all three of us engrossed. (Though Eli tried to tease Clark from time to time, pointing to something in the text and leaning across to me, as though challenging the language: "What? What?" Clark asked, till Eli wickedly grinned. I am reminded of a moment later on, in the south, in Krishnarajasagara Ecological Reserve, where a directional sign read: LOOK OUT FOR CROCODILES. I took a photograph of Eli standing beside these words, with the same grin on his face.) What was our role? Simply to read. Clark, and India, and Clark's own tumbles into India (as re-told in *Days and Nights*) were asking us to laugh at the stamped fabric of our own lives and start embracing the chaos we'd been resisting.

Passing Through

We kept moving, south by air to industrial Bangalore in the subcontinent's interior; then in a hired car to 'sleepier'[8] Mysore (where the nineteenth-century maharajah's palace, converted into a hotel, had been built to replicate the Capitol in Washington, D.C.). Night flights to coastal Madras (now Chennai) and Calcutta (now Kolkata) took us east and north; then it was back to Delhi, the circle completing. Not without interruption: the flight from Bangalore to Madras had been booked to arrive somewhat later than the connecting flight to Calcutta was scheduled to leave; the flight from Calcutta to Delhi was cancelled because weather observers in Bombay had signalled Delhi that the runways in Calcutta were too fogged in to use. Bureaucracies, hierarchies, responsibilities, order. But the talks went well: the universities already offering coursework in Canadian literature, the students interested in Laurence, Atwood, Layton, Ondaatje,

Birney ("The Bear on the Delhi Road"), eager to hear more. Clark and Eli read from their work, the students tuning in to the link between politics and irony.[9] I spoke about Lowry, and Laurence, and the ambiguities of identity and voice in an increasingly diverse world. All three of us listened to the students, their dismissal of the idea of landscape as anything more than mere backdrop, their demand for more data on gender, minorities, and class.

Everything around us here embodied India — multi-lingual translations, political debates, academic inquiries; also the actions of cricket players on the *maidans*, cumin sellers in the markets, petroleum-wealthy foreigners in flowing white robes (wearing "knuckle-sized diamonds on their fingers," wrote Eli [Mandel 103]) in the ornate lobby of the Taj in Bombay. We saw, began to absorb, *Indian* dimensions of diversity — though again and again we were told "Too bad you're not seeing the Real India." We looked for more. In Bombay we walked part way along Marine Drive, past Chaupati Beach, reading the contrast between the oily ocean refuse and the sleek new business towers at Nariman Point, where engineers and manual labourers (women, children, men, hammering rocks into roadway) were every day extending India farther into the Arabian Sea.[10] On Chamundi Hill outside Mysore, perhaps because of the heckling grey monkeys that clambered over the giant black statue of Shiva's gate-keeper, placid Nandi the bull, we were somehow drawn less to Hanuman the monkey god than to the elephant god Ganesh, remover of obstacles. In Somnathpur, at the Keshava Temple, the complexities of thirteenth-century Hoysala architecture awed us — layer on layer of carved elephants, lions, goddesses, dancers, Vishnu, Krishna, erotic friezes, medieval stone depicting stillness as illusion. Stone moved here, as though alive. Like the call of a *paan-wallah* drifting in the heavy air. Like the pungency of marigolds. In Calcutta Clark took us to meet Paritosh Sen, Bengal's leading modernist painter—who had read his Forster, and who turned to Eli, saying, "'Everything is linked to everything else ... "only connect" ...'" (Mandel 107). Clark felt at home.

He was also not at home. Except in words. In everyday experience he has lived in a geography not so much of borders as of border-crossing, inheriting pluralities. In essays and stories—those leaps of literary faith called fictions[11]—he inhabits the spaces that time and travel open to impression, configuration.

Into Language

Passing time, we sometimes tested each other's observational skills: How many different modes of travel did we see on the road in a ten-minute period? Was there ever a moment when the landscape was empty of people? Who could tell what direction we were taking? Who knew ... what each of us knew? Clark knew all the world capitals, cartography a passion. "Where's Bamako?" he might have asked, his voice puckish, artful, wily. (Did he know it came from a word meaning "River of Crocodiles," I wonder in 2013, a war disrupting Mali as I write. Perhaps he did, even then.) Possibly none of us, reading the proofs of Clark's half of *Days and Nights in Calcutta*, especially so early in our circuit round India, realized right away all that we were learning, even up in the air.

Later on, much became clear. We were being educated to Clark's India as well as our own. And when Clark asks "What is the 'real' Bombay, the real India, the real anything for a fiction writer?" (*Days and Nights* 18), his question is as literary as it is empirical, and his answer is "texture":

> Start at Nariman Point, where India comes as close in texture to America as it ever can. ... For a Westerner, there is enough unknown even on the steps of the Air-India Building, or with friends and family, and especially on the streets of any Indian city, to satisfy all his tastes for texture and design. To seek more is greed. *Bom baim, Mum bai*. Trust only texture. (*Days and Nights* 18-19)[12]

Texture is what his portion of *Days and Nights* seeks to construct and display. He records encounters with strangers, some of whom become family at a distance; observations of behaviour, some of which privileges him but also sets him aside in a special category; fears and discoveries. In Bharati's words, "fear is not an affliction; it merely is a way of ordering a confused world" (*Days and Nights* 188) — but while Clark learns to understand, he sheds naïveté only by degrees, and even then mainly through "translation" (*Days and Nights* 153). He records what he is told, repeats gossip as record. Perhaps more than anything else, he knows *telling* to be true:

> [India's] heart is in gossip, in telling tales. ... Since aversion in the joint family is impossible and psychology in the Western sense nonexistent, what replaces it is its older world image: tales. ... Nothing is left out. ... How is an outsider to understand? Literally? — certainly not. ... Indian conversation consists of a world of tales, endlessly intertwined, coy and squalid, symbolic and literal. ... (*Days and Nights* 152)

Bharati Mukherjee's half of the book adjusts perspective. In passages of documentary journalism, she explains experiential differences between social assumptions and forms of social contact in Montreal and those in Calcutta (expectations that guide shopping expeditions, or the rules that govern children's play). In tales, by contrast, she reveals (especially through *tone*, which alters how the reader receives meaning) how gossip functions to issue cautions, share reactions to uncertainty and departures from convention, and disclose the myths that underpin family history.[13] Clark speaks of how "Everything moves, simultaneously" (*Days and Nights* 32); Bharati writes of "EMBLEMS" (*Days and Nights* 167). And (with an irony drier than that of Clark's amused confessions of awkwardness), she alludes to an America "touched more by the presentation of tragedy than by tragedy itself," where "History can be dealt with in thirty-second episodes" (*Days and Nights* 168). She observes that in India, "Events have no necessary causes; behavior no inevitable motive. Things simply *are*, because that is their nature" (*Days and Nights* 168). And she tangentially adds, as though not seeing any need for confirmation, "Going to India was Clark's idea" (*Days and Nights* 168).

But just as self-effacement does not mean disengagement, so does disengagement not mean withdrawal: such is the appeal of *Days and Nights in Calcutta*, and such the lesson that we early co-traveller readers of Clark's proofs were learning to hear in its language. Listen especially to the rhythm of his first sentence, some five lines and fifty-six words long, which begins:

> Eight months later in an ancient courtyard outside the city of Baroda, in the Indian state of Gujarat, in hot, dry, still, postmonsoon October, I would be sitting barefoot,

at the card table of a bearded *sadhu* in dingy robes....
(*Days and Nights* 3)

Reading this sentence again, I am struck by the carefully constructed specificity of place and moment, shaped through the deliberate sequence of alternating prepositions (*in, outside, of, in, of, in, at, of, in*), but also by the crafted tension that undercuts the specificity, the contrast between the apparently empirical location and the *sadhu*'s non-empirical reading of Clark's fortune, the paradox created by *would be*, constructing the future in the past.

With each succeeding preposition, the specificity is pushed into a further *interior*: an interiority of both position and perspective. The reader is warned: the perceptions to follow will be conveyed through the writer's ears and eyes. But the Clark who writes these words, who at once feels pain and finds opportunity for laughter in the act of remembering (and thinking about mortality), also admits that he hears in translation: his sister-in-law Ranu is with him, turning the *sadhu*'s Marathi and Gujarati into English. All, that is, except for one phrase, which is directly conveyed in English, "'Big bank balance'" (*Days and Nights* 3).

Whether this phrase is to be heard as part of the prediction or as a request for payment is left tonally ambiguous, its irony potential, intent undisclosed. So what initially might seem to be a long and gangling sentence reads on re-examination to be remarkably economical.[14] As though unrolling a bolt of cloth, Clark's opening words put on display the strategy that his half of *Days and Nights* will follow. They create the illusion of concrete observation and in the same breath the complex reality of whatever in the culture functions intangibly.

"'Amazing'" (*Days and Nights* 3), Clark says to the *sadhu*, or to Ranu, or to both. It is his first recorded word in the book, and it, too, is ambiguous: Is the speaker deferring judgment? Is he already entering a maze of meaning? Or is he inviting the reader — the tourist-outsider-companion in the country of Blaise, suffering wonder, cauterizing pain — to follow him, from outside, *in*.

And Back Again

Days and Nights in Calcutta can be read as a postscript to "Going to India," the short story Blaise collected in his first volume, *A North American Education* (1973), or as a preface to any number of subsequent stories, but perhaps particularly those in the integrated story sequence called *The Meagre Tarmac* (2011), which tells of Indian professionals who have immigrated into the United States and of their children who have grown up there and claimed separate lives. Each has found a version of success and accommodation — and an unbalancing dissatisfaction. A wife leaves, unable to adapt; a husband grows apart, tempted by distance and accessibility; one half of a family wants to return to India while the other half insists on staying put; a child gives up one tradition but only imitates what appears to be another. Money, open sexuality, customs of food and dress: such are the determiners of what looks like power. Characters bristle, rebel, elbow their way up, drift, dwindle, shrug, concede. The word 'proper' is endlessly redefined.

"America," says Pronab, the narrator of "Man and Boy," the closing story in the collection, "gave me everything I ever wanted. But somehow, I, or America, could

not deliver on what I really needed" (*The Meagre Tarmac*
163). He adds:

> We could learn to imitate Americans, but we never
> understood "It", the essence. Back in St. Xavier's we ...
> were taught that nothing of importance in the world
> had escaped our notice. And that is true: nothing of
> value had escaped us. All that we missed was the trivia,
> the silliness — in other words, the essentials. (*The Meagre
> Tarmac* 174)

In *Days and Nights*, writing early on about his in-laws in
Calcutta, Clark had hinted at this possibility. "In infinitely flexible, tolerant, elastic India, obedience to the
father was the brittle cord. Vijay had bent it twice; he is
a tough, lonely man" (*Days and Nights* 57). The passage,
suggesting "allegory" in its reflections on Bharati and
Ranu, continues:

> The Bengali Brahmin through whom the twentieth
> century has flowed; his wife who has followed him
> everywhere but remained untouched; his daughters
> who will make contributions to knowledge as import-
> ant as his own, but who have traded something in the
> bargain — their innocence, perhaps, their *place* in some
> ongoing, creative flow. The daughters have lost their
> place in the joint family that is India; they are inherit-
> ors of their father's double vision, but the sad fact is
> that the double vision cannot be passed on. The daugh-
> ters will suffer agonies their father never knew — mod-
> ern India is in for agonies the world has never known
> — and it seems almost impossible to avoid or interfere.
> (*Days and Nights* 57)

Culminating in "Man and Boy," *The Meagre Tarmac*, with its insights into the complicated nature of success and displacement, takes the reader through a mirror version of *Days and Nights in Calcutta*. Confronting the predicaments of roots and belonging that unsettle and *de-scribe* all the characters, the sequence of stories also cumulatively probes the cultural agonies of twenty-first-century America, presented here as a second subcontinent of drift.

Throughout "Man and Boy," the narrator, Pronab, has been composing a version of his life, choosing finally to move back from America to India. At the end he meets his prospective editor, Ms. da Cunha, herself out of the conventional mainstream, a contemporary business-woman, feminist, Goanese. Summarily, she dismisses his rags-to-riches manuscript; it won't reach proofs, let alone publication. Telling him the world is no longer interested in *that* life story, she reflects on what she wants:

> "I want the part of your life before you controlled it. ... What are the real things that gnaw at you, Pronab? — that's what we never hear from immigrants, that's what we want to know. There are men from ... all over the world just like you, brilliant men, accomplished men, still nursing grievances, nursing unrequited lust, bitterly going through the motions. They carry scars; they're hollowed out. I know them. I'm one of them. We've bridged huge gaps, but parts are still missing."
> (*The Meagre Tarmac* 177)

The Real India, in short — imprinted by its own essential trivia perhaps — remains as elusive as ever here, as all 'real' identities do: lives constant and constantly changing, borders fixed and fluid, sensibilities as carapaced as convention but also vulnerable to storytelling, whether gossip and tale or scholarship and memoir. This state of in-between is Clark Blaise's subject and perennial metaphor. As readers, watching over his shoulder and listening in while conversations multiply and drift, we're invited to be companions through the precise details of personal trait that he chooses to cast as fiction,[15] the cycles of style that he shapes into narrative, and behind them, always, the politics of place and time.

Notes

1. My references to Eli are based partly on memory but primarily on his own notebook of this journey, "India: The Invisible Country," published in *Life Sentence*. Speaking of exile and home, he writes of "the tide of my own life…, the absence that is presence" (Mandel 95). Observing Ann's "nervousness" (Mandel 95), he was perhaps expressing his own; Ann was constantly reassuring him.
2. I draw the impressions in this paragraph largely from Eli's memoir, where he comments on Ranu's "sardonic laugh" (Mandel 95).
3. Partners' expenses were covered privately.
4. One concern at the time was to try to differentiate Canadian writers from those in Imperial Europe and the United States, whether arguing thematically or formally. Clark Blaise's work, like that of several other writers with cross-border experience or affiliation, represented one of many challenges to easy generalizations about a national culture.
5. As recently as 2013, Hillary Clinton, then Secretary of State for the United States, observed: "In my line of work, we often talk about the art of diplomacy as we try to make

people's lives a little better around the world. But ... art is also a tool of diplomacy.... It is a universal language in our search for common ground, an expression of our shared humanity" ("The Diplomacy of Art").

6. The Applebaum-Hébert Report, commissioned in 1980 and released in 1982, would reconfirm the cultural importance of this political decision; it recommended the establishment of Canadian Studies programs at home and further support for Canadian Studies abroad — a far-reaching policy that was soon enacted, with positive results, then arbitrarily suspended in 2012, with immediate negative reactions around the world.

7. For a more detailed discussion of borders and border fields, see my study *Borderlands: How We Talk about Canada*.

8. 'Sleepier' only by comparison. I am also alluding to the version of Mysore which is rendered as the 'sleepy' town of Malgudi in the novels of the great Indian novelist R.K. Narayan (1906-2001).

9. Eli's "First Political Speech" was a particular favourite.

10. The continuing extension of this Mumbai site is one of many signs of how the India of 1977 grew into the technologically advanced post-industrial state of 2013. In the same space of time, India's population further urbanized and more than doubled, from c. 630,000,000 to over 1,240,000,000.

11. "No writer," Blaise observes in "The Cast and the Mold," "is comfortable confronting his theme head-on; it's practically impossible to say precisely what you want to say *and* to gain the effects you want to gain. ... [B]ecause the artist's message is mindful of so many things..., the message is necessarily coded, textured, qualified. The writer trusts instead to the diligence of the reader and to time itself being on his side" (*Selected Essays* 173).

12. In context, these comments emerge from Blaise's reflection on differences between Canada and the United States: "The textures of American and Canadian life are as proximate as separate societies can be, but if fiction has eyes and ears, attention to texture will disclose the difference" (*Days and Nights* 18). For the attentive writer, Blaise goes on, even ostensible similarities will prove "as superficial as those between sugar and salt. To present texture and design without distortion was the job of fiction as I understood it. And it was the only way I had to present India. Between Canada and the United States you had to stand very close; you had to take in everything" (*Days and Nights* 18). His unstated question follows: How close can an outsider get to the "everything" of India?

13. A poem in my *Underwood Log*, alluding to Mukherjee's later *Tree Bride* trilogy (which records an Indian woman's departure for America), draws on this sensibility, reading in part: "Bharati writes: *Tara Lata is five years old and headed / deep into the forest to marry a tree–* // transpires the folk story's family history, told by one / at the end of the line ... // ... perhaps ... // ... she's wed the baobab, / the saurian shape that thunder takes // in the rain: maybe she's wrapped her arms / in epiphytes around its branches, / feeds on air and aspiration, dreams serpentine, / watches as her footprints walk away –" (65).

14. Cf. Blaise's argument, in "To Begin, To Begin," about the importance of first sentences in stories (*Selected Essays* 167-72).

15. Cf. Blaise's comment, in "On Ending Stories," about his own writing practice, his fondness for an ending that closes off a "nightmare" of a day at school "with questions about the promised land" or one that rounds off "a tale of generational conflict, sexual discovery, disillusionment (all that

stuff that won't let go of me) with a deliberately skewed vision taken from a different time and place, emphasizing the titanic force of connectedness, on the one occasion it had indisputably happened" (*Selected Essays* 178).

Works Cited

[Applebaum, Louis, and Jacques Hébert.] *Report of the Federal Cultural Policy Review Committee*. Ottawa: Information Services, Department of Communications, Government of Canada, 1982.

Birney, Earle. "The Bear on the Delhi Road." *Selected Poems 1940-1966*. Toronto: McClelland and Stewart, 1966. 14.

Blaise, Clark. "The Cast and the Mold." *Stories Plus: Canadian Stories with Authors' Commentaries*. Ed. John Metcalf. Toronto: McGraw-Hill Ryerson, 1979. 27-29. Rpt. in "How Stories Mean." *Selected Essays*. By Clark Blaise. Ed. John Metcalf and J.R. (Tim) Struthers. Windsor, ON: Biblioasis, 2008. 172-75.

-----. "Man and Boy." *The Meagre Tarmac: Stories*. Windsor, ON: Biblioasis, 2011. 163-78.

-----. "On Ending Stories." *Making It New: Contemporary Canadian Stories*. Ed. John Metcalf. Toronto: Methuen, 1982. 32-38. Rpt. in "How Stories Mean." *Selected Essays*. By Clark Blaise. Ed. John Metcalf and J.R. (Tim) Struthers. Windsor, ON: Biblioasis, 2008. 175-79.

-----. "To Begin, To Begin." *The Narrative Voice: Short Stories and Reflections by Canadian Authors*. Ed. John Metcalf. Toronto: McGraw-Hill Ryerson, 1972. 22-26. Rpt. in "How Stories Mean." *Selected Essays*. By Clark Blaise. Ed. John Metcalf and J.R. (Tim) Struthers. Windsor, ON: Biblioasis, 2008. 167-72.

Blaise, Clark, and Bharati Mukherjee. *Days and Nights in Calcutta*. Garden City, NY: Doubleday, 1977.

Clinton, Hillary. "The Diplomacy of Art." *Vanity Fair* Feb. 2013. Web. 30 Jan. 2013. <http://www.vanityfair.com/politics/2013/02/hillary-clinton-art-embassies>.

Mandel, Eli. "India: The Invisible Country[:] December 1976 to January 1977." *Life Sentence*. Toronto & Victoria: Porcépic, 1981. 91-109.

New, W.H. "22°36′N 88°24′E." *Underwood Log*. Lantzville, BC: Oolichan, 2004. 65-66.

-----. *Borderlands: How We Talk about Canada*. Vancouver: UBC P, 1998.

Clark Blaise:
The First Fifty Years, 1940–1990

Catherine Sheldrick Ross

Clark Blaise is a master of a form on the border of auto-biography and fiction — what he calls "'personal' fiction."[1] When you read the first six books (of now about twenty titles) from *A North American Education* (1973) through *Resident Alien* (1986), what is striking is the extent to which they all seem to be part of one larger, ongoing work. Ranging in form from short stories and novellas and novels to a travel memoir and autobiography, these six works create a unified Blaisean world. At the centre of each fiction is a perceiving self, engaged in remembering, inventing, imagining, and presenting the conditions of his own existence. Blaise's own life supplies many of the raw materials of place and incident, but remembered situations are transformed and reshaped anew from one story to the next.[2] Typically in the works published during the period being considered here, the stories are told in the first person by a male narrator who looks back on significant events of his life, trying to make sense of things. This narrator is always an outsider, partly because his Canadian parents are never quite assimilated into American life. Yet the most significant fact about the parents is their differences from each other. They represent the antipodes of the son's imagination. The triangle formed by the perceiving I-character and his parents is a recurring design element in this ongoing Blaisean work.

But what is the reader's experience of reading a Clark Blaise fiction? In Italo Calvino's *If on a winter's night a traveller*, readers talk about the kinds of books they would like to read — for example, "'The novels I prefer ... are those that make you feel uneasy from the very first page'" (126) — and the very next chapter is the opening chapter of just that sort of fiction. What sort of description would call forth a Clark Blaise book? Perhaps "The book I'm looking for is one that creates the texture of a life poised on the lip of a volcano" or "The books that interest me present a self constantly reinventing himself out of the givens of his own experience."

The givens cannot stand on their own, of course. Take the most incontrovertible facts of a life: time and place of birth. "I was born in Fargo, North Dakota, in 1940" is the first sentence of the autobiographical fragment "Memories of Unhousement" in *Resident Alien* (165). The flat understatedness of this beginning suggests an unselfconscious assertion of identity and belonging.[3] However, it soon becomes apparent that Blaise is never unselfconscious: sentences that sound casual are the result of deliberate craft. Identity, in particular, cannot be taken for granted but must be strenuously achieved, as Blaise suggested to Geoff Hancock:

Anyone who led a life as tenuous as I did, fraught with almost daily evidence of evanescence, is obviously going to be concerned with establishing a place and a name and an identity for himself that he could not have established in life. I did not ever have a sense of place, or belonging, in my life. So I had to create it, fabricate it, in my art. That's why my stories and novels have such a strong genealogical impulse. I don't think I have ever written anything in which I did not in some way say, "I was born in this place or that place." Or, "My mother or father or grandparents were born in this place." This is all a kind of fraud. I was born in a town that I've never seen. I moved from Fargo, North Dakota, when I was six months old, and I've never been back. (Blaise in Hancock, "Interview: Clark Blaise" 31)

The other side of things

By age fifty, Blaise had published two collections of short stories, *A North American Education* (1973) and *Tribal Justice* (1974); two novels, *Lunar Attractions* (1979) and *Lusts* (1983); one travel memoir, *Days and Nights in Calcutta* (1977); one book in which three short stories and a novella are sandwiched between autobiographical fragments, *Resident Alien* (1986); and one work of investigative journalism, *The Sorrow and the Terror: The Haunting Legacy of the Air India Tragedy* (1987). With the exception of the last book, this body of work is concerned initially with finding or inventing an identity and later with deconstructing an identity. Again and again, Blaise goes back to the essential experiences of his life and rearticulates them, reshapes them, dreams them over again.[4]

Reading the fiction and the autobiography, we are confronted by a sensibility preoccupied with interpretation. Blaise has taken on the hermeneut's task of penetrating the surface of things and revealing the secret, concealed meanings. "A writer," Blaise has told Hancock, "is always trying to suggest the other side of things" (Blaise in Hancock, "An Interview" 54). Blaise adds, "[My] stories ... tend towards a kind of confirmation and towards the discovery of that which you wanted to keep hidden, and to a kind of confirmation of what you hoped was not true" (Blaise in Hancock, "An Interview" 55). In the Blaisean world, events seem random and lives are subject to chance episodes of pain and violence. As Blaise put it in an interview with me:

> I want to write a fiction which is sufficiently broad to contain random, chaotic, accidental qualities. There's nothing more moving in fiction to me than the sense of an authentic randomness. I want to create a fiction that is sufficiently broad so that it can contain the notion of all of the accidents and contradictability that are part of life itself.[5]

But the typical Blaisean persona is driven to interpret —to find the hidden meaning in what seems like randomness, to push towards some terrifying peripeteia.

The first accident to be interpreted has to do with the mystery of birth and of origins, the theme of many of his stories. "[T]he only Canadian writer born in Fargo, North Dakota" (*Resident Alien* 165), Blaise has repeatedly explored the significance of his "accidental placement inside an emblematically Canadian family" (*Resident Alien* 175). A recurrent episode in the stories and novels is the character who has a sense in early adolescence that his identity has been tampered with in some profound way when he discovers that his family name is not what he had always supposed: not T.B. Doe but Thibidault in "The Thibidault Stories" in *A North American Education*; not Desjardins but Gardner in "The March" in *Tribal Justice*; not Porter but Carrier in *Resident Alien*. And, we might add, not Blaise but Blais.

A related mystery is his parents' apparently incongruous relationship. Blaise's French-Canadian father, Léo Roméo Blais/Blaise — furniture salesman and long-distance traveller — was handsome, extroverted, charming, and untrustworthy. Described in *Resident Alien* as one of the "dark, self-destructive, violent sociopaths" (27), this father is the prototype for the fictional fathers in Blaise's stories, the tattooed ex-boxers and wrestlers who like sexy women and flashy cars. The father represents glamorous, untamed potency. Says Blaise, "it was a legacy I wanted to claim. Myself as gipsy, as criminal, outcast" (*Resident Alien* 39). In contrast, Anne Marion Vanstone, his upright, resolute English-Canadian mother from Wawanesa, Manitoba, was one of the "[b]right, confident, assertive, informed people" (*Resident Alien* 27). The daughter of a man of substance — a prairie doctor who later became the driving force behind the Wawanesa Mutual Insurance Company — she graduated in 1927 in art from Wesley College (now the University of Winnipeg), taught school in various prairie towns, and in the early 1930s became a student of design in Dresden, Germany, often making trips to the Bauhaus in Dessau. "To me it's an extraordinary thought," said Blaise, "that she was this girl from prairie Canada in the midst of the Bauhaus studying interior design with high functional modernism" (Blaise in Ross). Fleeing Germany in 1933 when Hitler came to power, she went to Prague, then to London, and then home to Canada in 1937. Called back to Montreal to be head decorator at Eaton's, she met Léo Blais, furniture salesman on the floor. This was the accidental encounter that transformed her life and set up the tortured relationship examined in much of Blaise's fiction.

Interpreting his own life much as one would a literary text, Blaise looks for the one event that gives meaning and structure to the whole. He finds it in his parents' break-up when he was nineteen. This event is also offered as a key to interpreting his work. It accounts, he says, for the continued presence of child and adolescent characters in the fiction: "... I am dependent on a world made explicable by my mismatched parents in their desperate marriage. So long as they are together, all things are possible. ... I write from an undisclosed adult perspective at a point in time after their break-up, looking back to a time before it happened, when the [*potential*] for divorce, the *logic* for divorce, the *imperative* for divorce, was temporarily set aside" (*Resident Alien* 12). The family situation is a microcosm for the opposition of cosmic forces held perilously, for a time, in some sort of balance. The stormy relationship between his parents seems to have brought into alignment for Blaise a series of polarities: French and English; glamour and reliability; the life of the body and the life of the mind; the raw and the cooked.[6] Blaise specializes in writing about a character divided in his loyalties. This character feels pulled by the opposed forces that are personified by his mother and his father, but he withholds final commitment. In fact, the typical Blaise character is a compulsive border-crosser.

Cardinal points

Blaise himself has been a man on the move for most of his life. Most commentators on Blaise's work have remarked upon the themes of uprootedness, dislocation, and alienation, which they relate to Blaise's own experience. That move from Fargo when Blaise was six months old was the first of many: he moved thirty times by the end of the eighth grade and attended twenty-five different schools. He spent his childhood in Alabama, Georgia, and north-central Florida, later in the American midwest, Cincinnati, and Pittsburgh, but always returned to his mother's family in Winnipeg whenever his father "ran out of work, or was run out of work, or town" (*Resident Alien* 167). So more polarities were added to Blaise's experience, ready to be exploited later in the fiction and autobiography: swampy south and cold north; all-night journeys following maps across the great American desert and the homecomings; seedy disreputability and established social position. The cardinal points of the world of a Blaise story were set early.

The first was Florida. Blaise spent the years from six to ten in the swamplands of north-central Florida soaking up images of a fecund, watery world teeming with monstrous life: swamps full of alligators and primitive lungfish; social orders full of nightmarish cruelty and legendary poverty. He says, "And so the images of the unconscious were planted early and privately by the peculiar wealth of southern poverty, and I grew to believe in the coexistence, or the simultaneity, of visible and occult worlds: duplicities, masks, hidden selves, discarded languages, altered names, things not being what they seemed" (*Resident Alien* 14). Fertile, raw, unevolved, the Florida that Blaise recreates as the setting for many of his stories is a place of buzzing insects, purple-black muck, and underground lakes — it is the primitive and unhumanized.

Another cardinal point is Canada. In *Resident Alien*, Blaise recalls how his mother would tell him stories of a heroic girlhood, walking to school in North Battleford, Saskatchewan, at sixty-three below zero: "Down in musty Florida, she'd told me the story of walking on crusty snow that sounded like avalanches, of flinching from footsteps two blocks away, of tasting blood down her throat as capillaries exploded" (27). Blaise remembers coming to Canada for refuge when he was five, following an assault charge against his father in Pittsburgh, and again when he was ten, following one of his father's frequent business failures. Canada is associated with the houses of his Winnipeg grandparents and uncle: large, formal establishments with libraries and guest rooms, built for prosperous, accomplished people. Later he associated Canada with the voice of the CBC that crackled over the airwaves, speaking "of continuity, assured values, a unified voice" (*Resident Alien* 29).

In his fiction and autobiography, Blaise describes a child with an insatiable appetite for facts who is apprenticing as a polymath. Narrator David Greenwood of Blaise's first novel, *Lunar Attractions*, is typical: "Fish guides, bird guides, atlases, insect books, and star charts all fascinated me in my first ten years. I was helpless before those lists. I stayed in bed one entire summer attempting to memorize them all" (*Lunar Attractions* 13). The most important book for David Greenwood in *Lunar Attractions* (31), for Frankie Thibidault in "The Salesman's Son Grows Older" (*A North American Education* 150), and for Blaise himself in "The Voice of Unhousement" (*Resident Alien* 10) is the atlas. Starting by memorizing facts—names of countries, capitals, important geographical features—this child went on to creating his own personal mythology. Here is David Greenwood, describing his god-like power over his imagined world:

But now I was only beginning. I started with familiar continents or with the outlines of ancient empires, and I carved them into new divisions. ... Then I abandoned the familiar continents [al]together. I created countries of my own: oceans, rivers, and mountains of my own; developed their own cities and coastal towns, networks of road and rail; drew for hours with ruler and hard pencil the city maps.... Gradually these new maps replaced the old, the "real" ones, on my walls and in my affections. I could ... stare into those cities of my invention, ... watch ... as enemy bombers suddenly strafed them.... That was also me, dropping a fountain pen on my creation from a few inches above my elaborate chart. (*Lunar Attractions* 34)

It appears that Blaise the writer deals similarly with the facts of his own experience, sometimes using these facts without much change and sometimes cavalierly transforming them into new imagined patterns. Blaise went to high school in Pittsburgh, for example, and so did Norman Dyer in "Grids and Doglegs" in *Tribal Justice*, David Greenwood in *Lunar Attractions*, Richard Durgin in *Lusts*, and Phil Porter in "Identity" in *Resident Alien*. The gritty industrial landscape of Pittsburgh is the setting for a cluster of experiences represented in different ways from book to book: the retail furniture business with its insider language of the floor, markets, territory, traffic, and the road; baseball games and batting averages; sexual discovery with girls like Wanda Lusiak in *Lusts*, "the kind of girl who married early" (13); clubs for bright adolescents who get together to play chess and discuss archaeology, anthropology, and astronomy; occult signals from distant cities pulled from the airwaves by rabbit-ears and directional antennae.

An apprenticeship in writing

For Blaise, escape from Pittsburgh in 1957 came in the
form of admission to Denison University in Granville,
Ohio. While still a Geology major in his sophomore year
he took a writing course from Paul Bennett (to whom his
fifth book, *Lusts*, is dedicated). Writing "Broward Dowdy" as his last story for that writing course was decisive.
He switched his major to English and began his appren-
ticeship to the craft of writing. The same devotion once
shown in learning the names of fish, birds, and stars, he
began to give to literature: he resolved to read a book a
day, he started a book reviewing column for the weekly
student paper, he co-edited two campus literary magazines to which he contributed his own stories and poems,
and he won campus writing awards. What Blaise has
since called "[t]he luckiest move in my writing life" (*Resident Alien* 19) followed graduation from Denison, with
acceptance in 1961 to the ten-member summer writing
class in creative writing offered by Bernard Malamud at
Harvard. Blaise entered the Writers' Workshop at the
University of Iowa in February, 1962. The first day in
Iowa City he was introduced by workshop director Paul
Engle to the Calcutta writer, Bharati Mukherjee, who
had come from India to attend the Writers' Workshop
— "so formal, so proper, so beautiful, I thought of her
name as Miss Missmukherjee" (*Resident Alien* 24). In
September 1963, he married her. Blaise graduated from
Iowa in 1964 with an MFA, having written as his thesis
a short story collection called "Thibidault et fils" (Struthers, "A Checklist" 214). By the fall of 1964, Blaise seemed
to be settling into the life of an American academic and
writer: he was married, had an infant son Bart Anand,

and had started his first teaching job at the University of Wisconsin in Milwaukee.

But some unassimilated residue of Canadianness inherited from his parents realigned his life and set him on a new course that lasted for fourteen years. Later he said, "I don't know what it is that made Canada so real to me that it became a compulsion to go back to it. But in a sense I reversed the flow of history. I did something that an immigrant shouldn't do" (Blaise in Ross). Blaise came to Montreal in 1966 and remained for twelve years until 1978, the longest time he has ever stayed in one place. In the first year in Montreal he taught night classes at McGill and wrote "North America," a second version of an early novel, extant parts of which are held in manuscript in the University of Calgary collection.[7] Later he taught modern fiction and creative writing at Sir George Williams / Concordia while Bharati pursued a parallel career, teaching English at McGill and writing fiction.[8] Their second child, Bernard Sudhir, was born. Montreal, Blaise says, took "the place of my warring parents" (*Resident Alien* 30), presumably by providing a similar locus of opposites held together under pressure. The city seemed to empower Blaise as a writer: "A new kind of unforced, virtually transcribed story (new for me, at least) was begging to be written.... I'd never been so open to story, so avid for context" (*Resident Alien* 32).

Moreover, Montreal gave Blaise a sense that he had not experienced in the United States of being part of a community of writers, of what Margaret Laurence has called one's "tribe" of writers.[9] Blaise became a member of the Montreal Story Teller Fiction Performance Group, started by John Metcalf in late 1970.[10] The storytellers, consisting of Hugh Hood, John Metcalf, Clark Blaise, Ray

Smith, and Raymond Fraser, gave their first reading, Hugh Hood notes, "on a fearsomely cold afternoon in February, 1971" (Hood 12). During the five years that the group existed, they gave more than fifty readings in universities, colleges, CEGEPs, high schools, and bookstores. John Metcalf recalls the long car journeys to and from readings as "taken up with Hugh and Clark swapping baseball trivia.... Clark often detailed yet another financial reversal. On the day he told us his house had burned down, we all, I think, accepted the news as somehow unexciting and *inevitable*" (Metcalf, "Telling Tales" 24-25).

The Story Tellers promised to do their best to make their stories both interesting and related to the lives of the hearers. Blaise often read one of his Montreal stories, "Eyes," which Hugh Hood recalls "used to fascinate audiences in such settings, especially the menacing closing lines concluding, 'and your neighbours would turn upon you.' These listeners obviously appreciated the contrast between what Clark was describing, and his quiet, neat, self-contained personal appearance" (Hood 19). Further describing their reading styles, Hood notes:

> We all read rather effectively. Of the other four, the one whom I'd least have expected to be a success on the platform was Clark Blaise, but he was an amazingly persuasive reader. He insinuated his histrionics, rather than allowing you to see that he was acting the story out. He would stand there in dark, unobtrusive clothes, looking what he is, a grave, supernally intelligent artist, and enthral the audience by some recital of a series of terrific disasters, never raising his voice, but managing to chill everybody's imagination very sufficiently. (Hood 16)

Getting published

Blaise's work was first published in book form as part of Clarke, Irwin's anthology *New Canadian Writing, 1968*.[11] Blaise's "Author's Introduction" to his four stories showcased in this volume is remarkable for its apologetic tone: "It is easier to criticize these stories than to explain or defend them" (68). The piece is equally notable for the elaborate, not to say self-conscious, interpretation that Blaise provides of his own stories. For example:

> In each an adult voice of unspecified age and circumstance describes a test that he failed years earlier, and the deeper chaos that has resulted. Each narrator has struggled for enlightenment or recognition: for a living history with a meaning, a tolerant regionalism, a compromise with official power, and each has been deceived. The failure stems not from a lack of nerve or ambition or courage or even intelligence..., but rather from a sudden contact with infinity. ... These are stories ... about final visions and about men with only passing claims to promise and potency. It is the hint of unfathomable complexity, the insolent infinity that defeats our humanity, that interests me more than the delineation of individual character. (Blaise, "Author's Introduction" 68)

Blaise had been writing seriously for almost fifteen years by the time he published his first collections of stories, *A North American Education* (1973) and *Tribal Justice* (1974). These two volumes are interconnected in various complicated ways, both in terms of the history of their writing and in terms of their themes and concerns. Many of the stories in *Tribal Justice* were written considerably earlier than the stories in *A North American Education*.[12] Blaise has said that "North America," the second version of his early novel, was written in Montreal in 1966-67 and "became the Ur-manuscript to *A North American Education* and to parts of *Tribal Justice*" (Blaise in Struthers). And as he explained to John Metcalf, a single manuscript containing many of the stories in the first two books was rejected by various Canadian and American publishers, who all gave the same response: the stories were good, but too literary to be commercially successful (Metcalf, "Interview" 79). Published eventually by Doubleday Canada, the two collections never became bestsellers but were critical successes, got onto reading lists of Canadian literature courses, and established Clark Blaise as a distinguished writer of short fiction.

In these two books, central characters variously called Frankie Thibidault, Norman Dyer, and Paul Keeler present facets of the composite Blaisean character that readers have since come to recognize. This character with his Florida childhood, Pittsburgh adolescence, and Montreal adulthood looks back, with an elegiac sense of loss, at significant moments of experience. The tone of mourning can be heard, often at the end of a story, as the narrator draws attention to his awareness of "everything else around us crumbling into foolishness" (*Tribal Justice* 104). For example, "I who live in dreams have suffered something real, and reality hurts like nothing in this world" (*A North American Education* 37). Or, "I'm still a young man, but many things have gone for good" (*A North American Education* 161). The title story of *A North American Education* ends with a celebration of lost innocence: a fragile but triumphant moment of closeness with the father when the narrator

is very young. Although an offshore hurricane is ready
to strike, narrator Frankie Thibidault remembers that it
was "the best day of fishing we'd ever had, and we walked
hand in hand for the last time, talking excitedly, dodging
coconuts, power lines, and shattered glass, feeling brave
and united in the face of the storm. My father and me.
What a day it was, what a once-in-a-lifetime day it was"
(*A North American Education* 184).

The stories are not so much plots as they are arrange-
ments of materials held together by a human voice or
presence. A juxtaposition of details achieves significance
in relation to some cataclysmic and transforming event.
Many stories contrast two time periods — the time before and the time after the central character's recognition of an unnamable horror. Sometimes the character,
while still a child, is put into the role of eavesdropper or
Peeping Tom and learns something about his parents
that shakes his sense of identity. At other times, the
event triggering recognition of the terror beneath the
surface may be an encounter with the sub-human world
of insects, leeches, or lungfish — disturbing evidence of
something raw, primitive, unhumanized. In "Extractions
and Contractions," a father notices "glistening shapes
staggering from the milky foam" while he scrubs the
family's apartment and thinks, "*My child has roaches*, his
belly is teeming, full of bugs, a plague of long brown
roaches is living inside him, thriving on our neglect" (*A
North American Education* 56).

Going to India

Although the first two books deal mostly with the Florida,
Pittsburgh, and Montreal experiences, one story in *A*

North American Education points to India as a source of material — a source that becomes increasingly important in Blaise's work. "Going to India" centres on the narrator's intense uneasiness as he prepares to go to India and meet his wife's Brahmanical family. The story opens with the image of a child on a raft plunging over Niagara Falls. India, it is suggested, will involve a similar experience of terror and transformation.[13] This idea is given fuller development in Blaise's third book, *Days and Nights in Calcutta* (1977).[14] Part One written by Blaise and Part Two written by Bharati Mukherjee provide contrasting perspectives on the family's experiences spending a sabbatical year in India in 1973-74.

The shaping theme in Blaise's section of *Days and Nights* is the expectation of India as a place that turns the psyche inside out. Part One begins with details that indicate readiness for transformation. Between December 1972 and April 1973, Blaise fell on the ice and broke his left hand, his writing hand; in a moment of negligence the babysitter started a fire that burned down the family's rented house along with Clark's and Bharati's manuscripts, their furniture, Indian paintings, rugs, two thousand books, gerbils, and rows of avocado plants; and their new Volvo was destroyed in a multiple car accident. In Part Two, Bharati connects these mishaps: "Going to India was Clark's idea. I was surprised by his enthusiasm.... India, I warned, *would* be the fourth and fatal accident" (*Days and Nights* 168). Blaise, on the other hand, regarded India as a necessary test. Referring to his wish to write a novel (*Lunar Attractions*), he told John Metcalf in an interview before he left, "... I'm on my way now for a year in India to write a book that will show me I can do it now — or never" (Metcalf, "Interview" 77).

Blaise's part of *Days and Nights in Calcutta*, though

not the promised novel, itself possesses many of the earmarks of a novel: richly textured settings; a variety of different character types brought to life through telling detail; the depiction of cultural differences; an overarching design that holds in place the wealth of detail; and a perceptive centre of consciousness who registers his responses to selected events. As Blaise remarked to Barry Cameron, "... *Days and Nights* ... was a novel for me, very much a nonfiction novel, with a clear sense of myself-as-character, making me a little more naïve than I was, a little more priggish than I am, in order to, I hope, create a believable transformation of character by the end" (Blaise in Cameron 23). Blaise-as-character is shown confronting, with delight, frustration, and bafflement, the confusion and intensity of India. He says, "I felt engulfed by enough raw significance at every moment to drive me mad" (*Days and Nights* 151).

For someone with Blaise's compulsion to interpret and give shape to the raw material of experience, India presents the ultimate challenge. India, says Bharati at the beginning of her part of the book, "is full of uninterpreted episodes; there is no one to create heroes and define our sense of loss, of right and wrong, tragedy and buffoonery. Events have no necessary causes; behavior no inevitable motive. Things simply *are*, because that is their nature" (*Days and Nights* 168). But reading Blaise's part of *Days and Nights*, we are in the presence of an extremely intelligent narrator whose interpretive activity constantly strives to discover in the confusion some kind of shaped significance. Each specific detail is chosen and placed to illustrate, clarify, or explain some emotion, some aspect of Indian life. The contrast between the approaches taken by the two authors can be illustrated by an episode in the story "The World According to Hsü" in

Mukherjee's collection *Darkness*. The wife, Ratna, serves her cashew-lamb pilaf to dinner guests and begins to tell "hesitant anecdotes about pickpockets and beggars" seen on a recent holiday, but after dinner her husband, Graeme, will "shape and reshape the tropical confusion," showing slides he has taken that extract from the "chaotic greenery ... some definitive order" (Mukherjee 38).

Theme and variations

The next book was a novel, a form in which Blaise had long said he wanted to write. Not surprisingly, however, *Lunar Attractions* actually reads more like an interlocking collection of short stories centred on the same character. Narrator David Greenwood reconstructs, from an adult vantage point, the formation of his identity in terms of his relation to his parents, his response to school politics, his initiation into sexuality, and his development as a writer. So *Lunar Attractions* is, among other things, a *künstlerroman*, an account of the education of an artist. The book appeared in 1979, became a critical success, and won the fourth annual Books in Canada Award for First Novels ("Blaise of Glory" 3).[15] Readers responded to the work's rich texture and to the distinction of its prose, although some had reservations about its un-novel-like structure and what was felt to be its melodramatic plot elements. The source of the title is a poem, "Lunar Attractions," from a poetry collection by the narrator's forty-year-old female writing teacher, which contrasts the Apollonian and Dionysian poles of experience (*Lunar Attractions* 292-94). The book deepens motifs introduced in the two story collections: the focus on the sensitive child of warring parents; the presentation of a swampy Florida childhood and a gritty adolescence in a city named Palestra that closely resembles Pittsburgh; the concern with piecing together an identity; the elegiac sense that many things are gone for good; and the use of autobiographical elements. Blaise complicates this last point by stating on the acknowledgements page that "*Lunar Attractions* is fiction in the mode of autobiography, but that life was never lived."

Narrator David Greenwood/Boisvert grows up the only son of parents who to him were "not people, not personalities, but contending principles in the universe" (*Lunar Attractions* 11). The mother is a pale, genteel woman with a belief in order and civilization. The father is a dark, handsome, outgoing, philandering salesman, suited to hot sunbaked Florida and the life of the road. As an ex-boxer, he wants to make a man of his fat, asthmatic son, but the mother repudiates the violent world that the father represents: "'This is slaughter ...'" (*Lunar Attractions* 27), she cries, putting a stop to a boxing lesson. "'You'll never be like him. ... *This — these gloves —* this is all he knows. He had no chance — he used what God gave him and it brought him here. You must use *this'* — her fingers brushed my hair and gently buffed it out of my eyes — 'to get away from here and to get away from these people'" (*Lunar Attractions* 29). The son's unfulfilled yearning for his father's approval is a dominant theme introduced early. The novel opens with David Greenwood's memory of himself at the age of five, out in a boat with his father fishing on a Florida lake. What he sees, or thinks he sees, that day slices apart the placid surface of the lake and remains in his memory as an obsession:

> ... I have never completely rid it from my memory; it is the chord my imagination obsessively plays. Rising behind

> [my father] nearly as tall and thick as a tree trunk,
> hung for just an instant the gnarled, stony tail of a full-
> grown alligator. (*Lunar Attractions* 3-4)

After that moment everything changed: the narrator's father never took him fishing again and "[t]he shadow and the silence never lifted" (*Lunar Attractions* 5).

This early episode with the alligator is the first of several incidents similar in the way that David incorporates an event from his life into a fantasy world of terror and guilt. Digging in the sour purple-black Florida muck behind his house, nine-year-old David uncovers an alien "fin-headed monster" (*Lunar Attractions* 45)—a mudfish, it turns out—that he kills with his trowel and then later associates with the miscarried foetus of his baby sister. As a thirteen year old at the museum in Palestra (modelled on the Carnegie Museum of Natural History in Pittsburgh), he is fascinated and repelled by a stuffed *tableau vivant* titled *Nubian Lion, Attacking Bedouin and Camel* that seems to him to have the malignant "quality of nightmare" (*Lunar Attractions* 107). As an almost-fourteen year old, he is brought by police to the scene of the crime of transvestite Laurel/Larry Zywotko's murder and mutilation. These scenes become mental landscapes of David's attraction to the lunar nighttime world. He comes to the realization during his involvement with the Zywotko case that he is "on the side of fear, nightmare and of all unanswered things ... on the side of the caterpillars and not the butterflies, the whippoorwills and not the eagles" (*Lunar Attractions* 210).

By 1978, Blaise's twelve-year period of staying put was over. He left Montreal to become a Professor of Humanities at York University in Toronto. Then in 1980 he left Toronto, not without feelings of regret and resentment, to go to Saratoga Springs, New York, to share a position at Skidmore College with Bharati, teaching in alternate years.[16] The movements of the Blaise family over the next few years became complex and hard to follow. Between 1981 and 1985, they established a home base in Iowa City so that their sons Bart and Bernard could finish high school without the constant moves that had characterized Blaise's own growing up. Clark and Bharati alternated teaching at Skidmore and teaching in the Writers' Workshop at the University of Iowa so that until Bernie's graduation in 1985 at least one parent stayed in Iowa City. To complicate the story further, Blaise spent a semester in the fall of 1983 as a visiting lecturer in Fred Wah's integrated writing program at the David Thompson University Centre in Nelson, British Columbia. By the winter of 1984, Blaise was back in Iowa City; Bharati departed to be writer-in-residence at Emory College in Atlanta, where she wrote almost all the stories in *Darkness*. By the fall of 1985, Bharati was teaching in Montclair State, New Jersey, while Clark took his turn that fall as writer-in-residence at Emory College. In 1986 they moved, for a time, to New York City.

Well before Blaise left Toronto in 1980, he was working on his next novel, *Lusts*. He told Geoff Hancock, "I think of *Lunar Attractions* as the final work of my personal quest for identity. Hereafter I will be taking up questions very removed from autobiography, very removed from identity and locale. The novel I'm now working on has nothing to do with childhood, adolescence, or being Canadian, or French, or English" (Blaise in Hancock, "Interview: Clark Blaise" 30-31). And in an article in *Quill & Quire*, Blaise was reported as saying that his second novel was in the third person (Ryval 21). We can only assume some radical revisions were made to the text because the novel published in 1983 is essentially a first-person narrative, despite its epistolary form, and does include familiar autobiographical elements. Berkeley English Professor Rosie Chang has published a notice announcing that she is writing a biography of the late poet Rachel Isaacs (Durgin) and wants to hear from anyone with information about her. Ex-writer Richard Durgin contacts Rosie from his exile in Faridpur, Rajasthan, India, initiating a correspondence that consists of brief letters from Rosie and letters as long as thirty-five pages from Richard. The stated purpose of this correspondence is to uncover the mystery of why Rachel killed herself — the cataclysmic event that turned everything inside out for Richard and silenced him as a writer.

To provide a context for Rachel's death, Richard tells Rosie his own story, starting with his working-class childhood in Pittsburgh as a carpenter's son, continuing through his years as a scholarship student at an élite Kentucky university and his meeting with Rachel while at the Writers' Workshop at Iowa, and ending with their married life as writers in New York City. Like Blaise's earlier narrators, Richard takes an elegiac perspective on events. For example, "For most of my life I've been an accidental observer of a passing order" (*Lusts* 41). Or, "our lives are really a series of breaks, falls, bubbles, and crashes. Life refuses to assume a predictable shape. ... [I]t's not so much my day-to-day diminishment (graying, balding, sagging) as it has been a series of sharp, sudden, unforeseen breaks that brought me here" (*Lusts* 145).

As Richard tells his story, we begin to understand something of the complex attraction that drew together two people, Richard and Rachel, who were such opposites. This is Blaise's interpretation of his characters:

In *Lusts* I wanted to create something outside my experience. The character and his background are very much different from anything in my own experience. It's a totally imagined work. I had a sense of a character ... born in the centre of America — really working-class armpit America, Pittsburgh in the era of the 1940s and 1950s — who lusts for inclusion, lusts for a finer thing, lusts for just the will to lift himself into a finer, nobler world. But because of class, and because of the urgencies and hungers in his own background, he destroys just about everything he touches. // I wanted to talk about the limits, perhaps, of that kind of hunger. ... // I wanted to have the counterpoint to that character — the wife — be someone born on the rather effete rim of America who wants very much to enter the centre. The wife is someone who is born with all the privileges of America. She has been spared all the grime of America, but she then wishes to have it. So for her and for him there is kind of a tragic transection. // ... [I]t's ... a story of people fated to collide because each represents an idealization of what the other wants. (Blaise in Struthers)

Although some readers of *Lusts* have sensed the presence of Ted Hughes and Sylvia Plath or noted similarities between Richard's marriage to the eminent poet Rachel and Blaise's own marriage to Bharati, Blaise himself says that he has returned in this novel to the vexed pattern of his parents' relationship: "I've realized more and more that it's a portrait, really, of my parents ..." (Blaise in Struthers). Blaise remarks of Richard, "In a sense he's a lot like my father. That is, he's more a portrait of my father than he's a portrait of myself. In a very Americanized way. But it's the same thing, I think, that drove my father to be that kind of a violent person" (Blaise in Struthers).

A further source of interest in *Lusts* is the question of writing itself: the education of a writer; the nature of biography and autobiography; and the relation of biography to fiction. We are given samples of Rachel's autobiographical poems, Richard's autobiographical short stories, and Rosie's biography. Moreover, various characters provide comments of a literary-critical nature on their own and each other's work. We hear about Richard's fiction: his Pittsburgh-set fifties-style first novel called *Will You Be Coming out Again After Supper?* "about innocence and ambition and joining forces with the American dream" (*Lusts* 52); his sixties-style campus novel called *Smoke* about the American dream "turning to nightmare and spitting you out the bottom" (*Lusts* 52); and a lost novel, *Missing in Action*, "about a modern marriage between two decent artists, that ends tragically" (*Lusts* 50). After Rachel's death, Richard gave up writing fiction, but the account that he writes to Rosie Chang becomes the novel of redemption that he needs to write — "a novel-despite-itself" (*Lusts* 141). Rosie comments on this collaboration with Richard, saying that "the line between autobiography, biography, and fiction is a matter of emphasis that must continually be redefined: I am writing a biography of Rachel's life, incorporating your autobiography and a little of my own — and together we might be writing a novel" (*Lusts* 50).

Stories of unhousement

Blaise's sixth book, and arguably the best in the period up to 1990, gives further consideration to the boundary between autobiography and fiction. Introducing *Resident Alien*, he says: "This book is a journey into my obsessions with self and place; not just the whoness and whatness of identity, but the *whereness* of who and what I am. I call it an autobiography in tales and essay[s], though it contains some of the most thoroughly invented stories I have ever written" (2). Two so-called "autobiographical fragments," "The Voice of Unhousement" and "Memories of Unhousement," begin and end the book, enclosing the middle section made up of three short stories and a novella about the character Philip Porter / Philippe Carrier. Readers can therefore trace the shifting autobiographical and fictive forms taken by such motifs as the Florida childhood, the narrator's love for his father, or the final break-up of his parents' tortured relationship. At the same time, readers will notice many elements in Porter/Carrier's experience, such as his French Montreal Education in "North," that are totally imaginary. When I asked Clark Blaise what he could tell me about the writing of *Resident Alien*, this was the answer:

> I wanted to write about a world that was reasonably sunlit and clear and lucid from my mother's point of view and that was tortured and sick at its core from my father's point of view. I wanted to put the two together and show that it was possible in one life to live in both worlds, to have access to those worlds. I felt that as a real statement about how a segment of North America is. And I wanted also to be true to things that had died, things that had passed, things that are no more, like the South that I had known as a child, the Quebec that I had known, and the really twisted Jansenist Catholicism of the pre-René-Lévesque, pre-gentrified Montreal.

I wanted to be faithful to all of those experiences. I wanted to be faithful to a Canada that was still authoritatively British, confident. My sense of English Canada was always its confidence. I never knew a Canada that had an inferiority complex *vis-à-vis* anywhere. Especially the States. People in Canada *pitied* the States. ... So I wanted to be faithful to the fact that it was a Canada of virtue and rectitude and resolution and confidence. I wanted to get all of those things in. (Blaise in Ross)

Some portions of *Resident Alien* were written in 1983 while Blaise was teaching in the writing program at the David Thompson University Centre in Nelson, British Columbia. Because teachers were expected to produce writing each week to share with students, Blaise wrote short autobiographical pieces such as "A Passage to Canada" and "Mentors," which ended up in somewhat revised form in "The Voice of Unhousement." He also wrote the story "North" in Nelson, British Columbia, a setting that he says affected him as follows:

[A] sense of the urgency or the particularness of Montreal [came] flooding through me ... when I was sitting out there on the shores of Kootenay Lake in B.C. [laughter]. I was writing that story then and feeling very close to a world that I never knew. ... // I think I was responding sentimentally — in the good sense of 'sentimental', in the Flaubertian sense of 'sentimental' — to the realization that Montreal was now lost to me, was now taken from me. ... And I was responding to the tragedy in my life of being torn up from Canada. ... So, in a sense, I was projecting into a different character what I was going through. (Blaise in Struthers)

A short-cut to conveying the flavour of the Porter/ Carrier stories might be to talk about their titles. "South" and "North" refer to the cardinal compass points of Porter/Carrier/Blaise's journeys represented by Florida and Quebec. "Identity" is about a turning inside out that occurs when the narrator is twelve and discovers that he is not what he has always thought himself to be. When the Porter family flees Pittsburgh for Montreal in the middle of the night after his father assaults a man at work, the narrator is told that his real name is Philippe Carrier, not Philip Porter as he has always believed. The story ends with the family crossing the border into Canada and the mother's saying to her son, "'You can be anything you want to be'" (*Resident Alien* 75). "Translation" probably refers to a lot of things, among them the literal translation of Porter's autobiography, *Head Waters*, into a French edition, Carrier's *Les Sources de mémoire*, as well as the metaphoric translation of life into art and past into present.

One powerful theme in both the autobiographical and the fictional portions of *Resident Alien* is the stripping down of an identity. In "Translation," Blaise gives Porter the disease of epilepsy in order to suggest the provisional nature of our sense of self and sanity. In "Memories of Unhousement," the same theme of the precariousness of identity is suggested by the Alzheimer's disease that reduces Blaise's grandfather from the grand patriarch who built up Wawanesa Mutual to an old man who doesn't know his own name. Alzheimer's is the "family disease" (*Resident Alien* 178) that has since claimed Blaise's mother, who died in February 1987 in Winnipeg. Just as Blaise has treated his own childhood experience as emblematic of Canadian experience (*Resident Alien*

175), so he uses his family disease as emblematic of a twentieth-century experience of wiping out memory and identity, the progressive loss of both personal and cultural memory.

Blaise has not flinched from topics that are painful, and painful in a personal sense. In *The Sorrow and the Terror*, Blaise and Mukherjee collaborated on a book on the Air India tragedy of Flight 182, in which 329 people were killed by a terrorist bomb. Introducing the volume, they explained: "As Canadian immigrants ourselves, with twenty years' involvement in the Indian-immigrant life of North America, we were driven to write this book as citizens bearing witness" (*The Sorrow* ix).[17] The authors began research in January 1986, some six months after the disaster, motivated by their concern that this tragedy was being "unhoused" — treated by the Indian government as an overseas incident and considered by the Canadian government as an Indian event, despite the fact that the victims and the victimizers were Canadian citizens. The book they wrote, based in part on interviews with the bereaved families, is an elegy for the individual victims as well as an indictment of Canada's immigration policy.

What next? As he described his work in progress in 1988, two new books had been written and awaited publication and a third was in the planning stage (Blaise in Ross). According to Blaise, the two completed books differed substantially in their intended markets. "Embassy," a Graham Greene-esque adventure novel about a corrupt embassy on a Caribbean island, was ultimately abandoned as a result of Blaise's need to earn a living to help support his family. *Man and His World*, which was published by The Porcupine's Quill in 1992, he described as a tortured book of short stories whose themes included

Alzheimer's disease as well as the various dislocations and violence of the twentieth century. The third anticipated book, a novel with the working title "Brothers and Sisters," was to be about a man *sans identité*. Behind this book, said Blaise, lay the "sombre realization that a very few of us are denied an identity, and denied a community or a country or a history, that is truly our own. Now I'm a little bit more interested in the demolition of identity than I am in the establishment of identity or the painful accretion of shards of identity" (Blaise in Struthers).

Apart from the short story collection, *Man and His World* (1992), and a set of three lectures on literature, *Here, There and Everywhere* (1994), what Blaise did in fact publish in the decade following the period being considered here was a memoir, *I Had a Father: A Post-Modern Autobiography* (1993), and a novel, *If I Were Me* (1997), both of which pursue Blaise's lifelong engagement with the dilemma of identity and the writing of a life. During the decade or so after that, Blaise published his four-volume *Selected Stories* (2000-06), a new work of nonfiction about the invention of the concept of standard time, *Time Lord: The Remarkable Canadian Who Missed His Train and Changed the World* (2000), his *Selected Essays* (2008), and a new collection of interconnected stories, *The Meagre Tarmac* (2011). As Margaret Atwood put it in her review essay on *The Meagre Tarmac*, "Much of Blaise's work has circled around questions that were a little ahead of their time when he first began investigating them, but now seem highly contemporary: Who am I? Where am I? Where do I belong? Does nationality count for anything? Am I a part of all that I have met? What airport is this anyway?"

In the world of Clark Blaise, the self, caught between the poles of father and mother, French and English, the

United States and Canada, energy and order, North and South, West and East, continues to reinvent itself in works that confirm, despite all the losses, a human presence and a human voice.

Notes

1. Blaise uses this term in John Metcalf's "Interview: Clark Blaise": "I think the real reason I'm fond of 'personal' fiction is that two things move me in fiction — texture and voice. // *Texture* is detail arranged and selected and enhanced. ... By *voice* I am referring to the control, what is commonly referred to when we mention the 'world' of a certain author, the limits of probability and chance in his construction, the sanctions he leaves us for our own variations, what we sense of his own final concerns and bafflements" (78). This interview has been reprinted in John Metcalf and J.R. (Tim) Struthers, eds., *How Stories Mean* and as "Texture and Voice: An Interview with Clark Blaise" in J.R. (Tim) Struthers, ed., *Clark Blaise: The Interviews*.

2. Ann Mandel is writing about *A North American Education*, but she could be speaking of the whole Blaise canon when she says, "A rich presence of place and physicality of imagery becomes possible when the self is freed again and again from one story to the next, to see itself *there*, and then *here*, when each story is imagined *again*" (Mandel 27).

3. Readers who come upon the sentence "I was born in Fargo ..." have to consider that fewer than fifty pages earlier Blaise has made his character Philip Porter / Philippe Carrier speak slightingly of those "self-biographers who began their books with the fatal words, 'I was born ...'" (*Resident Alien* 117).

4. For Blaise's own account of his life and writing for his

first forty-five years, then a follow-up account discussing the next two decades, see "Autobiographical Essay: 1940-1984" and "Autobiographical Annex: 1985-2006" in his *Selected Essays*.

5. My interview with Blaise was conducted when he was in Guelph in November 1988 to participate in the conference "Coming of Age: John Metcalf and the Canadian Short Story" organized by J.R. (Tim) Struthers at the University of Guelph.

6. For an excellent discussion of the raw/cooked tension in Blaise's stories, see Robert Lecker, "Murals Deep in Nature: The Short Fiction of Clark Blaise."

7. The first version of "North America" — at that time entitled "The French and the Jewish War" — was written between 1962 and 1964 and destroyed one night in Iowa City in an episode described in *Resident Alien* (24). For details about the archival holdings of Clark Blaise materials at the University of Calgary, see Marlys Chevrefils, comp., *The Clark Blaise Papers*.

8. Up to 1990, Bharati Mukherjee had written five books in addition to the two that she co-authored with Clark Blaise: three novels, *The Tiger's Daughter* (1972), *Wife* (1975), and *Jasmine* (1989); and two collections of stories, *Darkness* (1985) and *The Middleman and Other Stories* (1988).

9. Commenting on the sense that Canadian writers have of being part of a tribe, Blaise said that in the United States "there's no community of writers.... That sense of a tribe of writers or a community of writers is not present. Everyone is an individual with their own career in mind. There's not a sense that you are creating the consciousness of your race" (Blaise in Ross).

10. For an account of the origin of the group, see Hugh Hood, "Trusting the Tale" (9).

11. Four of Blaise's stories were included in *New Canadian Writing, 1968*: "The Fabulous Eddie Brewster," "How I Became a Jew," "The Examination," and "Notes Beyond a History."

12. For details about the order in which the stories collected in *A North American Education* and *Tribal Justice* were actually written, see Robert Lecker, *An Other I: The Fictions of Clark Blaise* (36-37).

13. In fact, during his first visit to India in the summer of 1970, Blaise was confined to bed with hepatitis for two months of a three-month stay.

14. The title *Days and Nights in Calcutta* recalls that of Bengali film-maker Satyajit Ray's film *Days and Nights in the Forest*. In 1986, the book was reissued with a new joint epilogue by the authors, "How It All Turned Out...." A later edition, published in 1995, replaced the joint epilogue added in 1986 with a brief new prologue by Blaise and a brief new epilogue by Mukherjee.

15. In 1990, *Lunar Attractions* was reissued in a new edition featuring a new introduction by Blaise. Another edition, issued in 2015 by a different publisher, omitted Blaise's introduction.

16. Blaise has explained the reasons for moving: "Life in Toronto was simply unbearable in the late 1970s. ... It was a matter of having to choose between where I would make my home, the States, and what empowered me as a writer, which was Canada, the idea of Canada" (Blaise in Struthers). See also Mukherjee's article "An Invisible Woman" in *Saturday Night*, in which she explains that she left Toronto in anger at the racism she experienced there directed toward Indo-Canadians.

17. The title *The Sorrow and the Terror* echoes that of Marcel Ophuls' epic documentary film *The Sorrow and the Pity*, about French collaboration during World War Two with the Nazi occupation. A year after the book's original

publication, it was reissued with a different, much fuller introduction by the authors.

Works Cited

Atwood, Margaret. "Ariel or Caliban?" Rev. of *The Meagre Tarmac: Stories*, by Clark Blaise. *The New York Review of Books* 10 May 2012. Web. 14 Apr. 2014. <http://www.nybooks.com/articles/archives/2012/may/10/clark-blaise-ariel-or-caliban/>. Rpt. in *Clark Blaise: Essays on His Works*. Ed. J.R. (Tim) Struthers. Toronto: Guernica Editions, 2016. Essential Writers.

Blaise, Clark. "Author's Introduction." *New Canadian Writing, 1968: Stories by David Lewis Stein, Clark Blaise and Dave Godfrey.* Toronto & Vancouver: Clarke, Irwin, 1968. 67-68.

-----. "[Autobiographical Annex: Clark Blaise."] In "BLAISE, Clark, 1940- ." *Contemporary Authors: A Bio-Bibliographical Guide to Current Writers in Fiction, General Nonfiction, Poetry, Journalism, Drama, Motion Pictures, Television, and Other Fields.* Vol. 231. Project Ed. Julie Keppen. Farmington Hills, MI: Thomson Gale, 2005. Rpt. (rev.) as "Autobiographical Annex: 1985-2006." *Selected Essays.* By Clark Blaise. Ed. John Metcalf and J.R. (Tim) Struthers. Windsor, ON: Biblioasis, 2008. 209-21.

-----. "Clark Blaise: *1940- .*" *Contemporary Authors: Autobiography Series.* Vol. 3. Ed. Adele Sarkissian. Detroit, MI: Gale Research, 1986. 15-30. Rpt. (rev.) as "Autobiographical Essay: 1940-1984." *Selected Essays.* By Clark Blaise. Ed. John Metcalf and J.R. (Tim) Struthers. Windsor, ON: Biblioasis, 2008. 9-32.

-----. *Here, There and Everywhere.* Tokyo: Center for Intl. Programs, Meiji U, 1994. Meiji U Intl. Exchange Programs Guest Lecture Ser. 1.

-----. *I Had a Father: A Post-Modern Autobiography.* Reading, MA: Addison-Wesley, 1993. Toronto: HarperCollins, 1993.

-----. *If I Were Me: A Novel.* Erin, ON: The Porcupine's Quill, 1997. Rpt. (expanded) in *World Body.* Introd. Michael Augustin. Erin, ON: The Porcupine's Quill, 2006. Vol. 4 of *The Selected Stories of Clark Blaise.* 4 vols. 2000-06.

-----. *Lunar Attractions.* Garden City, NY: Doubleday, 1979. Toronto: Doubleday Canada, 1979. Introd. Clark Blaise. Erin, ON: The Porcupine's Quill, 1990. Sherbrooke Street 3. Windsor, ON: Biblioasis, 2015. ReSet Books.

-----. *Lusts.* Garden City, NY: Doubleday, 1983.

-----. *Man and His World.* Erin, ON: The Porcupine's Quill, 1992.

-----. *The Meagre Tarmac: Stories.* Windsor, ON: Biblioasis, 2011.

-----. "Mentors." *Canadian Literature* 101 (1984): 35-41. Rpt. in *Selected Essays.* By Clark Blaise. Ed. John Metcalf and J.R. (Tim) Struthers. Windsor, ON: Biblioasis, 2008. 33-41.

-----. *A North American Education: A Book of Short Fiction.* Toronto: Doubleday Canada, 1973.

-----. "A Passage to Canada." *Books in Canada* June-July 1985: 15-16.

-----. *Resident Alien.* Markham, ON: Penguin Books Canada, 1986.

-----. *Selected Essays.* By Clark Blaise. Ed. John Metcalf and J.R. (Tim) Struthers. Windsor, ON: Biblioasis, 2008.

-----. *The Selected Stories of Clark Blaise.* 4 vols. Erin, ON: The Porcupine's Quill, 2000-06.

-----. "Thibidault et fils." MFA thesis Iowa 1964.

-----. *Time Lord: The Remarkable Canadian Who Missed His Train, and Changed the World.* Toronto: Alfred A. Knopf Canada, 2000.

-----. *Tribal Justice.* Toronto: Doubleday Canada, 1974.

Blaise, Clark, and Bharati Mukherjee. *Days and Nights in Calcutta.* Garden City, NY: Doubleday, 1977. Rpt. with a new joint epilogue by the authors. Markham, ON: Penguin

Books Canada, 1986. Rpt. with a new prologue by Blaise and a new epilogue by Mukherjee in place of joint epilogue added in 1986. Saint Paul, MN: Hungry Mind, 1995.

-----. *The Sorrow and the Terror: The Haunting Legacy of the Air India Tragedy.* Markham, ON: Viking-Penguin, 1987. Rpt. with a new introd. by the authors. Markham, ON: Penguin Books Canada, 1988.

"Blaise of Glory." *Books in Canada* Apr. 1980: 3-4.

Calvino, Italo. *If on a winter's night a traveller.* Trans. William Weaver. Toronto: Lester & Orpen Dennys, 1981. International Fiction List.

Cameron, Barry. "A Conversation with Clark Blaise." *Essays on Canadian Writing* 23 (1982): 5-25. Rpt. as "To Create Histories Around Little Things: An Interview with Clark Blaise" in *Clark Blaise: The Interviews.* Ed. J.R. (Tim) Struthers. Toronto: Guernica Editions, 2016. Essential Writers.

Chevrefils, Marlys, comp. *The Clark Blaise Papers: First Accession and Second Accession: An Inventory of the Archive at The University of Calgary Libraries.* Ed. Jean F. Tener and Apollonia Steele. Biocritical Essay by Catherine Sheldrick Ross. Calgary: U of Calgary P, 1991.

Hancock, Geoff. "Interview: Clark Blaise on Artful Autobiography: 'I Who Live in Dreams Am Touched by Reality.'" *Books in Canada* Mar. 1979: 30-31.

-----. "An Interview with Clark Blaise." *Canadian Fiction Magazine* 34-35 (1980): 46-64. Rpt. as "Clark Blaise" in *Canadian Writers at Work: Interviews with Geoff Hancock.* By Geoff Hancock. Toronto: Oxford UP, 1987. 146-63. Rpt. as "Clear Veneer: An Interview with Clark Blaise" in *Clark Blaise: The Interviews.* Ed. J.R. (Tim) Struthers. Toronto: Guernica Editions, 2016. Essential Writers.

Hood, Hugh. "Trusting the Tale." *The Montreal Story Tellers: Memoirs, Photographs, Critical Essays.* Ed. J.R. (Tim) Struthers. Montreal: Véhicule, 1985. 7-22.

Lecker, Robert. "Murals Deep in Nature: The Short Fiction of Clark Blaise." *Essays on Canadian Writing* 23 (1982): 26-67. Rpt. as "Clark Blaise: Murals Deep in Nature" in *On the Line: Readings in the Short Fiction of Clark Blaise, John Metcalf, and Hugh Hood.* Downsview, ON: ECW, 1983. 17-58.

-----. *An Other I: The Fictions of Clark Blaise.* Toronto: ECW, 1988.

Mandel, Ann. "Useful Fictions: Legends of the Self in Roth, Blaise, Kroetsch, and Nowlan." *The Ontario Review* 3 (1975-76): 26-32.

Metcalf, John. "Interview: Clark Blaise." *Journal of Canadian Fiction* 2.4 (1973): 77-79. Rpt. in *How Stories Mean.* Ed. John Metcalf and J.R. (Tim) Struthers. Erin, ON: The Porcupine's Quill, 1993. 120-27. Critical Directions 3. Rpt. as "Texture and Voice: An Interview with Clark Blaise" in *Clark Blaise: The Interviews.* Ed. J.R. (Tim) Struthers. Toronto: Guernica Editions, 2016. Essential Writers.

-----. "Telling Tales." *The Montreal Story Tellers: Memoirs, Photographs, Critical Essays.* Ed. J.R. (Tim) Struthers. Montreal: Véhicule, 1985. 23-42.

Mukherjee, Bharati. "An Invisible Woman." *Saturday Night* Mar. 1981: 36-40.

-----. *Jasmine.* Markham, ON: Viking-Penguin, 1989.

-----. *The Middleman and Other Stories.* Markham, ON: Viking-Penguin, 1988.

-----. *The Tiger's Daughter.* Boston: Houghton Mifflin, 1972.

-----. *Wife.* Boston: Houghton Mifflin, 1975.

-----. "The World According to Hsü." *Darkness.* Markham, ON: Penguin, 1985. 37-56.

New Canadian Writing, 1968: Stories by David Lewis Stein, Clark Blaise and Dave Godfrey. Toronto & Vancouver: Clarke, Irwin, 1968.

Ross, Catherine Sheldrick. "The Sense of an Authentic Randomness: An Interview with Clark Blaise." Guelph, ON.

12 Nov. 1988. Collection of the interviewer, Catherine Sheldrick Ross. Ts. 19 pp. *Clark Blaise: The Interviews*. Ed. J.R. (Tim) Struthers. Toronto: Guernica Editions, 2016. Essential Writers. Print.

Ryval, Michael. "Confessions of a Reluctant Patriot." *Quill & Quire* Apr. 1979: 14, 21.

Struthers, J.R. (Tim). "A Checklist of Works by the Montreal Story Tellers." *The Montreal Story Tellers: Memoirs, Photographs, Critical Essays*. Ed. J.R. (Tim) Struthers. Montreal: Véhicule, 1985. 214-21.

-----. "Expressions of Your Breath: An Interview with Clark Blaise." Guelph, ON. 12 Nov. 1988. Collection of the interviewer, J.R. (Tim) Struthers. Ts. 28 pp. *Clark Blaise: The Interviews*. Ed. J.R. (Tim) Struthers. Toronto: Guernica Editions, 2016. Essential Writers. Print.

Light Through a Prism:
Clark Blaise's *I Had a Father:*
A Post-Modern Autobiography

Sandra Sabatini

Observe, observe perpetually.
— Virginia Woolf, "Montaigne" (qtd. in Bakewell 37)

The title of Clark Blaise's *I Had a Father* states what most would consider obvious. Everyone has a father of some kind, even if he is a sperm donor. But in times when notions of paternity and masculinity are challenged with such frequency — what is the necessity of the father when a turkey baster will work where required? — Blaise examines the artifacts and trace of his own father as though his gaze is the light and his father is the prism. Meaning spangles out and hits everything in its path, illuminating, colouring, obfuscating, and working practical magic on the stuff of memory. If the father is absent, Blaise says, the son will construct him. Not necessarily out of whole cloth, but out of memory, testimony, photographs, songs, locations, scents. Whatever comes to hand will be enlisted in the construct, so vital to identity and curiosity, so vital to the man and the writer that Blaise will become and the father and husband and friend and colleague that he will choose to be.

Blaise calls the work "A Post-Modern Autobiography"

and he is blunt and delightful about the ways the book resists classification, self-reflexively inquiring both of his readers and of himself whether he has written a book about his father, "born Léo Roméo Blais in 1905, in Lac-Mégantic, Québec" (ix), or about himself. It turns out to be both, as he states, without so much as a spoiler alert. In an interview with J.R. (Tim) Struthers, Blaise discloses the book's impetus: he is "trying to deal with the genetic impulse of a son who never *really* knew his father, nevertheless growing older and realizing that he is enacting the father's life almost helplessly" (Blaise in Struthers 34-35). His father is a mystery. Blaise confirms that his "fascination" with his father is "really an exploration of [his] own sense of incompleteness" (ix). His incompleteness, his sense of being unmoored, without identity, without country, his searching throughout childhood for a next potential hometown are themes that carry the book, discovered in a specificity of detail that calls to mind Montaigne, and, more precisely, Sarah Bakewell on Montaigne.

Bakewell's biography of Montaigne depicts a precursor to Blaise's detailed and persistent inquiry and the palpable impact of the writer's work:

In place of abstract answers, Montaigne tells us what *he* did in each case, and what it felt like when he was doing it. ... Exploring such phenomena over twenty years, Montaigne questioned himself again and again, and built up a picture of himself—a self-portrait in constant motion, so vivid that it practically gets up off the page and sits down next to you to read over your shoulder. ... [T]o read Montaigne is to experience a series of shocks of familiarity which make the centuries between him and the twenty-first-century reader collapse to nothing. (5)

Blaise is deeply engaged in constructing both a portrait and a self-portrait "in constant motion." From the first chapter, I experienced "shocks of familiarity" in the particularity of the memories conjured and rendered in this book. I felt the impact as soon as I read the front cover. The structure of the title itself is compelling — the title's declaration of ownership — *I* — of the summoning of the past — *Had* — of the significance and insignificance of the relationship — *a* — (the indefinite article) — *Father* — is so nuanced and deliberate. It is, on the surface, a simple declarative and yet the title elicits from me an immediate response.

Blaise begins with absences and gaps, so provocative. He doesn't know if his father "was sane or disturbed, a victim or a killer" (x-xi), or whether he is his father's "only child" (xi). He begins with what he does not know about his father and the reason this speaks to me so strongly is because I know about that beginning and I know about those gaps.

Clark Blaise had a father, but I did not. Or, rather, I had one for six years and then he died. He died suddenly and dramatically — electrocution and a catastrophic fall that he survived for a few tortured days. I went from rolling around on the red vinyl back seat of our giant Chrysler, while my dad took sharp corners on the way to the grocery store to increase the hilarity, to knowing how to sit still and quiet in an abruptly hushed house.

Here's what I remember. The hardwood floors were polished. My aunt, smoking, was giving my mother, also smoking, a home permanent in our dining room so that, I guess, my mother's hair would look nice for the visitation. Pink sponge curlers and hair permanent solution, sweetened ammonia dripping down my mother's plastic cape and toward her gin and tonic.

But my mother never drank gin and tonic.

I could smell the styling chemicals and the floor wax because I played at her feet, a chronic nuisance. The electric buffer stood unplugged and unstored in the corner of the room with the sewing patterns and fragments of pinking-sheared fabric. On my bed upstairs my mother had left a new outfit, red trousers and a matching turtleneck, to distract me from the sorrow she must have thought I felt. The house was full of whispering people who were related to me but whom I had never met. I remember their long-nosed sympathy and my own confusion. I was not sorrowful. I did not feel like a suitable object of pity. I played unchecked and unscolded with whatever took my fancy. Everyone was distracted. My mother, who had never written a cheque or done groceries, had to plan a funeral.

Everyone smoked. My brothers picked up the butts, the ones without red lipstick, and finished them off in the tall grass in the unmown back yard.

***

But I'm inventing some of this. Blaise gives me license. A book like his invites a strong personal response and thus my own brief "attempt to fashion continuity from fragments" (x). Fragments of ice hitting stemware as though someone was about to make a speech, fragments of conversation, fragrance of floor wax and cigarettes.

Here is Blaise's description of his father's trace, provoked in 1984 when Blaise took a position as writer-in-residence at Emory University in Atlanta and moved into a furnished apartment there:

> [T]he person who had preceded me in that apartment had left his traces in the air, on the walls, and in cigarette

burns on the porcelain rims of the lavatory—the toilet tank lid and the bathtub. It was as though my father was trying to reach me. I suddenly remembered the thin coat of talcum powder he left on the floor, the *Readers' Digest* whose pages would wrinkle and stick in the condensation water next to the yellow box of Serutan on the lid of the tank. I remembered how he prepared the regal acts of shaving in the morning or of settling back in the tub with a tumbler of Scotch and a cigarette, pinching it so it wouldn't roll into the water. He would linger in the tub till the Scotch was finished and his wet fingers had dissolved the Herbert Taryton. The residue of tobacco strands, pubic hair, and talcum powder would be left for the next bather to clean up. The wreckage of the bathroom was a kind of male statement—the lion at ease—but also a sign of his retreat from us. In the period of my growing-up, my father communicated more through his leavings than his presence. He left an eloquent trail. (3-4)

I feel both the ghostliness and the intimacy of this description: the necessary laxative, Serutan, the pubic hair, the leonine sense of dominion (someone else will clean up the father's mess), the stained fixtures, the *Readers' Digest*—that ubiquitous source of condensed information that Léo Blais could fold into his conversations, supporting his claims to a distinguished and formal education. Blaise excavates a sense of his father from the evidence he left behind. He can come to no conclusions. Instead, he sees himself as the cipher; the mystery of the father transferred to Blaise himself as he, in middle age, feels only his father's "encoding" (10) in opposition to the influence of the mother with whom he shared so many qualities and interests. But more on that later.

Léo Blais was a boxer. The metaphors abound and

Blaise holds each one up to scrutiny. His father was a boxer whose face he could never touch, who could easily weave away from his son, an image that reinforces the sense that the son is always seeking and never reaching the father. Blaise admits to being a participant in "a ragged little convention" (6) of adult sons reconciling with dying fathers, but the truth is that there is no reconciliation here: that the perpetual lack of the father supports and indeed insists on the postmodernity of the quest. Always seeking to understand, Blaise can only come to terms with the facts and the imaginings of his father's life as he perceives them and he is frank about confessing that his understanding is severely limited — his father "died with his stories intact, and if I am to bring him back I must reconstruct him from smoke" (12).

What a relief it would be to haul our neglectful, dead parents into the court of our scrutiny. To hear their stories and finally to have every detail of our childish frights and sorrows, confusions and rejections, at hand in order to ask "Why this?" and "Why this?" and "Why this, as well?" As if satisfaction would lie there. For Blaise proves that it does not. He can't help seeking, though. His father's example, his life and death, "must mean something" to Blaise, if only because, as Blaise says, "he's the only man with my genes who's been my age" (12). The statement reveals Blaise's concern with aging and with the connection to the male line of his family. How will he learn how to grow old? How will he know how to meet physical and intellectual decline if not by way of his genetic predecessor? All of these questions remain unanswered, but the process of discovering the parameters of the mystery is revealed in language, in characterization, in incidents divulging the depth of the narrator's curiosity and need. And that need resonates.

That's the power of the quest: to know the father is to know, for Blaise, the self. He writes about a party at which he asks another guest where she is from (34). He admits the question ought to be "Who are you?" (35). Pushing further, he reveals that what he's really asking is "Who am I?" (35). Or, as it occurred to me, "Who am I in relation to you?" This loss of the father underscores a fundamental loss of self against which we fatherless are always testing the bounds of identity. I wonder what kind of woman I would have become if my father had lived. He was old already when he died. Sixty-one and more than twenty years older than my mother. The chances are good that even if his accident had not killed him, his smoking and drinking might have shortened his life anyway. If I could sit him down, along with my chain-smoking mother, and ask how they could both be so frivolous with their lives, robbing me of my parents, of their solidness, of their welcome, of my own genealogy, which I will now never know, would I be satisfied with the answer? They had most likely done the best they could. And what's the point of hearing that? I've said it myself to my own children. They don't believe me and I'm alive to insist on it.

What would Blaise's own sons say about the fact that their parents moved house twenty-six times in the first twenty-nine years of marriage (110)—a significant improvement on Blaise's father's rate? Blaise says his father "valued no friendships or commitments, denied his family, expressed no nostalgia, held nothing sacred," so that Blaise himself is now "a man of revisitations, sentiment, heritage, obligation, and letters. I've let nothing, and no one, go" (31). It's a great way to rebel. Blaise chooses to become a solid citizen, father, husband in opposition to, rebellion against, the example set for him.

The consistent trope of the autobiography centres on maps (boundaries, territories, paths) and how these shape identities. Blaise considers his father's ability to memorize maps, an ability born of necessity for a salesman who learned "proper American English" (30) by singing Bing Crosby songs. Blaise writes:

> He memorized maps, the same way I did. Like a local bus station announcer, he could rattle off the town names in order between any two cities on any southern highway. He knew the secret things that weren't on the maps but were vital in the South — speed traps, speakeasies in the dry counties, one-armed bandits in the back of certain gas stations. My world lay folded on my lap in two dimensions. His was the road and the life on the shoulders, unrolling under the hood ornament, in three dimensions. (18)

Blaise returns to notions of maps and boundaries throughout the book, but what strikes me in this passage is the blatant admiration. Blatant and, for me, a bit confusing.

Blaise sees his father as savvy, having a street knowledge that can't be measured, a rascal who knows his way around speakeasies and speed traps, who knows the road. Yet this is a representation that Blaise both sets up and tears down. His father is an adulterer, an itinerant liar, whose shady past, failures, marriages, business ventures are mined for meaning. But here it's evident that Léo's knowledge comes from lived experience; Blaise's is less admirable because it comes from books and two-dimensional maps. At least, this is what he seems to be saying. And here is where my sense of engagement falters. The conflation of his father's identity with his own in photographs, in the telling of lies (through fiction or autobiography for Blaise), in the love of maps and geography is understandable, but at times I find myself resistant to the characterization of the father as an admirable man.

I admit this resistance may come from my life as a mother. A fatherless and then motherless mother, an orphan really, who feels the longing for a father, but who knows intimately the potency of the mother.

And the fact is, I wanted to hear more about Blaise's mother. In the unpublished essay "The Zen of Writing," Blaise reminisces how at age ten in a Springfield, Missouri schoolyard he would occupy himself at recess by breaking open rocks to find hidden veins of quartz. The metaphor illustrates the artist's need to find what's hidden. He considers how "Every rock contained a story." What compels him is not what is manifest. Blaise considers his mother and her life to be fully known. He is candid about her influence on him: she went to college and lived in Continental Europe and then England, training to become an artist, before returning to live in Montreal. There she made an inexplicably bad marriage to Léo Blais, an uneducated French-Canadian furniture salesman who claimed to have been educated at Harvard, the Sorbonne, and Tufts Medical School, and who had already been divorced twice — all things she discovered only after their marriage. Her commitment to her young son and her endurance throughout the difficulties of marriage to Léo Blais are touched on in *I Had a Father*, but these self-prescribed limits of the book made me seek out other writing by Blaise that engages more fully with his mother and considers the ways she supported him and inspired him.

Blaise's mother was a woman whose descriptions of meals could make Blaise's "mouth water for something [he had] never tasted" ("Tenants of Unhousement" 84). His mother "was the progressive; more adventurous and more independent than the cautious Manitoba family that formed her" ("Tenants of Unhousement" 83). Her language grounded him; she took him as a child to meet "the only writer in central Florida" (105), Marjorie Kinnan Rawlings, the author of *The Yearling*. While Blaise admits to admiring his mother and her ability to tell stories ("Tenants of Unhousement" 85), she does not inspire the same heroic sensibility or the same artistic response that his father does. Indeed, although his mother proved a secure, constant influence, Blaise declares that her openness robbed him of the ability to write about her, at least in his fiction. She lacked mystery. He explains, "My mother told me everything about herself. I think there's really nothing from her life that she left secret. It was all laid out for me. I had all the tools, all the details. She was a wonderful storyteller, and she told me all the stories of her life" (Blaise in Struthers 31).

By contrast, Blaise adds, "My father told me *nothing*, nothing at all, including [his] earlier marriages, his name, his upbringing" (Blaise in Struthers 31). Blaise states that he could write about his father because his father's motivations and decisions, his affairs, his criminal record, his rum-running, all remained a mystery. His father, as *terra incognita*, remains not only the undiscovered country, but the undiscoverable country whose secrets and ambiguities will provide inspiration and impetus for Blaise's own creative life. On the other hand, Blaise's mother, by being trustworthy and devoted, loses mystery and, therefore, influence. It hardly seems fair.

In *I Had a Father*, Blaise characterizes his mother's intellect as "high-mediocre" and his father as "touched with genius" (74). A genius liar, who "lied to everyone about his origins" (50) with lies both tacit and explicit, is the one to inspire both longing and admiration. The conflicting sentiments underscore for me the notion that we seek what we lack. As a boxer, his father was a superb physical specimen and would not have suffered a single day, as Blaise did, from being "the classic schoolyard punching bag" ("A Delayed Disclosure" 199). Léo's physicality is eloquent, but he is, for all that, physical yet absent. And this absence makes him an object of desire in a way that the very present mother is not.

Blaise had his mother with him throughout his maturing and into his middle age. She contained as much as she could the chaos of the family's itinerant life and provided what seems to me to be consistent attention and care. When Blaise was ill as a boy with *amytonia congenita*, a form of muscular dystrophy that went undiagnosed, his mother was his saviour. He describes her care of him: "She read to me, even though I didn't respond. She took me to doctors, finally finding one who prescribed a new wartime thyroid extract" ("A Delayed Disclosure" 199). According to Blaise, "My mother didn't give up" ("A Delayed Disclosure" 199). He describes her as an artist, as the one who taught him values, who gave birth to him "at a grandmother's age" ("A Delayed Disclosure" 197) of thirty-seven and barely survived the pregnancy. Indeed in many respects her commitment to her family came at a cost.

Blaise asserts that his mother survived her pregnancy because he "was the first," born "before [his] mother had built up antibodies against [his] father" ("A Delayed Disclosure" 197). His parents were fundamentally incompatible at even the cellular level in their competing Rh factor blood types. But it took his mother a long time to be able to withdraw from the devastation of the marriage, to move into a rooming house, and, finally, to escape to her family in Canada. *I Had a Father* focusses on Blaise's father, but haunting every page is Blaise's mother, the opposite essential whose presence shaped him as much as or more than his often absent father.

Blaise had a father and what a father he was. A man of maps and cigarettes and lies. A man whose trace provokes years of memories. Léo, as Blaise recalls him, is more an anti-father who lived on the margins of stability and who rarely succeeded at his endeavours. But his lies won him his wife and seemed to keep her uninformed of his various lovers through decades of marriage. He must have questioned what the good would be of plain dealing when lying won him most of what he achieved.

In "Tenants of Unhousement," Blaise agrees with his mother's characterization of Léo as a sociopath (94). Léo was also a man of rage, a rage for which there is little direct evidence apart from one dramatic explosion, but many references. When Blaise does research for the book, he meets a cop from Manchester, New Hampshire who knew his father and who said he "'musta bin a real bastid'" ("A Delayed Disclosure" 201). As well, Blaise discusses his father with a cousin who tells him she was warned as a child "'not to hang around Uncle Léo too much'" ("A Delayed Disclosure" 201). She refuses to explain, only saying that "'[a] boy shouldn't know bad things about his father'" ("A Delayed Disclosure" 201). But Blaise wants to know about his father. The bad and the good.

And though Blaise was in his fifties at the time of that conversation, his cousin refers to him as a boy. This is important for I think Blaise sees himself as a boy and always will see himself that way in relation to his father. This is the book's fulcrum. How do you face all that you know and intuit about a person whose life, decisions, habits, turns of phrase, whose ability to beguile and cajole and carve an unusual and peripatetic life for himself, had such impact and influence on you? Blaise refers to Québec as "a blank for me to fill in" (29), but it is not only Québec that is a void to him. These are his questions: How do you come to know the father? How do you contain him within yourself?

The answer is you don't. There are mysteries and in some cases there are mysteries that break you.

***

Blaise is candid about the break-up of his parents' marriage when he was in college. He describes himself as being

> ... There and not-There, a migratory bird. The night that my father attacked my mother, tearing up the contract of their marriage by breaking her nose and blackening both eyes, I was sprawled on a half-sofa in an upstairs room, reading. That was the nature of my breakdown: I suddenly couldn't go on with my college life, my geology studies, my labs, my fraternity, all the social futilities. I couldn't even get off the couch. She came to the door, a few minutes after the garage door slammed and said, "I must have walked into something."
>
> Life without my parents' unspoken, unacted erotic violence is literally unimaginable to me — that is, not available to my imagination — which guarantees I'll always be a son and not a husband or a father in everything I write. Life after their divorce seems lacking in pain and moral authority. In order to imagine stories, I need the shelter of their marriage, their complications

> and polarities. Within their marriage, within the world
> of my growing-up, all things are possible. (71)

Blaise's rendering here is disturbing and provocative. There is the series of breaks — the mother's nose, the marriage, and his own breakdown. The framework that contained him breaks and he breaks with it.

The language divulges the tension in Blaise's own response. He can't imagine life without the "unspoken, unacted erotic violence" of his parents. He sees that their divorce reveals a life lacking in both "pain and moral authority," which seem to be fundamental components of Blaise's identity and his ability to write or even to imagine. He withdraws as his father does, though instead of clinging to another woman, as Léo does, Blaise clings to reading — "Whenever he entered, I gripped my book all the harder, rather than intervene" (71). Instinctively, he holds to the hard material of the book even though the text has, for a time, deserted him.

And yet he resolves. He recovers, dropping out of school and reading a book a day and working as a busboy for a semester. "Those thousands of books," he writes, "unassigned and unlectured upon, read without guidance or credit or commentary, ... are my education" (76). It's hard to think of a breakdown as a gift, but in this case the time away from study and from his father permits Blaise the chance to immerse himself in the medium that he would make his own.

There is nothing linear in the telling of this story. Blaise admits to structuring the book "to isolate certain moments that have remained memorable, pivotal, poignant, and to forget about the flow" (202). I engage with the book as it comes, swimming in metaphor, in "deeper pools" (202) along with Blaise. In one of the final lyric passages, Blaise declares:

> The memories laid down early are like the lakes and paths and creeks of the Florida landscape I knew. Every shovel-strike brought up water. My memories pool to the outline of their deepest depressions, the smells of a Florida night, the heat from cracked concrete under-foot, the fishy smell of large lakes, the sense of promise with each toss of the baited hook, the sweet hibiscus blooms black inside with ants and gnats, the sour pur-ple muck too acid for growing things, and a thousand other sense impressions that must have bitten and stung me at the time, to remain so vivid after forty-five years. (179)

The metaphors here are layered and lush and resonate with the richness of the portrayal of Léo. Blaise is the writer as creative autobiographer, plunging into the depths of what he can recollect and construct from ex-perience and sense impressions. The pooling memories rise from a great depth; they are fragrant and dark and polyvalent — the concrete is cracked; hibiscus bloom but are filled with ants and gnats; the ground is too acid for growing; and Blaise's hook is baited as he casts into the past to lure quicksilver incidents, flashing from depths to fashion his father vividly and without apology. It is a completely captivating moment. It provokes in me the scent of whisky and cigarettes and the faint trace of my father's aftershave.

Our parents invade us and haunt us and, I think, we invade and haunt them right back. In an essay by Connie Rooke that considers a story, "Irina," by Mavis Gallant

— about whose work Blaise once commented, "I'd say I derive satisfaction only from Mavis Gallant, among Canadians" (Blaise in Hancock 148) — Rooke reveals the impact of children upon the grandmother who is the story's main character. Rooke says the children are a consoling and invading force (29), providing comfort even as they vanquish us. If there is consoling here on Blaise's part, it is in reference to himself. The invasion is obvious in the author's gaze, scrutinizing the minutiae of his father's life and making it his own. Blaise had a father and he lost him. The point seems to be that he had him at all. And Blaise contradicts himself, at least as far as the soil is concerned. His past has provided bountiful material for growing the fiction of his life. And Blaise comes to maturity, the son of a storytelling mother, a storytelling (lying) father, and marries a storytelling wife who bears two sons, two new sons who, themselves, come from a storytelling family.

In his essay "The Border as Fiction," Blaise writes: "There is a border mentality that can take liberty with borders as they are drawn, and that seeks to arrange things more coherently" (47). Blaise, multiplying metaphors that encapsulate ways of invading borders that separate the evident from the concealed — the cracking open of rocks, the shovelling of Florida earth, and the baited hook — blurs the boundary between his father and himself and admits to becoming his father. The book concludes with the story of the pumpkin that his father had carved one Hallowe'en and then discarded in the snow: "In the spring, all the seeds had sprouted, and the pumpkin had replicated itself at least a hundred times" (204). The image resonates for obvious irresistible reasons. In an earlier scene, when Blaise visits his ninety-two-year-old Aunt Lena, she calls him "'Lee'" (143). He reflects, "I've become my father, at last" (143).

Works Consulted

Bakewell, Sarah. *How To Live or A Life of Montaigne in One Question and Twenty Attempts at an Answer.* 2010. London: Vintage, 2011.

Blaise, Clark. "Autobiographical Annex: 1985-2006." *Selected Essays.* By Clark Blaise. Ed. John Metcalf and J.R. (Tim) Struthers. Windsor, ON: Biblioasis, 2008. 209-21.

-----. "The Border as Fiction." *Selected Essays.* By Clark Blaise. Ed. John Metcalf and J.R. (Tim) Struthers. Windsor, ON: Biblioasis, 2008. 43-56.

-----. "A Delayed Disclosure." *Selected Essays.* By Clark Blaise. Ed. John Metcalf and J.R. (Tim) Struthers. Windsor, ON: Biblioasis, 2008. 197-207.

-----. *I Had a Father: A Post-Modern Autobiography.* Toronto: HarperCollins, 1993.

-----. *Resident Alien.* Markham, ON: Penguin Books Canada, 1986.

-----. "Tenants of Unhousement." *The Iowa Review* 13.2 (1982): 83-98.

-----. "The Zen of Writing." 1996. Collection of the author, Clark Blaise. 11 pp.

Gallant, Mavis. "Irina." *From the Fifteenth District: A Novella and Eight Short Stories.* Toronto: Macmillan of Canada, 1979. 225-43.

Hancock, Geoff. "Clark Blaise." *Canadian Writers at Work: Interviews by Geoff Hancock.* Toronto: Oxford UP, 1987. 146-63. Rpt. as "Clear Veneer: An Interview with Clark Blaise" in *Clark Blaise: The Interviews.* Ed. J.R. (Tim) Struthers. Toronto: Guernica Editions, 2016. Essential Writers.

Rooke, Constance. "Waiting for a Final Explanation: Mavis Gallant's 'Irina'." *Fear of the Open Heart: Essays on Canadian Writing.* Toronto: Coach House, 1989. 27-40.

Struthers, J.R. (Tim). "Part of the Myth: An Interview with

Clark Blaise." *Carousel* 9 (1993): 27-46. Rpt. as "Part of the Myth: An Interview with Clark Blaise" and "Looking East: An Interview with Clark Blaise" in *Clark Blaise: The Interviews*. Ed. J.R. (Tim) Struthers. Toronto: Guernica Editions, 2016. Essential Writers.

Mitteleuropa Mothers in Montreal: Central European Correspondences Between Mavis Gallant and Clark Blaise

Stephen Henighan

Only two Canadian writers have published retrospective collections of their short stories under the title *Montreal Stories*. Both Mavis Gallant's *Montreal Stories* (2004), selected and introduced by Russell Banks, and Clark Blaise's *Montreal Stories* (2003), introduced by Peter Behrens, represent a sustained engagement with the city where Anglophone and Francophone Canada collide, sometimes mingle, yet often coexist in a state of mutual aloofness. Belonging to different generations, genders, and educational backgrounds, Gallant, the self-trained woman journalist, then long-term independent writer born in 1922, and Blaise, the male MFA graduate and creative writing professor born in 1940, take acutely personal, sometimes parallel, approaches to Montreal. For both writers, the city represents a lost point of origin, a place to which they gravitated after the disorientation of being shunted from one school to another in childhood and adolescence. Commenting on the reported seventeen schools she attended, Gallant jokes: "Some people have been to more. Clark Blaise has been to seven times as many, I think" (Gallant in Hancock 89).

Born in Montreal, Gallant was prised away from its streets at the age of ten by her father's early death, "possibly a suicide" (Grant 1), and her mother's indifference. Her decision to return from New York at eighteen, as dramatized in her autobiographical short story "In Youth Is Pleasure," confirmed her identity as a Canadian, rooted the definition of her Canadianness in English-French dualism, and converted Montreal into the point of departure against which she would measure her more than sixty years of observation of European societies. Belonging to a generation that reached adulthood before the 1947 Canadian Citizenship Act created the categories of the Canadian citizen and the Canadian passport, Gallant asserted her Canadianness as an expression of her sense of exile against a legal order which gave her the choice of being British, like her father, or American, as her mother was becoming. As Gallant's fictional alter ego, Linnet Muir, remarks in "In Youth Is Pleasure": "I did not feel a scrap British or English, but I was not an American either. In American schools I had refused to salute the flag" (*Montreal Stories* 107). Gallant insists on her national identity as the foundation of her being. As she would later write: "A Canadian who did not know what it was to be Canadian would not know anything else: he would have to be told his own name. [...] I suppose that a Canadian is someone who has a logical reason to think he is one. My logical reason is that I have never been anything else, nor has it occurred to me that I might be" (*Home Truths* xiii). If Canadianness is essential for Gallant, it is also anchored in negation: a definition of being that becomes irrefutable once one dissents from both Britishness and Americanness.

For Blaise, also, residence in Montreal was a return and a hiatus. Never having lived there, except for a transitory stay of a few weeks at the age of six, he identified the city from the U.S. Midwest as the potential cure for the psychological malaise bequeathed to him by his mixed English-Canadian and French-Canadian parentage, which had been amplified into an identity crisis by his parents' divorce. Upon arriving in 1966, Blaise explains, "I re-entered a world I had never made, Montreal, and determined I would become the son I might have been, and would assert authority over an experience I could and should have had, but never did. Confusion remained, but at least I would be the French and English son of befuddlement, the crown prince of Canadian identity" (*Montreal Stories* [1]). The product of a poor white child-hood spent largely in the pre-civil rights Deep South, adolescence in Pittsburgh, and a Midwestern education at Denison University and the University of Iowa, Blaise struggled to locate himself within the regional literary traditions of the United States. He claims that his early Southern stories read like parodies of Erskine Caldwell (*Resident Alien* 20-21); at that stage, at least, he felt he had nothing to say about the Midwest. In his first teaching job, in Milwaukee, Blaise listened to CBC radio at night: "it moved me. It spoke (as Canada always spoke to me) of continuity, assured values, a unified voice. [...] I was coming north" (*Resident Alien* 29). Yet Blaise crossed the border only after selling short stories with Canadian themes to the literary journals *The Tamarack Review* and *PRISM International*. He constructed himself as a Canadian through his fiction, then moved to Canada to become the person he had imagined.

For both Gallant and Blaise, adult life in Montreal was an experience of their twenties, the decade that places an indelible stamp on identity. Blaise lived in Montreal from the ages of twenty-six to thirty-eight — "the longest, by far, that I have lived in a single place; Montreal will remain my city for life" (*Resident Alien* 30). Gallant, having spent her childhood in and around the city, returned from Ontario and New York to live in Montreal from the ages of eighteen to twenty-eight. On taking up residence in the city, both writers recovered the French they had learned in childhood. For Blaise, who had grown up hearing his father's French in remote U.S. outposts, it was "bilingualism-or-bust" (*Selected Essays* 30); as he writes of his early years in Montreal, which coincided with the rise of Québécois nationalism, "'The Frencher the Better' was my motto to cover any encroachment on the aboriginal rights of the English" (*Resident Alien* 31). Blaise lampoons his own Francophile zeal in the character of Norman Dyer, the exuberant transplanted American English-as-a-Second-Language instructor in "A Class of New Canadians": "When stopped on the street for directions, he would answer in French or accented English" (*Montreal Stories* 51). In spite of this ironic self-regard, a rediscovery of the French language and the identities it conferred was crucial to Blaise's self-reinvention as a Montrealer and a Canadian. By the same token, the first act of Linnet Muir in "In Youth Is Pleasure," upon her return to Montreal, is to take "a taxi to the east end of the city—the French end, the poor end" (*Montreal Stories* 111). Hidden away from English, Linnet finds that French is "a frozen language that started to thaw" (*Montreal Stories* 120). Gallant, who had learned to read in both languages in early childhood (*Home Truths* xv), would go on to use French — albeit the French of France rather than of Quebec — as her everyday language for most of the last sixty years of her life. Her decade of adult life in Montreal enabled her to shed her conspicuously English surname, Young, and, by way of a

short-lived marriage to a jazz musician from Winnipeg
who had a French-Canadian father, acquire the camou-
flage of the Francophone surname Gallant. Blaise, whose
father had added an "e" to Americanize his *Québécois-
de-souche* surname of Blais, invested his portmanteau
identity with both French-Canadian and English-Canadian resonances.

Gallant and Blaise were the products of U.S. literary
institutions and putatively "English" mothers. Having
been confirmed in their literary vocations by *The New
Yorker* and the Iowa Writers' Workshop respectively,
both writers suffered indifference or hostility in Canada
for being "too American." Gallant's almost lifelong association with the flagship magazine of the U.S. literary
establishment became a liability in the nationalist
atmosphere of the late 1960s and 1970s. This tension was
exacerbated by the fact that her early books were initially published in New York and did not appear in separate
Canadian editions (few Canadian publishers issued fiction in the 1950s). By contrast, Alice Munro's later *New
Yorker* publications were not held against her since her
early work had appeared in Canadian literary journals
and her first books were published in Toronto as part of
the CanLit wave of the late 1960s and 1970s, prior to her
breakthrough into the *New Yorker*'s pages. Where Munro
was applauded as a Canuck who had made it big on
Broadway, Gallant was regarded as someone who was
not authentically Canadian, did not live in the country,
spoke with a pre-1945 Anglo-Montreal accent that many
Canadians regarded as "English," and wrote highfaluting
stories about European culture. Canadian newspapers,
as Gallant wryly noted, tended to spell "expatriate" as
"expatriot" (*Home Truths* xii). These prejudices receded
after Gallant was awarded the 1981 Governor General's

Award for English Fiction, though in certain obscurant-
ist quarters they persisted into the new millennium. In
2014, John Semley offered readers of *The Globe and Mail*
this caricature of Gallant's career: "Gallant has no particular use for Canada, and vice versa. Her first books of
stories were only made available stateside, thanks in
part to the author making no effort to court a Canadian
publisher" (R18). This inanity takes into account neither
Gallant's overt engagement with her Canadian identity
in her fiction, and in the autobiographical passages cited
above, nor the enfeebled condition of the Canadian publishing industry in the 1950s.

Blaise, regardless of his origins, remained part of the
Canadian literary and cultural world as long as he was
teaching at Concordia University in Montreal (and later,
for two years, at York University in Toronto). After leaving Canada in 1980, an exit embittered by his wife Bharati Mukherjee's parting denunciation, in an article published in *Saturday Night* magazine, of Canada, which she
declared to be more racist than the United States, and of
Canadian multiculturalism, which she characterized as
"implied consent given to racism" (38) by government
policy, Blaise was regarded in Canadian literary circles
as an apostate, if not an infidel. Having embraced Canada as the solution to the identity crisis caused by his
parents' divorce, Blaise then divorced himself from his
country as part of saving his own marriage (Blaise in
Smith), by endorsing his wife's assault on the policy that
succeeded English-French bilingualism as the definition
of Canadian identity. For younger generations, the pre-
eminent Canadian city was Toronto, not Montreal; starting with the appointment of the first federal Multiculturalism Minister in 1972 and in more pronounced form
from the 1980s onward, the country's defining trait was

now multiculturalism rather than bilingualism. By rejecting both Toronto and its favoured ideology, Blaise condemned himself to marginalization in Canadian literary circles. He disappeared onto a succession of U.S. campuses and was omitted from anthologies such as Jane Urquhart's *The Penguin Book of Canadian Short Stories* (2007). John Metcalf, his former colleague from the Montreal Story Teller Fiction Performance Group, continued to publish Blaise's stories and essays in Canada, from his editorial posts at The Porcupine's Quill and Biblioasis. Blaise's internationally published nonfiction book, *Time Lord* (2000), was well received. Yet only many years later, when Blaise published an exceptionally strong short story collection that could be read as an overt exploration of multiculturalism, *The Meagre Tarmac* (2011), did a tentative rapprochement occur that re-admitted Blaise to the fringes of the Canadian literary canon.

Gallant and Blaise adopted Canadian identities in response to the conundrum of having parents who came from different cultural backgrounds, then separated. While this strategy illuminates the two writers' embrace of Canadianness, it does not explain the construction of Canadian identity as a medium for sounding out cultural complexity. Gallant attributed her long-term fascination with the mingling of culturally distinct yet rootless people in post-1945 Europe to her experiences as a young woman in Montreal. As Linnet Muir narrates in "Varieties of Exile": "In the third summer of the war I began to meet refugees. There were large numbers of them in Montreal — to me a source of infinite wonder. I could not get enough of them" (*Montreal Stories* 149). In a parallel vein, Blaise credits his adoption of a cultural range broader than the mere mingling of English and French in Canada, or the positing of Canadian versus

American identities, to the dovetailing of his upbringing with his marriage to Calcutta-born Bharati Mukherjee: "I can speak with assurance as a Southerner, an American suburbanite, an American ethnic, a Canadian, and I can speak with assurance in some ways as someone with a memorable experience of India and certainly as a wanderer through Europe" (Blaise in Cameron 10). Both of these explanations are persuasive up to a point; but they are not sufficient. The missing influence is that of the two writers' mothers, whose surface labels — alternately "American" and "Quebec English" in Gallant's case, "English-Canadian" in that of Blaise — conceal a subterranean immersion in Mitteleuropa, the richly syncretic arc of interlocked cultures and territories with large minority populations, exemplified by the Austro-Hungarian Empire until its dissolution in 1918, that endured as both an idea and a reality from Germany to the borders of Turkey until the Second World War, and then the Cold War, consigned this formation to nostalgic memory as a lost proto-multicultural paradise.

Linnet Muir, Gallant's fictional alter ego, states in "In Youth Is Pleasure": "My mother, on the other hand — I won't begin to describe her; it would never end — smiled, talked, charmed anyone she didn't happen to be related to, swam in scandal like a partisan among the people. She made herself the central figure in loud, spectacular dramas which she played with the houselights on [...]. You can imagine what she must have been in this world where everything was hushed, muffled, disguised: She must have seemed all they had by way of excitement, give or take a few elections and wars" (*Montreal Stories* 117). Critics have made a mistake in not taking this description at face value and learning more about the extraordinary, alarming woman who gave birth to Mavis

Young. Gallant's terse summary of her "beginnings," in her introductory essay to the *Selected Stories*, as "wholly Quebec, English and Protestant, yes, but with a strong current of French and Catholic" (xv) suppresses the question of who her mother was; the essay provides considerable detail about her father, but none about her mother, who was neither English nor Protestant, and about whom she tended to say almost nothing beyond, "I had a mother who should not have had children, and it's as simple as that" (Gallant in Verongos). In the days of Gallant's childhood and young adulthood, prior to the Canadian Citizenship Act, as Linnet notes, "you were also whatever your father happened to be, which in my case was English" (*Montreal Stories* 107). When Gallant describes her background as "English," she is taking advantage of the definitions prevalent during her youth to cancel out association with the mother who horrified and rejected her yet whom, it is now clear, she also covertly admired and emulated. At the time of Gallant's death in February 2014, virtually all newspapers echoed *The New York Times* in repeating the incorrect statement, "Ms. Gallant, who was born in Montreal to an American mother [...]" (Verongos). It is astonishing that none of the book-length studies of Gallant's work, published by Neil K. Besner, Lesley D. Clement, Judith Skelton Grant, Janice Kulyk Keefer, Grazia Merler, Danielle Schaub, and Karen E. Smythe, provides the names of Gallant's parents. Only Grant offers a more detailed, albeit not entirely correct, account: "her mother, Canadian (but raised in the United States) of mixed heritage — German, Breton, Rumanian" (Grant 1).

Born Benedictine (or more likely Benediktine) Weissman (later Anglicized to Wiseman), probably in 1899, either in Montreal or in Romania, Gallant's mother was

regarded by her family as "one of the best known women
in Montreal" ("Mother Tells Story"). Much more research
needs to be done, but the available outlines illustrate
Wiseman's importance to her daughter, in spite of their
ghastly relationship, as a model of artistic ambition, female independence at any cost, and a paradigm of the
cultural complexities of Central Europe. By the age of
fourteen, Weissman, who was popularly known as Bennie, had written a play that was produced in Montreal;
according to her mother, in her late teens she wrote a
book "which was published" ("Mother Tells Story"). In
1913, according to York University criminologist Amanda
Glasbeek, Bennie left Montreal, "cropped her hair,
donned her brother's clothing, and became Jimmy" (92),
who worked during the day as a clerk at a Toronto department store and at night singing at a nickelodeon,
where she won a $20 singing prize for young men ("No
Slit Skirts"). Later U.S. police records indicate that Bennie's age at the time of this bout of gender-bending would
have been fourteen, though *The Toronto World* said that
she was seventeen; Glasbeek reports that Bennie left a
husband behind in Montreal (92), but this, like Bennie's
claim to be older than she was, may be simply a convenient lie she told the police. After two months in Toronto,
"Jimmy" was arrested at the corner of Yonge and Queen
Streets by a Constable McBurney, who recognized her
from a picture he had looked up after having her pointed
out to him earlier in another part of the city by individuals who believed that "her appearance as a boy was not
natural" ("No Slit Skirts"). Unmasked as a cross-dresser,
she was tried for vagrancy. Newspaper accounts remarked on her defiance in court and her unrepentant
pride at having earned men's wages of $7 a week ("Girl
Dressed as a Youth"). On being questioned about her

cross-dressing, she answered: "What chance is there for a girl?" (Glasbeek 92). She later explained to the Magistrate: "I just hate being a girl. That's why I'm dressed as a boy. I have not done anything wrong. As a girl I couldn't get work, and I'll just go back to boys' clothes whenever I get a chance" ("Girl Dressed as a Youth"). Bennie's disdain for women who accepted the lower wages paid to females was echoed years later by her daughter's fictional alter ego, who describes refusing to sit in the "women's section" of an office where she had applied for work: "'But I won't sit there.' Girls were 'there,' penned in like sheep. I did not think men better than women — only that they did more interesting work and got more money for it" (*Montreal Stories* 113). Gallant's insistence on a quasi-gender-bending form of female independence was not the only trait she gleaned from her mother. Her later fame for devastating put-downs was also a legacy from Bennie. *The Toronto World* provided this report of the conclusion of Bennie's trial: "Passing out of the door she encountered the grinning policeman who [had] arrested her. 'I am sorry for you, so sorry!' she said, at which the grin disappeared and Constable McBurney visibly lost two inches of his five foot eleven" ("Boy-Girl Expresses Pity").

In April 1921, Bennie was arrested again, in New York State, for cohabiting with R.O. Earl, an American who, like William Faulkner, had enlisted in the Canadian Army during the First World War. More importantly, Earl was married with children. He had rented a room in the Weissman home on St. Catherine Street in Montreal in June 1920 and had begun "to pay attentions to the daughter" ("Mother Tells Story"), who was then employed as a clerk in a downtown store. When Mrs. Weissman asked Earl to leave, Bennie went with him. Between July 1920 and March 1921 they travelled together, at one point being spotted in the Detroit train station. Even though Bennie insisted that the affair was platonic, writing to her mother, "We realize that in sin we cannot be happy" ("Mother Tells Story"), she was the one charged by police when they were arrested at a town near Utica, New York ("Romantic Weissman Girl"), then taken to Syracuse for questioning. The housekeeper they had engaged supported them by saying, "There was no suggestion of impropriety" and that, "The couple had been very industrious and were saving up for a home" ("Mother Tells Story"). In spite of this testimony, in the summer of 1921, Bennie served a three-month sentence in a penitentiary in Jamesville, just outside Syracuse, as punishment for her purportedly immoral relationship with a married man. She was then "deported as an undesirable alien" ("Romantic Weissman Girl"). The deportation makes clear that, contrary to many claims, Gallant's mother was not American; it is also unlikely, in spite of Grant's assertion, that she was "raised in the United States" (1) unless this phrase is a covert reference to her months on the lam with Earl and her time in prison. It is plausible that Bennie Weissman became a naturalized American years later, after moving to New York City in 1932 or 1933 with the man who became her new husband; but she was not an American a decade earlier, at the time of her daughter's birth.

When Bennie/Jimmy was released by the Toronto Women's Court in September 1913, it was reported that "She will be sent back to her parents properly garbed" ("No Slit Skirts"). When she was arrested in Syracuse in April 1921, her brother Nicholas made the trip to be with her. Bennie was deported from the United States that August. In October, she wrote to Syracuse Chief of Police Martin Cadin to inform him that she had married

Captain Albert Stewart Young, a recent British immigrant to Montreal; in her letter she gave Cadin the date
of her wedding and the church in which it had taken
place ("Romantic Weissman Girl"). In late December of
that year, however, Captain Young wrote to Chief Cadin
to state that he was "engaged to Miss Weissman, but that
his father, Colonel A.R. Young, has objected to the match"
("Romantic Weissman Girl"). Albert Young asked the police chief for a full account of Bennie's adventures in New
York State. Whatever he may have been told, and whatever their marital status may have been at this time (or
later), the couple had already conceived a child. Their
daughter, Mavis, was born on 11 August 1922. Since Gallant's contact with her mother after the age of ten was
intermittent and hostile — in the Linnet Muir stories, the
mother displays a "final unexpected upsurge of attention" (*Montreal Stories* 105) when the protagonist is fifteen — it is impossible to be certain how much of this
history the author knew. Gallant was aware that she had
a maternal grandmother in Montreal: the grandmother,
who died when Gallant was an adolescent, appears as a
character in another Linnet Muir story, "Voices Lost in
Snow." Grant's research suggests Gallant knew that the
Weissman family were ethnic Germans (Grant 1, 46); it
seems likely she also knew that her mother's family identified themselves as Romanians ("Mother Tells Story"),
even though her autobiographical stories, maintaining
the fiction of unadulterated British Isles ancestry, are
purged of such references. In the Linnet Muir stories her
parents, Albert and Benedictine, become Angus and
Charlotte. The fictional names make the father, who in
real life was born in England to a Scottish mother, more
Scottish; the mother is given a name that works equally
well in English, French, and German, though one that is

devoid of the Catholic resonances of Benedictine. The facts about Gallant's mother require a significant reassessment of her fiction, including both her depiction of gender and, particularly, her relationship with the cultures of Germany and Central Europe.

According to contemporary press reports, Bennie Weissman's mother was born in Breslau (today Wroclaw, Poland), which at that time belonged to the German Empire. "[B]ecause of the unpopularity of Germans in Montreal at this time" ("Mother Tells Story"), the mother refused to identify herself as German and insisted that the family was Romanian. Pervasive anti-German feeling during and after the First World War presumably also influenced the change of surname to Wiseman (although Bennie's jailing as "Weissman" in 1921 suggests that she retained her original surname on her identity documents). Both Bennie and Nicholas identified themselves to the U.S. media as Romanians, saying that their father was Romanian; Bennie said that she herself was born in Romania ("Romantic Weissman Girl"). One newspaper reported that she was fluent in five languages ("Romantic Weissman Girl"), while another newspaper said that she spoke English, French, German, and Romanian ("Mother Tells Story"); both of these claims exceed Gallant's statement that her mother spoke "German and some French" (Grant 1). The claim to fluency in Romanian is possible, yet doubtful since Bennie's German surname suggests that her paternal heritage was not ethnically Romanian but rather stemmed from one of the two large German-speaking enclaves that then existed in what is now Romania: the Saxons in Transylvania and the Swabians in the Banat region around the city of Timişoara. Both of these areas belonged to Austria-Hungary until the Treaty of Trianon incorporated them into Romania in 1920. Since Banat Swabians are usually Catholic, while most Transylvanian Saxons are Lutheran, Benedictine's ultra-Catholic name suggests that Gallant's grandfather (and possibly also her mother) came from the Timişoara region (this area is also the home of the contemporary minority-German Romanian writer, Herta Müller, winner of the 2009 Nobel Prize in Literature).

The culture of Germans in the quadrilingual (Romanian-Hungarian-German-Serbian) city of Timişoara, or in culturally mixed (Polish-Jewish-German) Breslau, incarnates Mitteleuropa syncretism. Gallant's own remarks sometimes inadvertently undermine her pose of being "English and Protestant" and her suppression of the ethnically German, Catholic-raised mother. "I had very young parents," she writes, "and they found it amusing to give me a simple text in English and have me rattle it off in French" (*Home Truths* xv-xvi). If Gallant's parents were truly "Quebec English," this scene would make no sense, since by definition English Canadians of the 1920s did not deign to learn the language of French Canadians, whom they regarded as their social inferiors. Even twenty years later, in the 1940s, Gallant was uniquely positioned as a journalist in Quebec because "I could interview French Canadians without dragging them into English" (*Selected Stories* xiv). The scene Gallant describes makes sense only if her parents spoke good French; in the 1920s, most Montreal Anglophones who spoke French were recent immigrants from Europe. In her autobiographical story "Wing's Chips," the narrator's father, who arrives in Canada only a year or two prior to his daughter's birth, distinguishes himself from other English Montrealers by speaking French rather than "noisily making fun of it" (*The Other Paris* 144). If the

Weissman family did come from Romania, where, as Gallant points out in her 1966 short story "Questions and Answers," being educated in French "was the fashion for Bucharest girls" of a certain background "thirty years ago" (*Selected Stories* 260-61), then Bennie, too, would have had a more positive attitude towards, and more knowledge of, the French language than mainstream Montreal Anglos. Bennie's decision to place her daughter in a French-language Catholic boarding school at the age of four, portrayed as culturally incomprehensible on the grounds that her parents were "both Protestants" (Verongos), makes more sense in light of her Romanian cultural influences and likely Catholic upbringing. The two expatriate Romanian women in "Questions and Answers" start out as "convent-trained, French-prattling" (*Selected Stories* 267) childhood friends. Did Gallant's mother place her in a French-language convent school because this was how she had been educated? Gallant's pose of being "English," when the truth was more complicated, echoes Bennie's assertion of being "Romanian."

This German-Romanian background casts Gallant's creative fascination with the human flotsam of Europe in the aftermath of the destruction of the cultural diversity of Mitteleuropa by two world wars in an unexplored light, suggesting that when she described uprooted Central Europeans, she was writing as a fellow inheritor of this legacy, not as the chilly, detached observer from the New World that she is often depicted as being. There was more of Joseph Roth in her, and less of Henry James, than has been allowed. This heritage helps to explain why Gallant, like Linnet Muir, "could not get enough" (*Montreal Stories* 149) of the refugees, many of them Central Europeans, who began to arrive in Montreal during the Second World War. It also elucidates her unexpected interest in Germany, the only country other than Canada and France to which she devoted an entire book, *The Pegnitz Junction* (1973). Furthermore, it is telling that while one of the only two stories in Gallant's first collection, *The Other Paris* (1956), that are set in Quebec is overtly about her father, the other may be read as being covertly about the legacy of "Romanianness" transmitted to her by her mother. "Wing's Chips," which fictionalizes a summer that Gallant spent with her father as a little girl, when he retreated to a village outside Montreal to paint, adumbrates her claim, reinforced by the interest in visual art that emerges in stories published later in her career, such as "The Doctor" and "Speck's Idea," that Gallant's sense of artistic vocation is a paternal inheritance: "My father [...] never thought of himself as anything but a painter" (*Selected Stories* x). "The Legacy," the second Quebec story in *The Other Paris*, which follows "Wing's Chips," portrays the mother's pose of Romanianness as a shackle. Marina Boldescu, growing up in a modest neighbourhood of Montreal, dreams of studying in France. After one of her brothers thwarts this plan, Marina becomes a teacher in the primary school from which she graduated. The story's forward action recounts events after the death of their Romanian immigrant mother, who, in a nod to Bennie's Catholic background, is a Greco-Catholic, a minority religious group in predominantly Orthodox Romania (*The Other Paris* 155). Her other brother foists upon Marina the ownership of the mother's successful shop, Rumania Fancy Groceries, which had been left to him in her will, blocking once again his sister's plans to go to France. Marina's dreamed-of route out of the neighbourhood becomes a "shifting and treacherous path that described a circle" (*The Other Paris* 172). In receiving this cultural legacy,

Marina condemns herself to fail to escape to France — in contrast to Gallant. At the story's close, Marina's brothers must physically subdue her to prevent her from destroying the shrines, plates, and glasses that they cherish as their inheritance from their mother. For Marina, by contrast, the Romanian legacy throttles her independence.

Gallant's suppression of her mother's Mitteleuropa background creates an elegant equation in which she herself becomes the quintessential Canadian, inhabiting a space between Britishness and Americanness. She needed her mother to be American so that she could be Canadian. She describes Bennie Weissman as emotionally unpredictable, yet not as a source of her own artistic ambitions or cultural outlook. When, in "Varieties of Exile," Linnet Muir says that she "tried to see Montreal as an Austrian might see it and to feel whatever he felt" (*Montreal Stories* 149), this exercise is depicted as deriving from her reading and her meetings with Central European refugees; yet it may also be an unacknowledged way of understanding the perceptions of a mother whose roots lay on the fringes of the Austro-Hungarian Empire. Gallant's literary ambitions must be to some degree a response to Bennie Weissman's status as a fledgling playwright as well as an absorption of Albert Young's self-discipline as a painter. At the same time, much more research is needed to corroborate the statements made to the press by the Weissman family. By 1926, the year Gallant turned four, her uncle, Nicholas, was masquerading as a French nobleman named "Count A. Paul Monte" in Milwaukee, where his wife had the telephone disconnected after he ran up monthly phone bills of $90 by talking to his countless female admirers ("Wife Too Good"). Ten years later, in 1936, *The Wisconsin Jewish Chronicle* advised its readers to "[w]atch out for a gentleman who calls himself Count Paul de Monte-fiore and claims to be a relative of the famous English family of that name...[.] His real name is Nicholas Wiseman [...]" ("Here and There"). Mavis Gallant was far from being the first member of her family who wove fictions about Europe.

Clark Blaise, too, obscures the maternal Mitteleuropa influence that channels his depiction of Montreal's cultural density. While Gallant saw her father as reliable and affectionate and her mother as uncaring and "half-crazy" (Schaub 3), for Blaise it is the Jack Kerouac-like father, Léo Roméo Blais, who left school at the age of nine, Americanized his name to Lee Blaise, married four or five times, had numerous girlfriends, was a boxer and a smuggler, held scores of jobs, and was jailed at least once (*I Had a Father* 3-13), who is mad, and the mother who provides an Anglo-Canadian continuity and stability that the author found neither in his father nor in the United States. Blaise recognizes his mother's crucial role in forging his own artistic consciousness: "Most male writers I know, or have read about, had artistically-inclined mothers trapped in unhappy marriages to resolutely feckless husbands" (*Selected Essays* 10). The oldest of ten children of a stern, British-descended Methodist doctor, Anne Marion Vanstone was born in Wawanesa, Manitoba, grew up there and in Saskatchewan, and qualified as a schoolteacher at Wesley College, which later became the University of Winnipeg (Ross, "Clark Blaise: Biocritical Essay"). In the stories he wrote during his years in Montreal, Blaise's dualistic vision of Canada slotted the mother into the category of English-Canadianness and duty, in opposition to the insurgent French-Canadian father. Blaise's impersonation of Québécois childhoods in stories such as "I'm Dreaming of Rocket

Richard" means that the English-Canadian mother figure is not always present. By contrast, in "The Fabulous
Eddie Brewster," one of Blaise's best-known stories, the
dualism is stark. The narrator's Québécois uncle, Étienne,
breaks all the rules. Reinventing himself as "Eddie Brewster," he makes it big in the U.S.A., eventually being elect-
ed mayor of a Florida town. Eddie's sister-in-law, the
narrator's very proper English-Canadian mother, dis-
courages Étienne's actions at each stage of his rise with
arguments such as, "what you plan is wrong, all wrong"
(*Tribal Justice* 42). While Étienne's adoption of American
audacity and unconcern for the consequences of his actions leads to success, the mother's Canadian insistence
on following the rules results in a retreat to drab Buffalo,
New York, the American city that is closest to Canada.
The father continues to take vacations in Florida with
the brother whose success he admires yet cannot emu-
late. The story concludes: "After their divorce several
years ago, my mother went back to Canada and now
teaches history in Regina" (*Tribal Justice* 46). The choice
of a city whose name invokes the colonial heritage of
Queen Victoria, and of the subject of history—lessons
from and about the past—recapitulates the constitutional dichotomy that portrays Americanness as consisting of "life, liberty, and the pursuit of happiness" and
Canadianness as residing in "peace, order, and good government." This dualism, like the English-French dualism
in Blaise's first three short story collections, *A North
American Education* (1973), *Tribal Justice* (1974), and *Resident Alien* (1986), obscures the origins of the author's
fascination with the cultural density of crossover identities, which derives not only from his parents' cross-cul-
tural marriage—his foundational duality—but also
from his mother's identification, during the pivotal years

of her late twenties and early thirties, with the culture of Mitteleuropa.

Born in 1940, Blaise is eighteen years younger than Gallant. Yet their parents belonged to the same generation. Though no firm data is available, Gallant's father, who died in 1932 (Schaub xiii) in his early thirties (*Selected Stories* x), would have been born in about 1900; her mother, who was twenty-two years old when she was arrested in New York State in 1921, was about the same age; Blaise's mother was born in 1903 and his father in 1905 (*Selected Essays* 10, 12). This common generational perspective means that all of these individuals inhabited as young adults a world in which Western Europe was defined by states such as France and Germany, which portrayed themselves as cohering around a single language and ethnicity, while Central Europe remained an unruly mixture of territories, encompassed by the Austro-Hungarian Empire until it dissolved at the end of the First World War. These territories persisted in their dishevelled state, in which no region was exempt from large minority populations and improbable cultural blendings, until Adolf Hitler's rampage into this area (ostensibly with the purpose of bringing its German-speaking minorities "back inside the Reich"), and the subsequent genocides of Jews and Roma, redrawing of borders, transfers of populations to new areas, and finally the imposition of Soviet suzerainty, obliterated Mitteleuropa and gave birth to "Eastern Europe." In the 1930s, however, novelists such as Robert Musil, Joseph Roth, Sándor Márai, and Mihail Sebastian, among others, continued to explore the Mitteleuropa legacy. In the 1980s, as the Cold War freeze began to thaw, Mitteleuropa enjoyed a revival, both as a nostalgic evocation of the past and as a tolerant possibility for the future — a hope that was dashed by the upheavals of the 1990s, such as the wars in former Yugoslavia and Moldova, and the rise of ethnic chauvinism in Hungary and Romania. The second wave of Mitteleuropa enthusiasm produced the memoirs of Elias Canetti, the travel writing of Patrick Leigh Fermor, and the early journalism of Timothy Garton Ash, as the melting away of "Eastern Europe" promised a return to a cultural configuration that would include a notion of Central Europe. Blaise's mother told him stories of this Europe which was "a unitary concept[...]. Prague and Budapest and Warsaw are as Western in her travels as Paris and London and Berlin" ("Tenants of Unhousement" 85).

Anne Vanstone was lured away from the Canadian prairies by the last years of Central Europe's pre-Second World War cultural syncretism. Like Mavis Gallant's mother, Blaise's mother spoke German (though not, apparently, the French of her future husband, whom she would meet in Montreal). Also like Bennie Weissman, Vanstone was an aspiring artist, in this case a designer. In 1929, as Blaise relates, just before the stock market crash that would set the stage for the European political upheavals of the 1930s, she "took off for Europe. She worked first in London, then, dissatisfied by the stodgy standards of local design, removed herself to the centre of modernism, Germany. She enrolled in an art school in Dresden, and took classes in Dessau, at the Bauhaus. With the closing of the schools in 1933, she escaped to Prague, using her German, and stayed there till 1935 when friends suggested she leave. With a Canadian passport, she'd found herself suddenly desirable in the eyes of many older, interesting, accomplished men. But she returned to London for a year, then back to Canada" (*Selected Essays* 200).

Blaise portrays his mother's European years as the core of her cultural education, even though her immersion in Modernism and the last gasp of Mitteleuropa failed to disabuse her of certain prejudices typical of many English Canadians of her generation, such as a dislike of Catholicism. Like Gallant's mother, Anne Vanstone was more interested in art and personal independence than in starting a family. Both Blaise and Gallant were only children of parents who separated. Where Gallant's mother "should not have had children" (Gallant in Verongos), Anne Vanstone internalized a certain societal shame at giving birth to her first child at what in those days was the venerable age of thirty-seven: "there was something trashy about carrying a baby at a grandmother's age" (*Selected Essays* 197). As a boy, Blaise would speculate about how, if his mother had married one of the men she had met in Europe, "I would be English or German or Czech or Hungarian" (*Selected Essays* 203). In this way, Mitteleuropa identity slipped beneath the surface of Blaise's life to occupy the powerful position of the road not taken; this is distinct from Gallant's portrait of Marina Boldescu in "The Legacy," which depicts identification with Central European culture as a pitfall avoided. At the same time, Blaise's factual error in attributing to his mother "a Canadian passport" (*Selected Essays* 200) more than a decade before such an object existed (in the 1930s, Canadians travelling in Europe used British passports) insists on the integration of his mother's acquired Mitteleuropa, Modernist veneer into the Canadian essence she transmits to him. Yet, in Blaise's *A North American Education* (1973) and *Tribal Justice* (1974), this essence remains subterranean; it informs the fictions' depictions of cultural richness, but does not disrupt their dualistic patterning. More than a decade later, in *Resident Alien* (1986), the impact of the maternal Mitteleuropa influence on Blaise's depiction of Canadian English-French dualities becomes discernible. Only once Blaise returned in 1980 to the United States, where the struggle to weld a Canadian identity from the warring halves of his own personality (and of Canada's personality during the turbulent 1970s) receded from his fiction, arguably leaving him bereft of his most urgent themes, did the mother's Mitteleuropa past begin to come to the surface.

Blaise's first two collections dramatize tensions between English Canadians and French Canadians, between Canadians and Americans, between Southern and Northern U.S. sensibilities, or, as in "Snow People" and "The March," plumb the contradictions of Franco-American identity. They are, as the first collection's title indicates, tales of North American Educations. The only stories that venture outside North America's borders are "Going to India," an autobiographical story about a white Montrealer's plane journey to Calcutta to meet his Indian wife's family, and the novella "Continent of Strangers." The latter piece, in which the creative writing student protagonist is lured to Europe by a girl who once interested him, who in turn loses interest in him as soon as he arrives in Germany, thins the weight of European culture to tourist pablum: the protagonist "spent a day in Lübeck, visited Buddenbrooks House and walked the streets that Tonio Kröger had known" (*A North American Education* 107). The story revolves around the banal question of whether two young Midwesterners are going to sleep together. The dénouement takes place in Sweden, a country that lies outside the arc of the traditional Anglophone Grand Tour of Europe, is far from Mitteleuropa, and was exempt from the two world wars. The story reflects early 1960s $5-a-day American antics in Europe. The particularities of place, usually Blaise's strong suit, get trivialized. As Robert Lecker concludes, "the experiential structures seem forced, and the narrative voice sounds contrived" (*On the Line* 29).

As long as Blaise was immersed in Montreal, or still held it as a recent memory, as in *Resident Alien*, contemporary Europe, as "Continent of Strangers" illustrates, dwindled to a tourist abstraction. The Mitteleuropa heritage, unacknowledged, shaped his evocation of Montreal, and arguably of other places. Speaking of his mother's stories of her life in Prague, Blaise observes: "[...] I have preserved a vanished central Europe from those stories—those cities of stone and brick without much neon; hand-hewn cities of cobblestones, narrow sidewalks and low skylines bowed before their steeples. Cities of narrow vistas through wavy glass, courtyards and horse-carts and streetcars and meticulous parks no larger than apartments. Cities of fogs and the narrow, ancient rivers like wider thoroughfares of a more viscous material, still pumping through the city centers. Prague, Budapest, Paris, Cologne: she liked cities that still had their uses for fresh water, cities that treated their rivers like retired dignitaries, still capable of light official duties" ("Tenants of Unhousement" 84).

The love of cities with cobblestones and rivers may explain Anne Vanstone's decision to settle in Montreal upon her return to Canada. Certainly, barring intimidatingly Francophone Quebec City, it was the Canadian city that bore the closest physical resemblance to Mitteleuropa. As the binary tensions of the 1970s slipped away, maternal Mitteleuropa influences ceased to be a subterranean force in Blaise's fiction and became an overt element of his heritage. Rather than expressing his

mother's frustrated artistic designs through his examination of his father's Francophone heritage, he began to
examine those designs' origins. *Man and His World*
(1992), his first short story collection written from the
consolidated vantage point of a writer living in the
United States, who did not plan to return to Canada,
opens with "A Tour Around My Father," a story about his
far-flung paternal cousins, yet, in the manner of Gallant's two consecutive stories in *The Other Paris* that
gesture towards one parent then the other, the book's
second story, "Meditations on Starch," reflects on the
mother's wanderings. Blaise, in contrast to Gallant, is
overt about the maternal roots of his identification with
the Mitteleuropa heritage. "Meditations on Starch" portrays how the autobiographical narrator unconsciously
transmits his Central European obsessions, derived from
his mother's romance with a handsome Nazi sympathiz-
er in 1930s Prague, to his own half-Indian son: "So the
stories I grew up with and passed on to my son were an
idea of Europe that hasn't existed in eighty years, a Holy
Roman Empire in which a single language and a single
passport dominated all others and the rest of the world
suffered paroxysms of exclusion for not being European,
and, specifically, German" (*Man and His World* 29).

This early-twentieth-century "Holy Roman Empire"
informs the Montreal depicted by both Blaise and Gallant, injecting the English-French binary with a third
term that renders it more ductile and resonant, capable
of capturing the "varieties of exile," the "extractions and
contractions," that spring up to complicate relations
across the English-French divide. To conclude this discussion, I will look briefly at how this works in one Montreal story by each author. First, it should be stated that
the use of Mitteleuropa that is discussed here is distinct

from the "double exile" terminology that became common currency among Anglophone writers who lived in Montreal in the late 1980s. After the 1987 promulgation of the Meech Lake Accord (and even more so after the failure to ratify it in 1990), "double exile," which asserted that Anglophone Montreal writers were excluded from the national imaginaries of both Quebec and English Canada, served as a populist vulgarization of Gilles Deleuze and Félix Guattari's ideas in their book *Kafka: pour une littérature mineure* (1975) — often reduced to, "We're like the Jews of Prague at the time of Kafka" (David Solway in Diamond 6) — that Anglophone Montreal writers waved as a banner of defiant alienation when they decried that they were "heard neither in Quebec City nor in Toronto" (Solway 60). Neither Gallant nor Blaise was sufficiently immersed in Montreal life during this period — though Blaise was writer-in-residence at Concordia University in 1986-87 (Blaise, "Chronology of Salience" 19) — to be conscious of let alone accept this tendency, whose most vocal representatives were David Solway and Ann Diamond. By contrast, Gallant and Blaise drew upon Mitteleuropa models as a consequence of their respective mothers' reactions to a concrete engagement with Central European culture.

"North," written by Blaise after his departure from Canada — albeit during a term teaching at the David Thompson University Centre in Nelson, British Columbia in Fall 1983 (Blaise in Struthers) — and included in *Resident Alien* as the third of four stories about a family that flees from Pittsburgh to Montreal, abandoning its adopted name of Porter for the father's birth surname of Carrier, is the story that Blaise chose to lead off his *Montreal Stories*. It is the story that fits best with his announced intention, in his immersion in Montreal and its myths, to "become the son I might have been" (*Montreal Stories* [1]). Like Gallant's "In Youth Is Pleasure," "North" narrates a settling-in to Montreal after a return from the United States; like Linnet Muir, Philip Porter (later Carrier) lands in the city's working-class, French-speaking East End in an era of dire poverty and unquestioned Catholic dominance prior to the declericalization that occurred as a result of the Quiet Revolution which began in 1959. Carrier is sent to a French Catholic school ruled by ferocious nuns, where a girl named Thérèse Aulérie is assigned to him as a tutor. Thérèse turns out to be an assimilated Irish Quebecker whose grandfather spelled the family name "O'Leary." The story pivots on the irony of this adolescent friendship between "a Carrier who spoke no French" and "an O'Leary who read 'Archie' comic books but knew no English" (*Montreal Stories* 22). Yet the mordant dualisms — the mother's English-Canadian Protestant restraint, the father's family's pre-Quiet Revolution French-Canadian Catholic suspicion of Communism and Liberalism, which are seen as identical, and of the English language — are invested with a significance beyond the merely local by the obtrusion of a character from the mother's European past. This part of her life is alluded to only once: "[w]hen I came back from England [...]" (*Montreal Stories* 26). The mother's friend, Ella, who is a professor at McGill University, has short hair, smokes a pipe, and shares her apartment with another woman. The story does not highlight her sexual transgression against a repressed era, emphasizing instead her status as a Jewish refugee from Central Europe and a representative of a cosmopolitan culture that young Philip has been taught to regard with hostility. Ella offers to pay for Philip to attend an English private school that will prepare him for McGill: "You can live with us, and we will send you. I know professors, I know musicians, writers, artists. We go out every night, or we have people here who are leaders not just of this city, not just this country –" (*Montreal Stories* 29). Ella's references to Sigmund Freud, Albert Einstein, and Karl Marx contextualize by opposition the French-Canadian obscurantism in which, according to his mother, Philip is being raised, presenting it as not only backward but also a milder North American wing of the international fascism that obliged Ella to flee Europe. Philip responds to Ella's litany of Jewish cosmopolitan achievement by retorting sourly that an education outside the French-Canadian tradition simply teaches people "how to get electrocuted for being Russian spies" (*Montreal Stories* 31). This disparaging reference to the Rosenberg case closes off the third option as a possible escape hatch for Philip, who chooses to return to his East End school and the eternal flirtation of English-French dualism represented by his tutoring sessions with Thérèse. The possibilities represented by Mitteleuropa culture are nullified by the rootedness of Canadian history and social categories; yet through the wider-ranging maternal influences experienced by both the author and the narrator, this dualism expands to become something fuller and more resonant— "the clapper of the biggest bell in the world" (*Montreal Stories* 33)— than simply local history.

Speaking of his reading, Blaise states: "I'd say I derive satisfaction only from Mavis Gallant, among Canadians" (Blaise in Hancock 148). Even more significantly, in a conversation with J.R. (Tim) Struthers, Blaise responded to the question of which work of Gallant's he would recommend most highly by saying: "I've always been very drawn to the post-War German situation, so the stories in *The Pegnitz Junction* are very personally meaningful

to me" (Blaise in Struthers). Blaise's treatment of Montreal reprises motifs from Gallant's Montreal stories.
"Varieties of Exile," collected five years before "North,"
anticipates (or inspires) some of the cultural obsessions
of Blaise's story when Linnet says, "My dictionaries were
films, poems, novels, Lenin, Freud" (*Montreal Stories*
149). The two stories display analogous structures: in
"Varieties of Exile" the Mitteleuropa themes open the
story, yet, as in Blaise's story, are assimilated in stages
by English-French dualism. Linnet Muir's fascination
with European refugees who "came straight out of the
twilit Socialist-literary landscape of my reading and my
desires" (*Montreal Stories* 149) — again, the mother's background is suppressed — unfolds in tandem with her hesi-
tation over whether to marry: "I was nineteen and for the
third time in a year engaged to be married" (*Montreal
Stories* 149-50). These two tensions meld when, after
moving to Montreal's English-speaking Lakeshore suburbs to escape the summer heat, she witnesses the tedi-
ous existence of middle-class housewives who spend
their days at home. On the commuter train that she rides
to work in downtown Montreal, Linnet meets an older,
married English remittance man who shares her literary
enthusiasms and left-wing politics: "Frank Cairns was
something new, unique of his kind, and almost as good
as a refugee, for he was a Socialist" (*Montreal Stories* 160).
They lend each other Russian books. This friendship co-
incides with, and abets, Linnet's withdrawal from the
world of European refugees, and her rejection of her
identification with her teenage years in New York. Like
Philippe Carrier, Linnet puts the United States behind
her and embraces dualistic Canada: "I had become patri-
otic. Canadian patriotism is always anti-American in
part [...]" (*Montreal Stories* 164). To consolidate Linnet's

Canadian identity, Frank Cairns, who represents the English paternal principle — his resemblance to Linnet's English immigrant father becomes clear — must also be rejected. When people on the Lakeshore begin to gossip about Linnet's conversations on the train with a married man, she leaves this district, moves back downtown, and commits herself to Canada by marrying an English Canadian with a French-Canadian surname. Frank Cairns enlists for service in the Second World War and is killed in Italy, dying overseas like Linnet's father, and putting an end to her fascination with refugees: "They were going through a process called 'integrating.' [...] A refugee eating cornflakes was of no further interest" (*Montreal Stories* 169). Gallant would pursue her passion for Europeans during more than six decades' residence in Europe; Blaise's consciousness of the European influences on his fiction became explicit after he left Canada and returned, in person and in much of his fiction, to the United States. Yet in their respective *Montreal Stories*, both writers employed maternally derived Mitteleuropa imagery to tantalize narrators who drew on these cultural references in subterranean ways to lend density to the depiction of a bicultural Canada.

Works Consulted

Besner, Neil K. *The Light of Imagination: Mavis Gallant's Fiction.* Vancouver: U of British Columbia P, 1988.

Blaise, Clark. "Chronology of Salience." *An Other I: The Fictions of Clark Blaise.* By Robert Lecker. Toronto: ECW, 1988. 13-20.

-----. *I Had a Father: A Post-Modern Autobiography.* Reading, MA: Addison-Wesley, 1993.

-----. *Man and His World.* Erin, ON: The Porcupine's Quill, 1992.

-----. *The Meagre Tarmac: Stories.* Windsor, ON: Biblioasis, 2011.

-----. *Montreal Stories.* Introd. Peter Behrens. Erin, ON: The Porcupine's Quill, 2003. Vol. 3 of *The Selected Stories of Clark Blaise.* 4 vols. 2000-06.

-----. *A North American Education: A Book of Short Fiction.* Toronto: Doubleday Canada, 1973.

-----. *Resident Alien.* Markham, ON: Penguin Books Canada, 1986.

-----. *Selected Essays.* By Clark Blaise. Ed. John Metcalf and J.R. (Tim) Struthers. Windsor, ON: Biblioasis, 2008.

-----. "Tenants of Unhousement." *The Iowa Review* 13.2 (1982): 83-98.

-----. *Time Lord: The Remarkable Canadian Who Missed His Train, and Changed the World.* Toronto: Alfred A. Knopf Canada, 2000.

-----. *Tribal Justice.* Toronto: Doubleday Canada, 1974.

"Boy-Girl Expresses Pity for Constable: Benedictine Wiseman Is Handed Over to the Care of a Matron." *The Toronto World* 15 Sept. 1913: 4.

Cameron, Barry. "A Conversation with Clark Blaise." *Essays on Canadian Writing* 23 (1982): 5-25. Rpt. as "To Create Histories Around Little Things: An Interview with Clark Blaise" in *Clark Blaise: The Interviews.* Ed. J.R. (Tim) Struthers. Toronto: Guernica Editions, 2016. Essential Writers.

Clement, Lesley D. *Learning To Look: A Visual Response to Mavis Gallant's Fiction.* Montreal & Kingston: McGill-Queen's UP, 2000.

Deleuze, Gilles, and Félix Guattari. *Kafka: pour une littérature mineure.* Paris: Les éditions de Minuit, 1975.

Diamond, Ann. "Negative Capability: An Anglo Phone Saga." *Poetry Canada Review* 10.3 (1989): 5-7, 29.

Gallant, Mavis. *Home Truths: Selected Canadian Stories.* Toronto: Macmillan of Canada, 1981.

-----. *Montreal Stories.* Selected and with an introd. by Russell Banks. Toronto: McClelland & Stewart, 2004.

-----. *The Other Paris.* 1956. Freeport, NY: Books for Libraries, 1970. Short Story Index Reprint Ser.

-----. *The Pegnitz Junction: A Novella and Five Short Stories.* 1973. London: Jonathan Cape, 1974.

-----. *The Selected Stories of Mavis Gallant.* Toronto: McClelland & Stewart, 1996.

"Girl Dressed as a Youth Wins Prize for Singing: She Works as Clerk in Toronto Store for Two Months without Being Suspected of Masquerading." *Chicago Daily Tribune* 21 Sept. 1913: 2.

Glasbeek, Amanda. *Feminized Justice: The Toronto Women's Court, 1913-34.* Vancouver: UBC P, 2009. Law and Society Ser.

Grant, Judith Skelton. *Mavis Gallant and Her Works.* Toronto: ECW, 1989.

Hancock, Geoff. *Canadian Writers at Work: Interviews with Geoff Hancock.* Toronto: Oxford UP, 1987.

"Here and There." *The Wisconsin Jewish Chronicle* 27 Mar. 1936: 1.

Kulyk Keefer, Janice. *Reading Mavis Gallant.* Toronto: Oxford UP, 1989.

Lecker, Robert. *On the Line: Readings in the Short Fiction of Clark Blaise, John Metcalf, and Hugh Hood.* Downsview, ON: ECW, 1982.

Merler, Grazia. *Mavis Gallant: Narrative Patterns and Devices.* Ottawa: Tecumseh, 1978.

"Mother Tells Story of Daughter's Odd Romance Which Came to End Here: Meanwhile Benny Wiseman, Who Came Here from Canada with Married Man, 'Just a Pal,' Awaits Deportation Decision." *Syracuse Herald* 22 Apr. 1921: 7.

Mukherjee, Bharati. "An Invisible Woman." *Saturday Night*
    Mar. 1981: 36-40.

"No Slit Skirts for This Young Woman: Missing Montreal Girl
    Arrested in Toronto Was Wearing Attire of a Boy." *The
    Winnipeg Tribune* 13 Sept. 1913: 8.

"Romantic Weissman Girl Falls in Love Again, Chief of Police
    Hears." *Utica Morning Post* 29 Dec. 1921: 13.

Ross, Catherine Sheldrick. "Biocritical Essay." *The Clark Blaise
    Papers: First Accession and Second Accession: An Inventory
    of the Archive at The University of Calgary Libraries*. Comp.
    Marlys Chevrefils. Ed. Jean F. Tener and Apollonia Steele.
    Calgary: The U of Calgary P, 1991. xiii-xxxi. "Clark Blaise:
    Biocritical Essay." Special Collections, University of Cal-
    gary Libraries and Cultural Resources. 25 Oct. 2006. Web.
    27 Aug. 2014. <http://www.asc.ucalgary.ca/node/826>. Rpt.
    (rev.) as "Clark Blaise: The First Fifty Years, 1940-1990" in
    Clark Blaise: Essays on His Works. Ed. J.R. (Tim) Struthers.
    Toronto: Guernica Editions, 2016. Essential Writers.

Schaub, Danielle. *Mavis Gallant*. New York: Twayne, 1998.
    Twayne's World Authors Ser. 871.

Semley, John. "Gallant Wit." *The Globe and Mail* 16 Aug. 2014:
    R18.

Smith, Shaun. "The Invisible Canadian: After Decades Abroad,
    an Overlooked Master of the Short-Story Form Returns
    with a New Collection." *Quill & Quire*. Quill & Quire, Apr.
    2011. Web. 27 Aug. 2014. <http://www.quillandquire.com/
    authors/the-invisible-canadian/>.

Smythe, Karen E. *Figuring Grief: Gallant, Munro, and the Poet-
    ics of Elegy*. Montreal & Kingston: McGill-Queen's UP, 1992.

Solway, David. "Double Exile and Montreal English-Language
    Poetry." *Director's Cut*. Erin, ON: The Porcupine's Quill,
    2003. 59-66.

Struthers, J.R. (Tim). "Expressions of Your Breath: An Interview
    with Clark Blaise." Guelph, ON. 12 Nov. 1988. Collection of

the interviewer, J.R. (Tim) Struthers. Ts. 28 pp. *Clark Blaise: The Interviews.* Ed. J.R. (Tim) Struthers. Toronto: Guernica Editions, 2016. Essential Writers. Print.

Urquhart, Jane, ed. *The Penguin Book of Canadian Short Stories.* Toronto: Penguin Canada, 2007.

Verongos, Helen T. "Mavis Gallant, 91, Dies; Her Stories Told of Uprooted Lives and Loss." *The New York Times.* The New York Times, 18 Feb. 2014. Web. 16 Aug. 2014. <http://www.nytimes.com>.

"Wife Too Good to Bogus Count." *The Milwaukee Sentinel* 28 June 1926: 10.

I Once Was Lost but Now Am Found: Rereading Clark Blaise

Alexander MacLeod

One of the first university essays I ever wrote was on Clark Blaise. I was in an Introduction to Canadian Literature class and our professor, an expert on the Canadian short story, began the course with an assignment that was so deceptively simple I think it had to have been a trap. After the first week of class, we were told to pick any story ever produced by a Canadian and write six double-spaced pages about it. That was it. No list of preferred authors or topics to choose from, no outside sources required. No strict MLA formatting guidelines. Just pick a story, take an angle on it, and discuss the piece for six pages. It was, I realize now, what professors call a "response paper," an assignment that sets up a purposely exclusive relationship between the story and the student. In what turned out to be a mistake, I decided to tackle Blaise's "How I Became a Jew," one of four stories by him first showcased in *New Canadian Writing, 1968*, then included in his second full collection, *Tribal Justice*, and later in *Southern Stories*. This is one of Blaise's earliest works, a story that follows the misadventures of a boy named Gerald Gordon as he moves from rural Georgia to downtown Cincinnati in 1950 and enrolls for his first day of class at a recently integrated Junior High School.

I did what I could with my paper. I pulled the regular marathon-writing session the night before it was due, and I remember focussing a lot on the "symbolic import-ance" of an Abraham Lincoln statue that stands in front of Gerald's new school. In my general reading up to that point, I had learned just enough to know that if a writer puts an Abraham Lincoln statue into a story about the divisions between the North and the South in America, and if he mentions it more than once, and if that statue is "greenish" and trapped "behind black iron bars" (*Southern Stories* 110) — then that certainly qualifies as "signifi-cant." As far as I was concerned, a corroded Abraham Lincoln statue, wherever you found it, was "symbolically important" and if you had the feel for it, you could "re-spond" to that image for at least six pages and make a good case. I submitted my paper confidently.

When the marks came back, I was less than pleased. My professor thought this was mid-to-low B-level work. In his comments, he observed that I only had "the start of something" and that I hadn't fully developed my argu-ment. He congratulated me for choosing a fairly obscure selection, but warned me to be careful in the future. "There's more going on here than you can see," he said. "You need to take more time with this. Blaise is tricky."

Tricky — that was the word for Blaise. I'm not sure if it was a compliment or a criticism, but the point was clear: students who, by their own free will, chose to write unassuming introductory undergraduate papers on Clark Blaise got what they deserved. If, like so many of his protagonists, they wandered into a Blaisean short story expecting to find an easy way out and some kind of satisfying resolution, then, inevitably, they were head-ed toward disappointment and already well on their way to an uncomfortable, probably embarrassing fall. As

I learned early on, Blaise was not a tour guide you could trust. Though he might lead you down to the gator-infested waters of the Florida swamps, or through the crumbling urban architecture of the American rust belt, or back and forth across the troubling borders of Quebec, even into the near-suffocating strangeness of India, you had to stay alert and keep your head up. You had to be careful because although he might inspire your confidence by expertly drawing your attention to all those details — to the smells, the sights and sounds, the histories of all these different places — in the end, like it or not, Blaise would turn on you. At almost exactly the moment you let yourself go, at almost exactly the moment you surrendered yourself to the story, that was when he dumped you into the heart of foreignness and left you there to fend for yourself in a hostile and suddenly incomprehensible world.

As anyone who has read more than a few of his stories will tell you, feelings of emptiness are everywhere in Clark Blaise's work. Over a career that spans more than five decades, he has presented us with perhaps our time's most comprehensive examination of modern displacement. His characters are literally "missing in action." They are personifications of longing, defined most clearly by what they lack. No connection is safe in Blaise's stories: fathers cannot be trusted; mothers carry unspoken, painful histories; friends have ulterior motives; words shake free of their meanings and get lost in translation. In the worst-case scenarios, even language itself dissolves into an emotionally devastating mess of malapropisms spoken by Alzheimer's patients who cannot recognize their children or remember their own names. Yet although Blaise's settings may vary widely, his preferred situations have remained fairly consistent throughout his career. Yes, the timing, culture, and climate of his stories are in constant flux, but his characters, whenever or wherever they are in time and space, invariably come face to face with what might be called the Blaisean void — that overwhelming feeling of loss that seems to permeate almost every corner of his fictional world. Examples pile up on each other, endless variations on that one fertile but familiar theme.

How do we respond, for example, to Foley, the lead character in "A Fish Like a Buzzard," who loses his brother in a Florida swamp and is left there at the story's conclusion to wait alone "till somebody [comes] along" (*Southern Stories* 24)? What about the adolescent protagonist in "The Unwanted Attention of Strangers" who spends "eight hours strolling from gate to gate" inside the Pittsburgh airport and slowly feels his "special place in the universe" fading away (*Pittsburgh Stories* 27, 29)? Then there are all those Thibidaults and their sons, and the shape-shifting Porter/Carriers. Is it even possible to follow them through all their transformations and their border-crossing traumas? And why should anybody care for that misguided collection of academics who are always trying to "find themselves" in Montreal? What about the other Gerald, Gerald Lander, the world-famous linguist and star of *If I Were Me*: Is there a real-life reader tired and world-weary enough to relate to this character as he wanders across the globe, sometimes searching, sometimes running from his strange and scattered family? Freddie Singh could easily be describing the whole fictional population of Blaise's universe when he observes, in "Man and His World," that "'We are the only animals who can get so lost'" (*World Body* 167).

All those years ago, when I was writing my first paper on Blaise, I couldn't quite see how all this absence could possibly fill up a story or a novel. While I focussed my attention on the symbolic significance of that Abraham Lincoln statue, I was actually looking away from the true centre of the story. The plight of poor old Gerald Gordon, struggling in Cincinnati in 1950, never got the attention it deserved. When I look back now, I can see him there, caught at the precise intersection of American politics, religion, race, region, and class, and I realize there is nothing accidental about his fate. I think of Gerald Gordon as a kind of prototype. Before all the Thibidaults, all the Dyers, the Porters, Carriers, and Landers, he was the very first Blaise narrator to be hung out to dry by his creator. (In *An Other I*, Robert Lecker gives 1961 as the date of composition for "How I Became a Jew" [36].) Stuck smack dab in the middle of the twentieth century and trapped between North and South, Black and White, Rural and Urban, Rich and Poor, Childhood and Adulthood, he is just a kid desperately trying to make sense of himself in an obstinate world that cares nothing for him or his struggles. It is impossible not to feel for him, and it is easy to understand why Gerald wants to imagine himself as one of the chosen few, one of those select people called into an ideal Israel, a home where only the best belong. As readers we know that Gerald, like so many of the Blaisean characters who follow in his footsteps, can never gain access to such a place and that he and all the others will remain forever on the outside. The boy is caught in a riptide of uncertainty that can do nothing but carry him away. Too much is going on in his life; forces are at work that he cannot understand. Back when I was a student in Introduction to Canadian Literature, I was in a similar position. I couldn't quite see what was going on with Gerald or with Blaise. I couldn't feel the impending crush. My professor was right. I only had the beginning of something.

***

The last essay I've written (this one) is also about Clark Blaise. In the interval between my first messy engagement with his work and this current effort, some things have stayed the same and many other things have changed. I teach Introduction to Canadian Literature now and, whenever I get the chance, I dutifully inflict Blaise on all my students. It has been a curious kind of conversation. Slowly, after years of reading and re-reading his work, and following the critical debate about it, and teaching the stories again and again, my central interpretation of Blaise's fiction project has changed in a fairly significant way. I simply don't look at these stories in the same way I used to, and when I think about Blaise's unique contribution to Canadian literature I find myself re-evaluating most of the critical assumptions I once held.

It is difficult to pin down the exact reason for my revisionist reading of Blaise's work, but I think the historical and cultural shifts that have reshaped the world around his fiction have played no small role. Since the middle of the twentieth century, those exterior social contexts, the real life that exists "out there," beside and beyond the experiences recorded in Blaise's pages, has been so radically reconstituted that it almost demands a corresponding shift in how we read these stories. Like a photographic negative, changing and even reversing as it develops, the true significance of Blaise's work is only emerging now. It may be that the writer so many people — myself included — once considered as the great chronicler of North American rootlessness may actually turn out to be quite a different figure.

There is nothing strange or revolutionary about the kind of critical rereading Blaise's work deserves. Such reappraisals happen all the time. Literary critics, scholars in other fields, and commentators at large often have to wait for some kind of distance to open up between the present and the past before they are able to chart the dominant cultural contours of any given period. In Canadian literary studies, we are only starting to look back and reclaim some of the underappreciated writers from the '60s, '70s, and '80s. We are only beginning to interrogate their work more carefully and only beginning to ask the right questions. What kind of world did these artists examine? What sort of revolutionary changes did they grapple with? Sociological statistics, census data, and other demographic indicators can tell us everything we need to know about declining birth rates, fractured families, the rise of the Interstate highways, the suburbanization of the North American landscape, and the always accelerating advance of travel and telecommunications technologies during this period, but the literature that actively confronted these forces also needs to be consulted. How did an entire continent turn itself so completely from the endlessly differentiated, rurally dominated patchwork of separate geographical realities that dominated economics and politics in the 1930s into the undifferentiated sprawling postindustrial landscape that now dominates our lives? What sort of cultural realignment literally "took place" during these years? Where is the literary record? Is there a writer who captured it — the slow but inexorable fade of one world and the undeniable, but equally gradual rise of its replacement?

The startling originality of Blaise's engagement with contemporary cultural geography is only starting to receive the careful attention it merits. In the whole history of Canadian and American literature, I do not think there is another writer whose work is more directly hard-wired to the revolutionary socio-spatial transformations this continent has experienced from the middle of the twentieth century to the present. Blaise grew up on the Interstate. The key events of his life are marked by border-crossings between states, provinces, nations, cultures, and languages. His work is at home in transit, comfortable with multiculturalism, finely attuned to the divide between rural and urban life, aware of the schism between high and low culture, and continually curious about the political, historical, and economic forces that make and re-make our social environments. Anthologies and course syllabi are crowded with many other writers who each dutifully captured and explored their own particular sectors of Canadian and American geography, but there is no writer more out-of-place than Blaise, no writer more sensitive to the bumps, bruises, and scars of "a North American Education," and no writer more valuable to us if we want to look back and retrace the route that has brought us here.

To fully appreciate Blaise's unique contribution, we have to realize that despite his overwhelming fascination with geography, his work is not regionalist fiction — at least not in the way we traditionally define that loaded and ambiguous term. We are not dealing here with a Faulkner, an O'Connor, or a Welty. In fact, Blaise's stories examine an entirely different kind of terrain. He is the native son of nowhere, the proud inheritor of a complicated family tree that reaches not backwards into history, but rather outward across social space. Blaise, quite clearly, does not "belong" to the South or to Pittsburgh or to Montreal or to Calcutta. Instead, in a fairly remarkable reversal, these places exist in his fiction only during those brief historical moments when they belonged to Blaise: the South provides the setting for the

adventures of young boys; the Midwest challenges adolescents; Montreal teases newly minted academics; and
globe-trotting world travels are reserved for wise, old
men. Every place we visit in Blaise's work is indexed to
this one lifeline, this one set of human experiences. The
stories are about places that have no real claim on Blaise.
They did not "produce" him according to the old clichés
of environmental determinism. Rather, precisely the opposite thing is unfolding here. Every location is limited
to the role it played in the development of one imagination. "Our lives are time zones," Blaise writes evocatively
at the conclusion of *Time Lord* (239). Personal histories
cannot be separated from the places where memory is
made. What Blaise calls the "*whereness*" of identity is at
least as important as its "whoness" or its "whatness" (*Resident Alien* 2). As he observes in an interview by Barry
Cameron, "everything I've done has been related to ...
how we understand where we have been placed and
what we are to become ..." (Blaise in Cameron 5).

How we read Blaise and how we interpret the dominant struggle in his fiction depends on how we approach
this issue of place-based identity. Does a character require a stable home before he or she can possess a stable
identity? Does environment determine destiny? Or is it
possible that those who no longer live in their native
lands — or those who could never claim such a connection to place — can still find ways to orient themselves
in foreign conditions, wherever they may be. In "Dark
Matter," Gerald Lander believes that for him "[t]he most
precious thing in the world [is] his belonging to a place
that subtly exclude[s] him — or ... his right to reject a
place that subtly include[s] him" (*If I Were Me* 87). It is a
purposely ambivalent statement. Lander simultaneously wants to be a part of and apart from the world he

inhabits. Unlike the child protagonists who figure so strongly in Blaise's early stories, Lander's reflections on membership and belonging often tend toward abstraction; he spends more time *thinking* about his relationship with place than he does *feeling* the brute physical or emotional pain of his various dislocations. Lander is a multilingual, world-travelling citizen of the globe. He has devoted his life to the pursuit of foreign languages, foreign grammars, foreign words and worlds. However, he longs for precisely the kind of rootedness he is not allowed to possess. "What country do you give for a man who has everything?" he asks himself in "Dark Matter" (*If I Were Me* 102). The freedom to travel widely and the opportunity to gain unlimited access to the world becomes its own kind of prison. The protagonists of Blaise's later stories often run to the foreign and away from the local because they have never experienced the traditional idea of home. They use their considerable intellectual gifts to uncover the rooted connections of others while simultaneously severing or discrediting whatever linkages they themselves might value. In one of his most poignant moments, Lander observes, in "The Banality of Virtue," that "[w]hen the whole world screws you up, it takes even more of the world's resources to straighten you out" (*If I Were Me* 43).

***

When I teach Blaise's stories in my own Introduction to Canadian Literature classes today, I am always surprised by the reactions I get. My students — coming as they do from a mix of cultural, linguistic, and economic backgrounds — never seem to identify with all that loss, the feelings of exile and exceptional loneliness that I once thought were undeniable in Blaise's work. Even when I bring in my maps and chart the many movements in Blaise's peripatetic career, and even when I quote from all those interviews and articles that have tried to uncover the autobiographical elements of Blaise's stories, the students still stubbornly turn away from any interpretation that sees Blaise as the lonely victim of a wandering childhood and itinerant parents. Instead, the best students, many of them the second-generation products of the kinds of night school adult-learners portrayed in "A Class of New Canadians," read these stories as an accurate record of their own experiences in the late twentieth and early twenty-first centuries. Rather than seeing Blaise as an exceptional outsider, they read him as an average, even archetypal contemporary figure — not an exile, but an obvious member of their tribe. When I present them with Gerald Gordon or Gerald Lander and I say, "Look at how alone he is," they shake their heads and say, "No, everybody is alone like that at some point."

After so many years of emigration and immigration, and after decades of cultural and linguistic inter-marriage, and after generations of ever-increasing personal mobility and travel, the world outside Blaise's fiction has caught up to lives led inside the books. When we reread these stories today, we see that Blaise's characters are not nearly as unusual as we may once have thought. Rather than imagining that they are lost and alone, it seems now that Blaise's characters are actually leading the way, carving out a path that millions have followed in recent decades. It may be true that two generations ago most of the North American population lived and died within fifty miles of the places where they were born, but that simply is no longer the case. "The past," as L.P. Hartley famously put it in his novel *The Go-Between*, "is a foreign country" and we do not live there any more. When scholars study Blaise's work, they are not reading anthropological reports on some strange group of lonely overeducated misfits who just can't fit in no matter where they go. If it were only possible to shake off the nostalgic fog that so often clouds our reading on the issue of place, we might finally see the mirror Blaise is holding up. We might finally understand that when we look at his people, we see ourselves — an entire population haunted by visions and stories of a stable home place that never actually belonged to us.

In one of his most candid, self-reflexive moments early in his autobiographical fragment "The Voice of Unhousement," Blaise provides the following description of his writing life: "I am like a dog tied to a post and then forgotten; I have sniffed every inch of my turf, I've dug it up, I've soiled it, I've hounded my life for meaning as though it were somehow prototypical, epic and exemplary, rather than sheltered, eccentric and utterly accidental" (*Resident Alien* 9). The introduction to *Resident Alien* contains a similar kind of self-evaluation. Here, Blaise claims that "[i]f I have any distinction at all as an author, it is through acting out, dramatizing, the background setting of a conventional existence and teasing from it the stuff of nightmare and wonder" (*Resident Alien* 2). Speaking with Barry Cameron, he argues that "there's nothing universal in my autobiography unless I choose to make it that way. Otherwise, it's a thoroughly singular and useless one" (Blaise in Cameron 10). Obviously, the most hostile critic Blaise has ever faced is Blaise himself. I think he treats his own work very harshly; I also think the hard lines Blaise uses to describe his own life have had a powerful effect on how his fiction is read. Are these stories "prototypical" or "eccentric," "conventional" or full of "wonder," "universal" or "singular and useless"? Everything depends on how we answer these questions. If Blaise's stories are about eccentrics acting out their strange lives in strange locales, then we can safely locate his work in the nineteenth-century genre of the local colour sketch and be done with it. In reading local colour stories, we imaginatively "escape" from our own lives and temporarily delight in the exotic experience of the foreign. But if Blaise's stories are typical and universal, then there can be no such separation between reader and character. There can be no easy division between the familiar "us" and the foreign "them." If, as I believe, the life Blaise is exploring in his fiction is far more conventional than even he would have us believe, then readers must go into these stories expecting to find themselves, expecting to have a deeper engagement with the world in which they live.

***

In the year 2000, two separate but closely related events occurred in Blaise's publishing career. While Knopf Canada was releasing *Time Lord*, Blaise's nonfictional but endlessly creative study of Sir Sandford Fleming and the invention of standard time, The Porcupine's Quill simultaneously launched a separate four-volume *Selected Stories* series that reclassified Blaise's short fiction according to his shifting fascination with different fictional landscapes. Rather than following the normal route and carving up a writer's career according to epochal changes in his personal history — from early to middle to late — The Porcupine's Quill decided, on Blaise's recommendation, that it would be more appropriate to divide his life work according to the seismic shifts of his fictional geographies. I do not know if the near parallel release of *Time Lord* and the *Selected Stories* series was a happy accident or the product of a careful strategy, but I know that each project was enriched by the presence of the other. At exactly the moment Blaise was using his new work to draw attention back to the underappreciated aesthetic qualities of our relationship with Time, The Porcupine's Quill was asking us to think again about Blaise's old work and the underappreciated sophistication of its aesthetic engagement with Space.

In the end, Blaise's work always comes back to these issues. Time and Space. History and Geography. The cognitive strategies we use to locate ourselves within the perpetually shifting borders of these two most fundamental attributes of human life. These are his core subjects. Blaise is fascinated by the intersection of the temporal and the spatial. Though he is obviously aware of Heisenberg and Einstein, Derrida, Foucault, and Saussure, and though he is clearly sensitive to the challenges of uncertainty, relativity, chaos, entropy, and deconstruction, Blaise continues to ask his stubborn questions and continues to wonder about how we find ourselves, even temporarily, in a world that can never be, and indeed never was, stable and unchanging. Like Fleming, Blaise measures his time by the mile and his distance by the hour. Maybe he was never as lost as he (or we, or I) thought. Perhaps his work is not a catalogue of absence, not an exploration of the void, not a perpetual sending away, but rather an acutely sensitive travelogue about a long, circuitous journey home to whatever home can look like in the twenty-first century.

Works Cited

Blaise, Clark. *If I Were Me: A Novel*. Erin, ON: The Porcupine's Quill, 1997. Rpt. (expanded) in *World Body*. Introd. Michael Augustin. Erin, ON: The Porcupine's Quill, 2006. Vol. 4 of *The Selected Stories of Clark Blaise*. 4 vols. 2000-06.

-----. *Montreal Stories*. Introd. Peter Behrens. Erin, ON: The Porcupine's Quill, 2003. Vol. 3 of *The Selected Stories of Clark Blaise*. 4 vols. 2000-06.

-----. *A North American Education: A Book of Short Fiction*. Toronto: Doubleday Canada, 1973.

-----. *Pittsburgh Stories*. Introd. Robert Boyers. Erin, ON: The Porcupine's Quill, 2001. Vol. 2 of *The Selected Stories of Clark Blaise*. 4 vols. 2000-06.

-----. *Resident Alien*. Markham, ON: Penguin Books Canada, 1986.

-----. *Southern Stories*. Introd. Fenton Johnson. Erin, ON: The Porcupine's Quill, 2000. Vol. 1 of *The Selected Stories of Clark Blaise*. 4 vols. 2000-06.

-----. *Time Lord: The Remarkable Canadian Who Missed His Train, and Changed the World*. Toronto: Alfred A. Knopf Canada, 2000.

-----. *Tribal Justice*. Toronto: Doubleday Canada, 1974.

-----. *World Body*. Introd. Michael Augustin. Erin, ON: The Porcupine's Quill, 2006. Vol. 4 of *The Selected Stories of Clark Blaise*. 4 vols. 2000-06.

Cameron, Barry. "A Conversation with Clark Blaise." *Essays on Canadian Writing* 23 (1982): 5-25. Rpt. as "To Create Histories Around Little Things: An Interview with Clark Blaise" in *Clark Blaise: The Interviews*. Ed. J.R. (Tim) Struthers. Toronto: Guernica Editions, 2016. Essential Writers.

Hartley, L.P. *The Go-Between*. London: Hamish Hamilton, 1953.

Lecker, Robert. *An Other I: The Fictions of Clark Blaise*. Toronto: ECW, 1988.

New Canadian Writing, 1968: Stories by David Lewis Stein, Clark Blaise and Dave Godfrey. Toronto: Clarke, Irwin, 1968.

Border-Crossing and the Moving Nation: The Stories of Clark Blaise

Andrew C. McKague

Clark Blaise's defiant insistence in his essay "The Smuggler's Son Grows Older" that "I am what you say I cannot be" reasserts the right and the responsibility of the contemporary artist to keep moving, to challenge and redefine perceived boundaries of place, time, nationality, race, ethnicity, class, language, the mind. Blaise's fiction reflects, and elaborates on, his experiences of border-crossing, alienation, dislocation — a state of perpetual "unhousement," to borrow the term he employs emphatically at the end of the same essay for the condition and the act of never being grounded for very long in one place. Of course we must not forget that writers' mastery of words — indeed writers' inventiveness — is, and needs to be, the pre-eminent factor in our appreciation of their works. Nevertheless, a biographical understanding of the fundamental if characteristically changing outlines of Blaise's life as an artist is critical to any discussion of his writing because of the profound relationship of his past to the intensely autobiographical dimensions of his fiction. Sources including the biographical section of Barry Cameron's *Clark Blaise and His Works* (1985), Blaise's detailed "Chronology of Salience" in Robert Lecker's *An Other I: The Fictions of Clark Blaise* (1988), Catherine Sheldrick Ross's "Biocritical Essay" in *The Clark Blaise Papers*

(1991), Roger K. Smith's introduction to the Blaise entry
in *Short Story Criticism*, Vol. 225 (2016), interviews by individuals such as Geoff Hancock, J.R. (Tim) Struthers,
and Alexander MacLeod, along with Blaise's own powerful autobiographical essay and update, first published in
1986 and 2005 then collected in his *Selected Essays* (2008),
and Blaise's new autobiographical annex written for J.R.
(Tim) Struthers' *Clark Blaise: Essays on His Works* (2016),
tell us of an extraordinary life lived and of a stellar body
of writing devised.

Blaise was born in Fargo, North Dakota in 1940 to an
English-Canadian mother (from Manitoba) and a French-
Canadian father (from Québec), attended some twenty-
five or thirty schools in the South and the central United
States and Canada during his youth, did a B.A. in English
and Geology at Denison University in Granville, Ohio,
and took his MFA at the University of Iowa. He moved to
Montreal in 1966, becoming a Canadian citizen in 1973
— the same year as he published his first book, the classic story cycle *A North American Education*. In Montreal
he taught at Sir George Williams University, later Concordia University, founded Concordia's popular graduate
program in Creative Writing, and, as described in his
essay "Portrait of the Artist as a Young Pup," was a member of The Montreal Story Tellers. After leaving Montreal
in 1978, Blaise has been on the run ever since, with a
longer than usual stretch, from 1989 to 1998, as Director
of the renowned International Writing Program at the
University of Iowa, then settling (more or less) in San
Francisco, with his wife, writer and professor Bharati
Mukherjee, until her retirement on June 30, 2013, at
which point the couple relocated back to New York City.
He has taught or lectured across Canada, in several
parts of the United States, and in many countries around

the world—"here, there, and everywhere," to echo the title of the three lectures he delivered and published in Japan in 1994.

From 2000 to 2006 the distinguished Canadian small press The Porcupine's Quill published a four-volume set entitled *The Selected Stories of Clark Blaise* which collects the author's finest stories in terms of location. Although this type of cataloguing is a rather precarious practice, given the constant movement in Blaise's works, examining a single story from each collection can serve as a way to explore the totality of Blaise's universe. Stories such as "South" from *Southern Stories* (2000), "The Waffle Maker" from *Pittsburgh Stories* (2001), "A Class of New Canadians" from *Montreal Stories* (2003), and "Did, Had, Was" from *World Body* (2006) illustrate simultaneously the locations and the dislocations of Blaise's world. As a means of furthering such critical exploration, various border theories and concepts can establish frameworks for understanding the forces which impinge on Blaise and his fictional protagonists. After briefly discussing these complementary theoretical resources, I plan to argue that—in addition to the commonality from story to story highlighted by these frameworks—each short story possesses its own distinctiveness: its own form of border-crossing, with characters sometimes succeeding and sometimes failing to make and to cope with change.

The importance of border-crossing in contemporary fiction should not be underestimated. On a planet where more borders of every kind are being constructed each year, the power of artistic border-crossing is something we should savour. I shall provide a multiple perspective on border theory, beginning first with theorist Mieke Bal, who mobilizes "travelling concepts" of literary criticism and interdisciplinary studies nicely mirroring

Blaise's depiction of movement. The ensuing segment
will concern travel writer, cultural critic, and novelist
Pico Iyer, who presents an optimistic portrait of global
culture in the contemporary world. And finally we can
proceed to key essays by Blaise himself for an up-close
take on what borders mean to him—before moving
across another border, of genre, to the four stories chosen
for discussion here.

Bal's *Travelling Concepts in the Humanities: A Rough
Guide* offers a relevant and progressive framework with
which to begin. For Bal there is something important to
be gained from a life lived on shifting terrain; problematic coordinates and frequent change have their benefits.
She believes that "To make your fortune, you have to
travel. Hazardous, exciting, and tiring, travel is needed if
you are to achieve the gain of new experience" (4). Not
only are the characters—or, as Bal conceives of them in
her study *Narratology*, the "actors" and "characters" and
"speakers" (5-9)—throughout Blaise's fiction gaining, if
sometimes losing, from their transitory ways of life, but
this essay, too, travels back and forth between theoretical border frameworks and fictive border-crossers.

What Bal in *Travelling Concepts* calls "a spirit of adventure" (23) is the positive energy which propels our
dreams. Of course the main interest in Bal's text centres
on the need for interdisciplinarity in the academy, so
that concepts can breathe (travel), instead of being confined, and tested, by methods of only one kind of training or approach. As opposed to scholars who demand
that "the 'correct' philosophical understanding of concepts" form the basis of critical method, for Bal "the primary concern is not 'correct' but 'meaningful' use" of
concepts (16-17). Typically Blaise's border-crossers likewise travel not to be 'right' or 'wrong', but to fight what-

ever binds and controls their collective selves — forever ungrounded.

In the *Harper's Magazine* article "The Last Refuge: On the Promise of the New Canadian Fiction," Iyer, author of *The Global Soul*, argues that ours is "a world in which more and more people are on the move and motion itself has become a kind of nation" (77). "The Global Soul" is a term which Blaise could have accepted decades before it was ever employed. Although those who live in this moving nation are in a constant state of disorder, each hopes ideally, Iyer argues in his book, to "make the collection of his [or her] selves something greater than the whole" (121). Iyer also proposes that this collection of selves can be compared to "a Global City" (121), with a collection of cultural communities gelling into something greater than one static entity. In a sense, then, despite the emphasis on place implied by Blaise's titles for individual volumes of his *Selected Stories*, it is worth gesturing towards the possibility that place really doesn't matter much at all — provided it's never fixed. What matters most is the entire "world body."

For members of the moving nation, as Blaise emphasizes in "The Smuggler's Son Grows Older," uncrossed borders aren't very stimulating because they involve entrapment in past practices. Global Souls — people who challenge norms for the good of others not for personal gain — can learn and teach more, Blaise like Iyer would say, by travelling than by staying still. Iyer notes in his book that "Global Souls are seen as belonging to a kind of migratory tribe, able to see things more clearly than those imprisoned in local concerns can, yet losing their identity often as they fall between the cracks" (140). While many of Blaise's characters possess that special ability to observe their surroundings keenly, they often lack the power to handle their fragmented selves, suffering a range of problems from emotional strain to mental deterioration. In his essay "The Border as Fiction," Blaise contends that "Borders, in fact, exacerbate instability. Borders are madness ..." (9).

Blaise has acquired a "border consciousness" (1), as he calls it in "The Border as Fiction," of the most sophisticated standard; few writers are capable of the authentic insight found in his blend of autobiographical fiction. In the same essay he remarks: "I look upon borders as zones of grace, fifty miles wide on either side, where dualities of spirit are commonplace" (1). For a man like Blaise, however, borders are in some ways troubling; they ask the questions of identity and purpose which, in "The Smuggler's Son Grows Older," he says he fears: "Who are you? What are you? Why have you come? How long will you stay?" Of course Blaise's concerns are not confined to matters of geography and "unhousement." His characters face the economic divide of the poor and the rich, battle the tensions of race and ethnicity, move amongst foreign cultures, and travel with their minds, be it jumping the links of time or sliding into mental deterioration. There are no definite answers; there is no fixed outcome.

The stereotypical borders of identity tell you that you cannot be two selves or more. The borders say that you cannot be from many places or homes — although in fact Blaise is, and so are most of his characters. Moving from place to place is the signature of Clark Blaise. But from the more obvious pictures of border-crossing, we can envisage much more. In "South," a man of uncertain age, profession, and residence looks back on a boyhood spent moving from town to town, on a time when his mother crossed racial and cultural borders, taking the family where she 'shouldn't', then passed a mental boundary as she later slipped into senility. "The Waffle Maker" portrays the borders and gaps of place and time as a jet-setting sixty-year-old writer looks back on a Pittsburgh adolescence, and a life, that has been. "A Class of New Canadians" depicts the challenges posed for a thirty-year-old teacher just arrived from the United States, and for his diverse adult students, by borders of nation and culture and language and economics when these are interwoven with Montreal politics. And "Did, Had, Was" crosses not only continental and national boundaries but also the border between a state of health and mental disease, the trial of a world-travelling journalist nearing retirement. Blaise has created an identity for his characters, for himself, and for contemporary readers out of his various crossings and has unpacked his findings in the remarkable fiction now collected in four interconnected volumes.

The story "South" describes the repeatedly destabilized situation of a poverty-stricken family in the Deep South in the year 1946. As a result of the boy's father being seriously injured in a car accident, and unable to work, the boy's mother is forced to sell her belongings gathered over a lifetime of motion. Although I selected this story on account of its acknowledgement of the problematic borders of race and class, "South" also reinforces the belief that something can be gained, not just lost, through moving from place to place. Years later, relating the story, the son remarks about his mother's preparation to sell her keepsakes: "she'd accumulated things in Europe and in England and then in Montreal.... She unwrapped them and cried; she tried to tell me the stories of their acquisition, the smuggling out" (124).

True to Iyer's desire for cultural integration, and to the mother's own progressive sense of border-crossing, she moves her family across culturally and economically imposed borders of race and class to a poor African-American neighbourhood on the east side of town, settling them in as the only white people on that side of the town's east/west, poor/rich, black/white border. Morally, the mother experiences a sense of victory; but in practice her progressive "concepts" do not travel well into the South of the mid-twentieth century. The mother's ideas and behaviour initially cause her son only embarrassment, as exemplified when he sees her approaching the east side of town: "I prayed she wouldn't cross over" (127).

By the end of the story, we learn that the mother, having had no luck in the racist South, not only sold all her prized possessions, but also left her husband, moved back home to Manitoba, and now has crossed another border, a medical one: she suffers acutely from memory loss. Here we see an example of someone forced to eliminate her various selves as a result of exhausting conditions, and then suffering further losses which are utterly out of her control, leaving her as a solitary shell of what she once was. She is left "alone in an apartment in Winnipeg" (129), forgetting whether she has eaten, forgetting to cook the food she has bought. Ironically, the son recognizes the importance of his mother's life only when she has passed a border into a place where he can no longer communicate with her. "Mother, why couldn't we love you enough?" (130) he is left wondering, now as then existing in the mythic shadows of his father.

The story "The Waffle Maker" presents another embattled protagonist, Lewis Morris — or, as he renames himself, Lew Morrison — striving to negotiate between the past and the present, reflecting on a life which has relied on border-crossing to create happiness and self-worth. Growing up in Pittsburgh, the so-called armpit of the United States, he watches his talented tap-dancing father, Lou Morris, miss out on a life which could have been if he had escaped the city. Years later, Lew notes of his father, "The problem was in the geographical co-ordinates of his life" (126). Another fraught relationship of the adolescent boy's is his thwarted love for a female exchange-student from India named Laxmi, who stays with the family until forced to leave Pittsburgh upon learning that a marriage has been arranged for her back home. A fixed "concept" such as Laxmi's arranged marriage can be seen as analogous to what concerns Bal theoretically in the academy. I would argue that these two experiences propel Lew into a border-crossing mind-set; in essence he must seize the world and control it.

As a sixteen-year-old, he drives out to the Greater Pittsburgh International Airport in order "to feel connected to a wider world and to watch glamorous people coming and going" (132). Iyer contends in *The Global Soul* that the airport (and we might add the airplane) is "the spiritual center of the double life: you get on as one person and get off as another" (42). Narrating "The Waffle Maker" at age sixty, while on board an airplane, Lew thinks back to the low-lifes and bullies from his school days and assumes that they're still stuck in Pittsburgh. For this border-crosser, movement allows for personal progression and identity formation, which, as Bal says of "concepts," operate "not so much as firmly established univocal terms but as dynamic in themselves" (11). Lew is a scriptwriter and playwright whose latest work — based on physicist Werner Heisenberg, discoverer of the uncertainty principle — confronts "the voices and judgement of history" (127). And in personal terms, although scarred by the experiences of his youth, Lew can now look back at Pittsburgh and reminisce fondly about his back pages

— even if, as I believe, this is only as a result of keeping on the move since he left. Indeed, at the very end of the story Lew alters course again, skipping the off-Broadway production of his new play to catch one plane then another in restless, uncertain, but for him essential pursuit of Laxmi and the qualities she embodies.

In "A Class of New Canadians," Norman Dyer is an example of border-crossing gone astray, despite, and, more importantly, because of, his dedicated efforts at self-advancement. Himself an exile from the United States recently arrived in Canada, Dyer teaches English as a second language and desperately tries to fit into bilingual Montreal by immersing himself in the language, literature, politics, and cultural textures of Québec. He compares his teaching, pretentiously, to that of "Joyce in Trieste, Isherwood and Nabokov in Berlin, Beckett in Paris" (52). Now that Dyer has found what he perceives to be the cultural centre of the universe, he tries to fix himself firmly into belonging. But for Dyer the goal is mastery, and our sense of his settledness in a state of smug self-satisfaction only increases as the story proceeds. Therefore, I would argue that Dyer is not border-crossing to improve his understanding of others or even to better himself — but instead to satisfy his fixation with being in the centre.

After teaching one of his classes he learns that students of his, such as Mr. Weinrot and Miguel Mayor, are learning English in order to leave Montreal and move around the world. Through his teaching Dyer would seem to be promoting movement — as advocated by thinkers like Bal and Iyer — but he actually wants no part of it. At one point Dyer feels "He wanted to turn and shout to Weinrot and to all the others that Montreal was the greatest city on the continent, if only they knew it as well as he did" (55). And at another point Dyer knowingly neglects to edit fully Mayor's letter seeking employment (outside of Canada), hoping Mayor will be forced to remain in Montreal for a while longer. We might say that it is Dyer's current resistance to classic Blaise "unhousement" which should warn readers that something is off.

"Did, Had, Was" concentrates on a character, the Québec-born world journalist Paul Picard, who has spent a lifetime travelling relentlessly across Europe, Africa, and Asia. Now, however, in the twilight of his career, with his contacts dying or losing power, Picard's memory begins to fade as he enters what he worries is the start of "mental bankruptcy" (132) — a condition from which his mother, like the narrator's mother in "South," suffered. Plans of retirement are put on hold as a result of a school of journalism offering him "a major commitment: The Picard Centre of International Communications" (129); even this name calls out "border-crossing." But gradually in "Did, Had, Was" Picard is seen to be losing grip on where he is and what he is doing at the moment.

While it could be argued that here we are observing an example of a mind made up of too many borders, leading to ultimate dislocation in the form of terminal illness, I wish to suggest that disorientation is a natural attribute of the Global Soul. When Iyer identifies the state of confusion commonly found at airports, "And so, half-inadvertently, not knowing whether I was facing east or west, not knowing whether it was night or day, I slipped into that peculiar state of mind — or no-mind — that belongs to the no-time, no-place of the airport" (59), he could well be describing Picard's psyche. At story's end Picard thinks that he is back in Montreal during his student days when he is actually in Paris decades later.

As Picard's mind freely jumps place and time, we learn about the many other borders he has crossed. Moral codes are broken by his overwhelming sexual desires; he depends on the sex trade, disregarding taboo practices no matter where he goes or what the cost. From years of observing torture and murder, Picard comes to straddle the line between reporting and feeling — he does both. Clear conclusions and perfect logic do not appeal to the probing psyche and accordingly Picard rightly, albeit tragically, refuses to cease crossing old and new kinds of borders. He remains intent on providing — if eventually only in his behaviour and no longer in his writing — the world with his discoveries. Picard had known from early adulthood his destiny to be a border-crosser. "He'd committed himself to instability," to "the intoxication of a journalist's freedom: to lay out a new course of study every day" (136), and he never turns back.

The four stories that I have selected offer examples of many types of borders and of different sorts of border-crossers. Although each story reflects a sense of geographical place, it becomes apparent that motion and change are the coordinates which truly matter in the world of Bal's "travelling concepts." The narrator's mother in "South" is equipped with steadfast border-crossing impulses, but ultimately falters because of social and medical conditions which prove too powerful, forcing her into a much-diminished state back in the place where she started. Lew Morrison set forth as a young man to better his existence by leaving Pittsburgh, has tried to enhance the lives of others through his art, and at age sixty recognizes the need to change again. In Norman Dyer we meet a character who makes an initial move to Montreal, but once there ironically sets limits for himself and others. Then in Paul Picard we find a character who, as a result of memory loss, no longer always knows where he is, yet carries on. Perhaps Paul Picard is the ultimate border-crosser in the Blaise universe. A man estranged from his surroundings, battling all conditions, keeping constantly in motion, unwilling to quit.

Works Consulted

Bal, Mieke. *Narratology: Introduction to the Theory of Narrative.* 2nd ed. Toronto: U of Toronto P, 1997.

-----. *Travelling Concepts in the Humanities: A Rough Guide.* Toronto: U of Toronto P, 2002.

Blaise, Clark. "[Autobiographical Annex: Clark Blaise.]" In "BLAISE, Clark 1940- ." *Contemporary Authors: A Bio-Bibliographical Guide to Current Writers in Fiction, General Nonfiction, Poetry, Journalism, Drama, Motion Pictures, Television, and Other Fields.* Vol. 231. Project Ed. Julie Keppen. Farmington Hills, MI: Thomson Gale, 2005. 50-57. Rpt. (rev.) as "Autobiographical Annex: 1985-2006." *Selected Essays.* By Clark Blaise. Ed. John Metcalf and J.R. (Tim) Struthers. Windsor, ON: Biblioasis, 2008. 209-21.

-----. "The Border as Fiction." *The Border as Fiction*; and *Borderlines and Borderlands in English Canada: The Written Line.* By Clark Blaise; and Russell Brown. Orono, ME: Borderlands Project, The Canadian-American Center, U of Maine, 1990. 1-12. Borderlands Monograph Ser. 4. Rpt. (rev.) in *Selected Essays.* By Clark Blaise. Ed. John Metcalf and J.R. (Tim) Struthers. Windsor, ON: Biblioasis, 2008. 43-56.

-----. "Chronology of Salience." *An Other I: The Fictions of Clark Blaise.* By Robert Lecker. Toronto: ECW, 1988. 13-20.

-----. "Clark Blaise: *1940- .*" *Contemporary Authors: Autobiography Series.* Vol. 3. Ed. Adele Sarkissian. Detroit, MI: Gale

Research, 1986. 15-30. Rpt. in "BLAISE, Clark 1940- ." *Contemporary Authors: A Bio-Bibliographical Guide to Current Writers in Fiction, General Nonfiction, Poetry, Journalism, Drama, Motion Pictures, Television, and Other Fields*. Vol. 231. Project Ed. Julie Keppen. Farmington Hills, MI: Thomson Gale, 2005. 37-50. Rpt. (rev.) as "Autobiographical Essay: 1940-1984." *Selected Essays*. By Clark Blaise. Ed. John Metcalf and J.R. (Tim) Struthers. Windsor, ON: Biblioasis, 2008. 9-32.

-----. "A Class of New Canadians." *Montreal Stories*. Introd. Peter Behrens. Erin, ON: The Porcupine's Quill, 2003. 51-59. Vol. 3 of *The Selected Stories of Clark Blaise*. 4 vols. 2000-06.

-----. "Did, Had, Was." *World Body*. Introd. Michael Augustin. Erin, ON: The Porcupine's Quill, 2006. 129-43. Vol. 4 of *The Selected Stories of Clark Blaise*. 4 vols. 2000-06.

-----. *Here, There and Everywhere*. Tokyo: Center for Intl. Programs, Meiji U, 1994. Meiji U Intl. Exchange Programs Guest Lecture Ser. 1.

-----. *A North American Education: A Book of Short Fiction*. Toronto: Doubleday Canada, 1973.

-----. "Portrait of the Artist as a Young Pup." *The Montreal Story Tellers: Memoirs, Photographs, Critical Essays*. Ed. J.R. (Tim) Struthers. Montreal: Véhicule, 1985. 65-72. Rpt. (rev.) in *Selected Essays*. By Clark Blaise. Ed. John Metcalf and J.R. (Tim) Struthers. Windsor, ON: Biblioasis, 2008. 147-55.

-----. "The Smuggler's Son Grows Older." *Clark Blaise, Proprietor*. Ed. J.R. (Tim) Struthers. *Short Story* ns 15.2 (2007): 57-64. Rpt. (rev.) in *Selected Essays*. By Clark Blaise. Ed. John Metcalf and J.R. (Tim) Struthers. Windsor, ON: Biblioasis, 2008. 65-74.

-----. "South." *Southern Stories*. Introd. Fenton Johnson. Erin, ON: The Porcupine's Quill, 2000. 123-30. Vol. 1 of *The Selected Stories of Clark Blaise*. 4 vols. 2000-06.

-----. "The View from Seventy-Five: Autobiographical Annex 2002-2015." *Clark Blaise: Essays on His Works.* Ed. J.R. (Tim) Struthers. Toronto: Guernica Editions, 2016. Essential Writers.

-----. "The Waffle Maker." *Pittsburgh Stories.* Introd. Robert Boyers. Erin, ON: The Porcupine's Quill, 2001. 125-42. Vol. 2 of *The Selected Stories of Clark Blaise.* 4 vols. 2000-06.

Cameron, Barry. "Clark Blaise (1940-)." *Canadian Writers and Their Works.* Ed. Robert Lecker, Jack David, and Ellen Quigley. Introd. George Woodcock. Fiction Ser. Vol. 7. Toronto: ECW, 1985. 20-89. Rpt. as *Clark Blaise and His Works.* Toronto: ECW, 1985.

Hancock, Geoff. "Clark Blaise." *Canadian Writers at Work: Interviews with Geoff Hancock.* By Geoff Hancock. Toronto: Oxford UP, 1987. 146-63. Rpt. as "Clear Veneer: An Interview with Clark Blaise" in *Clark Blaise: The Interviews.* Ed. J.R. (Tim) Struthers. Toronto: Guernica Editions, 2016. Essential Writers.

Iyer, Pico. *The Global Soul: Jet Lag, Shopping Malls, and the Search for Home.* 2000. New York: Vintage, 2001.

-----. "The Last Refuge: On the Promise of the New Canadian Fiction." *Harper's Magazine* June 2002: 77-80.

MacLeod, Alexander. "'Too Canadian for the Americans and too American for the Canadians': An Interview with Clark Blaise." *Essays on Canadian Writing* 79 (2003): 178-90. Rpt. as "Too Canadian for the Americans and Too American for the Canadians: An Interview with Clark Blaise" in *Clark Blaise: The Interviews.* Ed. J.R. (Tim) Struthers. Toronto: Guernica Editions, 2016. Essential Writers.

Ross, Catherine Sheldrick. "Biocritical Essay." *The Clark Blaise Papers: First Accession and Second Accession: An Inventory of the Archive at The University of Calgary Libraries.* Comp. Marlys Chevrefils. Ed. Jean F. Tener and Apollonia Steele. Calgary: The U of Calgary P, 1991. xiii-xxxi. "Clark

Blaise: Biocritical Essay." Special Collections, University of Calgary Libraries and Cultural Resources. 25 Oct. 2006. Web. 10 Apr. 2007. <http://www.asc.ucalgary.ca/node/826>. Rpt. (rev.) as "Clark Blaise: The First Fifty Years, 1940-1990" in *Clark Blaise: Essays on His Works*. Ed. J.R. (Tim) Struthers. Toronto: Guernica Editions, 2016. Essential Writers.

Smith, Roger K. Introduction. "Clark Blaise (1940-)." *Short Story Criticism*. Vol. 225. Ed. Lawrence J. Trudeau. Detroit, MI: Gale, Cengage Learning, 2016. 73-75.

Struthers, J.R. (Tim). "Angles of Vision: An Interview with Clark Blaise." *The New Quarterly* 13.3 (1993): 113-29. Rpt. as "In the Beginning: An Interview with Clark Blaise" in *Clark Blaise: The Interviews*. Ed. J.R. (Tim) Struthers. Toronto: Guernica Editions, 2016. Essential Writers.

-----. "Part of the Myth: An Interview with Clark Blaise." *Carousel* 9 (1993): 26-46. Rpt. as "Part of the Myth: An Interview with Clark Blaise" and "Looking East: An Interview with Clark Blaise" in *Clark Blaise: The Interviews*. Ed. J.R. (Tim) Struthers. Toronto: Guernica Editions, 2016. Essential Writers.

Reading by Twilight:
Nathaniel Hawthorne, Clark Blaise,
and the Technology of the Short Story

Graeme Northcote

You can do one or the other, but not both at once.
—J. Hillis Miller, **Hawthorne & History: Defacing It** (55)

*... as in poetry, a good first sentence of prose
implies its opposite.*
—**Clark Blaise, "To Begin, To Begin" (159)**

1. Reading by Twilight

In his preface to *Twice-Told Tales*, Nathaniel Hawthorne
proclaims that his collection, "if you would see anything in
it, requires to be read in the clear, brown, twilight atmosphere in which it was written; if opened in the sunshine,
it is apt to look exceedingly like a volume of blank pages"
(xxiii). In *Hawthorne and History: Defacing It*, J. Hillis Miller argues that Hawthorne's "lament for his inability to
bring together realism and allegorical meaning echoes
through all Hawthorne's prefaces to his volumes of short
stories" (55). In Miller's ensuing analysis of "The Minister's Black Veil," he speaks to the incommensurability in
storytelling of realism and its apparent counterpart allegory, which "has a remorseless power of disembodiment"

that "dissolves the solidity of realistic representation" (55). However, what Miller perceives as simply a lament for this supposedly unalterable truth can also be read as Hawthorne's answer to this question of a supposed dichotomy between realism and allegory.

In *The Language of Allegory*, Maureen Quilligan describes the effect of allegory as "precisely the disjunction between thing said and meaning meant" (27), whereby the very inconsistency of the surface materials of a text is crucial to forming the abstract pattern ultimately created (28). With this perception in mind, Hawthorne's comment takes on new meaning. In the clarity and certainty of full daylight, his volumes appear as "blank pages" precisely because of the incoherence of their surface meaning. The literal content of the text paradoxically lacks any degree of substance. It is only in twilight that the meaning of the stories begins to unfold. Rather than interpreting this as a failure of the text, might we not see it as an allegory for the particular way in which stories necessarily function to produce meaning?

Twilight occupies the space between light and dark, where the certainty of objective illumination begins to break down. It is a space of dark patches where light does not reach, where only the subjective imagination of the beholder can penetrate. These apparently blank pages, according to Hawthorne, "are not the talk of a secluded man with his own mind and heart, ... but his attempts ... to open an intercourse with the world" (xxiii); in other words, the tales were never supposed to be invested with a single objective meaning, visible in the light of day. Rather, they were created as deliberately shadowed texts, designed to be read in twilight. It is the reader who is called upon to produce the meaning of the text, to utilize reason and imagination in order to read between the tenuous patches of illumination. Realism and allegory cannot coexist when the text is examined according to reductive, essentialist principles demanding a definitive and discoverable meaning. Hawthorne instead proposes a reading by twilight, according to the principles of a dynamic "intercourse" amongst reader, text, and author that occurs within and through the shadowed regions of the text. Only through this approach can the apparent opposition between allegory and realism be resolved. And despite his avowed disillusionment, Hawthorne speaks directly to this dynamic in the preface to *Twice-Told Tales*, where he claims that "even in what purport to be pictures of actual life, we have allegory ..." (xxiii).

Once again, Hawthorne's meditations can be better understood in relation to the work done by Quilligan. In her discussion of the nature and function of allegory, she claims that it "works horizontally, rather than vertically, so that meaning accretes serially ... in the self-consciousness of the reader, who ... creates the meaning of the text" (28). In other words, allegorical texts proceed in a linear process of interpretation and abstraction. Levels of meaning are coexistent at any given point, and are co-created by the reader upon navigating gaps or disjunctions in the horizontal narrative structure, forming divergent, intertwining threads of interpretation through a text.

By situating the appropriate (that is, productive) reading of his fiction temporally, Hawthorne suggests a parallel understanding. His contention is that meaning is not stable, and cannot be charted in clear levels across all hours of the day. Indeed, if the text itself is regarded as stable, it loses all meaning, becoming blank pages.

The reader produces meaning serially, by entering the twilight of each day, the spaces of the force that Blaise identifies in the title of his story "Dark Matter."

Dark matter must be understood as narrative gaps, a branching pattern of fissures in the narrative that simultaneously fractures the literal meaning of the text and transcends it by creating broader abstract patterns and connections, which we call allegory. Rather than positively producing fixed narrative content, it negatively produces spaces of narrative possibility from which the reader subjectively constructs meaning according to the patterns of illumination that came before. This process is inherent to all allegorical texts, but more importantly it can also function in realist texts. Just as the day transitions into night, realist fiction, by utilizing narrative gaps, has the capacity to shift in and out of the allegorical spectrum of understanding.

Blaise's short fiction, often possessing the veneer of realism, masters the technique implicitly established by Hawthorne centuries ago in the nuanced mechanics of his own tales. Both authors employ specific kinds of narrative devices and systems that allow for the collapse of realism and allegory within their writings, such that the texts operate on both levels, either simultaneously throughout, or periodically in relation to nexus points in the narrative. In this respect, Blaise can be seen as Hawthorne's spiritual successor as craftsman of the short story.

2. Hawthorne's "The Minister's Black Veil: A Parable"

Among Hawthorne's many works of short fiction, "The Minister's Black Veil: A Parable" stands as his most explicit engagement with the concept of dark matter. The story is centred on a deceptively simple and modest artifact: a folded piece of black crape hung as a veil over the visage of one Parson Hooper of the town of Milford. This one object catalyzes an extreme response from the townsfolk, who suddenly perceive the figure with fear, suspicion, and disgust, despite the fact that he remains otherwise the near-saintly public servant whom they have always known. Ultimately, Father Hooper is ostracized from the community solely because of the mystery of the veil and what it *could* be hiding or symbolizing.

When he first appears in the text, Hooper walks "[w]ith this gloomy shade before him ... at a slow and quiet pace ... as is customary with *abstracted* men" (26, emphasis added). The word "abstracted" operates here on multiple levels, suggesting both a characteristic of Father Hooper's personality, and his ontological status as a veiled figure within the text. Through the mechanism of the black veil, a literal patch of darkness in the narrative, the figure of Mr. Hooper has been abstracted not only from the community, but also from the story itself. Mr. Hooper no longer exists as a definite subject; the veil has nullified any specific identity, to the extent that a spokesman for the townsfolk "'can't really feel as if good Mr. Hooper's face was behind that piece of crape'" (26) at all. Rather, the crude technological apparatus establishes the parson as a human question mark, a conceptual bundle of possible relations to various explanatory frameworks. The speculation from the community focusses on the veil's significance *in relation to* a variety of imagined transgressive *behaviours*. In other words, the veil exists in the cultural imagination as a purely contextual symbolic construct, without intrinsic meaning. Likewise, the figure behind the veil ceases to be Mr. Hooper and instead becomes an abstract entity, whose nature is entirely dependent upon the (unknown) context of its existence and interactions.

What lurks behind the veil is dark matter. It is the invisible force that shapes the material signs of the realist narrative. The veiled Father Hooper is the hollow exoskeleton of that emptiness. However, the narrative spaces created by the black veil are not devoid of meaning, but rather suffused with it. They are spaces of "pure" meaning, with form but no fixed content. The black veil is impenetrable, and all we truly know of what lies beyond is that, whatever it may be, it is roughly Hooper-shaped. This not only produces the abstraction of the character within the text, but allows him to function allegorically as well as realistically.

As if to emphasize the dual nature of Father Hooper as both a realistic and an allegorical figure, Hooper himself, in the story's second-last paragraph, provides an allegorical interpretation of the veil in a speech on his deathbed. This speech is oddly abstracted from the action of the narrative, with no direct reference to any of the characters present. Just as Father Hooper is crossing over into the realm of the dead, his speech seems to cross borders as well, rising above the realist narrative to address the reader directly.

Decrying the hypocrisy of those that judge him because of the simple fold of crape, he exclaims, "'I look around me, and, lo! on every visage a Black Veil'" (37). Hooper seems to at last be offering the reader answers as to the meaning of what the minister calls "'the symbol beneath which I have lived and die!'" (37). Hooper invites a reading of the veil as a symbol of alienation within a community, the invisible, self-imposed barriers that separate individuals emotionally and spiritually from one another.

While Hooper's address is a classic example of allegorical form, it seemingly disrupts the coherence of the realist narrative. While on the surface the ending of the story resolves the allegorical meaning of the text, it ultimately does nothing to resolve the realist meaning of the narrative. Father Hooper's motivation, the origin of the black veil, remains a mystery. On the surface, this splits the narrative into two threads of understanding: one allegorical, and one realist.

In the final two paragraphs of the story, there is a jarring fracture between these allegorical and realist readings of the text, highlighted by the abrupt shift in both the tone and the focalization of the narrative. Hooper's speech in the second-last paragraph constitutes a culmination of the allegorical framework of the text; it explicitly focalizes the allegorical figure of Father Hooper for the first time, and through his words seemingly draws the symbols and themes of the preceding narrative to a definitive conclusion. The source of conflict within the town has died, and with his dying breath he has seemingly relayed the long-sought answer to the question of the black veil. Except that the story isn't quite over.

The final paragraph disrupts and counterbalances every element of the one preceding it. In spatiotemporal terms, a close, intimate focus on the last moments of Father Hooper's life suddenly pans outward at a rapid pace. Focalization shifts from Hooper to the community itself, indicated by the use of the impersonal pronoun "they" rather than specific names or figures, and by the tone of the narration reading like a projection of the communal voice. In contrast to the prolonged, even languid, textual attention to Hooper's final moments, the final paragraph features a rapid and startling acceleration through time. The corpse's journey from deathbed to coffin spans a single sentence — the intervening distance, time, and action completely nullified. The final sentence catapults the reader from the moment of the burial into the present, explaining, "The grass of many years *has* sprung up and withered on that grave, the burial-stone *is* moss-grown, ... and good Mr. Hooper's face *is* dust; but awful *is* still the thought, that it mouldered beneath the Black Veil!" (37, emphasis added).

The jarring spatiotemporal shift in the narrative signals the subtler disruption of the allegorical reading and resolution already established. The final paragraph firmly grounds the text in a realist narrative, conceptually distancing the reader from the allegorical force of Father Hooper's speech. The mysterious and darkly profound figure of the earlier portion of the narrative now simply "fell back upon his pillow, a veiled corpse" (37), with nothing left to say either literally or figuratively. The corpse is buried, grass grows and withers, moss spreads across the tombstone ... and the body turns to dust, emphasizing the physicality of Father Hooper and his very human connectedness to the natural cycle of life and death despite the communal perception of his ethereal otherworldliness.

We are effectively left with two endings to "The Minister's Black Veil": one allegorical, and one realist. The apparently jarring dissonance between the two seems to support Miller's initial reading of the text as speaking to the incommensurability of realism and allegory. However, the narrative dark matter established by the black veil serves to tie together the disparate threads of the story. The realist and allegorical narratives intertwine in order to produce meaning in ways that neither could alone.

Father Hooper dies veiled, and "[s]till veiled, they laid him in his coffin, and a veiled corpse they bore him to the grave" (37). The continued emphasis on the veiled body simultaneously reinforces the realist physicality of Father Hooper and his allegorical abstraction. His body crumbles to *dust*. He has literally faded away to *nothing* beneath the black veil. Allegory and reality converge, as the physical presence of Father Hooper becomes identical to his existential presence within the text. Without even bones to mark his identity, with his face shrouded until it no longer exists, Hooper truly could have been anyone, with any conceivable history and agenda. The resolution proffered by this figure on his deathbed is undermined by the continued presence of the black veil. The ending reminds us that despite surface appearances there is no moment of revelation; the veil is *never* removed, and never will be.

Miller has noted that many critics have combed through the text to offer a realist framework to explain Hooper's actions and the imagery that surrounds him. Diverse, even contradictory interpretations are possible because of the impenetrable nature of the black veil. The narrative spaces can be filled with any content that seems to fit the contours of the contextual frame. However, that same impenetrable quality means that no realist explanations can be established with certainty. The Hooper-shaped dark matter remains, allowing the figure to be everything and nothing, to fit a given realist narrative, and at the same time to defy it, to transcend it, to function abstractly on an allegorical level. Each of the final two paragraphs ends with

the same two words: "Black Veil!" This repetition signals that the text is functioning as both allegory and
realism, uniting the two endings in the shared production of meaning.

"The Minister's Black Veil: A Parable" is thus truly
a twice-told tale, as the title of the collection in which
it was published announces. The duality of the story's
ending, understood in relation to the oft-ignored subtitle, can be read as an answer to the very dilemma
Hawthorne himself raises in the preface. The moral of
this parable *is* the black veil, not what lies beyond, the
twilight space itself that splits the tale in two, making
it neither wholly allegorical, nor wholly realistic, but
both at once.

3. Blaise's "Salad Days"

Nowhere is this complex interplay between realism and
allegory more evident than in Blaise's sequence of stories
about psychologist Dr. Gerald Lander, first published as
the volume *If I Were Me* and later republished, with one
additional story ("Migraine Morning"), as part of Blaise's
collection *World Body.* The story "Dark Matter," in particular, offers a profound and compelling meditation on
the nature and production of meaning, a structural exploration of human experience as a conflation of the
mythic and the mundane, of allegory and realism. The
story follows Gerald Lander during his trip to Tel Aviv,
but simultaneously follows the character's existential
revelations, operating on both realistic and allegorical
levels. The narrative implicitly serves as a subtle articu-
lation of the theory of allegory as dark matter, focussed

through the character of Lander and his theories pertaining to the practice of language.

In order to understand how the figure of Gerald Lander functions to illuminate dark matter within this text, we must first turn to an earlier story in the sequence. "Salad Days," which comes second after "Strangers in the Night," operates as a key for how to read and interpret not only "Dark Matter" but also Lander himself. Nominally, "Salad Days" is a story of a young Lander, student of the Freudian method, attempting to decipher the Alzheimer word-salads of his dying mother. More importantly, however, it is also a metafictive exploration of allegory and the production of meaning within human experience. Lander's process of translation involves a sequential deconstruction of his mother's words into their component syllables, sounds, and associations. He takes each word not as a definite symbol with a fixed content, but as a bundle of possible allusions and correlations. The *chair* his mother speaks of, Lander interprets as referring to "himself, the person *in* the chair across from her" (18). Likewise, he interprets the word *painting* as "[p]ain, perhaps, just plain pain," a word that "connected all her angers, her rage, at food being thrust at her, at strangers entering her room" (18).

In both cases, it is crucial to note that the words do not function metaphorically, as parallel hierarchies of meaning, but rather metonymically, as horizontal contextual frameworks. There is no direct substitution of symbols for subjects; rather, Lander's process of translation is fundamentally metonymic, conceptualizing the word-salad as a fragmented puzzle, whereby every piece, however isolated and incoherent, embodies structural cues suggesting what to place within the empty spaces in order to produce a coherent meaning. Consequently, a reading of "Salad Days" needs to recognize Blaise's engagement with metonymy, specifically in relation to Roman Jakobson's seminal essay on the subject, entitled "Two Aspects of Language and Two Types of Aphasiac Disturbances."

Jakobson positions metaphor and metonymy as opposing poles, producing meaning in very different ways. Or in the terms of this present discussion, narrative dark matter produces meaning metonymically, and not metaphorically. This is evident from the fact that the empty narrative spaces that constitute dark matter cannot reasonably be understood as direct symbolic substitutions for anything except *other* empty spaces. Metaphor is an equation, whereby symbol x = subject y. Let us do the math; 'nothing' cannot equal 'something', emptiness cannot stand for substance. By contrast, metonymy functions much differently, producing meaning according to contiguity, or the contextual framework surrounding the metonym itself. Accordingly, Jakobson articulates a series of examples whereby "*Fork* is substituted for *knife*, *table* for *lamp*, *smoke* for *pipe*, *eat* for *toaster*" (125). The same pattern is evident in the word-salad pairings of Lander's 'translation', whereby a word like *chair* stands in for the subject sitting on it. These metonymic symbols accrete meaning through the subjects associated with them, whereby particular symbols or subjects are made to embody other contextual elements, one puzzle piece alluding to adjacent forms, or even to the puzzle as a whole.

The chair does not represent Lander; nor is the act of painting a metaphor for anger and pain and helplessness. Rather, his mother's 'language' functions as a fractured framework which builds around the dark matter of her inner consciousness. Meaning comes from the contextual details and associations that Lander projects into the dark matter behind his mother's words. The patterns of meaning that Lander reads into the word-salad in order to formulate his supposed 'translation' are produced through the act of his own subjective interpretation, filling in the gaps with his own experience and knowledge of his mother's life. In other words, Lander is essentially reverse-engineering metonymic content into the empty narrative spaces within his mother's word-salads, perfectly illustrating the way in which dark matter produces meaning within a text.

Lander's process directly parallels Quilligan's horizontal conceptualization of allegory. Lander attempts to navigate the linguistic gaps of dark matter through a sequential examination of each individual word, its possible interpretations and connections, slowly compounding contexts in order to establish patterns of meaning. While Lander claims to have 'discovered' the hidden meaning of his mother's word-salads, the text implies otherwise. Although this story is very short, almost an eighth of it is devoted to a verbatim quotation of one of Lander's harshest critics, who posits that "'sometimes gibberish, even a beloved mother's gibberish, is just noise'" (20), that Lander has, to use Freud's term, 'projected' meaning into an empty space where no such hidden meaning exists. Such a perspective is anathema to Lander, because meaninglessness is "[t]he one thing he could not imagine" (17).

Blaise's use of a direct quotation instead of paraphrasing Lander's critics seems to be a deliberate effort to contrast concrete, stable, and structured language with the fragmented gibberish of Lander's mother. Blaise presents us with two perspectives, each singularly limited: a reductive imposition of stable, objective meaning into a subjective space, and a reductive nihilism dismissing the possibility of any meaning whatsoever. The thrust of the narrative should be understood as somewhere in the middle, synthesizing elements of both of these two extreme philosophical and linguistic views while simultaneously transcending them. The nature of dark matter is such that it inherently and necessarily disrupts definitive interpretation of the 'true' hidden meaning of a text. At the same time, dark matter is inherently meaningful, functioning as a black hole, shaping the meaning of the text around it according to subjective interpretation that is inevitably and necessarily 'projected' into it.

"Salad Days" situates Lander as embodying the existential quest for 'true meaning', for answers hidden within the shadows of dark matter—except that Blaise reveals to us that there is nothing hidden within dark matter save what we place there. It functions metonymically, with no fixed content, only shifting meanings that operate in relation to particular contextual structures, patterns ultimately perceived and filled in by subjective readers. There is no substance to a black hole. It exists as pure gravity, visible and relevant only insofar as it shapes and incorporates elements of the universe around it. The material substances of reality, the laws of time and space, are bent and transformed as they enter a black hole. Analogously, realist narratives take on allegorical dimensions when they are reshaped through the interpretive forces of narrative dark matter.

4. Blaise's "Dark Matter"

The production of allegory through dark matter serves as a fundamental thread running through the core of Blaise's story "Dark Matter." Lander's journey within the text, exploring and struggling with the nature of his diasporic identity (both as a Jewish man and as a travelling academic and self-described universal citizen), is simultaneously an exploration of and a struggle with the nature of dark matter, with the allegorical structure of human experience. The most explicit indication of this reading lies at the exact centre of the narrative, when a contemporary of Lander's, economist Joel Kaminsky, explains the concept of dark matter. It is, he claims, "the invisible weight of the universe…, the stuff that's as heavy as everything we can see, only we have to take even its existence on a kind of theoretical faith" (93).

Dark matter is articulated as the force that binds things together and flings them apart, just as narrative gaps simultaneously fracture a narrative and encourage the abstraction of allegorical patterns that unify the narrative. Interestingly, in the story Kaminsky explicitly suggests that such a concept could be applicable to Lander's own studies of the human mind. More implicit is the parallel that can be drawn between 'celestial mechanics' and the existential mechanics of human experience. What this suggests is that human experience is structured according to certain systems or mechanics, of which dark matter is an integral element. Likewise, it encourages the reader to consider the mechanics of the short story itself, the way in which the narrative is structured in relation to dark matter.

"Dark Matter" opens with a meditation on how "A normal life of eighty years can be expressed as a parabola" (81), a series of scattered but connected points articulated as a clear arc rising, peaking, then coming to a rest according to the equations of the curve itself. This opening signals that Lander's fundamental struggle within the text is with the nature of his own diasporic identity. His decision whether or not to remain in Tel Aviv reflects the existential quest revealed in "Salad Days." It embodies a tension between rooting himself both geographically and conceptually within the sphere of Jewish identity and remaining a transient global citizen with an identity diffused across a multiplicity of locales, relations, and ideas.

To lay down roots in Tel Aviv is to accept the graceful descent of his life's parabola, to follow it to its natural end-point. To continue travelling is to disrupt the rules of the equation, to bend the line and scatter the points on the graph. What is crucial about this struggle is that the forces acting upon his decision are largely implicit, even invisible. The reader can feel the invisible weight of political and ethnic tensions and the nebulous threat of violence throughout the story, sensed only indirectly through conversations with various characters until the very end. Likewise, the family narratives of his son and daughter, his marriage and divorce, are left untold. The precise pattern of Lander's travels is never aligned into a coherent path, and the push and pull of cultural politics on his psyche remains understated and undeveloped. His motivations represent the area beneath the curve of the parabola, the uncalculated value that holds up the structure of his life.

The same sense of fractured identity and obscured motivations is apparent within the other characters in "Dark Matter." They, like Lander, are contorted around narrative gaps, with identities split between the present and the distant past, with scant mention of the implied forces that shaped the transition between the two. Gershon becomes Gerald; Arnie becomes Ari; Davia becomes Aviva. Each character has undergone dramatic transitions, geographically and otherwise. The changes in names, in location, success, and marriage, all imply a sharp division between past and present selves. And yet, as Lander interacts with Ari and Aviva, we find that all three characters act, by virtue of their proximity, as a synthesis of their apparently disparate identities. Gerald is called back to his identity as Gershon through his interaction with Ari, which seems to plant the idea of rooting himself in Tel Aviv. Similarly, Aviva is called back to her identity as Davia through her interaction with Gerald, her former lover. The final word of the story is her name, Davia, which she has signed in a letter addressed to Gershon. Even as Gerald Lander's life appears to have come to an end, a letter expresses relief at his survival, and addresses him by his old name.

The ambiguous significance of names within the story evokes a sense of identity as a multiplicity, with different lives, different choices, existing simultaneously. Lander exists as both Gershon and Gerald, and as such is both alive and dead. This effect is established through the presence of narrative dark matter. Because, as Blaise himself argues in his essay "To Begin, To Begin," the beginning of a story ultimately implies its opposite. In "Dark Matter" we are not given the parabola of Gershon/Gerald's life, or that of Arnie/Ari's life, or that of Davia/Aviva's life. What we are given are two points. Where they began, and where they are. This means we cannot easily reconcile these identities into a single, coherent life story with a single, coherent meaning. We are able to project wildly different curves leading to and from either point, to imagine them as completely separate lives and identities, which nonetheless occupy the same spaces within the narrative.

It is no coincidence that immediately before the detonation of the bomb at the end of the narrative, the man whom Dr. Lander spots reading a Hebrew newspaper is "his ancient double, the man in a dream of so many years" (102). This is an allusion to the first Gerald Lander story, "Strangers in the Night," in which he sees another version of himself in the night, "His double. ... The other Lander" (14-15). In Tel Aviv this double, this alternate version of himself, panics and dashes frantically from the hotel. Dr. Lander stayed in the vicinity and was therefore presumably (although not necessarily) caught in the blast, while the other Lander, who had been reading the newspaper, presumably (although not necessarily) was long gone by the time the bomb went off and therefore survived to receive Davia's letter. The narrative dark matter, which created this disjunction of identity, therefore allows for a dual reading of the text. From a realist perspective, Gerald Lander simply spotted a figure that uncannily resembled one from a long-ago dream, immediately following which he had a sudden and profound epiphany. However, the passage also functions allegorically, representing the branching possibilities of fate and identity, the sudden expansion of consciousness to reflect the true multiplicity of human experience. In the passage Lander identifies himself as lion and zebra, predator and prey. The divisions of language, of time and memory, are revealed as illusions. In this sense the figure of Lander at that moment truly operates as a multiplicity of beings, spanning multiple points in time and even multiple possibilities for the present.

By the end of "Dark Matter," Gerald Lander has transcended his function as a merely realistic character, additionally taking on allegorical dimensions, so that he simultaneously functions as a mythic figure, a multiplicity of ideas and identities. The quotation from Sartre's

Saint Genet that Blaise uses as an epigraph for the following newly-added story, "Migraine Morning"—"Indeed, it is not unusual for the memory to condense into a single mythic moment the contingencies and perpetual rebeginnings of an individual human history" (105)—effectively underlines this transformation and stands as a statement of Blaise's own technique. Through consciously structuring Lander's story around textual gaps and elements of dark matter, Blaise, like Hawthorne before him, collapses the division between realism and allegory.

5. The Technology of the Short Story

The narrative structures that Blaise and Hawthorne employ in order to establish spaces of dark matter within the text can benefit greatly from being considered in relation to Marshall McLuhan's theories regarding the phenomenology of technology. Hawthorne and Blaise engage with realist depictions of technological artifacts or systems specifically because these involve the conceptual negation of space and time within human experience. In other words, the technostructures that McLuhan discusses in works such as *The Gutenberg Galaxy* and *Laws of Media* produce *in reality* the conceptual dark matter that Hawthorne and Blaise utilize allegorically *in fiction*. Technology, broadly understood as artificial constructions or external tools and systems designed to extend or accelerate natural human capacities, therefore functions as the perfect realist mechanism through which to produce narrative dark matter and enable simultaneous allegorical reading of a text. But that is matter for another essay.

Works Consulted

Blaise, Clark. "Dark Matter." *World Body*. Introd. Michael Au-
    gustin. Erin, ON: The Porcupine's Quill, 2006. 81-104. Vol.
    4 of *The Selected Stories of Clark Blaise*. 4 vols. 2000-06.

-----. *If I Were Me: A Novel*. Erin, ON: The Porcupine's Quill,
    1997. Rpt. (expanded) in *World Body*. Introd. Michael Au-
    gustin. Erin, ON: The Porcupine's Quill, 2006. Vol. 4 of
    The Selected Stories of Clark Blaise. 4 vols. 2000-06.

-----. "Migraine Morning." *World Body*. Introd. Michael Au-
    gustin. Erin, ON: The Porcupine's Quill, 2006. 105-11. Vol.
    4 of *The Selected Stories of Clark Blaise*. 4 vols. 2000-06.

-----. "Salad Days." *World Body*. Introd. Michael Augustin.
    Erin, ON: The Porcupine's Quill, 2006. 17-20. Vol. 4 of *The
    Selected Stories of Clark Blaise*. 4 vols. 2000-06.

-----. "Strangers in the Night." *World Body*. Introd. Michael
    Augustin. Erin, ON: The Porcupine's Quill, 2006. 13-15. Vol.
    4 of *The Selected Stories of Clark Blaise*. 4 vols. 2000-06.

-----. "To Begin, To Begin." *How Stories Mean*. Ed. John Met-
    calf and J.R. (Tim) Struthers. Erin, ON: The Porcupine's
    Quill, 1993. 158-62. Critical Directions 3. Rpt. in "How
    Stories Mean." *Selected Essays*. By Clark Blaise. Ed. John
    Metcalf and J.R. (Tim) Struthers. Windsor, ON: Biblioasis,
    2008. 167-72.

-----. "Yahrzeit." *World Body*. Introd. Michael Augustin. Erin,
    ON: The Porcupine's Quill, 2006. 113-17. Vol. 4 of *The Se-
    lected Stories of Clark Blaise*. 4 vols. 2000-06.

Doubleday, Neal Frank. *Hawthorne's Early Tales, a Critical
    Study*. Durham, NC: Duke UP, 1992.

Halliday, Sam. *Science and Technology in the Age of Haw-
    thorne, Melville, Twain, and James: Thinking and Writing
    Electricity*. New York: Palgrave Macmillan, 2007.

Hawthorne, Nathaniel. "The Minister's Black Veil: A Parable."

Twice-Told Tales. 1837. Introd. Rosemary Mahoney. New York: The Modern Library, 2001. 25-37.

-----. "Preface to Twice-Told Tales." *Twice-Told Tales.* 1837. Introd. Rosemary Mahoney. New York: The Modern Library, 2001. xxi-xxiv.

Jakobson, Roman. "Two Aspects of Language and Two Types of Aphasic Disturbances." *On Language.* Ed. Linda R. Waugh and Monique Monville-Burston. Cambridge, MA: Harvard UP, 1990. 115-33.

Lodge, David. *The Modes of Modern Writing: Metaphor, Metonymy, and the Typology of Modern Literature.* Ithaca, NY: Cornell UP, 1977.

McLuhan, Marshall. *The Gutenberg Galaxy: The Making of Typographic Man.* Toronto: U of Toronto P, 1962.

McLuhan, Marshall, and Eric McLuhan. *Laws of Media: The New Science.* Toronto: U of Toronto P, 1988.

Miller, J. Hillis. *Hawthorne & History: Defacing It.* Cambridge, MA: Basil Blackwell, 1991. The Bucknell Lectures in Literary Theory.

Quilligan, Maureen. *The Language of Allegory: Defining the Genre.* Ithaca, NY: Cornell UP, 1979.

The Other Side of Things: Clark Blaise's "Notes Beyond a History"

Robert Lecker

In a statement that serves to describe his own art, Clark Blaise says:

> A writer is always trying to suggest the *other* side of things. He's trying to create a subject and an object, not only the centrepiece but the frame, and sometimes he feeds the frame first and withholds the picture. Other times he gives the picture and withholds the fact that he's going to hang it in the garage next to an old nudie calendar. Sometimes it may be a very beautiful thing to be deliberately destroyed.... It's always a matter of working by indirection and by surprise and by suggestion, which means that everything you state directly has a shadow meaning, implied. (Blaise in Hancock 54)

Since Blaise is a writer given to fictionalizing his life and his aesthetic development (as he says in *Resident Alien*, he is "wedded ... to the epic of my own becoming" [9]), we can never take his self-critical pronouncements at full face value. The face is always masked. But Blaise's words do point to two aspects of his work that critics tend to ignore. First, they direct us to the fact that Blaise is preoccupied with binaries. "The *other* side of things" evokes a world of otherness and proliferating opposites that seldom merge: subject counters object, centrepiece repulses frame, picture subverts setting, narrative preys on fact. My list is merely a departure point; for Blaise, everything is structured in twos. And as I will try to show, this two-sidedness is by no means a purely thematic concern. By entertaining "the *other* side of things" we can understand the profound dualism central to Blaise's approach to narrative strategy and form. Second, Blaise's words direct us to the realization that what is *said* in his stories always covers a deeper level of meaning or consciousness that can only be exposed by probing beneath a deceptively finished surface. Blaise is right to argue that the language of his stories "reveals its kinship to poetry" ("To Begin, To Begin" 22). It demands to be read as "a single metaphor and the exfoliation of a single metaphor through dense layers of submetaphors" (Blaise in Hancock 56).

My sense is that the "single metaphor" most fascinating to Blaise is connected with "the *other* side of things" so central to his life as art. This connection is subtly displayed in "Notes Beyond a History" — one of Blaise's most powerful and most representative stories — yet few readers have commented on its form or structure. In an earlier commentary I suggested, briefly, that "Notes Beyond a History" is "concerned with a morality of *seeing*" that involves the narrator in a search for "the imagined story beyond the recorded history," for the "'mythic moment' which may define an entire period in one's life" (Lecker 51, 52). True, but I ignored the formal implications of "the *other* side of things." Barry Cameron recognized that this "densely textured, richly descriptive story ... explores 'the other side' of Florida, of history, through a dialectic between the primitive and the civilized, memory and history, myth and fact" (Cameron 65), but space restrictions made it impossible for him to follow the exfoliation of this dialectic. So I return to it now, hoping to reveal the other side of Blaise's world by allowing myself to make connections, to pause, to double back, to play, to live in and out of this two-sided space.

* * *

The opening. Draw a map of the geography described in the first two paragraphs. The other side jumps out at you. On one side there is Theodora Rourke's "stone cottage that was a good eighty years old" and "set far back" from the lake near which she lives. She "had not wanted to see the lake." "She didn't need the water." And "she was ninety-two." That's *her* side. Now draw "the hedge at the side that separated us from Theodora Rourke." "We" (the Sutherlands) lived in a four-year-old "fine Spanish-style home of tawny stucco," surrounded by "a rich Bermuda lawn reaching to the water." She: divorced from the water, surrounded by "two hundred yards of twisted trees" that had once been a Valencia grove, self-contained, reclusive, timeless in her mystery. We: reaching for the water from a contrived lawn, reaching the lawn from a contrived house, imbuing the house with a contrived history that allows Sutherland to say, "we've always been known as the leading family and one of the oldest."

She/We. From the first sentence, in the first paragraph, on the first page, the narrator (why is he tagged only by a *sur*name?) tells us that, like the geography surrounding him, he is split. Watch him enumerate the divisions that plague him from the start. "I should divide the history of Oshacola County into 'Modern Era' and 'All

Time' so that both the Rourkes and the Sutherlands could enjoy their prominence." "We were the first family of Lake Oshacola," but she "had come with the place." She was comparable in stature to Cy Young; we reached the less stellar prominence of Early Wynn. She knew the landscape when it was untamed, when the lake was "but an ocean of alligators, the breeder of chilling fevers." We knew the lake from the groomed stretches of our Bermuda lawn. Let the hedge dividing their properties become a line between signifiers:

Rourke	*Sutherland*
"stone cottage" (ca. 1852)	"Spanish-style home" (1928)
"set far back" from the beach	"fifty yards from the beach"
"She didn't need the water"	"reaching to the water"
"an ocean of alligators"	"a rich Bermuda lawn"
"the Rourkes had come with the place"	"We were the first family of Lake Oshacola, then"
Cy Young	Early Wynn
"All Time"	"Modern Era"

It is clear that Sutherland sees the Rourkes as others representing an other*ness*. But the dividing force behind his opening words is not simply the desire to enumerate difference. The "shadow meaning, implied" is that Sutherland desperately wants to cross the hedge, to move out of the tamed, recognized, protected world of his "Modern Era" and into the mysterious, eternal, and hidden realm of "All Time" aligned with Rourke.

On one level this desire implies Sutherland's unhappiness with his own past and what it forced him to become. He wants to be other than what he is. Yet his assertion of difference, and the obsessive she/we dichotomy he sets up, speaks powerfully of his need for identification with Rourke. The more he divides himself from the other side the more we know he wants it. But why? To claim priority of social status? It's more. Rourke represents something other than permanence, prestige, and lineage in social terms. She represents a narrative realm that Sutherland, as speaker, must penetrate if his "notes beyond a history" are truly to go *beyond* the history embodied in his family, his home, his tale. History, then, becomes a metaphor for the narrative world that enfolds him in the safety of recognized progression and place. History is known, named, mapped, controlled, just as the story aligned with history will be locked into Sutherland's landscaped consciousness: "a rich Bermuda lawn," "a fine Spanish-style home."

All false. His problem: to go beyond the lawn, the house, the history, and find *another* world, ungroomed but stable, something that will last, something "set far back" from the "Modern Era" in a period that resists change. A mythical world? Sutherland seems to be saying that his story (his life) will only be fulfilled when he manages to escape the social and narrative conventions that have limited his life as a man. In this sense, his attempt to resurrect Rourke's story speaks for his need to regress, to find the childlike consciousness that once allowed him to be drawn into an experience without distancing himself to describe it.

If this is true, then we know the problems his maturation has brought: to be severed from experience, removed from mystery, caught in time, place, death. To move back in time is to evade this death, reverse progression, and inhabit an eternal, immutable realm. But eternity can be problematic: it promises no death, and without death there is no reason to write. One writes against death. Blaise writes against death. Sutherland writes against his death. To keep telling the story, to go beyond history, he must paradoxically recognize that he must never go beyond it. The opening of the story confirms his profound but repressed consciousness of this paradox informing every word he writes. He wants to cross the hedge; he fears crossing it. He wants permanence; he wants change. He wants to be "the first family of Lake Oshacola"; he wants to be its last. The binaries move on.

The second two paragraphs introduce a new set of "other" sides that enlarge upon the implications of those we already know. The mythical dimension of Rourke's life is now aligned with Catholicism, a religion strange to Sutherland in his childhood, not only because "we had no admitted Catholics in Hartley," but also because Catholicism is a "conspiracy" of unknown rituals and rites whose power is predominantly narrative. For Sutherland, Catholicism is a story his mother tells, a nightmare tale of "Black Sisters" who "walked in loose black robes ... and then at night they shed their robes and took to flight." By crossing the hedge and entering Rourke's domain Sutherland might penetrate a new kind of story diametrically opposed to his own, which is characterized by whiteness, daylight, learning, history—things that can be known. This story, his story, is pointedly aligned with his mother, who, as "a south Georgia disciple of Tom Watson," was repelled and fascinated by "everything strange" about Rourke. By enclosing the m(other) view within a single paragraph, Sutherland conveys both the dichotomies of faith that haunted him as a child as well as his desire to find a surrogate mother who will provide him with a new narrative life. Two worlds keep warring; Sutherland tries to win both wars.

He can't. For even within these separate worlds the

other side appears. As soon as Sutherland describes his mother's realm he feels compelled to describe his father's in other terms. While she was a "poor tormented woman" who taught her children "to love each other, Florida, F.D.R., and the Christ of her choice," he was "a Hartley man with education," an "old father" characterized by his "white suits, stoutness, and eclectic learning." Mother was obsessed with "collecting the goods on Theodora Rourke." Father stood for "wisdom," "self-righteousness," "justice," "legality," "history." The oppositions *within* Sutherland's family ultimately reflect the oppositions he finds *outside* through his impression of Rourke's domain. These oppositions further reflect a dilemma Sutherland confronts: if he chooses to go beyond history he simultaneously chooses to go beyond the father who embodies history and ultimately to reject him. One of the reasons Rourke's existence fascinates him is that (as we soon discover) her world is fatherless. The implication is that only by abandoning a literal and figurative father can Sutherland find the narrative and personal freedom his telling so desires to find. But in this conflict, as in all his conflicts, Sutherland can never abandon either of the other sides. He wants to lose his father, yet without him he must answer for everything he does. He wants to be "freed ... for my manhood" and to remain the protected child. He wants to invent a new story of himself but realizes that he has only his history to tell. When he wonders why his brother became "a builder of rockets ... and left me here in Hartley, a teacher," we know. His brother, who *is* named, managed to leave his past for the future symbolized by the "Apollo moon probes" he designs. Tom got to the other side. But Sutherland remains caught in the story of his past as he dreams of transcending the stable world he so loves.

Now there is a break, a demarcation point in the narrative that tells us a frame has been made. The frame: story of a man telling the story of his youth as he wonders how to become that youth; story of a youth telling the story of his maturation as he wonders how to become a man. My description of the frame is meant to suggest the personal pull Sutherland feels between development and regression, but it also describes a structural pull that determines narrative perspective. When the story opens, Sutherland remembers the other side as another time; his viewpoint is retrospective. Then, having confronted the dilemma posed by his recognition of time past, he tries to evade memory by focussing on his present. But because the present provides no solace he tries to evade it by focussing on his past. For Sutherland, then, the other side of things is temporal as well as spatial.

The second section of the story finds him in his air-conditioned office, "wrapped in tinted glass," eight floors above the Lake Oshacola of his childhood. There is no mystery here. Sutherland has become the product of his family's rich Bermuda lawn. And Oshacola itself ("beautifully landscaped now") is the product of that "civilizing" impulse that wants to make the wilderness "humanized," ordered, safe. Sutherland would like to believe that he can control his environment. He imagines himself as inhabiting a fortress from whose height his view "commands the lake." Then he wonders: "If eight floors of perspective can do *this* to Oshacola, why shouldn't Tampa be creeping slowly to my front lawn?" Notice that the idea of commanding the landscape reminds Sutherland of his lawn; in other words, his need for control is linked to the safety of his "civilized" childhood. Moreover, he is not interested in subduing the landscape through physical intervention. His methods of obtaining command are expressed in terms of elevated perspective, as if he could dominate the landscape through his vision. Sutherland's problem, however, is that he confuses elevated perspective with true vision. While the height he inhabits may seem to provide a commanding view, Sutherland is actually defeated and trapped — in his office, in his memories, in his dreams of grandeur. To obtain true vision he must abandon his false commanding view, get back to ground level, tear up the Bermuda lawn, cross the hedge to Rourke's world (remember: "She didn't need the water"). Sutherland still needs it because his self-understanding is intimately tied to the lake and its surrounding terrain. He knows that "not only has the lake been civilized, but so has my memory, leaving only a memory of my memory as it was then," and he wonders why "places are always remembered as larger and more unruly" than they now appear to be. The answer, of course, is that as a child he had not yet developed the perspective that allows him to believe he is in control, he had not yet abandoned his sense of the "clusters of snakes threshing mightily on Theodora Rourke's warm sand beach."

Now he has. Why? Because he never left the father image that controlled his early life. Even today, he admits, he is "more than a little bit my father's son." The father's son is tied to an imposed perspective, to a view of life seen from safe distance. Sutherland claims that "what I see with my eyes closed, books shut, was also true." That's not enough. You can't tell us you *choose* to see truth this way because you're a "shrewd man." You can't choose to have true vision. Either you shut your books, go beyond history, and live in the truth of your imagination or you remain sanitized and air-conditioned, overlooking the lake. You can't have it both ways. But that's how you want it. Is that why you tell us about seeing things with your eyes closed and then give us a documentary, historical view of Hartley with your eyes (and books) wide open? Does it matter how many people lived in Hartley in 1932? Why have you gone back to the years of your childhood? Does it matter how many cars there were, or whether the buildings were dark brick? Where are *you* in the picture you paint? Still thinking of your father and the power he had. He "knew them all," all those Hartleyans you would never know. Still thinking of your brother and how he managed to escape. That pizza stand you imagine near "the complex at the Cape." Is that near where Tom builds his Apollo moon probes? Let's find out *your* name. You won't tell. You hide behind your surname, your father's name, and give us facts. Then you try to convince us that "history is all about" knowing "that *change* merely reflects the unacknowledged essence of things." History, for you, is about knowing the way things are. That kind of knowing has been your project. Rourke fascinates you because she represents mystery and a spiritual essence that will never be fully known. If you get to that other side, you might see with your eyes closed, books shut.

Try. The third section of the story finds Sutherland crossing the hedge that has obsessed him since he was a child. Theodora Rourke wants him to deliver the Jacksonville paper. This means that he must now enter her domain; their relationship is bound to change. It does. As soon as Sutherland receives the invitation to make contact with Rourke he gives her a new and significant name. Now she is "Big Mama" to him, the Big Mama who will in some way become a surrogate mother to the paperboy who is reluctant to cross borders and enter a new life. His entrance to her world marks a conversion experience for Sutherland and a turning point in the story: now he will be introduced to a way of seeing (and by extension, to a way of knowing) that subverts the linear, pragmatic modes of perception aligned with his family and his childhood. I say his "entrance" to underscore the sexual implications of Sutherland's initiation. This is the first time we see him conscious of making entry to an unknown world that is explicitly signed as a female domain. He hesitates "at the foot of the steps to Big Mama's back porch," but finally he does "go inside." I'm forcing things here. The truth is that Sutherland "followed Big Mama inside, but not into the house." Although Sutherland does not go right inside Big Mama's place ("How I wanted to step inside"), it is clear that some culmination takes place on the porch as Sutherland peers into the parlor and eats a piece of cake impregnated with the image of Christ.

What is the nature of this culmination? On one level, it is aesthetic. The house is filled with "paintings and photos" while "the tables were piled with metal and porcelain objects that reflected the pale sunlight like the spires of a far-off, exotic city." Rourke is obviously connected with two kinds of art, one that represents life as "vivid" and "eternally moist, eternally in the sun," and another that sees it as "exotic," "far-off," "faint," and "vague." Her house bridges the gap between the immediate and the imagined, between verisimilitude and vision. This is the bridge Sutherland tries to find in his own art — a way of telling that will enable him to turn his past into a vision that he can fuse with the hard reality of his present. His conversion involves the knowledge that two worlds can be housed together when borders are crossed. On another level, the culmination is spiritual. Sutherland realizes that his religious training has fixed him in history, rather than in the "All Time" he associates with Rourke and her belief in "His immortal body."

I want to be able to say that Sutherland embraces this body, that he does transcend the self-limitations he is coming to understand. But the fact is that at this point in the story he still rejects the knowledge that is offered to him; he refuses to go *all the way* inside. This explains why he will not eat the holy wafer his cake crumbs have become ("I pressed the last crumbs into a wafer and let it drop back on the plate"), why he cannot understand Rourke's quivering prayer sounds, and why he bolts from the room ("my only chance to get away before she could drain my blood into a cup"). Although this section ends with Sutherland's evasion of Big Mama, it is clear that something in him has changed, for now he is ready to touch the line that divides Sutherland from Rourke. "I threw myself into the brier hedge between our proper-ties." I threw myself a bit beyond my history.

Not for long. The next section finds Sutherland con-templating history again, listing the "facts" about Rourke that will be recorded in his *History of Hartley*. At the very mention of this title we know that Sutherland will fail in his attempt to get beyond the book that defines his life and his mode of perception. Although his narrative might be seen as an attempt to subvert history, it is only a brief interlude in the life of a man who has chosen to be "responsible" for "records" and "facts." I begin to lose faith in Sutherland, want him to throw away the history and give up the data. He won't. His security, now and always, is tied to what is known. Look at the information he provides about the Rourkes. The only thing interest-ing about the "facts" is that Theodora's husband, like Sutherland's father, was a state senator and judge. The implications of this kinship are important, for they cast Bernard Rourke in the role of surrogate (and absent) father to Sutherland; and as we have already seen, Theodora acts as his Big Mama. So Sutherland wants new parents, replacement parents, a replaced life. The details he provides tell us he is unhappy with what he has become. But at the same time, his refusal to become anything other than what he is suggests that the influence of his safe, Bermuda-lawned childhood has been overpowering, crushing in its safeness, crushing in its ability to deprive him of his manhood.

This word—"manhood"—is the one I wanted to reach in order to explain Sutherland's opening description of the "discovery that determined my life." He is going to tell us about "the old canal" connected with Rourke's origins. But first, he gives us "a word, historically, on the old canal scheme." The explicit connection Sutherland makes between word, history, and geography indicates that his upcoming narrative will reveal something about his own life and art. Now picture Florida, limp phallus of the South, and wonder why Sutherland is so preoccupied with "a dream of the Mighty Ditch" that could be "a natural divider between the productive and enlightened north of Florida and the swampy, pestiferous south." For Sutherland, the mighty ditch would cut the phallus hanging from the body; the "natural divider" he contemplates is only an outward symbol of the much deeper psychological and sexual division he fears he will experience as a man. Sutherland is obsessed with division because he wants to remain whole. (Remember the hedge that divides him from Rourke, the glass that divides him from Hartley, the canal that divides him from his past.) Whole? Unsullied by Rourke, unsullied by time, unsullied by the act of telling. If Sutherland inhabits the canal, then, he also inhabits a dividing line. Things may change. Does anything change for Sutherland that August morning on the old canal?

He is fishing with Tom. A "black, blunt" tub comes into view, poled by a tall man in black robes. The man lands on Rourke's "scummy beach." Sutherland realizes he is "a Catholic priest." Maybe Rourke is dead. The priest leaves. They follow him. They get lost. They find a wide ditch banked with mud and crushed stone. The ditch narrows. Gray shanty shapes appear. Then "two boys, our age," who were "squatting in the water on either side of the dike," emerge.

I follow the Sutherland boys away from their home. Watch them get lost. Wait for the significance of their journey to appear. Get bored. I know that the voyage is symbolic. When I first read the story I wrote that the search for Rourke's secret "is clearly a heart of darkness voyage that deliberately refuses light" (Lecker 53). But this refusal is not part of Sutherland's attempt to affirm Rourke's mysteriousness or his own, as I claimed. He refuses to acknowledge what is blatantly revealed: that Rourke's ancestry is not noble, eternal, or socially elevated in the conventional sense he respects. Her blood may be mixed. And she seems connected to the albino boys who play along the ditch (when Sutherland sees them he "seemed to be looking into the opaque, colorless eyes of Big Mama, and into the bleeding side of Jesus"). More important, she is linked to a people that reject Sutherland and call for his immediate death. Big Mama's "tribe" wants to kill Sutherland. My mother and her family want to kill me, the son. My mother wants me dead.

Any reader would say that Rourke wants nothing of this; she is *already* dead and never cared much for Sutherland anyhow. Yet it is precisely through her death, through her absence, through her neglect of this boy, that she signals her desire to leave him alone, out in the open, prey. She offers him up to a metaphorical death.

Sutherland retreats from the metaphor, pulls away from Big Mama, tries to go back to a time when innocence was easy. Back to the Bermuda lawn. Back to his side of the hedge. "I started paddling backwards...." "We were reeling backwards now, as fast as I could paddle." Reeling back into known time, history, daylight, commanding views, sterility, record-keeping, death. Sutherland cannot win. To pursue the unknown is to find death; to return to the known is to find death. Death, death, death. Death in life. What are the narrative implications of this oxymoronic stance? Sutherland is *sentenced*. For him, there is no safety in language or form. No solace offered by tradition. No way of telling that can ground the teller in time and guarantee his safe passage to eternity. No way of beginning that does not acknowledge every sense of the end. No way of ending that does not lament every lost beginning. No way out.

Faced with these narrative implications, Sutherland can only continue to write. Yet the mode of narration he resorts to in the last section of the story shows how completely he has failed to find the other side he claimed to want. He goes right back to the "records" that offer him a haven from the other side. This historical haven allows his tone to change: before, it could be involved, frightened, variable in its pace; now, it is reportorial, direct, rational to the point of obsession. Listen to him recite the facts about Spanish or Creole populations, about Big Mama's estate, about her husband's paintings, about how he is not concerned with her genes "in any quasi-legal sense — only historically." He means *personally*, but by now the personal and historical are synonymous — a sign of Sutherland's failure to transcend his ordered past and the ordered narrative he fashions to enclose that past. This is why he substitutes the personal for the historical when in the next sentence he tells us that Rourke "is one of many who have left scars on my body and opened a path that time has all but swallowed up." "Scars on my body": initiation into the other side.

Sutherland is right when he suggests that this initiation "opened a path" for him that was inevitably "swallowed up." But does he recognize that by recording time — by telling — he swallows up himself? In a final attempt to identify with Rourke he compares her "lost people" to the "two children" who found them: "they too are only wanderers." Nonsense. Tom is eminently located in his Apollo moon probe quest. And you, Sutherland, are ensconced in your air-conditioned office, meditating on your narrative quest. You won't step outside, break the glass, make the passage you want come true. So you sit there telling us your tale of loss and think the story you tell has power. Wrong. There is power, but it is the power of rampant impotence. We follow you, amazed by how little you've done, shocked by how little you've grown. In the end, your story has the power of absence; it is a story thriving on its inability to be told. Perfectly, *nothing* happens to mark its closure. So confess your failure. Tell us you know you write out of nothing but your castrated consciousness. I turn the page and wait to see if you will redeem the final lines. Confess: "I live in the dark, Tom in the light." Yes. Confess more: "my experience that afternoon" did "compel me to become a historian" and did "prevent me from becoming a good one." Yes. Go on: Tom, "eyes skyward," is "indifferent to it all" while everything around me is "crumbling into foolishness." Is this the sudden end? Did I push you too far, turn you into something other than what you wanted to be? I don't care. Your other side might be mine. Let me start over. Come closer. Now tell me your story again.

Works Cited

Blaise, Clark. "Notes Beyond a History." *Tribal Justice.* Toronto: Doubleday Canada, 1974. 91-104. Rpt. in *Southern Stories.* Introd. Fenton Johnson. Erin, ON: The Porcupine's Quill, 2000. 97-108. Vol. 1 of *The Selected Stories of Clark Blaise.* 4 vols. 2000-06.

-----. *Resident Alien.* Markham, ON: Penguin Books Canada, 1986.

-----. "To Begin, To Begin." *The Narrative Voice: Short Stories and Reflections by Canadian Authors.* Ed. John Metcalf. Toronto: McGraw-Hill Ryerson, 1972. 22-26. Rpt. in "How Stories Mean." *Selected Essays.* By Clark Blaise. Ed. John Metcalf and J.R. (Tim) Struthers. Windsor, ON: Biblioasis, 2008. 167-72.

Cameron, Barry. "Clark Blaise (1940-)." *Canadian Writers and Their Works.* Ed. Robert Lecker, Jack David, and Ellen Quigley. Introd. George Woodcock. Fiction Ser. Vol. 7. Toronto: ECW, 1985. 21-89. Rpt. as *Clark Blaise and His Works.* Toronto: ECW, 1985.

Hancock, Geoff. "An Interview with Clark Blaise." *Canadian Fiction Magazine* 34-35 (1980): 46-64. Rpt. as "Clark Blaise" in *Canadian Writers at Work: Interviews by Geoff Hancock.* Toronto: Oxford UP, 1987. 146-63. Rpt. as "Clear Veneer: An Interview with Clark Blaise" in *Clark Blaise: The Interviews.* Ed. J.R. (Tim) Struthers. Toronto: Guernica Editions, 2016. Essential Writers.

Lecker, Robert. "Murals Deep in Nature: The Short Fiction of Clark Blaise." *Essays on Canadian Writing* 23 (1982): 26-67. Rpt. in *On the Line: Readings in the Short Fiction of Clark Blaise, John Metcalf and Hugh Hood.* By Robert Lecker. Downsview, ON: ECW, 1982. 17-58.

Story and Allegory, the Cast and the Mold: Reading Clark Blaise's "The Birth of the Blues"

J.R. (Tim) Struthers

The assembling and publication between 2000 and 2006 of the four-volume Porcupine's Quill edition of *The Selected Stories of Clark Blaise* sets forth for our own and later generations the extraordinary contributions Blaise had made by that time to a uniquely challenging and exciting genre whose intricacy, density, and resonance have been rightly celebrated by distinguished critics such as Mary Rohrberger, Charles E. May, and Susan K. Lohafer in the United States, and, here in Canada, most importantly, John Metcalf. For more than a half-century starting with the publication in 1962 of his first story, "A Fish Like a Buzzard," Clark Blaise has presented readers with work after work infused with all he has learned from endless physical and mental travels, limitless reading, and extensive reflection on and teaching of literature, charging his writing with every iota of knowledge and feeling and imagination and craft he possesses. And not only can we savour individually each selection in Blaise's series, as Mavis Gallant advised about reading her stories (xix): we get to enjoy two volumes of brand-new stories by him. Beginning in 2011 with *The Meagre*

Tarmac, a book much praised by Margaret Atwood among others; then likely by 2017 another group of linked stories — or, I would say, similarly to *If I Were Me* (1997) and *The Meagre Tarmac* (2011), another novel-in-stories — to be titled *Entre-Nous*.[1]

Time after time, into a long succession of mesmerizing new creations, Clark Blaise has funnelled as much as we would consider possible by the greatest of the many short fiction writers whose work he admires: Nathaniel Hawthorne, Anton Chekhov, Thomas Mann, James Joyce, William Faulkner, Ernest Hemingway, Bernard Malamud, Mavis Gallant, Flannery O'Connor, Alice Munro. Blaise's own list, which he cordially provided when I asked if he would make up a nine- to ten-player starting line-up of personal favourites, is of course far more intriguing, even if he did choose to increase the number not only by naming "a couple of bench-players" as he admitted, but also in some instances by citing entire nations of story writers as if they were single players. "Two that you might not know," Blaise began, citing publications from the early 1960s, "are Curtis Zahn (*American Contemporary*) and Irvin Faust (*Roar Lion Roar*)." Then he proceeded with his list of various classics: "Hemingway. Some of Updike, same with Cheever. Alice [Munro] and Hugh [Hood] were early favourites, hence influences. The Irish, the Russians, the Germans (Mann and Handke though the latter's Austrian), Calvino, Borges, the usual suspects I guess. Carver was a classmate, so no influence on me except as cautionary. Mishima" (Blaise, Message 3:49 p.m. 4 Nov. 2015). OK, so I only got 3 out of 10. (Or 10 out of 10 if you look at it my way.)

In order, both in terms of date of publication and in terms of choice of subject, the four volumes that form *The Selected Stories of Clark Blaise* are: first, *Southern*

Stories (2000); second, *Pittsburgh Stories* (2001); third, *Montreal Stories* (2003); and, fourth, *World Body* (2006). The overall geographical and personal trajectories of the series offer a fictional counterpart to the shape of Blaise's autobiographical experiences: first, as a child in the American South; next, as an adolescent in Pittsburgh; later, as a young man and a young writer in Montreal; and then — and now — as a world citizen, a world writer. Of more specific interest is a comparable feature in the structure of each individual book. For as I argued in my earlier essay on "A Fish Like a Buzzard" from *Southern Stories* (2000), opening stories are typically selected for that purpose because they represent a striking illustration of (and an inviting welcome to) that artist's work and world. In addition, opening stories are frequently designed to function, or at least may be viewed, as a kind of disguised essay: a work intended to introduce that artist's theory and practice of the short story, to serve not only as fiction but also as metafiction.

In my earlier essay I drew on Blaise's "To Begin, To Begin" and "On Ending Stories," the first and the third of a highly insightful group of three brief essays on the short story originally commissioned by John Metcalf and now assembled at my suggestion as a single composite-essay, "How Stories Mean," in Blaise's *Selected Essays* (2008). In the present essay I will be citing "The Cast and the Mold," the second of Blaise's three pieces, and then his seminal essay on Hawthorne and Melville written for the landmark volume *A New Literary History of America* (2009). Blaise introduces the central metaphor of "The Cast and the Mold" as follows: "That cold, attractive entity we call a story is often a casting, something plastic poured into a mold, allowed to set, and then extracted, polished, and exhibited. The plastic is event; the mold is something akin to impulse, a trigger, an urgency to set it all down. A hall of castings is a book, like this one" (173). Blaise then asks: "And what of that shaggy, disreputable, rusting, unlovely thing called a mold? That larger, encompassing, all-embracing *world* that contained all the delicate flutings within its heavy, iron-or-clay shell?" (173). And he responds: "Usually it's lost to us, smashed open by the artist as he extracts his finished product. And yet, I would argue, it very often *is* the story; it contained the story and gave it form and guided that molten flow in a thousand invisible ways. But once the flow had hardened, its purpose was served. It disappeared" (173). Or, rather, he suggests, the mold vanishes until the reader remakes it. "The reader's job," Blaise observes, "like the archaeologist's, is to reconstruct that mold, [to] re-imagine it" (173).

Blaise emphasizes that it is the reader's responsibility to see not only the "shimmering reflection" (172) of a story's surface but also "far below the surface" (172). This suggestion is comparable to, and perhaps consciously or unconsciously echoes, Hemingway's famous image in his nonfiction work about bullfighting, *Death in the Afternoon*, that compares writing to an iceberg (192): something presenting an astonishing beauty above the surface yet concealing a horrifying force underneath. When we apprehend a story fully in this manner, Blaise states, "We see structure and purpose and meaning and metaphor and we see the hidden nine-tenths of everything superficial in the story. We see, in fact, that the story was only a single example of something much larger, more diffuse, and practically unnamable" (172-73). In sum, we see story as *allegory*.

***

In trying to discern the structural principles, the key components, the ways in which language is used in "The Birth of the Blues," I wish to suggest five different levels — psychological or developmental, social or historical, moral, mythical, and metafictional — on which I see the story operating. This technique reflects what Blaise, in his very important essay on Hawthorne and Melville, describes as the capacity for "expanding the frame of conventional storytelling by deepening and darkening it" ("1850, August 5" 280), an ability that Melville developed from reading Hawthorne's tales. Thus, "in a word," Blaise contends of Melville, "he had discovered the power of allegory" ("1850, August 5" 280). To illustrate each of these five different levels of allegory in "The Birth of the Blues," I will make reference to what in this story, as in "A Fish Like a Buzzard," Blaise chose as the story's governing metaphor: the funnel.

First, on a psychological or developmental level, we can regard the funnel of prophetically dark clouds that gather over the head of Frank Keeler's mother in the story's opening paragraph as a metaphor for the then four- or five-year-old boy's Freudian need to gain initial knowledge of his own sexuality through interacting with his mother. Second, socially or historically — the story begins in 1944 — the funnel clouds clearly evoke the militarily conclusive but humanly catastrophic dropping of atomic bombs by the United States on the Japanese cities of Hiroshima and Nagasaki the very next year, in August 1945. Third, on a moral level, we can regard the funnel of dark clouds as a metaphor for Frank's frustration with the difficulty of making the kind of choice represented by the supposedly easy distinction between the weeds and the radishes in the family's archetypal garden — in this case, a wartime Victory Garden — where this story, and therefore the collection as a whole, symbolically opens.

Fourth, on a mythical level, and more specifically on a biblical level, we may note, as can be said of Joyce's title for "A Little Cloud" in *Dubliners*, that frequently clouds —here in "The Birth of the Blues," the funnel of dark clouds — can be a metaphor for the presence of God: beneficent or vengeful, just or whimsical, as such a God may be (for a biblical use of clouds that likely influenced Joyce, see Note 1 by Margot Norris in Joyce, "A Little Cloud" 57). In the same vein, Blaise, during the discussion period following a first public reading of his story "The Kerouac Who Never Was" on June 29, 2012, remarked in reply to a question I asked about the God-like appearance in that story of a figure out of the fog: "I've come to the conclusion that every story has a God. In fact, a story *better* have a God [laughter] to lift it from experience into metaphor" (Blaise qtd. in Struthers, "To Elevate Experience"). Every story benefits from being given a pattern of metaphors. Every story benefits from being made into an allegory.

And fifth, and perhaps most importantly, on a metafictional level, the funnel also serves as a metaphor for the dynamics and the power of the genre of the short story— so brilliantly conceptualized by Clark Blaise in "How Stories Mean" and other essays and reviews (see Struthers, "The World of Clark Blaise" 248-56) and so boldly practised by him in now about seventy collected stories (see Struthers, "A Checklist of Works by Clark Blaise to 2015"). As Blaise remarked in an interview by Geoff Hancock in 1980, "the great challenge" for a writer is "to find language that fits the things that do not yield to language" (Blaise in Hancock 53). Continuing, Blaise observed: "most of what critics and editors call 'new' or 'exciting' concentrates on *formal* inventiveness, without realizing that one sentence of great writing (in a traditional formal shell) can be as 'avant-garde' as the latest breakthrough in form" (Blaise in Hancock 53). Thus, for Blaise, "dazzling innovations in form are simple face-liftings if they do nothing fresh with language as well" (Blaise in Hancock 53). The metafictional dimension, while it is only one of many levels on which the language of a Blaise story functions, nevertheless is absolutely crucial: it being the most sophisticated way but also the clearest way for him to guide us about how to read a particular story or indeed his entire *oeuvre*.

Moreover, in a story such as "The Birth of the Blues" that treats language equally as medium and as subject, it is surely possible to regard the word "storey" (spelled with an e) — which Blaise employs in his description of the "old five-storey apartment house" (20) that Frank visits with his father — as a homonym for, as punning on, the word "story" (spelled without an e). Especially in light of the widely-used metaphor of "the house of fiction" introduced by Henry James in the preface to his novel *The Portrait of a Lady* (46) then applied to the short story by Caroline Gordon and Allen Tate through the title they chose for their popular anthology, *The House of Fiction* (1950; 2nd ed., 1960). And tell me: Do you think there was any way I could have resisted trying to identify exactly five levels of allegory here when this building has exactly five storeys? Yet as witty as Blaise's writing is, it also carries a serious message. Namely, whatever his subject may be on one level (the literal level, the level of image and plot, the level of what many critics term "representation" — call that "storey" with an e), his subject on another level (the figurative level, the level of metaphor and allegory, the level of what Blaise in "The Birth of the

Blues" terms "transformation" [17, 22] — call this "story" without an e) is the workings of fiction and its basis in the nature of language.

***

Blaise himself, in his essay "1850, August 5; A Literary Party Climbs Monument Mountain: Nathaniel Hawthorne and Herman Melville," demonstrates the significance of the idea of allegory not only for talking about the originating works of American or, we may say, North American fiction, but also for understanding the entire history of the short story. As for Melville, so for later writers of the twentieth century and now the twenty-first century: "The American short story," Blaise argues convincingly, "derives from Hawthorne in the way that Russian literature crawls from under Gogol's overcoat" (280). To this Blaise adds: "Think of the Black Sabbath rituals in Cheever's suburbs — masks of a gin-drowned Eden — or Raymond Carver's marital cul-de-sacs containing a hint of divinity, or Flannery O'Connor, or Bernard Malamud, among dozens" (280). He concludes: "It's the subtle manipulation of allegory that lends density, foreboding, and multiple interpretations to the simple screen of narrative presentation" (280).

Or, indeed, think of the stories written by Clark Blaise himself. For as we can appreciate in the critical writing of many poets, fiction writers, dramatists, and other artists — including the two very important Canadian critics discussed by B.W. Powe in *Marshall McLuhan and Northrop Frye: Apocalypse and Alchemy* (2014) — an essential feature of Blaise's essay on Hawthorne and Melville is that while it speaks directly of its chosen subject, it speaks indirectly of much more, including the author's own personal vision and creative practice. (As Harold Bloom has argued, "The quest of contemporary criticism is for method, and the quest is vain. *There is no method other than yourself*" [413].) Blaise's essay focusses primarily on what the older Hawthorne was able to teach the younger Melville about the potency of crafting their writing as allegory; but it also cites the work of key short story writers immediately preceding or contemporary with Blaise; then it expands further to invite readers to reflect on the work of unidentified "dozens" of others. Including, I am sure, the author of the story "Flying a Red Kite," which Blaise first read as an MFA student at Iowa (Blaise, "Portrait" 148-49), and of the only half-jokingly titled story "An Allegory of Man's Fate": Blaise's fellow Montreal Story Teller Hugh Hood. Beyond all of this, of course, Blaise's comments on Hawthorne and Melville reveal much about the aesthetics, the writing style, of another story writer unnamed but everywhere present in the essay — its author, Clark Blaise.

"I'd say that my stories are structured around social signifiers in the way that Catholic signifiers inform Hugh's stories," Blaise observed (Blaise, Message 12:58 p.m. 31 Oct. 2015). Thirty-five years earlier — in an answer to Geoff Hancock's question "Is every story an allegory about reality, in quotes, or a metaphor for some aspect of reality?" (Hancock in Hancock 56) — Blaise remarked that his stories are "not ... allegory in the sense that, say, Hugh Hood's stories are. I don't have the moral patience or the scruples for allegory but I would imagine they are all metaphors" (Blaise in Hancock 56). Yet Blaise's use of the qualifier "not ... allegory in the sense that, say, Hugh Hood's stories are" clearly admitted of the possibility, even early in his writing career, that each "house of fiction" he built might be an allegory in some other sense. And certainly Blaise's answer now, as his essay on Hawthorne and Melville powerfully attests, would be in the affirmative.

***

In much the same way that we can see five levels in the story "The Birth of the Blues," so can we make five associations with the name of the once classy apartment house that carpenter, plumber, man-of-all-trades Joe Keeler and his at this point twelve-year-old son Frank visit one Saturday afternoon in order to fix an overtly sensual woman's plumbing—make of that crude jokey cliché what you will. (Indeed, one topic that Blaise considers in some detail in this story, as Carol Shields also wittily treats it in her story "The Metaphor Is Dead — Pass It On," is the debasement of language to mere clichés.) Blaise describes the building as "an old five-storey apartment house with gilt numbers above the door and a name in gold leaf painted on the transom: ALHAMBRA" (20)—the number of floors definitely making the idea of discerning five different aspects not only to the story's overall design but also to the building's particular name seem appealing, especially upon learning that the number of the woman's residence is "apartment 5" (20). Similarly enticing is a passage by Blaise about the Alhambra's architectural style that situates "The Birth of the Blues" in a direct line descending from classic twentieth-century short stories including both James Joyce's "Araby," as discussed by Robert M. Luscher in his essay on *Pittsburgh Stories* (68-69, 70), and, I would think, F. Scott Fitzgerald's "Babylon Revisited": "the whole thing must have been put up in the Moorish period of the mid-twenties, when buildings were all named Babylon and Araby" (20).

In exploring possible associations of the name Alhambra, we may start autobiographically with certain
facts about the suburb of Pittsburgh called Mount
Lebanon that Blaise discovered principally during the
seven years of his adolescence spent mainly in that city.[2]
"'The Alhambra' and 'The Granada'," Blaise recalled,
"were real apartment buildings (not terribly elegant) in
Mount Lebanon, now demolished" (Blaise, Message 9:32
a.m. 31 Oct. 2015). Second, since the visit to the Alhambra involves a sexual awakening for twelve-year-old
Frank of the type that would interest the Freud of *Three
Essays on the Theory of Sexuality* (1905), and since the
presence of Freud is so strongly evident, both parodically
and seriously, in situations and images here, we can regard the name as functioning on a sexual level. Hence
the final syllable, "bra," in Alhambra can be interpreted
as a verbally playful reference to the alluring attire — "a
brassiere" (21) and not much more — of the nearly naked
woman whom Frank glimpses down the hall while she
is dressing and putting on her make-up, arousing his
adolescent libido. Moreover, the middle syllable, "ham,"
in Alhambra suggests not only the momentarily exposed
fleshy parts of the woman's legs, but also a teller of jokes,
the subject of the Freud of *Jokes and Their Relation to the
Unconscious* (1905), thereby giving us a third way of interpreting Alhambra — linguistically, in terms of the
play of language.

Fourth, in the context of the history of short fiction,
the name given by Blaise to the apartment house also
recalls the title of the semi-fictional *The Alhambra: A Series of Tales and Sketches of the Moors and Spaniards*
(1832) by Washington Irving, whose earlier *The Sketch-
Book of Geoffrey Crayon, Gent.* (1819-20), now commonly
called *The Sketch-Book*, stands at approximately the

beginning of North American short fiction (see May, *The Short Story* 6-7, 24-25). And fifth, in the still wider cultural context of diverse visual arts, specifically the history of film and the history of architecture, the name Alhambra, as Blaise has suggested, "[g]oes back to silent films, *The Sheik*, Valentino, etc." (Blaise, Message 9:32 a.m. 31 Oct. 2015) —while also undoubtedly being calculated to echo ironically the name of the famous fourteenth-century Moorish-style palace in Granada, Spain, which provided Irving with the inspiration for his book *The Alhambra*. By permitting what Blaise in his essay on Hawthorne and Melville calls "multiple interpretations," the name Alhambra succeeds in summoning up years and years of personal, sexual, linguistic, literary, and still wider cultural contexts. Talk about the capacity of a highly compressed artistic form to expand powerfully! —as Blaise argues in his essay "The Craft of the Short Story" and in various interviews including the one we conducted in 2007, "An Expanded Moment, Not a Contracted One" (now revised and retitled "Learning To Read, Learning To Write").

***

On a literal level, the level of image and plot, in terms of what many critics designate by the word "representation," "The Birth of the Blues" presents contrasts between the old and the new concerning the history of housing ("an old five-storey apartment house" [20] like the Alhambra as opposed to newer suburban dwellings with "lawns as green as Forbes Field in June" [19]), along with contrasts between the old and the new concerning the history of public transportation (the soon-to-disappear "old heroic" [19] type of trolley on which father and son travel to the Alhambra as opposed to the "sleek new" [24] type of trolley on which they return home). At the same time, on a figurative level, the level of metaphor and allegory, in terms of what we may designate by Blaise's word "transformation" (17, 22), we are intended to think of such details metafictively — as being meant to prompt meditations (consider Blaise's choice of title for his story "Meditations on Starch," which includes a visit to Bergasse 19, the Freud House, in Vienna) about contrasts between the old and the new in another respect: the changes from established past practices to possible future practices of literary form and technique and style.

In sum, we are granted the opportunity to envision a changing continuum, the evolving tradition of the short story, that Clark Blaise's "A Fish Like a Buzzard" and "The Birth of the Blues" and every other story by him takes as its responsibility to engage with, to define itself in terms of or against, and, ultimately, to transform, in giving birth to something new. Metaphorically, Blaise emphasizes the importance of the concept of "transformation" (17, 22) to the ever-changing history of the short story by means of two parallel scenes in "The Birth of the Blues." The first describes how "fascinated" (17) Frank is early in his life at seeing his mother use their gas oven — a disturbing image in a story set during the Second World War — to make something out of wax in the hope of eliminating multitudes — another distressing image in a story set during the Second World War — of tiny facial hairs to make her skin tellingly "pink and smooth" (17). Here we are told that Frank "liked the slow process of transformation, like blueing in the washtub, the tab of orange worked into the bowl of margarine, this third thing, whatever it was" (17). The second portrays another "transformation" (22) that Frank witnesses a few years later, at age twelve, when he sees the nearly naked woman at the Alhambra getting ready for a date with her fiancé. These are scenes that concentrate not on "representation" but on "transformation" — a term Blaise employs not once but twice to suggest not only that we should view these two scenes as being linked but also that we should comprehend the nature of all creative work as involving, first and last, "transformation" or, we might well say, "metamorphosis."

At the end of "The Birth of the Blues," the reader is left with a dual feeling of intense dismay and intense delight. Dismay as signalled from the beginning of the story by the author's darkly prophetic use of the title of the 1926 song "The Birth of the Blues," a phrase subsequently adapted for the title of the 1941 film *Birth of the Blues* starring Bing Crosby. Dismay at so much of what this story alludes to, describes, anticipates. (The general "mold" for this particular "cast" being, in addition to the coming-of-age story, the war story — as was the case with Blaise's early story "Broward Dowdy.") Yet, simultaneously, delight. Delight at imagining — since, as I like to say, "There's a 'Tim' in 'optimism'" — that Frank might conceivably mature into someone like the well-informed third-person narrator of the story. Or someone like the precocious Richard Durgin, the fiction-writing fictional character in Blaise's second novel, *Lusts* (1983), to whom Blaise originally, and very interestingly, attributed authorship of this story.[3] Or someone as truly exceptional as Clark Blaise himself.

Delight, that is, at imagining Frank maturing to a point where he would be able, precisely like Clark Blaise, to look back perceptively on his own past — however unsettled and unsettling it was — and give lasting shape to it, find continuing meaning in it. And definitely delight from realizing that once again we are being afforded the pleasure of engaging in deeply aesthetic, deeply personal ways with the infinitely resonant work of a writer who is contributing as much as any individual can to remaking, enriching, revitalizing the genre of the short story.

Here is a very special individual who, in brilliantly transforming his experiences, the possibilities of story, and language itself, succeeds also in profoundly transforming *us*.

Notes

1. In "The View from Seventy-Five: Autobiographical Annex 2002-2015," written on 10 February 2015 exactly two months before his seventy-fifth birthday, Blaise described *Entre-Nous* as follows: "My final book, in this unlikely cluster of my seventy-fifth year, is again a novel, made up of two novellas and three stories, narrated by Richard (Dickie) Fréchette, a Franco-American boy born some sixty-five years ago into a poor, French-speaking, intensely Catholic (hence intensely atheistic) family in Winooski, Vermont. His older brother, Paulie, wants to be the new Kerouac, but develops the ancestral disease; their father dies from mesothelioma, strongly represented in Québec on account of unregulated asbestos mining around the town of Asbestos; and Paulie has to drop out of high school and get a job. Dickie's lifelong quest is Betsy Robitaille, the parish superstar whose French mother takes her back to Strasbourg (after her father dies, at thirty-eight) to complete her education, but Betsy calls him over. A scholarship is arranged, and so at fourteen Richard Fréchette finds himself a European schoolboy, living in a house with the girl of his

dreams." And yet, as Blaise cautions us, "If you haven't already guessed, be careful of what you dream."

Looking ahead to how he envisions the book developing, Blaise remarked: "With time, though, the old Vermont community of Québec immigrants begins to assimilate, standards change, and Dickie's life, I hope, will be seen as an embodiment of how a community dissolves, and re-converges." He then concludes: "The book is called *Entre-Nous*. It is a record of my own reconnection with my French origins, much in the way I connected with 'my' Indian origins in *The Meagre Tarmac*."

2. The Pittsburgh era of Blaise's life totalled seven years. He arrived in the city with his parents in late 1952 or early 1953, three to four months before his thirteenth birthday, completed grade eight there and spent his high school years there, then, after enrolling at Denison University in Granville, Ohio to begin his undergraduate studies in September 1957, continued to return — to "791A Cooke Dr., Pittsburgh 28, PA (it was a row of small brick duplexes)," he noted (Blaise, Message 4:44 p.m. 17 Nov. 2015) — until his parents' break-up at Christmastime in 1959. "I wasn't in Pittsburgh really from the time my mother split in '59," Blaise recalled; "I was forced to leave school, and went South. It's a foggy period. I really didn't have an address since the house was up for sale, my mother was in a boarding house, my father was in Mexico, etc." (Blaise, Message 7:58 a.m. 27 Oct. 2015). Most likely, Blaise speculated, "It wasn't 1952 when we arrived in Pittsburgh, unless it was late in the year; I'd say now it was 1953 because I remember one of my first Pittsburgh headlines: Kiner Traded" (Blaise, Message 7:58 a.m. 27 Oct. 2015).

Of his specific Mount Lebanon connections, Blaise observed: "We lived in Castle Shannon, which neighbours

Mount Lebanon, but was very poor and didn't have a high school. Castle Shannon students were free to choose South Hills High or Mount Lebanon and nearly all of them chose South Hills since Mount Lebanon was for the college-bound and set a very high standard. I noticed this week an on-line listing of 'best cities' in Pennsylvania, and #1 was Mount Lebanon. So it would be true to say we never lived in Mount Lebanon, but also true to say I was in Mount Lebanon every day for school, and on weekends I worked at my father's furniture store, also in Mount Lebanon (but at the border with another outer suburb, Upper St. Clair, which also lacked a high school, so all of its students filtered into Mount Lebanon for 9th grade)" (Blaise, Message 4:00 p.m. 17 Nov. 2015).

3. Though in many respects obviously written by Blaise, and in *Pittsburgh Stories* (2001) reclaimed by him as his own composition, "The Birth of the Blues" seems somehow imprinted by a different perspective or voice—one distinct from Blaise's at about forty years of age when he wrote the story, but distinct, too, from Blaise's even at the same young age as Richard Durgin when "The Birth of the Blues," as *Lusts* recounts, won Durgin "*Atlantic* magazine's undergraduate talent search for 1959" (96).

I inquired of Blaise: "What I find myself wondering is what sense you would have of the difference in perspective, or in all that you mean when you use the word 'voice,' between Richard Durgin and yourself: between Durgin and yourself, first, at the same young age Durgin was when he is said to have written this story; then between Durgin and yourself, second, at the age you were, more than twenty years later, when you invented Durgin and wrote 'The Birth of the Blues' for him" (Struthers, "Richard Durgin" 3:54 p.m. 19 Nov. 2015).

Blaise responded: "Durgin in that story as it appeared in the novel is very much the embittered proletarian son of the bitter, carpenter father, out for vengeance, and his revelation at the end is to transcend his father's cloistered world of tit-for-tat retaliation. The story was written, rather like the stories inside the essays of *Resident Alien*, to be part of the context of the full book, but able to stand alone, at, I think, some loss. But they are parts of a slowly revolving mirror, reflecting or losing things as they make their rotation" (Blaise, Message 4:57 p.m. 19 Nov. 2015).

Continuing my line of thought, I remarked: "There is something very, very intricate going on here, especially when the impact of pulling the story out of its original context and presenting it at the beginning of the second volume of your *Selected Stories* is also considered. Because I feel as if I'm at least a little out of my depth here, and maybe *way* out of my depth here, I'd like to pursue this a little further if you would be so kind.

"I suppose one way of pinpointing what I'm puzzled about," I suggested, "would be to begin with a phrase like 'Richard Durgin's Style.' What I find myself feeling or intuiting since I think that I'm barely at the stage where I can begin to talk about it analytically—though I suppose we could say that all analysis may very well rely on feeling or intuiting this or that—is some hint I have, to draw on the carpentry metaphor because Frank's father is a carpenter, that 'The Birth of the Blues' is somehow *uniquely* framed by what I am calling 'Richard Durgin's Style.' I'm thinking of ways in which the unidentified third-person narrator of the story so strongly articulates certain things—certain oppositions, for example, or what the narrator (and you) would call 'equivalences.'

"Or," I proposed, "I could express this, I suppose, as a sense on my part of a different tone framing this story." Then I asked: "Would it be fair to use a word like 'harsher' to describe this story's tone — versus the tone you yourself would have taken in writing a story at the young age when Durgin purportedly writes 'The Birth of the Blues' or the tone you yourself would have taken at the time you actually wrote the story? And for that matter, though the story is told in the third person (and in past tense), what are the characteristics of that narrator versus, say, a young Richard Durgin, a young Clark Blaise, an older Richard Durgin, an older Clark Blaise?

"Put differently," I then asked, "would you suspect that you consciously and perhaps very possibly also half-consciously or even unconsciously somehow adapted your style to write a story meant, originally, to be the creation of Richard Durgin? And, if so, could you say how?" (Struthers, "Richard Durgin's Style" 8:43 a.m. 20 Nov. 2015).

With characteristic perceptiveness, good humour, and conciseness Blaise answered: "That's the joy of critical analysis, Tim. I just write them, unconscious of any complication. I can see there are different shades of interpretation when you rip a story from one context and put it in another. The story doesn't change, but its presence changes the context. Put in *Pittsburgh Stories* it plays a different role than it does in *Lusts*, *non*? One is sexual, the other is geographical" (Blaise, Message 9:48 a.m. 20 Nov. 2015).

In response, I suggested: "You say of the two different contexts represented first by *Lusts* (1983) and then by *Pittsburgh Stories* (2001) that 'One is sexual, the other is geographical.' I find it very interesting that a seemingly simple switch in context — and thus in the story's perceived subject — could dramatically change our sense of the story's narrative point of view: from a more involved or intimate voice for a work focussed more on sexuality to a more detached or distanced voice for a work focussed more on geography.

"Furthermore," I stated, "when 'The Birth of the Blues' is transferred from *Lusts* to *Pittsburgh Stories*, we lose sight of Richard Durgin completely. And that, it seems to me, means that in the context of *Pittsburgh Stories* the identity of the third-person narrator of 'The Birth of the Blues' is left more mysterious (though very possibly still informed, but now invisibly, by qualities of what I called 'Richard Durgin's Style'). To wit, the narrator seemingly imagined purely by you in the context of *Pittsburgh Stories* could appear somewhat different in sensibility and even age from the narrator seemingly imagined purely by Richard Durgin though of course ultimately by you in the context of *Lusts*.

"Earlier you summarized such matters using a very compelling image: 'they are parts of a slowly revolving mirror, reflecting or losing things as they make their rotation.' And how fascinating it is to see what each allows us to imagine!" (Struthers, "The Same Story Seen Differently Because of Alternative Contexts" 12:20 p.m. 22 Nov. 2015).

Blaise answered: "I would agree with your conclusions. The *Pittsburgh Stories* 'version' is a lesser work, because of its context" (Blaise, Message 6:05 p.m. 22 Nov. 2015).

To this I replied: "The same story yet arguably *more* mysterious for stripping it of the original Richard Durgin frame, I would say. And isn't that sort of unending impact what any writer *dreams* of achieving?" (Struthers, "The Same Story Yet Arguably *More* Mysterious" 6:36 p.m. 22 Nov. 2015).

Acknowledgements

A much earlier and much shorter version of this essay was presented on 17 June 2010 as part of The Border as Fiction: The 11th International Conference on the Short Story in English, held at York University in Toronto. For their support, friendship, inspiration, and in some instances particular help at various times over the past ten years while I have been doing concentrated research, interviewing, critical writing, and editorial work on Clark Blaise, I would like to thank Clark Blaise, William Butt, Marlys Chevrefils, Ailsa Cox, Alan Filewod, Alec Follett, Ajay Heble, Eleni Kapetanios, G.D. Killam, Susan K. Lohafer, Robert M. Luscher, Kelsey McCallum, Andrew C. McKague, John Metcalf, Marianne Micros, Michael Mirolla, W.H. New, Graeme Northcote, Catherine Sheldrick Ross, Paul Salmon, Ron Shuebrook, Joy Struthers, Masa Torbica, Will Wellington, and Kelly Wighton.

Works Consulted

Atwood, Margaret. "Ariel or Caliban?" Rev. of *The Meagre Tarmac: Stories*, by Clark Blaise. *The New York Review of Books* 10 May 2012. Web. 4 Nov. 2015. <http://www.nybooks.com/articles/archives/2012/may/10/clark-blaise-ariel-or-caliban/>. Rpt. in *Clark Blaise: Essays on His Works*. Ed. J.R. (Tim) Struthers. Toronto: Guernica Editions, 2016. Essential Writers.

"The Birth of the Blues." Music by Ray Henderson. Words by B.G. Buddy De Sylva and Lew Brown. 1926.

Birth of the Blues. Dir. Victor Schertzinger. Paramount Pictures, 1941.

Blaise, Clark. "1850, August 5; A Literary Party Climbs Monument Mountain: Nathaniel Hawthorne and Herman

Melville." *A New Literary History of America*. Ed. Greil Marcus and Werner Sollors. Cambridge, MA: The Belknap Press of Harvard UP, 2009. 278-83.

-----. "[Autobiographical Annex: Clark Blaise]." In "BLAISE, Clark 1940- ." *Contemporary Authors: A Bio-Bibliographical Guide to Current Writers in Fiction, General Nonfiction, Poetry, Journalism, Drama, Motion Pictures, Television, and Other Fields*. Vol. 231. Project Ed. Julie Keppen. Farmington Hills, MI: Thomson Gale, 2005. 50-57. Rpt. (rev.) as "Autobiographical Annex: 1985-2006." *Selected Essays*. By Clark Blaise. Ed. John Metcalf and J.R. (Tim) Struthers. Windsor, ON: Biblioasis, 2008. 209-21.

-----. "The Birth of the Blues." *Pittsburgh Stories*. Introd. Robert Boyers. Erin, ON: The Porcupine's Quill, 2001. 15-25. Vol. 2 of *The Selected Stories of Clark Blaise*. 4 vols. 2000-06.

-----. "Broward Dowdy." *Tribal Justice*. Toronto: Doubleday Canada, 1974. 3-14. Rpt. in *Southern Stories*. Introd. Fenton Johnson. Erin, ON: The Porcupine's Quill, 2000. 41-50. Vol. 1 of *The Selected Stories of Clark Blaise*. 4 vols. 2000-06.

-----. "The Cast and the Mold." *Stories Plus: Canadian Stories with Authors' Commentaries*. Ed. John Metcalf. Toronto: McGraw-Hill Ryerson, 1979. 27-29. Rpt. in "How Stories Mean." *Selected Essays*. By Clark Blaise. Ed. John Metcalf and J.R. (Tim) Struthers. Windsor, ON: Biblioasis, 2008. 172-75.

-----. "Clark Blaise: *1940-* ." *Contemporary Authors: Autobiography Series*. Vol. 3. Ed. Adele Sarkissian. Detroit, MI: Gale Research, 1986. 15-30. Rpt. in "BLAISE, Clark 1940- ." *Contemporary Authors: A Bio-Bibliographical Guide to Current Writers in Fiction, General Nonfiction, Poetry, Journalism, Drama, Motion Pictures, Television, and Other Fields*. Vol. 231. Project Ed. Julie Keppen. Farmington Hills, MI: Thomson Gale, 2005. 37-50. Rpt. (rev.) as "Autobiographical Essay: 1940-1984." *Selected Essays*. By Clark

Blaise. Ed. John Metcalf and J.R. (Tim) Struthers. Windsor, ON: Biblioasis, 2008. 9-32.

-----. "The Craft of the Short Story." *Proteus* [Southampton Coll. of Long Island U] (2003): 220-27. Rpt. in *The Southampton Review* 1.1 (2007): 22-28. Rpt. in *Canadian Notes & Queries* 72 (2007): 28-31. Rpt. (rev.) in *Selected Essays*. By Clark Blaise. Ed. John Metcalf and J.R. (Tim) Struthers. Windsor, ON: Biblioasis, 2008. 181-90.

-----. *Entre-Nous*. Forthcoming likely by 2017.

-----. "A Fish Like a Buzzard." *Silo* [1] (1962): 1-18. Rpt. (rev.) in *Southern Stories*. Introd. Fenton Johnson. Erin, ON: The Porcupine's Quill, 2000. 13-24. Vol. 1 of *The Selected Stories of Clark Blaise*. 4 vols. 2000-06.

-----. "How Stories Mean." *Selected Essays*. By Clark Blaise. Ed. John Metcalf and J.R. (Tim) Struthers. Windsor, ON: Biblioasis, 2008. 167-79.

-----. *If I Were Me: A Novel*. Erin, ON: The Porcupine's Quill, 1997.

-----. "The Kerouac Who Never Was." Short Story Traditions: Bridges to Modernity and Beyond. 12th International Conference on the Short Story in English. Society for the Study of the Short Story. North Little Rock, AR. 29 June 2012. Reading. *14: Best Canadian Stories*. Ed. John Metcalf. Ottawa: Oberon, 2014. 70-79. Print.

-----. *Lusts*. Garden City, NY: Doubleday, 1983.

-----. *The Meagre Tarmac: Stories*. Windsor, ON: Biblioasis, 2011.

-----. "Meditations on Starch." *Man and His World*. Erin, ON: The Porcupine's Quill, 1992. 27-37. Rpt. in *World Body*. Introd. Michael Augustin. Erin, ON: The Porcupine's Quill, 2006. 119-28. Vol. 4 of *The Selected Stories of Clark Blaise*. 4 vols. 2000-06.

-----. Message to the author. 7:58 a.m. 27 Oct. 2015. E-mail.

-----. Message to the author. 12:22 p.m. 27 Oct. 2015. E-mail.

-----. Message to the author. 9:32 a.m. 31 Oct. 2015. E-mail.

-----. Message to the author. 12:58 p.m. 31 Oct. 2015. E-mail.

-----. Message to the author. 3:49 p.m. 4 Nov. 2015. E-mail.

-----. Message to the author. 4:00 p.m. 17 Nov. 2015. E-mail.

-----. Message to the author. 4:44 p.m. 17 Nov. 2015. E-mail.

-----. Message to the author. 4:57 p.m. 19 Nov. 2015. E-mail.

-----. Message to the author. 9:48 a.m. 20 Nov. 2015. E-mail.

-----. Message to the author. 6:05 p.m. 22 Nov. 2015. E-mail.

-----. *Montreal Stories*. Introd. Peter Behrens. Erin, ON: The Porcupine's Quill, 2003. Vol. 3 of *The Selected Stories of Clark Blaise*. 4 vols. 2000-06.

-----. "On Ending Stories." *Making It New: Contemporary Canadian Stories*. Ed. John Metcalf. Toronto: Methuen, 1982. 32-35. Rpt. in "How Stories Mean." *Selected Essays*. By Clark Blaise. Ed. John Metcalf and J.R. (Tim) Struthers. Windsor, ON: Biblioasis, 2008. 175-79.

-----. *Pittsburgh Stories*. Introd. Robert Boyers. Erin, ON: The Porcupine's Quill, 2001. Vol. 2 of *The Selected Stories of Clark Blaise*. 4 vols. 2000-06.

-----. "Portrait of the Artist as a Young Pup." *Canadian Literature* 100 (1984): 35-41. Rpt. (rev.) in *The Montreal Story Tellers: Memoirs, Photographs, Critical Essays*. Ed. J.R. (Tim) Struthers. Montreal: Véhicule, 1985. 65-72. Rpt. (rev.) in *Selected Essays*. By Clark Blaise. Ed. John Metcalf and J.R. (Tim) Struthers. Windsor, ON: Biblioasis, 2008. 147-55.

-----. *Resident Alien*. Markham, ON: Penguin Books Canada, 1986.

-----. *The Selected Stories of Clark Blaise*. 4 vols. Erin, ON: The Porcupine's Quill, 2000-06.

-----. *Southern Stories*. Introd. Fenton Johnson. Erin, ON: The Porcupine's Quill, 2000. Vol. 1 of *The Selected Stories of Clark Blaise*. 4 vols. 2000-06.

-----. "To Begin, To Begin." *The Narrative Voice: Short Stories and Reflections by Canadian Authors.* Ed. John Metcalf. Toronto: McGraw-Hill Ryerson, 1972. Rpt. in "How Stories Mean." *Selected Essays.* By Clark Blaise. Ed. John Metcalf and J.R. (Tim) Struthers. Windsor, ON: Biblioasis, 2008. 167-72.

-----. "The View from Seventy-Five: Autobiographical Annex 2002–2015." *Clark Blaise: Essays on His Works.* Ed. J.R. (Tim) Struthers. Toronto: Guernica Editions, 2016. Essential Writers.

-----. *World Body.* Introd. Michael Augustin. Erin, ON: The Porcupine's Quill, 2006. Vol. 4 of *The Selected Stories of Clark Blaise.* 4 vols. 2000-06.

Bloom, Harold. "Criticism, Canon-Formation, and Prophecy: The Sorrows of Facticity." *Poetics of Influence: New and Selected Criticism.* Ed. John Hollander. New Haven, CT: Henry R. Schwab, 1988. 405-24.

Donoghue, Denis. *Metaphor.* Cambridge, MA: Harvard UP, 2014.

Faust, Irvin. *Roar Lion Roar and Other Stories.* New York: Random House, 1964.

Fitzgerald, F. Scott. "Babylon Revisited." *Babylon Revisited and Other Stories.* New York: Charles Scribner's Sons, 1960. 210-30.

Freud, Sigmund. *Jokes and Their Relation to the Unconscious.* Trans. James Strachey. Ed. Angela Richards. London: Penguin, 1991. Vol. 6 of *The Penguin Freud Library.* 15 vols.

-----. *Three Essays on the Theory of Sexuality.* In *On Sexuality.* Trans. James Strachey. Ed. Angela Richards. London: Penguin, 1991. 31-169. Vol. 7 of *The Penguin Freud Library.* 15 vols.

Frye, Northrop. "The Expanding World of Metaphor." *Myth and*

Metaphor: Selected Essays, 1974-1988. By Northrop Frye. Ed. Robert D. Denham. Charlottesville: UP of Virginia, 1990. 108-23.

Gallant, Mavis. Preface. *The Selected Stories of Mavis Gallant.* Toronto: McClelland & Stewart, 1996. ix-xix.

Gass, William H. "Metaphor." In "The Biggs Lectures in the Classics." *Life Sentences: Literary Judgments and Accounts.* New York: Alfred A. Knopf, 2012. 267-88.

Gogol, Nikolai. "The Overcoat." Trans. Andrew R. MacAndrew. *Elements of Fiction: An Anthology.* Ed. Robert Scholes and Rosemary Sullivan. Canadian ed. Toronto: Oxford UP. 117-43. Rpt. in *Elements of Fiction.* Ed. Robert Scholes and Rosemary Sullivan. 3rd Canadian ed. Toronto: Oxford UP, 1994. 91-114.

Gordon, Caroline, and Allen Tate, eds. *The House of Fiction: An Anthology of the Short Story with Commentary.* New York: Charles Scribner's Sons, 1950. 2nd ed. New York: Charles Scribner's Sons, 1960.

Hancock, Geoff. "An Interview with Clark Blaise." *Canadian Fiction Magazine* 34-35 (1980): 46-64. Rpt. as "Clark Blaise" in *Canadian Writers at Work: Interviews with Geoff Hancock.* By Geoff Hancock. Toronto: Oxford UP, 1987. 146-63. Rpt. as "Clear Veneer: An Interview with Clark Blaise" in *Clark Blaise: The Interviews.* Ed. J.R. (Tim) Struthers. Toronto: Guernica Editions, 2016. Essential Writers.

Hawthorne, Nathaniel. *Mosses from the Old Manse.* 1846. Introd. Mary Oliver. New York: The Modern Library, 2003.

-----. *The Snow-Image and Other Twice-Told Tales.* Boston: Ticknor, Reed, and Fields, 1852.

-----. *Twice-Told Tales.* 1837. Introd. Rosemary Mahoney. New York: The Modern Library, 2001.

Hemingway, Ernest. *Death in the Afternoon.* New York: Charles Scribner's Sons, 1932.

Hood, Hugh. "An Allegory of Man's Fate." *Dark Glasses*. Ottawa: Oberon, 1976. 130-43.

-----. "Flying a Red Kite." *Flying a Red Kite*. 1962. Introd. Hugh Hood. Erin, ON: The Porcupine's Quill, 1987. 185-96. Vol. 1 of *The Collected Stories*. 5 vols. 1987-2003.

Irving, Washington. *The Alhambra: A Series of Tales and Sketches of the Moors and Spaniards*. Philadelphia: Carey & Lea, 1832. 2 vols.

---. *The Sketch-Book of Geoffrey Crayon, Gent.* 1819-20. Ed. and introd. Susan Manning. Oxford, Eng.: Oxford UP, 2009. Oxford World's Classics.

James, Henry. "Preface to 'The Portrait of a Lady'." *The Art of the Novel: Critical Prefaces*. Introd. Richard P. Blackmur. New York: Charles Scribner's Sons, 1962. 40-58.

Joyce, James. "Araby." *Dubliners: Authoritative Text, Contexts, Criticism*. Ed. Margot Norris. New York: W.W. Norton, 2006. 20-26. A Norton Critical Edition.

-----. "A Little Cloud." *Dubliners: Authoritative Text, Contexts, Criticism*. Ed. Margot Norris. New York: W.W. Norton, 2006. 57-70. A Norton Critical Edition.

Lohafer, Susan K. *Coming to Terms with the Short Story*. Baton Rouge: Louisiana State UP, 1983.

-----. *Reading for Storyness: Preclosure Theory, Empirical Poetics, and Culture in the Short Story*. Baltimore: Johns Hopkins UP, 2003.

Luscher, Robert M. "In Search of Lost Time: Clark Blaise's *Pittsburgh Stories* as a Short Story Sequence." *Clark Blaise, Proprietor*. Ed. J.R. (Tim) Struthers. *Short Story* ns 15.2 (2007): 65-88.

May, Charles E. *Edgar Allan Poe: A Study of the Short Fiction*. Boston, MA: Twayne, 1991. Twayne's Studies in Short Fiction Ser. 28.

-----. *"I Am Your Brother": Short Story Studies*. Garden Grove, CA: Amayzing Editions, 2013.

-----. *The Short Story: The Reality of Artifice*. 1995. New York: Routledge, 2002. Genres in Context.

McLuhan, Marshall. *The Interior Landscape: The Literary Criticism of Marshall McLuhan 1943-1962*. Ed. Eugene McNamara. New York: McGraw-Hill, 1969.

-----, with Wilfred Watson. *From Cliché to Archetype*. New York: Viking, 1970.

Metcalf, John. *An Aesthetic Underground: A Literary Memoir*. Toronto: Thomas Allen, 2003.

-----. *Freedom from Culture: Selected Essays 1982-92*. Toronto: ECW, 1994.

-----. *Kicking Against the Pricks*. Downsview, ON: ECW, 1982. Rev. ed. Guelph, ON: Red Kite, 1986.

-----. *Shut Up He Explained: A Literary Memoir Vol. II*. Windsor, ON: Biblioasis, 2007.

-----. *What Is A Canadian Literature?* Guelph, ON: Red Kite, 1988.

Mitchell, W.J.T. "Representation." *Critical Terms for Literary Study*. Ed. Frank Lentricchia and Thomas McLaughlin. 2nd ed. Chicago: U of Chicago P, 1995. 11-22.

Northcote, Graeme. "Reading by Twilight: Nathaniel Hawthorne, Clark Blaise, and the Technology of the Short Story." *Clark Blaise: Essays on His Works*. Ed. J.R. (Tim) Struthers. Toronto: Guernica Editions, 2016. Essential Writers.

O'Connor, Frank. "My Oedipus Complex." *Collected Stories*. Introd. Richard Ellmann. New York: Alfred A. Knopf, 1981. 282-92.

Ovid. *The Metamorphoses of Ovid*. Trans. Mary M. Innes. Harmondsworth, Eng.: Penguin, 1955.

Powe, B.W. *Marshall McLuhan and Northrop Frye: Apocalypse and Alchemy*. Toronto: U of Toronto P, 2014.

Rohrberger, Mary. *The Art of Katherine Mansfield*. Ann Arbor, MI: U Microfilms Intl., 1977.

-----. *Hawthorne and the Modern Short Story: A Study in Genre.* The Hague, Neth.: Mouton, 1966.

Scholes, Robert. *Fabulation and Metafiction.* Urbana, IL: U of Illinois P, 1979.

The Sheik. Dir. George Melford. Famous Players-Lasky, 1921.

Shields, Carol. "The Metaphor Is Dead — Pass It On." *Various Miracles.* Toronto: Stoddart, 1985. 102-04.

Singer, Sandra. "Self-Healing through Telling Someone Else's Intimate Story: Clark Blaise's *Lusts*." *Clark Blaise: Essays on His Works.* Ed. J.R. (Tim) Struthers. Toronto: Guernica Editions, 2016. Essential Writers.

Struthers, J.R. (Tim). "A Checklist of Works by Clark Blaise to 2015." *Clark Blaise: Essays on His Works.* Ed. J.R. (Tim) Struthers. Toronto: Guernica Editions, 2016. Essential Writers.

-----. "Endings and Beginnings: Reading Clark Blaise's 'A Fish Like a Buzzard'." *Short Fiction in Theory and Practice* 1.1 (2011): 7-23.

-----. "An Expanded Moment, Not a Contracted One: An Interview with Clark Blaise." *Clark Blaise, Proprietor.* Ed. J.R. (Tim) Struthers. *Short Story* ns 15.2 (2007): 123-44. Rpt. (rev.) as "Learning To Read, Learning To Write: An Interview with Clark Blaise" in *Clark Blaise: The Interviews.* Ed. J.R. (Tim) Struthers. Toronto: Guernica Editions, 2016. Essential Writers.

-----. "Richard Durgin." Message to Clark Blaise. 3:54 p.m. 19 Nov. 2015. E-mail.

-----. "Richard Durgin's Style." Message to Clark Blaise. 8:43 a.m. 20 Nov. 2015. E-mail.

-----. "The Same Story Seen Differently Because of Alternative Contexts." Message to Clark Blaise. 12:20 p.m. 22 Nov. 2015. E-mail.

-----. "The Same Story Yet Arguably *More* Mysterious." Message to Clark Blaise. 6:36 p.m. 22 Nov. 2015. E-mail.

-----. "To Elevate Experience into Metaphor: An Interview with Clark Blaise." *Clark Blaise: The Interviews*. Ed. J.R. (Tim) Struthers. Toronto: Guernica Editions, 2016. Essential Writers.

-----. "The World of Clark Blaise: A Bibliography of His 'Occasional' Critical Writing, Autobiographical Writing, and Nonfiction Writing." *Selected Essays*. By Clark Blaise. Ed. John Metcalf and J.R. (Tim) Struthers. Windsor, ON: Biblioasis, 2008. 223-80.

Tambling, Jeremy. *Allegory*. Abingdon, Eng.: Routledge, 2010. The New Critical Idiom.

Thompson, Reg. "All Things Considered: Alice Munro First and Last." *Alice Munro: A Souwesto Celebration*. Ed. J.R. (Tim) Struthers and John B. Lee. *Windsor Review* 47.2 (2014): 5-9.

Waugh, Patricia. *Metafiction: The Theory and Practice of Self-Conscious Fiction*. London: Methuen, 1984. New Accents.

Wilde, Oscar. "The Critic as Artist." *Intentions*. 1891. Rpt. in *The Artist as Critic: Critical Writings of Oscar Wilde*. Ed. Richard Ellmann. 1969. Chicago: U of Chicago P, 1982. 340-408. Rpt. in *Intentions*. Amherst, NY: Prometheus, 2004. 93-217. Literary Classics.

Zahn, Curtis. *American Contemporary*. Introd. Herbert Gold. New York: New Directions-San Francisco Review, 1963.

Opening "Eyes"

Ray Smith

In his reminiscence of The Montreal Story Tellers, John Metcalf says this of the public readings of Clark Blaise:

> Clark Blaise's stories ran on wheels, as it were; Clark gave the impression that he was merely the almost invisible track on which they ran. The stories are so beautifully crafted and balanced in terms of their rhetoric that Clark seemed almost to disappear behind them. This was, of course, an illusion. Clark was never openly dramatic, never given to gesture, but he read fluently and *urgently* and with a fierce grip on the audience which tightened relentlessly. It was rather like watching an oddly silent pressure-cooker which you knew was capable of taking the roof off at any moment. This feeling of *contained* power, typical of Clark's performing style, was also somehow connected with Clark's temperament. I've never seen Clark not in control of himself but I'd pay large sums of money not to be there if or when. ("Telling Tales" 31)

Since first reading it more than thirty years ago, I have several times returned to this paragraph, savouring its perfect description of Clark on the stage, musing on the preposterous notion of Clark as railway tracks, admiring the audacious and precisely judged italics. And I have pondered how Clark did it, how he still does it in story after story, despite his excursions into a variety of styles, forms, voices, and modes. While the power is evident in Clark's public performance, it is also there in the progression of words on the page.

The three of us met about 1969, and a year or so later with Hugh Hood and Raymond Fraser formed the Montreal Story Teller group, doing readings in schools and universities. Clark and John are in many ways alike: they prefer short stories, they write with precision and economy, and they continually work from autobiographical materials. Perhaps the most important similarity is their bi-nationalism: John was born and raised in England, but has become a Canadian; Clark, with Canadian parents, was born in the States, but has lived in and has written about both countries. Clark has the added *frisson* of a third national connection through his marriage to Bengali-born Bharati Mukherjee.

Clark and John were consistently the best readers of the five. With his perfect pacing and precise modulation, John, like Clark, is always a powerful reader, but does not exhibit the sense of "*contained* power" which he says is characteristic of Clark. If we look through "Eyes," the story Clark most often read on stage, we can understand that when read "fluently and *urgently*" the unsettling incidents of the voyeur and the butcher shop would ensure that Clark's "fierce grip on the audience [...] tightened relentlessly." But what is the origin of the power, and how is it put on the page so that it grips us in the first place? In order to understand this, I shall examine the first two paragraphs of "Eyes."

In his "Portrait of the Artist as a Young Pup" Clark describes the period in which he wrote the story:

I was writing very openly, in the late sixties, of Montreal. The city was drenched with significance for me — it was one of those perfect times when every block I walked yielded an image, when images clustered with their own internal logic into insistent stories. A new kind of unforced, virtually transcribed story (new for me, at least) was begging to be written — stories like "A Class of New Canadians," "Eyes," "Words for the Winter," "Extractions and Contractions," "Going to India," and "At the Lake" were all written in one sitting, practically without revision. (66)

This passage reminds me of an incident in *War and Peace*. Near the middle of the novel Natasha Rostov tries an unfamiliar peasant dance; the point of view in the second paragraph is of a peasant woman:

> Where, how and when could this young countess, who had had a French *émigrée* for governess, have imbibed from the Russian air she breathed the spirit of that dance? [...]
>
> Her performance was so perfect, so absolutely perfect, that Anisya Fiodorovna, who had at once handed her the kerchief she needed for the dance, had tears in her eyes, though she laughed as she watched the slender, graceful countess, reared in silks and velvets, in another world than hers, who was yet able to understand all that was in Anisya and in Anisya's father and mother and aunt, and in every Russian man and woman. (604)

Natasha's identification here with the Russian people is central to the novel. Similarly, Clark's identification with Montreal is central to his life and writing at that time, and is the source of the power of the images, of the insistent stories, imbibed from the Montreal air. But how does he get it on the page, how does he establish it first in the reader?

In "To Begin, To Begin," Clark argues that "The most interesting thing about a story [...] is its beginning, its first paragraph, often its first sentence," adding, "The first paragraph is a microcosm of the whole, but in a way that only the whole can reveal" (158). (This essay and two others by Clark, as well as John's interview with him, all appear in *How Stories Mean*; all contain useful information about Clark's approaches to writing, especially openings.) Here is the opening of "North":

> In the beginning, my mother would meet me at the "*Garçons*" side of Papineau School. She might have been the tallest woman in the east end of Montreal in the early fifties. I was walking with my friend Mick. I was thirteen, and he was older but smaller. From the neck up he looked twenty. He was in my cousin Dollard's class. He had discovered me on the first day of school, standing by the iron gate looking puzzled. "Take the garkons," he had advised, under his breath. *Garkons* was an early word in my private vocabulary. In the beginning, I had to trust strangers' pronunciations, or worse, my own. (15)

In the beginning was the word, and the word was strange, private, mispronounced, the door to another world. The first sentence suggests that the mother is nurturing, protective, perhaps over-protective; the second, that she is different from and perhaps superior to the other mothers. She is the generic mother of most of the stories, inspired by Clark's own mother, as the father is inspired by

Clark's father, the boy inspired by Clark. The *"Garçons"* entrance, for a boy who as a grown-up is writing in English, suggests an aspect of the theme which Clark has continually, perhaps obsessively, pursued throughout his career: frontiers and borders, the difference, the strangeness, of here and there, of me and them. One of the corollaries, defamiliarization, is evident from the mother's height, and from the Irish-named Mick, another half-outsider at Papineau School. Mick is another generic Blaise character, the unintellectual companion with street smarts — or, like Broward Dowdy in the *Southern Stories*, swamp smarts. His job is to guide the puzzled narrator through the iron gate, the *"Garçons"* door, to initiate him into the recondite vocabulary of there and them.

***

This opening paragraph of "North" contains not just this story, it contains most of Clark's entire *oeuvre*. "Eyes" also begins with immediacy:

> You jump into this business of a new country cautiously. First you choose a place where English is spoken, with doctors and bus lines at hand, and a supermarket in a *centre d'achats* not too far away. You ease yourself into the city, approaching by car or bus down a single artery, aiming yourself along the boulevard that begins small and tree-lined in your suburb but broadens into the canyoned aorta of the city five miles beyond. And by that first winter when you know the routes and bridges, the standard congestions reported from the helicopter on your favourite radio station, you start to think of moving. What's the good of a place like this when two of your neighbours have come from Texas

and the French paper you've dutifully subscribed to arrives by mail two days late? These French are all around you, behind the counters at the shopping centre, in a house or two on your block; why isn't your little boy learning French at least? Where's the nearest *maternelle*? Four miles away.

In the spring you move. You find an apartment on a small side street where dogs outnumber children and the row houses resemble London's, divided equally between the rundown and remodelled. Your neighbours are the young personalities of French television who live on delivered chicken, or the old pensioners who shuffle down the summer sidewalks in pyjamas and slippers in a state of endless recuperation. Your neighbours pay sixty a month for rent, or three hundred; you pay two-fifty for a two-bedroom flat where the walls have been replastered and new fixtures hung. The bugs *d'antan* remain, as well as the hulks of cars abandoned in the fire alley behind, where downtown drunks sleep in the summer night. (45)

For comparison, here is the opening of Metcalf's "Gentle as Flowers Make the Stones," written about the same time:

Fists, teeth clenched, Jim Haine stood naked and shivering staring at the lighted rectangle. He must have slept through the first knocks, the calling. Even the buzzing of the doorbell had made them nervous; he'd had to wad it up with paper days before. The pounding and shouting continued. The male was beginning to dart through the trails between the *Aponogeton crispus* and the blades of the *Echinodorus martii*.

Above the pounding, words: "pass-key," "furniture," "bailiffs."

Lackey!

Lickspittle!

The female was losing colour rapidly. She'd shaken off the feeding fry and was diving and pancaking through the weed-trails.

Hour after hour he had watched the two fish cleaning one of the blades of a Sword plant, watched their ritual procession, watched the female dotting the pearly eggs in rows up the length of the leaf, the milt-shedding male following; slow, solemn, seeming to move without motion, like carved galleons or bright painted rocking-horses.

The first eggs had turned grey, broken down to flocculent slime; the second hatch, despite copper sulphate and the addition of peat extracts, had simply died.

"I know you're in there, Mr. Haine!"

A renewed burst of door-knob rattling. (113)

Finally, two excerpts from Hugh Hood, the first the opening of "Le Grand Déménagement" from *Around the Mountain*:

Suppose you move here the end of August, say. You arranged with your *propriétaire* for a lease which, no matter what your wishes, will terminate on April 30th the next year, or more probably the year after, giving you a *terme de bail* of twelve plus eight, or a total of twenty months. A lease in Montréal ends on April 30th. Useless to plead its inconvenience, if you only mean to stay nine months, or fifteen, because the custom is invariable. So God ordained it; so it remains. (81)

And the opening of the title story from the collection *The Fruit Man, the Meat Man & the Manager*:

> A grocer named Morris Znaimer managed the Green-
> wood Groceteria, up on Greenwood Avenue next to the
> university, for over seventeen years, in partnership
> with Jack Genovese, fruit and vegetables, and Mendel
> Greenspon, an experienced butcher but not kosher.
>
> Mister Znaimer took care of grocery inventory and
> the beer, and he also did the accounting and book keep-
> ing, supervised the cash desk and checkout counter with
> a girl named Shirley to help, and decided about charge
> accounts and billing; he had hardly any bad-debt items
> because he was a shrewd judge of credit. (188)

The greatest contrast between Hugh and the other
two is immediately obvious: while they are concerned
with the self, Hugh writes of the world. He says in his
"Author's Introduction" to *Around the Mountain* that he
wanted it to be "a work that would carry on its face an
innocent air of immersion in this world, the fallen secular community" (11). He does not quite say that the book
is a prose epic of love to Montreal. And while he mentions *The Prelude* and *Purgatorio* as sources of reference,
he might also have mentioned a favourite book of his,
Turgenev's *A Sportsman's Sketches*, with its evident love
of the Russian countryside and its people, and a similar
interest in the world the self sees, hears, feels. In his
introduction to *Around the Mountain* Hugh remarks, "I
remember the city as it struck me during my first four
or five years there, fascinating, swarming with suggest-
ive details like the possibility of endless linguistic joking"
(16). Compare with Clark's remark, quoted above: "The
city was drenched with significance for me — it was one
of those perfect times when every block I walked yielded
an image, when images clustered with their own internal logic into insistent stories." But while Clark's love of

Montreal is one of the cardinal points of the compass of his soul, it remains secular and personal. Hugh's love is, was, religious as he makes clear in his introduction to *Around the Mountain*: "'Look at the creation, see how it is made, how wonderfully, how marvellously'" (13). The immanence of the divine in all things is central to Hugh's view of the world. To write of the world outside of himself as Turgenev does, but to put into words the presence of God, is thus for Hugh a kind of sacred duty. While Clark and John write of the self seeing, Hugh writes of what the self sees which is the presence of God. What Clark calls a "canyoned aorta" is the appalling Decarie Expressway: "'And this also,' said Marlow suddenly, 'has been one of the dark places of the earth.'" On the way to a Story Teller reading Hugh really did extol the beauty of the Decarie. I was aware back then of Hugh's Catholicism, but certainly had no idea of its pervasive power: if God ordained Quebec's moving day practices, perhaps He ordained the Decarie. I was flabbergasted when Hugh remarked casually that the title characters in "The Fruit Man, the Meat Man and the Manager" are allegorically the Trinity, and "Greenwood" the Garden of Eden. I'll return to Hugh from time to time; suffice it to say that his work is entirely unlike that of Clark and John.

The excerpt from John's story makes clear an important contrast with Clark — the interleaving or juxtaposing of two elements, here the noise at the door and the dying fish. Interleaving provides a major structural principle for John, and examples can be found in scenes throughout his work. The connection between the noise and the fish is causal, but typically John does not at once make this clear, and the "them" which are made nervous is deliberately enigmatic. Indeed, the core structure of the story is Jim Haine's translation from Latin of a Martial epigram interleaved with the hostility, vulgarity, and incomprehension of the world. One might say that in this story *John Wesley* Metcalf demonstrates most effectively his belief that the devil is immanent in all things, with the fragile exception of art, and that is why "Gentle as Flowers Make the Stones" is the quintessential Metcalf work.

Also evident from the excerpt is John's greater concern for words and the succinct saying of them. I don't mean that Clark and Hugh don't care about words, but that John's interest is insistently in the foreground. The Latin is obvious, and prepares us for Martial's poem, but we might note *pancaking, flocculent, beaking* (113, 113, 114), and the later *vouchsafed* and *coir* (123, 124). And of course the point of the story is Jim's obsession with getting right the words and their arrangement on the page. Clark may have written the late sixties Montreal stories at one sitting; John has always laboured over his work as Jim Haine does, endlessly rearranging words in patterns on the page. Here John has deployed each sentence with meticulous care; indeed, John should always be read sentence by sentence (obviously), but each sentence savoured in turn as a thing of beauty in itself. By contrast, each of Clark's sentences, no matter how delicious, impels us on to the next, with no sense that we miss something by rushing forward.

***

Returning to "Eyes," we likely notice on the page the paradoxical "jump [...] cautiously," but I doubt audiences would hear it — I certainly didn't. The paragraph continues with a sketch of the comfortable but alien English — Texan! — suburb where nonetheless "These French are all around you."

Let me here deal with the voice and tense. Second person and present tense, long considered uncongenial in English, have enjoyed a recent vogue. This baffles me. When I encounter an opening such as "You dream obsessively that you're a butterfly," I reply, "No, I don't" and stop reading. "You have just had your first period" suggests the author has a questionable grasp of human anatomy. I'm not sure why they work in "Eyes," though probably because I am enough like Clark's "You" that the identification is not grotesque. On first hearing him read it, I probably sighed, but soon enough found myself falling into the incantatory spell of his voice, of the progress of the story. I think my ear simply edited the incoming "You" to "I" or "He," and I'll do the same here to avoid the ludicrous. Clark addresses the issue in his interview with John (Metcalf, "Interview" 124).

The narrator, his wife, and child begin the cautious steps into the strange, beguiling, almost frightening city. In "North," the boy has been uprooted from Pittsburgh or Cincinnati and dropped into the shock of French Montreal for several years at about puberty; in "Eyes" the adult narrator has returned of his own accord, curious to re-explore this other side of himself. His remembered or learned French is sufficient for *centre d'achats* and *maternelle*, and for the oblique reference to François Villon in "the bugs *d'antan*." That he is an educated man of the world is also implied in the detail about the French newspaper and the reference to London and later to Barcelona. Indeed, he is, as usual, a version of Clark.

All fiction writers dig into their own lives for materials. The convenience is obvious. One is not surprised that David Lodge sets his comedies in an academic setting, that Nabokov favours characters with a Russian background, or that Alice Munro developed the town of

Jubilee, Ontario. Clark Blaise and John Metcalf both use autobiographical material more than most other writers. The lives of nearly all their central male characters follow their own lives. The parents and the settings constantly reappear. Clark and John do not just delve into their own lives, they quarry them, strip mine them. However, separating the autobiographical and the fictional is largely a futile exercise, and with Clark or John a project suitable only for particularly anal-retentive or masochistic Ph.D. candidates. I may perhaps add that I have always accepted that despite disclaimers Metcalf's "Private Parts" is literally, as the subtitle has it, "A Memoir."

But while one may use one's own life with considerable freedom, discretion is advisable when representing others. Clark and John have both been happily married to admirable and forgiving women for many years, and while both have included aspects of their wives in their work, both have been wisely diplomatic. Were John to publish a dark portrait of Myrna Metcalf, he would soon be pricing prosthetic testicles. Clark could face the greater humiliation of appearing, warts and all, in a novel by Bharati — and with sales in the tens of thousands.

Metcalf and Blaise treat the fictional wife slightly differently. While both concentrate on the narrator, Metcalf more often includes the wife significantly in his stories; Martha in "Polly Ongle" and Sheila in "Travelling Northward" are both sources of minor conflict, and are at most only anecdotally inspired by Myrna. Helen, in "The Nipples of Venus," might well be a closer portrait of Myrna, and is a participant in the later action, but is an entirely sympathetic character. In Clark's stories by contrast, the wife is almost always independent of the action, busy with her own career, busy with the children. This is even largely true in their partnered nonfiction book, *Days and Nights in Calcutta*. Anjali, the wife in "Going to India" whose interest in the cockpit crew perhaps troubles the narrator, comes closest to Metcalf's practice. The wife in "Extractions and Contractions" seems a reasonable but light sketch of Bharati; the wife in "Eyes," "a north-Europe princess from a constitutional monarchy" (46), is clearly at most a displacement, is but the unknowing object of the voyeur rather than a participant in the action, and is not with the husband at the movie or in the butcher shop; in "He Raises Me Up," Erika's most important line is, "'Wake me when he comes back'" (93).

The difference is not, as I may seem to suggest, a matter of cosmetic or domestic discretion. The power in the stories of both John and Clark comes, in part, from their concentration on the perceptions of central male characters. However, while Clark sticks rigorously to the subject, John is more likely than Clark to make asides or take a tangential route through the story. John likes to savour incidents, words, people as Clark usually does not. Examples from "Single Gents Only" are David's train trip, the phrase "'Hold a woman by the waist and a bottle by the neck'" (5), the dotty grandfather. In "The Nipples of Venus," the hero spends several appropriately languid hours contemplating lizards in an outdoor café (289-93). On the page, Paul Denton's extended reflection on his son in "Polly Ongle" (226-27) might appear excessive; anyone who has heard John perform its irritation mounting to rage will understand the point; this speech and the final confrontation with the son in the park (269-84) frame the story. The meandering path of "The Years in Exile" is uncharacteristic but appropriate for a narrator reflecting on a life. I should note that over time Clark has himself become more tangential, as in the stories in *Man and His World* (1992) or in the more recent "Life Could Be a Dream (Sh-boom, Sh-boom)" in *Montreal Stories* (2003).

But he is not tangential in "Eyes." Let us consider now the perfect efficiency of what is there and what is not.

***

The opening paragraph of "Eyes" sketches the family's life through the first winter. We learn at once that the story is set in a largely French-speaking city. Montreal is not named, but because Clark wrote the story just after the city hosted the world's fair Expo 67 (its theme was "Man and His World") he may have assumed North American readers could deduce it. Though the bridges suggest it, the fact that the city is on an island is not mentioned, nor is the city's defining feature, Mount Royal. This is a particularly intriguing contrast to Hugh's *Around the Mountain* which appeared in 1967, a year before Clark wrote "Eyes" and when Clark "was reading all the Canadian literature I could get my hands on, reading Canadian exclusively[...]. Of course I knew Hugh Hood's work — he went all the way back to my Iowa days when I'd read *Flying a Red Kite*" ("Portrait" 66). From the route into the city centre via "the boulevard that begins small and tree-lined in your suburb but broadens into the canyoned aorta" a Montrealer can deduce that the family is likely living in Ville St. Laurent or Côte St. Luc and getting downtown via the Decarie Expressway, speculations irrelevant to anyone else. Is it an apartment, or a rented house? What do we know of the landlord, the janitor, or the neighbours except that two are Texans? (Compare in Metcalf's "Gentle as Flowers Make the Stones" Jim Haine's enraged building superintendent, or his neighbour Mrs. McGregor with her note, "They are all FLQ in this building. Signed: the Lady Next Door. (Scottish)" [120].) What is experienced on the car or bus ride? Not even a brief anecdote. (Compare the memorable bus ride in Hood's "Flying a Red Kite.") If "These French are all around you," why not an illustrative encounter? (Compare, in Metcalf's "Polly Ongle": "'*Tabarouette!*' said the waitress, depositing on their table a bowl of potato chips. 'Me, I'm scared of lightning!'" [240]) We may wonder about "the French paper you've dutifully subscribed to [which] arrives by mail two days late." This intellectual obviously doesn't take one of the lurid tabloids, and the large-circulation broadsheet *La Presse* would be delivered. In fact, it must be the thin, austere *Le Devoir* (The Duty) which he coyly names in "dutifully subscribed." (Dare we suspect him of implying the even more coy "The 'Eyes' of Texas are upon you" in the same sentence? No, we dare not.) For Montrealers, the most stunning omission from an American's first winter here is the brutal, implacable cold. However, it is irrelevant in the context, and we might note that Clark and Bharati came here after several years at the University of Iowa, so they would have experienced winters about as cold as Montreal's.

The second paragraph, beginning "In the spring you move," is equally concise. Quite possibly, Clark does not deal with the eccentricities of moving day in Quebec because he knew Hugh's "Le Grand Déménagement." More likely, he did not even consider it because it would stop the narration dead. The details of the second neighbourhood are just as tightly concentrated, almost epigrammatic: "where dogs outnumber children and the row houses resemble London's" (45) and the later "stewardesses who deposit their garbage in pizza boxes" (47). Clark declines to colour the passage with Hugh's delectation of neighbourhood detail, or with either the interleaving or the tight vignettes which so characterize John's work. When he wants them, Clark will use these processes: "Among the Dead" opens like one of Hugh's Montreal surveys, although Hugh has never, to my knowledge, suggested Montreal is ugly or will break your heart; "Extractions and Contractions" and "He Raises Me Up" both use interleaving, if not with John's insistence, while later in "Eyes" Clark presents the Johnish vignettes of the Greek gangster movie (47-48) and the slim blond girl and the young Greek in the Salonika suit (48).

In the first two paragraphs, Clark deftly and swiftly sketches the first frantic fourteen months in Montreal without using any of the elements we have noted in John's and Hugh's excerpts. He has gripped our attention, then tightens it with the voyeur incident (45-47). But what is the source of the "*contained* power" John wrote of? If the source is hinted at in my remarks about Natasha's dance, its appearance on the page is suggested by an excursion into Jane Austen's writing of *Persuasion*.

***

Textual analysis of variant drafts is a dry study, often yielding little to any but the obsessive-compulsive. Most of Jane Austen's manuscripts have been lost, but we do have her holograph of a draft of the final two chapters of *Persuasion*. Here is the beginning:

> With all this knowledge of M^r E — & this authority to impart it, Anne left Westgate Build^{gs} — her mind deeply busy in revolving what she had heard, feeling, thinking, recalling & forseeing everything; shocked at Mr Elliot — sighing over future Kellynch, and pained for Lady

Russell, whose confidence in him had been entire. —
The Embarrassment which must be felt from this hour
in his presence! — How to behave to him? — how to get
rid of him? — what to do by any of the Party at home? —
where to be blind? where to be active? — It was altogether a confusion of Images & Doubts — a perplexity,
an agitation which she could not see the end of — and
she was in Gay S^t & still so much engrossed, that she
started on being addressed by Adm^l Croft, as if he were
a person unlikely to be met there. ("Appendix" 238)

Here is the finished version:

Anne went home to think over all that she had heard.
In one point, her feelings were relieved by this knowledge of Mr. Elliot. There was no longer any thing of
tenderness due to him. He stood, as opposed to Captain Wentworth, in all his own unwelcome obtrusive-
ness; and the evil of his attentions last night, the
irremediable mischief he might have done, was considered with sensations unqualified, unperplexed. —
Pity for him was all over. But this was the only point of
relief. In every other respect, in looking around her, or
penetrating forward, she saw more to distrust and to
apprehend. She was concerned for the disappointment
and pain Lady Russell would be feeling, for the morti-
fications which must be hanging over her father and
sister, and had all the distress of foreseeing many evils,
without knowing how to avert any one of them. (199-200)

Like Jane Austen's other heroines, Anne Elliot, the most mature and arguably the most intelligent of them, must sift
through misunderstandings and deceptions to see truth
and achieve happiness. Hampered by lack of knowledge,

she cannot easily understand; hampered by propriety, she cannot act. The line through the novel is only lightly the plot, such as it is (the odious Mr. Elliot is never a serious contender for Anne's hand); the compelling interest for the author is clearly the sequence of Anne's thoughts.

In the quoted passages Anne has just learned the truth about Mr. Elliot and is pondering the effect this will have on herself and others. We can only wonder how many other revisions intervened; at a guess, not many. But the draft we have gives an intriguing glimpse into Jane Austen's main concern in composition. She writes throughout in brief phrases and questions broken with dashes, almost in telegraphese, noting the sequence of Anne's responses as *aides-mémoire*, and in the final version reorders, amplifies, clarifies them. This is consistently true throughout both the draft and the final copy. She also makes significant improvements in the ensuing action, dropping the encounter with Admiral Croft which leads to Wentworth's proposal, delaying the proposal, and dramatizing the revelation that Wentworth has never ceased loving Anne. Yet her main concern remains the same — the sequence of Anne's thoughts.

Can we take seriously Clark's claim that he wrote "Eyes" in a single draft and almost without revision? The story is about 2,000 words, quite possible for a single sitting by a writer as fluent and driven as Clark was, although it was perhaps done in several three-hour sessions over several days. (Jane Austen was also fluent, perhaps driven: she finished the 80,000-word *Persuasion* in about a year, and the much longer *Emma* in fourteen months.) Clark told John, "I write a first draft longhand, then I type a working draft from the longhand that is so haphazard I don't even capitalize. Then I go through with pen and type again. I might cut 40% and add about 15%. Then I'll cut a little and add a little less" ("Interview" 120). The facsimile of the Jane Austen draft page shows an even more economical 20% and 5% revision, though obviously without the rough typescript, and the next draft would have needed greater rewriting. The fact that Clark does not use interleaving, which needs considerable revision for balance, suggests a largely satisfactory first draft with the sort of revision he mentions. And Clark has always been fluent: despite obligations of family, despite continual teaching and travel, he has produced two or three times the work of the painstaking and more leisured Metcalf. If we take him at his word — and we have no reason to doubt him — I suspect Clark's draft of the opening of "Eyes" might be as illuminating as Jane Austen's. Could he have laid down the draft first paragraph with anything like the conciseness of the fair copy? Did the draft Hughishly name the city, the rivers around the island, Mount Royal, the particular suburb? Did it Johnishly describe the apartment (as he does the second apartment) or dramatize an encounter with the janitor or a mortifying misunderstanding at the supermarket in the *centre d'achats*? Did he toy with a sentence or two on the tradition of moving day before stroking it out? Did he really limn the second neighbourhood with such epigrammatic brevity? I am inclined to take Clark at his word, and assume that his first draft was even closer to the finished than is Jane Austen's.

But this is idle speculation. Although I know he and Bharati are in Bombay at the moment and I could e-mail the questions to Clark and perhaps get a reply in a few hours, I shall not. He might not remember, might tell me to read the story as it stands, might offer some naughty misdirection; he might even lie. In any case, Barthes has declared the author is dead, so modern critics would dismiss my speculations and Clark's reply as irrelevant.

Henry Austen wrote of his sister:

> Of personal attractions she possessed a considerable share. [...] Their assemblage produced an unrivalled expression of that cheerfulness, sensibility, and benevolence, which were her real characteristics. [...] She delivered herself with fluency and precision. Indeed she was formed for elegant and rational society, excelling in conversation as much as in composition. [...]
>
> If there be an opinion current in the world, that perfect placidity of temper is not reconcileable to the most lively imagination, and the keenest relish for wit, such an opinion will be rejected for ever by those who have had the happiness of knowing the authoress of the following works. Though the frailties, foibles, and follies of others could not escape her immediate detection, yet even on their vices did she never trust herself to comment with unkindness. ("Biographical Notice" 3-4)

With some allowance for time and gender, this could well be a description of Clark. "I've never seen Clark not in control of himself but I'd pay large sums of money not to be there if or when." The issue I have been addressing is John's observation of "this feeling of *contained* power" in Clark's reading, and by extension in the work on the page. It is not, as we have seen, delivered in the ways John and Hugh achieve their undeniable power, but can be seen in the Jane Austen excerpts. Despite their "cheerfulness, sensibility, and benevolence," Jane Austen and Clark Blaise attack their material with such single-mindedness of subject and ruthlessness of execution that, were it widely known (to adapt the closing line of "Eyes"), the eye would blink and their neighbours would turn upon them.

Works Cited

Austen, Henry. "Biographical Notice of the Author." *Persuasion.* By Jane Austen. 1817. Ed. John Davie. Introd. Claude Rawson. Oxford, Eng.: Oxford UP, 1990. 1-7. The World's Classics.

Austen, Jane. "Appendix: The Original Ending of *Persuasion.*" *Persuasion.* By Jane Austen. 1817. Ed. John Davie. Introd. Claude Rawson. Oxford, Eng.: Oxford UP, 1990. 238-51. The World's Classics.

-----. *Emma.* 1815. Ed. James Kinsley. Introd. David Lodge. Oxford, Eng.: Oxford UP, 1990. The World's Classics.

-----. *Persuasion.* 1817. Ed. John Davie. Introd. Claude Rawson. Oxford, Eng.: Oxford UP, 1990. The World's Classics.

Barthes, Roland. "The Death of the Author." *Image — Music — Text.* By Roland Barthes. Selected and trans. Stephen Heath. New York: Hill and Wang, 1977. 142-48.

Blaise, Clark. "Among the Dead." *Montreal Stories.* Introd. Peter Behrens. Erin, ON: The Porcupine's Quill, 2003. 83-89. Vol. 3 of *The Selected Stories of Clark Blaise.* 4 vols. 2000-06.

-----. "Broward Dowdy." *Southern Stories.* Introd. Fenton Johnson. Erin, ON: The Porcupine's Quill, 2000. 41-50. Vol. 1 of *The Selected Stories of Clark Blaise.* 4 vols. 2000-06.

-----. "Extractions and Contractions." *Montreal Stories.* Introd. Peter Behrens. Erin, ON: The Porcupine's Quill, 2003. 61-72. Vol. 3 of *The Selected Stories of Clark Blaise.* 4 vols. 2000-06.

-----. "Eyes." *Montreal Stories.* Introd. Peter Behrens. Erin, ON: The Porcupine's Quill, 2003. 45-50. Vol. 3 of *The Selected Stories of Clark Blaise.* 4 vols. 2000-06.

-----. "Going to India." *Montreal Stories*. Introd. Peter Behrens. Erin, ON: The Porcupine's Quill, 2003. 107-22. Vol. 3 of *The Selected Stories of Clark Blaise*. 4 vols. 2000-06.

-----. "He Raises Me Up." *Montreal Stories*. Introd. Peter Behrens. Erin, ON: The Porcupine's Quill, 2003. 91-96. Vol. 3 of *The Selected Stories of Clark Blaise*. 4 vols. 2000-06.

-----. "Life Could Be a Dream (Sh-boom, Sh-boom)." *Montreal Stories*. Introd. Peter Behrens. Erin, ON: The Porcupine's Quill, 2003. 159-68. Vol. 3 of *The Selected Stories of Clark Blaise*. 4 vols. 2000-06.

-----. *Man and His World*. Erin, ON: The Porcupine's Quill, 1992.

-----. "North." *Montreal Stories*. Introd. Peter Behrens. Erin, ON: The Porcupine's Quill, 2003. 15-33. Vol. 3 of *The Selected Stories of Clark Blaise*. 4 vols. 2000-06.

-----. "Portrait of the Artist as a Young Pup." *The Montreal Story Tellers: Memoirs, Photographs, Critical Essays*. Ed. J.R. (Tim) Struthers. Montreal: Véhicule, 1985. 65-72.

-----. "To Begin, To Begin." *How Stories Mean*. Ed. John Metcalf and J.R. (Tim) Struthers. Erin, ON: The Porcupine's Quill, 1993. 158-62. Critical Directions 3. [See also "The Cast and the Mould" and "On Ending Stories," *How Stories Mean* 163-65 and 166-69.]

Blaise, Clark, and Bharati Mukherjee. *Days and Nights in Calcutta*. Garden City, NY: Doubleday, 1977.

Conrad, Joseph. "Heart of Darkness." *Heart of Darkness and Other Tales*. Ed. and introd. Cedric Watts. Rev. ed. Oxford, Eng.: Oxford UP, 2002. 101-87. Oxford World's Classics.

Hood, Hugh. *Around the Mountain: Scenes from Montréal Life*. 1967. Introd. Hugh Hood. Erin, ON: The Porcupine's Quill, 1994. Vol. 4 of *The Collected Stories*. 5 vols. 1987-2003.

-----. "Author's Introduction." *Around the Mountain: Scenes from Montréal Life*. 1967. Erin, ON: The Porcupine's Quill, 1994. 9-29. Vol. 4 of *The Collected Stories*. 5 vols. 1987-2003.

-----. "Flying a Red Kite." *Flying a Red Kite.* 1962. Introd. Hugh Hood. Erin, ON: The Porcupine's Quill, 1987. 185-96. Vol. 1 of *The Collected Stories.* 5 vols. 1987-2003.

-----. "The Fruit Man, the Meat Man and the Manager." *The Fruit Man, the Meat Man & the Manager.* Ottawa: Oberon, 1971. 188-97.

-----. "Le Grand Déménagement." *Around the Mountain: Scenes from Montréal Life.* 1967. Introd. Hugh Hood. Erin, ON: The Porcupine's Quill, 1994. 81-91. Vol. 4 of *The Collected Stories.* 5 vols. 1987-2003.

Metcalf, John. "Gentle as Flowers Make the Stones." *Standing Stones: The Best Stories of John Metcalf.* Introd. Clark Blaise. Toronto: Thomas Allen, 2004. 113-35.

-----. "Interview: Clark Blaise." *How Stories Mean.* Ed. John Metcalf and J.R. (Tim) Struthers. Erin, ON: The Porcupine's Quill, 1993. 120-27. Critical Directions 3. Rpt. as "Texture and Voice: An Interview with Clark Blaise" in *Clark Blaise: The Interviews.* Ed. J.R. (Tim) Struthers. Toronto: Guernica Editions, 2016. Essential Writers.

-----. "The Nipples of Venus." *Standing Stones: The Best Stories of John Metcalf.* Introd. Clark Blaise. Toronto: Thomas Allen, 2004. 285-308.

-----. "Polly Ongle." *Standing Stones: The Best Stories of John Metcalf.* Introd. Clark Blaise. Toronto: Thomas Allen, 2004. 219-84.

-----. "Private Parts: A Memoir." *Standing Stones: The Best Stories of John Metcalf.* Introd. Clark Blaise. Toronto: Thomas Allen, 2004. 19-86.

-----. "Single Gents Only." *Standing Stones: The Best Stories of John Metcalf.* Introd. Clark Blaise. Toronto: Thomas Allen, 2004. 1-18.

-----. "Telling Tales." *The Montreal Story Tellers: Memoirs, Photographs, Critical Essays.* Ed. J.R. (Tim) Struthers. Montreal: Véhicule, 1985. 23-42.

-----. "Travelling Northward." *Adult Entertainment.* Toronto: Macmillan of Canada, 1986. 140-201.

-----. "The Years in Exile." *Standing Stones: The Best Stories of John Metcalf.* Introd. Clark Blaise. Toronto: Thomas Allen, 2004. 137-55.

Tolstoy, L.N. *War and Peace.* Trans. and introd. Rosemary Edmonds. 1957. Rev. ed. 2 vols. Harmondsworth, Eng.: Penguin, 1978. Bk. 2, Pt. 4, Ch. 7, 599-607. The Penguin Classics.

Turgenev, Ivan. *A Sportsman's Sketches.* 1896. Trans. Constance Garnett. Library Ed. London: William Heinemann, 1920. Vols. 8-9 of *The Novels of Ivan Turgenev.* 17 vols. 1920-22.

Villon, François. "Ballade des dames du temps jadis." *Le testament et poésies diverses.* Ed. Barbara Nelson Sargent. New York: Appleton-Century-Crofts, 1967. 31-33.

The Mini-Cycle in Clark Blaise's *Resident Alien*

Allan Weiss

In an article published in the Fall 2009 issue of the journal *Short Story*, I described a form I called the "mini-cycle": a miniature story cycle composed of only a few stories —usually three— linked by character, setting, and/or theme. In the mini-cycle, the stories constitute a unified set and may have little or no connection to the other stories published in the same story collection or cycle. An early example in Canadian literature of the three-story mini-cycle, or perhaps story trilogy, is "The Extraordinary Entanglement of Mr. Pupkin," "The Fore-Ordained Attachment of Zena Pepperleigh and Peter Pupkin," and "The Mariposa Bank Mystery" in Stephen Leacock's *Sunshine Sketches of a Little Town* (1912). The book as a whole is a story cycle unified by setting, while these three stories form a smaller unit within the cycle's overall framework recounting the love story between Peter Pupkin and Zena Pepperleigh. A more recent Canadian example of the three-story mini-cycle is "Chance," "Soon," and "Silence" in Alice Munro's *Runaway* (2004). In the same year, Denise Roig published *Any Day Now* (2004), a story collection made up entirely of six trilogies, which Roig calls "trios."[1]

Scholars of the story cycle (e.g., Ingram, Struthers, Lynch, Nagel) —also known as the "short story sequence"

(Luscher, Kennedy), the "short story composite" (Lundén), and the "composite novel" (Dunn and Morris), among other terms — see it as a liminal form between the story collection and the novel. The book-length story cycle simultaneously offers the sort of individual moments of experience and perception one expects from a collection of unrelated stories and the unifying narrative arc one associates with the novel. The story cycle refuses the over-all development of the novel, depicting the life or lives of its protagonist(s) as fundamentally fragmentary and dis-jointed, comprised of discrete illuminations and dra-matic incidents rather than a single, cohesive evolution.

If the story cycle lies somewhere between the story collection and the novel, then the mini-cycle can be seen as a liminal form between a set of unrelated stories in a collection and a novella.[2] Like the novella, the mini-cycle delves in some detail into the experiences of a single pro-tagonist or, more rarely, examines a particular theme or setting. On the other hand, the mini-cycle permits a more kaleidoscopic vision, portraying separate events and epiphanies as the main character moves toward maturation or fuller understanding.

From *A North American Education* (1973) and *Tribal Justice* (1974) onward, Clark Blaise has frequently experi-mented with the form of his story collections, seeking ways to unify related or unconnected narratives beyond the confines of any given short story. One particularly interesting example of his use of the mini-cycle form ap-pears in the middle fiction section of *Resident Alien* (1986); "The Porter/Carrier Stories" consists of a trilogy plus a novella, thus combining the liminal form with the more conventional novella of approximately fifty pages. Presumably, Blaise could have written Philip Porter's / Philippe Carrier's story as a single, longer work of fiction, yet chose to divide his narrative into three linked short stories and one text that is approximately as long as the other three combined. Analyzing Blaise's trilogy and its relation to the novella reveals what he achieves by employing this complex structure.

The four texts portray Philip Porter's / Philippe Carrier's struggles as he seeks his identity and geographical and social place. The Montreal-born (81) child of Canadians now living in the United States, and the son of a man who cannot settle in any one city or town for very long, Phil finds himself living on and crossing borders throughout his life. Two major events shape his destiny more than any other: a childhood incident that triggers the onset of epilepsy, and his father Reg's assault of his manager that requires the family to flee from Pittsburgh to Montreal, Quebec, Reg/Réjean's home town. Phil endures constant moves and even a radical change of name in the process of crossing geographical, temporal, emotional, and other borders; indeed, as Graham Huggan has argued, he is characterized more by his lack of secure, certain home and identity than by any specific national, cultural, or even linguistic selfhood (62).

The stories in the trilogy are largely chronological, beginning with Phil's earliest experiences in the American South and proceeding through his movement northward to Canada. The titles explicitly refer to this transition and provide an interesting comment on it: "South," "Identity," and "North." It is worth noting that the story "Identity" and Phil's identity lie between geographical locations; as Robert Lecker writes, like Phil himself the story is a border entity, and so both text and character are equally liminal (191-92). The novella that follows is entitled "Translation": here, the linguistic, cultural, temporal, and other dualities present in the trilogy come together, as Phil meets his Québécois translator and finds himself in constant motion between English and French, past and present, South and North, and so on (see Lecker 199-200).

The mini-cycle, then, reflects an overarching shift in geography, whose primary aim is to portray Phil's mutable status. The stories are unified less by plot than by the various polarities that constitute his identity and place in the world. In his study of the book, Robert Lecker goes into some detail about two of the primary dualities that define — if such a word can be used of the protagonist — Phil's life and self: past and present, and self and other, especially author and character. Lecker focusses on Blaise's growing self-reflexivity as he blurs the boundary between himself as author and the persona he adopts in his fiction (see especially the discussion on 162-65). As Lecker demonstrates, Blaise melds autobiography and fiction, life and art, real and assumed self to suggest that the artist's truest identity is a dynamic one that encompasses both poles of such seeming binaries. In the process, Phil must either reconcile or come to terms with the irreconcilability of his mythologized early childhood of security and certainty in an idealized family and the 'divorce' (in many senses of the term) that permeates his later childhood and upbringing (see Lecker 176).

Lecker's detailed and sensitive analysis effectively illuminates the four texts' treatment of Phil's progress from boy to man and from character (in his own story) to author. Identity is the main theme of the story trilogy and novella, and Blaise's depiction of Phil's identity emphasizes its ever-changing nature. A study of the mini-cycle's form reveals how that shifting selfhood is represented by a number of motifs that recur throughout, with his name changes as only the most obvious example. The form as well as the thematic content reflects the fluid nature of self and the need to adopt various perspectives in order to view any identity — but especially an artist's — in its truest form. Thus, each story possesses its own internal structure while at the same time foreshadowing later stories and/or alluding to previous ones.

The references to North American, and specifically American, geography are among the clearest ways Blaise connects the short stories in the trilogy. "South" opens with a direct reference to its setting: "It was the South" (47). In this story, Phil is six or seven years old, and the family is living in three rooms in their landlady's house, but must move when Phil's father is seriously injured in a car accident. We learn early on, however, that Reg — as he is known in the United States — is not an American but a Canadian, and Phil's mother Hennie is also a Canadian whose relatives back home provide financial assistance (48). Canada is thus portrayed as a source of help and even salvation at the beginning of the trilogy. Bereft of resources, the family is obliged to move, so Reg is both immobilized and forced to become mobile by his accident. As a salesman, however, Reg had always been peripatetic, and Phil recounts the many geographical shifts he had already been required to undergo even by this early age:

> I had started kindergarten outside of Atlanta and had put in a chunk of first grade in Gadsden, Alabama, and we had come to Leesburg, Florida, at the end of the first grade, before my father's accident, so that I was remembered by a few kids when second grade started. I usually didn't have that advantage. Most of the moves

in our life were timed for summer, so that each September I began a new school. In Leesburg, Florida, in 1946, I had a small history. (50)

In their new home, the Porter family lives as a white family in the eastern and predominantly black part of town, and in the American South much of one's social position depends on where one lives. As Phil says,

It was a small town in those days, and a child revealed everything about himself from the direction he nosed his bicycle in from the stands outside of school. Each cardinal compass point indicated who and what you were, what your father did and what your prospects in life were going to be. I was an exception because our little laundry shed of a house was the last white-occupied structure on that side of town. (51)

His mother refuses to respect these racial barriers and crosses the social as well as geographical border separating black and white "by walking into Niggertown and running her hands over the heads of little girls and then standing in the yards calling up to women of her age, 'I'm your new neighbour. We live just on the other side of the streetlight there. I hope you'll come over for tea some afternoon'" (52). His best friend, Grady Stanridge, meanwhile, is securely ensconced in the western white part of town, and the second half of the story details a visit Phil pays to his friend's house. With its title, its earlier references to Canadian cities, and these contrasts between east and west, "South" thus presents, implicitly or explicitly, Phil's four cardinal compass points, and as we will see provides a foundation for the social and cultural implications of geography the entire trilogy depicts.

In "Identity," Phil is twelve years old, and the story recounts his life in Cincinnati and then Pittsburgh. Haunting the tale is the variety of memories Phil has of the onset of his epilepsy; the past, in the form of his early days in other parts of the United States, keeps intruding as he struggles with the mystery of his condition's origins. He is certain that it began when he had a tricycle accident, yet we are by no means sure where or how it might have happened, and in fact his mother's version of what led to the condition calls into question whether the accident took place at all (62). Once again, geography is a significant theme, especially the degree to which Phil has no true home: "Let more bones break, more moves be made. Those early memories are from Cincinnati — a freak appearance in our lives, a town that did not claim us — from deep in America, a country, as it turned out, that did not claim me either" (63).

In Pittsburgh, meanwhile, Phil is portrayed on the roof of his apartment building trying to draw in distant television stations through a set of rabbit-ears. He sees his greatest achievement as succeeding in capturing signals from "Channel Nine in Steubenville, Ohio, or Seven in Wheeling, West Virginia ... there was rumoured to be a Channel Ten in Altoona and a Channel Three downriver in Huntington, West V[i]rginia" (64). It appears, then, that what makes Pittsburgh special to Phil is not so much its own existence as its ability to act as a doorway to the rest of the continent. If Phil has a geographical identity, Lecker argues, it is North American rather than any specific or local one, and the signals symbolize his efforts at communicating beyond the self and the local (182).

At the end of "Identity," Phil comes home to find his mother frantically packing; that they are moving yet again does not surprise him:

> Inside were half-packed boxes, all over the place, where
> selections of our things had been thrown in…. We'd
> moved many times before, and usually under bad con-
> ditions — to towns we didn't know and where we had no
> address. Those moves were chance things: pack up the
> car, flee a city and travel to a place where a job might
> be waiting. Then find an apartment after a few days in
> a squalid hotel, unpack, put the boy in school. (71)

Usually, she prepares for their moves very carefully, but
clearly something has gone wrong: "She was a careful
packer, and this was not careful packing" (71). As it turns
out, this is no ordinary move: Reg has assaulted his manager, as we learn in the final story of the trilogy, and
must move not merely out of town but out of country.
The family heads north, and as they reach the border
Hennie says to Phil, "'In a minute we'll be going into
Canada. Canada is where your father and I come from….
We're going to Montreal. We have relatives in Montreal'"
(74). Now, Canada is more than a site of aid; it has become a refuge.

As a result, Phil is no longer an American, if he ever
was one. Hennie continues, "'Our name will change
when we go over the border. Forget all you ever kn[e]w
about Porter. Our real name is Carry-A. Like this — see?'
She showed me a plastic-coated green-framed card with
an old picture of my father on it. I couldn't pronounce
the name, but the letters bit into my brain. Réjean Carrier" (74-75). Phil asks, "'What's my name?'" and his father
simply tells him to "'shut up'"; his mother, however, says,
"'You can be anything you want to be'" (75). Phil's lack of
certain identity now becomes a liberating as well as dis-
orienting aspect of his life. Blaise could have explained
in "Identity" Reg's need to flee from justice, but chose

instead to delay revealing the reason for the move in order to provoke in the reader the sense of dislocation that Phil feels. As Blaise establishes throughout the first two stories, Phil seldom knows the circumstances behind the family's frequent moves and so has become somewhat used to the constant and unexpected uprooting he endures, and even inured to not knowing why they move.

In "North," the final story of the trilogy, Phil is living in Montreal; while he does not move in this story, geography continues to play an important role in his life. The city is divided into the English west and the French east, much as Leesburg was divided into a white west and a black east. Furthermore, his school has two separate entrances, one for the boys and one for the girls. As Lecker observes, "The initial distinction between boys and girls is gradually broadened to include a host of related polarities: male and female, father and mother, Catholic and Protestant, French and English, experience and innocence, age and youth. Carrier's movement 'north' and over the border traces his attempt to bridge the gaps between all these polarities" (191). Phil is required by history and his French Catholic school to obey these geographical strictures, but like his mother prefers to ignore them whenever possible. His new friend Mick tries to place him geographically; Mick asks, "'Where you from —the States? Vermont?'" and after replying, Phil notices that "Pittsburgh rang no bells for Mick Fortin. He only knew the cities that sent us tourists—Burlington, Plattsburgh, and half of Harlem, plus the cozy loop of the old NHL" (80). For Phil, Pittsburgh is now a memory, one he compares to the television signals he used to seek: "In memory, Pittsburgh came bursting through like a freak radio signal" (85).

Phil's sexual awakening is a major theme in the story,

and he gleefully finds himself tutored by a girl named
Thérèse Aulérie who represents the equally distant and
mysterious realms of the French-Canadian side of Montreal and femininity. While he recognizes the truth of his
mother's view that the francophone neighbourhoods are
dreary, what counts for him is how appealingly alien
Thérèse's world is:

> I came to think of my five hours a week with Thérèse
> as my parole from solitary. I came to understand my
> mother's use of the word "drab" to describe the inter-
> iors and the streets, the minds and souls and conversa-
> tions of east-end Montreal. One big icy puddle of frozen
> gutter water, devoid of joy, colour, laughter, pleasure,
> intellect or art. School and home and church and the
> narrow east-end streets that connect them are the
> same colour even now in my memory, linked in a lan-
> guage that I didn't understand except through its
> rhythms. (91)

Note how Blaise combines in this paragraph a depiction
of what Thérèse means to Phil, a description of her environment, and a reference to her language; for Phil, the
personal, the geographical, and the linguistic are one.

Phil and his family live in the district of Hochelaga,
but Hennie yearns to have her son become part of the
English community, represented by McGill University:
"'Some day you'll go here,' she said. 'I don't care what it
takes or if you graduate from French school or American
schools — they'll have to let you in'" (93). Milton Street,
Pine Avenue, and Prince Arthur become the boundaries
and markers of this more privileged world as Hennie
takes Phil to visit an old professor friend. Phil rebels and
wants nothing more than to return to his French school,

resisting his mother's efforts to cross into the English area of the city, and thereby rise in class, through him.

The family is living with Reg's brother Théophile, and Dollard, Théophile's son, is Phil's guide to the French-speaking and Catholic world to which Reg—now Réjean once more—has brought his family. Ironically, Dollard later gets a job at Steinberg's, a supermarket owned by English-speaking Jews, while we learn that "Two of Théophile's sons-in-law got big jobs in the States" (103), reversing the geographical migration of Réjean and the rest of the Carrier family. Phil once again tries to connect to distant cities and what is now a foreign country through a set of rabbit-ears:

> We got a television set, the first anyone had seen, even though Canadian television was barely launched, rudimentary. That didn't stop me from buying the wires and rigging some rabbit-ears and tying them to our chimney in an attempt to coax something, anything, from the air. Burlington, Plattsburgh—those towns that provided night-time English radio in my room —where were you when it really counted? Even KDKA in Pittsburgh came in, most nights. (103)

Now, Phil is looking backward, to a remembered home, seeking some certainty in an existence marked by perpetual change, and enacts his desire by trying to reverse both time and space. "North" presents the many pressures Phil faces to conform to other people's definitions of him, pressures coming from his immediate and extended families, from his present school and one that, through his mother, beckons to him. He reacts by refusing to conform, and seeking his identity in a much broader and even international context.

Of course, the physical migrations Phil unwillingly experiences symbolize and trigger other changes as well.[3] For example, with each move he must learn a new language, and so each story portrays Phil's linguistic as well as geographic transitions. Even in the United States, with its single national language, Phil must negotiate the many shifts in language he encounters in moving from state to state and from South to North. In "South," Phil says that he likes the newspapers in foreign languages and typefaces that his mother uses as packing material: "I liked foreign-looking things. Some of the newspapers were in Gothic face. Some of them were in French" (49). In the next paragraph, Phil says that the family hires "'a coloured man'" (49) to move them into their new house in "Niggertown" (52, 54): Phil is being taught the racist language of 'his' people, the town's whites. He is thoroughly embarrassed by the way his mother showers him with endearments no one else in the town would use: "She had the Canadian custom of smothering me with 'dears' and 'darlings' and even 'preciouses' in every conversation, and she even extended the custom to my little friends, as she called them. The one acceptable term of endearment—honey—she never used" (53).

In "Identity," the French language makes its first appearance in the trilogy but only in association with sex. Phil's friend is Peter Humphries:

His mother was divorced—*divorcée* was one of those words, probably the only one, that a 1952 Pittsburgh kid pronounced in a self-consciously French way, to imbue it with its full freight of accompanying *negligées* and *lingerie* and *brassières* and of other things that came off in the night and suggested a rich inner life.... (65)

Thus, Phil sees her as representing pure sensuality and associates her with a certain sort of language; his mother and his friend use different words for her: "My mother called her 'The Slut.' — Peter called her 'her' and 'she'" (68).

The most radical linguistic change Phil undergoes is of course the switch from English to French. Suddenly, he metamorphoses from an English-speaking American to a francophone Québécois, and as "Identity" ends and "North" begins we see him in full transition from one cultural identity to another. It is noteworthy that the motif of radio and television signals returns on the final page of "Identity" to mark this shift, as the family crosses into Canada: "My father found a radio station playing strange music in a foreign language" (75). The opening of "North" features the anglicization of the French word for 'Boys'; he meets his newest friend, another English-speaker in a French school, when Mick sees him baffled by the signs on the school: "'Take the garkons,' he had advised, under his breath. *Garkons* was an early word in my private vocabulary. In the beginning, I had to trust strangers' pronunciations, or worse, my own" (79). Thérèse, like Phil, has a name that crosses the linguistic border; just as Porter is an anglicized version of Carrier, Aulérie is a francized version of her "vrai *nom*," O'Leary (89). Thus, as Lecker notes, names continue to represent linguistic divisions and ironic contradictions: Mick Fortin, whose surname is French, is an anglophone, while Thérèse, whose real surname is English, is a francophone (192).

Phil begins to learn French, but his mother has a much more difficult time: "In a week I knew some nouns and adjectives; no verbs, no sentences. French neutralized my mother's education; she was like a silent actress"

(81). For her, the language represents all that is strange and even potentially dangerous:

> She was one of those western Canadians of profound good will and solid background, educated and sophisticated and acutely alert to conditions in every part of the world, who could not utter a syllable of French without a painful contortion of head, neck, eyes and lips. She was convinced that the French language was a deliberate debauchery of logic, and that people who persisted in speaking it did so to cloak the particulars of a nefarious design, behind which could be detected the gnarled, bejewelled claws of the Papacy. (82)

Hennie's continuing efforts to put Phil in an English school constitute a threat to his own efforts to assimilate: "English would obviously be easier, but not necessarily preferable. I wanted to belong, and no one I knew in Montreal spoke English, except my mother" (82). Théophile, a member of the St-Jean-Baptiste Society, will not hear of Phil's attending any but a French school, and that settles the question. Yet even though it is clearly impossible, Phil remembers that he studied and spoke to his classmates in English — clear signs of the unreliability of memory, a theme that takes on ever-increasing importance as the mini-cycle continues.

The linguistic and cultural divide between Phil and his French-Canadian compatriots shrinks as he learns from and teaches Thérèse; while she shares Catholic doctrine with him, he shares knowledge about the habits of American teenagers with her (90). In a sense, Phil becomes the ultimate translator, acting as a communication link (much like the television and radio signals) between English and French, the United States and Canada, boys and girls, and many other dualities. Throughout the story, Phil navigates carefully through a liminal space bordered by but not fully a part of these worlds. "North" ends with the French-named Phil and the English-named Thérèse sharing a thoroughly bilingual Sunday meal at Murray's Restaurant:

> I'd ordered and paid in English, and she'd been terribly impressed. She'd promised me she'd do it, but had gotten too embarrassed at the last moment. We were walking behind a group of old ladies in white gloves and wide-brimmed hats, the tea-drinking ladies of Westmount, and Thérèse had been frightened of them, afraid of what they might be saying about her. Just gossip, I said, mindless things, and I translated some of it, to reassure her. She shook her head and acted ashamed. *"Sh'peux pas[!]"* she declared, pounding the side of her head with her fists, *"Idiote!"*, then giggled. *"Mais tu peux, non[?]* You hunnerstan' every word, [*non?*] Smart guy!" She took my hand in both of hers and swung my arm like the clapper of the biggest bell in th[e] world. (105)

Phil's bilingualism represents his ability to cross borders, although that ability is due mainly to the fact that he has no definite home, whether national or linguistic.

The trilogy also portrays the degree to which geographical and linguistic changes reflect and produce shifts, especially deterioration, in Phil's and his family's social status. They are never rich, always living a precarious existence because of Reg's job, but they are at least reasonably independent at the start of the trilogy. What occurs is a growing gap between Hennie's social expectations and pretensions and the reality of the family's decline in fortunes.

"South" begins with an account of Reg's accident. As Phil says, "Until the accident we had been surviving in town" (47). When Reg is sent home, he is confined to one of the BarcaLoungers he had been selling; in a symbolic sense, then, he is trapped by the insecure job he holds. As a consequence of his immobility, and the exhaustion of financial help from others, the family has to sell off Hennie's most valuable possessions and move. Phil's description of her luxury items reveals both her alienation from her current social position and Phil's alienation from her:

> My mother's family was well-to-do, and my mother was a woman of taste. She'd been a decorator, and she'd accumulated things in Europe and in England and then in Montreal, where she'd met my father. Those things—Meissen things, Dresden things, Prague things, sketches she'd done in German and British museums, water-colour renderings she'd done for clients in Montreal, heavy silverware in a rich, burgundy velvet-lined case, candlesticks, cut-glass bowls, little framed paintings and etchings and cameos done on p[or]celain or ivory—they meant nothing at all to me. She unwrapped them and cried; she tried to tell me the stories of their acquisition, the smuggling out. They meant nothing at all, to my shame. A BarcaLounger now—that was a valuable thing. (48-49)

Phil identifies more with his father's taste and lifestyle. The family moves to the black neighbourhood, and it seems they have had to surrender even a 'proper' address:

> The new place was actually larger than the three rooms.
> It might have been called a house — it was detached but
> set back from the street, as a garage or a laundry house
> might have been. It gave us an address with an "A" at
> the end — something new in all our travels, "a sign" my
> mother said. (49)

However, to Hennie's distress, it even lacks indoor plumbing (50).

Hennie simply cannot fit in; she lacks friends, and refuses to adapt to Southern and poor — that is, working-class — ways (see especially 51, 53). On the other hand, she and Phil like liver: "We got it for ten cents a pound, since it wasn't considered fit for white consumption. It was assumed, whenever I was sent out to buy it, that we were getting it for our cleaning lady. I tried to keep my mother from going for it, since I knew she wouldn't go along with my lie" (53). The South has its own form of class consciousness, much of it based on race, and Phil discovers that fact when he visits his friend's house. Grady Stanridge lives in a house that contrasts sharply with Phil's own: "His house was Florida Moorish, with a tile roof, Mexican grillwork and rows of tall, narrow windows, curved on top" (53). The Stanridges have an extensive garden and Mrs. Stanridge has her own set of 'valuable' possessions to which she clings as forcefully as Hennie did to her artworks, ceramics, and so on.

When a purportedly antique purple flowerpot appears to go missing (the garish colour perhaps signalling its true worth), Mrs. Stanridge blames her son and then her new cleaning lady. Phil sees the flowerpot on a shelf and points it out to her. Mrs. Stanridge says, "'I promise I ain't never hiring a white woman to do coloured work again!'" (56). The identity of the cleaning lady is not made explicit here, but Phil informs us in the next paragraph that Hennie has been reduced to cleaning "other people's houses while I attended school and my father reclined on his BarcaLounger" (56). One cannot help concluding that Hennie is Mrs. Stanridge's new cleaning lady, particularly when Mrs. Stanridge complains, "'And her acting so superior. Like she was too good to clean a white lady's house'" (55). If she is indeed referring to Hennie, the latter has clearly suffered a very humiliating social descent, as Lecker notes (178).

"South" is ostensibly about Phil's relationship with his father, whose employment and medical problems determine the family's economic and social fate. Yet the story deals more profoundly with Phil's inability "to see his mother" (57) in any meaningful way. Toward the end of the story, he tells us that as a boy he "deliberately mythologized" (56) his father, and never understood his mother's higher-class background or the price she paid, the sacrifices she made, in and for her marriage. Eventually she does leave her husband, returning to Winnipeg to become a schoolteacher (56), and Phil finally acknowledges how much he has neglected her in his hero-worship of his undeserving but more colourful father:

> how easy it is for a boy and for a young man and even for a man now embarked on middle age to see his mother as nothing exceptional in the universe, nothing at all, an embarrassment in fact, against the extravagance of his father.
>
> Mother, why couldn't we love you enough? (56-57)

The family's decline in social position is made painfully evident in "Identity," although here Blaise's point is to demonstrate the unreliability of memory (see Lecker 179-80). In trying to recall the trigger of his epilepsy, for example, Phil first remembers his father sitting in a Queen Anne chair, then immediately dismisses the idea as impossible (61). By the time they reach Pittsburgh, the Porters can no longer afford a house; they are living in an apartment building, and both parents have to work to make ends meet (63). When they are forced by Reg's assault to flee the United States, they have to leave their furniture and take only what they can carry in the car. They cannot even stay in a hotel, but hide out in a motel parking lot looking for a licence plate to steal. In the course of her marriage, Hennie has gone from living in a house to renting an apartment to sleeping in a car (74).

Like "South," "Identity" presents us with Phil's ignorance of his parents' true selves, and of all they had subjected each other to and endured. The opening paragraph links the story to the earlier one: "Porter, Reg and Hennie. My parents for several years. Mysteries to me, to each other. Gone now, even in name" (61). At the end, the identities of all three family members become uncertain, as Phil learns that Porter is not their true surname. Suddenly, they must all become Carriers. The entire family's social place, in terms of class, ethnicity, heritage, and so on, undergoes a thorough revolution. As represented by the various legal documents that lie scattered around their old home in Pittsburgh (73), the only legacy his parents pass down to Phil is the lack of a clear set of personal or social boundaries.

In "North," Hennie's efforts to re-establish her former social position involve trying to direct Phil's education so that he will become what she used to be. She desperately wants him to attend McGill and thereby avoid becoming like her husband's family. Now, Phil and his

parents must live with Théophile — they do not even have
a home of their own — and as we have seen there arises
immediate conflict between Théophile and Hennie over
where Phil will go to school. Hennie's view is that "English was the only language for an intelligent boy who
didn't want to become a priest" (82). When his mother
brings him to Eaton's, Phil learns later that his mother
had been head of the store's furniture department, and
Reg/Réjean had been one of her salesmen. She then expresses her bitterness at what she has become: "'I de-
serve it all, don't I? Sleeping on a floor in Hochelaga. No
wonder they don't want to remember me — I must look
a sight'" (92).

As a way of asserting her English and higher-class
identity, Hennie takes Phil for tea and scones at the cafeteria upstairs (92-93), and to visit her professor friend,
Ella. Hennie, Ella, and Dolly, Ella's presumed lover, have
concocted a plan for Phil, a way for him to attend an
English school; as Ella tells him,

> "You can live with us, and we will send you. I know pro-
> fessors, I know musicians, writers, artists. We go out
> every night, or we have people here who are the leaders
> not just of this city, not just this country — "
>
> " — the *world*, darling. Ella is known all over the world."
>
> "That's not the point. The point is, we want to share
> this — what should I call it? Power? Connection? Good
> fortune?" (99-100)

Phil escapes, insisting that he be allowed to return to the
French school where he has at least established some
sense of belonging and identity. Referring to his father,
but by extension himself as well, Phil says at one point,
"The future would always be insecure" (104). He chooses

that insecurity over both status and the prospect of being who his mother wants him to be (someone much like herself, or more exactly her former self). He would rather remain the social border-crosser he has become, and find his own way through life.

One other extremely important transition Phil undergoes in each story and in the trilogy as a whole is his sexual awakening. In "South" he is somewhat too young for such feelings, and yet the way he describes his father indicates that much of Reg's appeal for him lies in the father's virility. Reg is

> the manly force in my life, the dark, romantic, French, medieval, libidinous force in my life, the foreign element in my life, believing somehow that his eighteen siblings, his six wives, his boxing career, his violence and his drinking and his police record, his infidelities, in some way ennoble *me*, tell me I'm not just the timid academic son of my mother's rectitude. (56)

It is in "Identity" that Phil experiences lust for the first time, to some extent for his own mother in an admitted case of "Oedipal longings" (70) but mostly for Peter's. Phil associates Mrs. Humphries with everything sensual and feminine, and the story's humour largely derives from his fumbling for knowledge:

> Being with Peter, the only friend I had, was like standing at the tip of an enormous funnel; all the sexual knowledge available to pubescent, provincial Americans in 1952 was swirling past me, and not a precious drop was wasted, not with Peter and his mother nearby. I wasn't in their apartment that often ... but every time I entered it I was struck by the fumes of something lurid. (66)

When Peter dresses up in his mother's clothes, thereby violating Phil's growing sense of the differences between male and female, the friends avoid each other for some time. The masquerade Peter engages in parallels and prefigures the change in identity the Porter family will enact when becoming Carriers at the end of the story.

In the meantime, Phil finds his mother at her sexiest when she is scrambling to pack what she can as they're preparing to leave the United States. As in other areas of his life, Phil sees sexiness not as fitting a clear-cut set of defined features but as transcending any commonly accepted image:

> Sexiness, if I am now to lift it from any immediate context or application to any particular woman, is (for me) an appearance that borders on slovenliness. Sex will never embrace me in tennis shorts, in a bikini, or in any fetishistic combination of high heels and low neckline. Sex is the look that says, "Help me out of these clothes," or shows that things she's wearing are a constriction, not an attraction. (72)

Later, as Phil becomes a teenager in "North" and the adult portrayed in the novella "Translation," he continues to define his sexuality in terms of his relationship with his mother.

In "North," Phil develops an infatuation for Thérèse, his tutor; she does not dress or wear make-up in the manner of the American teenage girls he knew, but Phil finds her attractive nevertheless (87). She is his "parole from solitary" (91) and salvation from the drabness of the French-Canadian world. In the final scene of the story, as noted above, Phil and Thérèse share a moment of mutual admiration and, perhaps, recognition after he has ordered their lunch in English. What she does not know is that he earned the money for their outings by distributing flyers for a strip club, a business to which his friend Mick had introduced him. His sexuality is now connected to a very cynical pursuit; the raw lust he experienced at twelve has transformed into a more practical outlook at sixteen.

Thus, each of the three short stories is structured with its own narrative arc, while the trilogy as a whole features a more extended arc that brings Phil from childhood innocence and a stronger sense of self to teenage experience and a refusal to be defined. Phil's sexual maturation understandably progresses from story to story as he grows up, and his romantic view of his parents is replaced by passions and then pragmatism. Meanwhile, motifs of national, cultural, linguistic, and other dualities inform the individual stories and the trilogy as a whole. Themes and images recur, yet each story treats them somewhat differently, communicating through its distinct nature the fragmentary, contradictory, fluid, and ultimately boundless identity Phil develops. Indeed, if he has any identity at all it is a kind of transnational, North American one, and the trilogy could be described as portraying Phil's 'North American Education', to allude to the title of Blaise's first story collection.

It would be useful now to relate the trilogy to the novella that carries Phil's narrative to its conclusion. "Translation" brings together the motifs in the three short stories, offering a kind of closure as Phil finally determines what childhood event brought on his epilepsy: an incident culminating in a scene involving his parents and a hot iron. Reg is now in a nursing home, and it is the scar on his body left by the iron that triggers Phil's memory. Phil is finally able to express his love for his father, and one can only hope that it is not too late for his father to get the message.

By the time "Translation" begins, Phil is in his forties, lives in the United States, and has reassumed his childhood name of Porter. He is a successful author of fiction and has now written an autobiography, *Head Waters*, which has been published in translation by a small Montreal press as *Les Sources de mémoire*. By moving back to the United States, Phil therefore has returned to his own headwaters in a sense. The plot of the novella, however, concerns Phil's meeting and relationship with his French-language translator, Madeleine Choquette, in Montreal. In this respect Phil is reenacting his childhood move with his family to Montreal, the place of his birth (81), and taking account of his headwaters there.

The novella revisits the themes and motifs of border-crossing we have analyzed in the trilogy, that is, the crossing of geographical, linguistic, social, and sexual borders. As Phil thinks back on his life, particularly since the period covered by "North," he pursues an affair with the older Madeleine — recalling his early Oedipal yearnings — and searches for his father. There is no room here to examine the novella in detail, but even a cursory reading reveals the extent of intertextuality between the novella and the earlier stories. Phil travels north once more, and his ongoing experience of and fascination with geography — places and their boundaries — are reflected in his perception of Montreal upon his return: "These were dangerous streets for Porter, the steep downtown slopes between MacGregor and Sherbrooke — Peel, Stanley, Drummond, Mountain — for it was in a tourist room between Burnside and St. Catherine on Peel that young Carrier had last lived with his mother" (136). Phil thus associates the city's geography with his movements through space, time, and social position. He is now using his American last name again, repeating while reversing the name change he undergoes at the end of "Identity," and the opening of the novella concerns the recurrence of Phil's epilepsy and his search for his condition's roots, recalling the first paragraphs of "Identity." Throughout "Translation," the narrative moves back and forth in time, from Phil's adulthood to childhood and back; that is, the largely, but not entirely, chronological sequence of the trilogy is countered, with the result that the stories' incidents are enriched by further detail.

Phil's relationships with his parents are the main concern of "Translation," as Lecker shows (see 204-08), and what happens is that in a sense Phil becomes his father while Madeleine becomes his mother. For example, the first line of section 7 is, "Porter dreaded the Canadian border. The simplest questions of an immigration officer were the imponderables of his life" (121). This is exactly the sort of fear that Reg expresses at the end of "Identity" when he tells Phil to keep his mouth shut. As for Madeleine, in her role as older woman she reminds one not only of Mrs. Humphries but also of Hennie. We learn that Madeleine is even the same age, fifty-two (144), as Hennie was when the latter died. Moreover, as intermediary between languages as well as romantic interest, Madeleine becomes another Thérèse. In addition, Phil learns more about who his father really was, even to the point of Phil's discovering he has a brother and sisters he never knew about (155-56). At the end of the novella Phil tries to communicate across the vast distances that have separated him and his father, in a manner reminiscent of his experiments with rabbit-ears. As we see, then, "Translation" is both a recapitulation of and a site of possible closure for the elements that structure the trilogy.

Blaise thus creates one novella and one trilogy that rests on the border between a set of independent stories and another novella. The three short stories possess their own internal structures, to a large extent (but not entirely) standing on their own as individual narratives. Yet each of the three stories enriches the other two, so that the whole trilogy exhibits a global unity created and reinforced by the stories' common features. Then Blaise provides a novella that mirrors and complements the trilogy while offering a slightly more coherent narrative that nevertheless presents a fragmentary, border-crossing vision through its varied spatial and temporal settings. Phil is shown throughout the middle fiction section of *Resident Alien* as a figure of contradictory, conflicting, and diverse identities. The structural fragmentation of the complete mini-cycle, then, reproduces Phil's inner being, and is therefore the most logical way for his life story and personality to be rendered dramatically for the reader.

Notes

1. For clear examples of the mini-cycle form in American fiction, see Robert Olen Butler's *A Good Scent from a Strange Mountain* (1992) and *Tabloid Dreams* (1996), which I discuss in an article in the Spring 2009 issue of *Short Story*.
2. For a discussion of the novella form, see Blodgett 56-59.
3. On the symbolism of geography and maps, see Huggan 56-57.

Works Cited

Blaise, Clark. *A North American Education: A Book of Short Fiction*. Toronto: Doubleday Canada, 1974.

-----. *Resident Alien*. Markham, ON: Penguin Books Canada, 1986.

-----. *Tribal Justice*. Toronto: Doubleday Canada, 1974.

Blodgett, E.D. "Forming Other Connections: Ethel Wilson's Novellas." *New Directions from Old*. Ed. J.R. (Tim) Struthers. Guelph, ON: Red Kite, 1991. Canadian Storytellers 1.

Butler, Robert Olen. *A Good Scent from a Strange Mountain*. New York: Henry Holt, 1992.

-----. *Tabloid Dreams*. New York: Henry Holt, 1996.

Dunn, Maggie, and Ann Morris. *The Composite Novel: The Short Story Cycle in Transition*. New York: Twayne, 1995. Studies in Literary Themes and Genres 6.

Huggan, Graham. "(Un)co-ordinated Movements: The Geography of Autobiography in David Malouf's *12 Edmonstone Street* and Clark Blaise's *Resident Alien*." *Australian and New Zealand Studies in Canada* 3 (1990): 56-65.

Ingram, Forrest L. *Representative Short Story Cycles of the Twentieth Century: Studies in a Literary Genre*. The Hague: Mouton, 1971.

Leacock, Stephen. *Sunshine Sketches of a Little Town*. 1912. Ed. Gerald Lynch. Ottawa: Tecumseh, 1996.

Lecker, Robert. *An Other I: The Fictions of Clark Blaise*. Toronto: ECW, 1988.

Lundén, Rolf. *The United Stories of America: Studies in the Short Story Composite*. Amsterdam: Rodopi, 1999.

Lynch, Gerald. *The One and the Many: English-Canadian Short Story Cycles*. Toronto: U of Toronto P, 2001.

Munro, Alice. *Runaway*. Toronto: McClelland & Stewart, 2004.

Nagel, James. *The Contemporary American Short-Story Cycle:*

The Ethnic Resonance of Genre. Baton Rouge: Louisiana State UP, 2001.

Roig, Denise. *Any Day Now.* Winnipeg: Signature Editions, 2004.

Struthers, J.R. (Tim). "Intersecting Orbits: A Study of Selected Story Cycles by Hugh Hood, Jack Hodgins, Clark Blaise, and Alice Munro, in Their Literary Contexts." Diss. U of Western Ontario, 1981.

Weiss, Allan. "Between Collection and Cycle: The Mini-Cycle." *Short Story* ns 17.2 (2009): 78-90.

-----. "Cycles within Cycles: Mini-Cycles in Robert Olen Butler's Fiction." *Short Story* ns 17.1 (2009): 65-80.

-----. "A Sextet of Trios." Rev. of *Any Day Now,* by Denise Roig. *Literary Review of Canada* July-Aug. 2005: 17.

Of Metaphor and Memoir:
Clark Blaise's *Lunar Attractions*

Mary Williams

Clark Blaise comments on *Lunar Attractions* (1979), his first novel, and on his autobiographical compulsion: "It's a novel about the total development of an individual. ... I think I will need the shell of autobiography in anything I do. ... I will continue to accept the shape of my life as it has been given to me" (Blaise in Hancock, "Interview: Clark Blaise" 30-31). *Lunar Attractions* chronicles narrator David Greenwood's physical, emotional, sexual, political, and, most vividly, artistic coming of age; it is a telling fragment of a life (focussing as it does on David from age five to age seventeen, and on his migration from a Florida swamp to a northern city), which constantly intersects Blaise's own. The mode of autobiographical memoir, initiated in his earlier short story collections *A North American Education* (1973) and *Tribal Justice* (1974), is again adopted in *Lunar Attractions*, to be extended and refined to an unprecedented degree of self-reflexivity.

* * *

Even the "germ" of an idea is a metaphor. Even if we manage to penetrate to the very heart of a Clark Blaise story, we are confronted with a metaphor, an equivalence, substitution. This is the nature of his art; his story is conceived that way: "I think of a story as essentially a single metaphor and the exfoliation of a single metaphor through dense layers of submetaphors. ... every sentence [must] in some way be a part of that metaphor" (Blaise in Hancock, "An Interview" 56). *Lunar Attractions* also conforms to this model. From its central metaphor, the novel generates layers of submetaphors that shelter and enhance the central metaphor, the story's core of meaning, as the folds of David Greenwood's brain shelter and enhance their imaginative core, "the fabled salt-machine that fell overboard and kept churning, eventually filling the seas" (11).

The central metaphor of *Lunar Attractions* is the text itself as a literal embodiment of the narrator's developing artistic awareness, of the tortuous rise of his creative power. David learns to perceive metaphor, to see equivalence between discrete aspects of his experience; he learns to write. As a metaphor, in turn, the text subsumes self-reflexive qualities in its structure, in its autobiographical implications, in its concerns with vision and madness, and, most importantly, in its form of memoir. Through the exfoliation of this single metaphor, Blaise ultimately renders *Lunar Attractions* a profoundly self-reflexive novel, one that reflects back on its author, its narrator, and itself as art.

Based on four fragments of the mind of its narrator, the text is structurally self-reflexive. Four verbal "pictures" of David's transforming brain are interspersed as regular supports throughout his narrative: his first shadowy recollection, a morass of melted crayons, a nightmarish *tableau vivant* in a museum, and "Over a thousand pages in four thick binders" (254) — letters sent and received from a legion of crackpot psychics and religious fanatics, aliens and con artists. The text is also divided — into three sections, a formation which aptly mirrors David's stance as he moves toward artistic voice and vision. He is perpetually the third: the most oblique angle of the triangle, the unlikely hybrid of contrasts. He is the "inheritor of my parents' ... contradictions" rather than their gifts (35-36); he is intellectually suspended in an indeterminate space between school friends Wesley, who champions "induction and elimination" (132), and Irving, who proceeds "not by logic but by analogy" (132); he is the force that can both fuse and divide Laurel and Larry Zywotko. The last, and by far the shortest, section of the novel is also the most fractured by chapter divisions (there are five, as compared with three and four in the longer first and second sections). Here, David must continually begin again. The section's fragmented structure reflects the proliferation of his already diverse range of interests toward the end of his narrative (the end of the development of his artistic awareness), and his equally rapid rejection of these interests — these miscarried "approaches to art" (154) — as his need to gain access to a definitive means of creative expression grows more acute. *Lunar Attractions* is also formally self-reflexive in that it concretely demonstrates the fundamental split in David's psyche. David has a ubiquitous second voice that dissents in italics — "A voice whispered to me, *this is crazy; you've done something crazy*" (89) — and qualifies in parenthesis — "Yet I have watched my father (let me say it now: I have watched my father like no son has ever watched his father)" (12).

The text is also self-reflexive in that it is the autobiography of both its author and its narrator. We see Blaise through David's unfolding life, of which *Lunar Attractions* is an embodiment. In a later piece, "A North American Memoir: Revenge," Blaise writes:

> ... I grew to believe in the co-existence, or the simultaneity, of visible and occult worlds: duplicities, masks, hidden selves, discarded languages, altered names, things not being what they seemed. Add to that the continual moves...[,] the social adjustments..., the tension of my parents' marriage, and the gifted memory, and the ego-thrust towards immortal vengeance, and you have the formative, pre-literate experience of an eventual artist (if lucky), or a functional neurotic. It still took a series of fortunate accidents and gifted teachers to coax the writer from all that unformed, possibly poisonous sludge. ("Revenge" 59)

David too discovers "hidden selves" everywhere (his unborn sister, the mudfish buried in the yard, Laurel, Sheila), discarded languages (his father's French, his mother's German), and altered names (he learns that his real name is not Greenwood but Boisvert, and that virtually everyone has an alias). Blaise emerges from "poisonous sludge"; David rises from "the nightsoil of my imagination" (19). For Blaise, things are not what they seem; for David, "even implacable principles are in contention" (30). In every detail of the passage quoted above, Blaise describes David's imaginative formation as he describes his own.

David's struggle to achieve artistic vision is the self-reflexive source of his art, because the struggle then becomes the subject of *Lunar Attractions* once that vision is achieved. The text is "proto-fiction" (154), the seminal product of the seminal experience. It is the only true means, after all others have been exhausted, to self-knowledge:

> Another thing I know—and I have learned it as I write—is that my kind of innocence, because it is so complicated, is the most dangerous, most corrupt kind of knowledge. We all "know" this, of course—what is propriety but the stench of repression? (155)

To write of the formation and demise of that corrupted innocence from the vantage point of hard-won creative sovereignty is to free the word "know" from quotation marks, to activate a real, unbounded self-knowledge.

The novel's concern with madness also has self-reflexive results. While David demonstrates his "paranoid schizophrenia" (82) through a myriad of "submetaphors," the most profound demonstration of his divided nature relates to the central textual metaphor. David acts both as the text's creator and as its audience. The most vivid example of this compulsion is found in a key passage situated almost exactly at the mid-point of the narrative. Here, the narrative flow is riven (bisected as neatly as its creator's personality), and interpretive commentary inserted. David tells us that "the digging episodes of my childhood and the map fantasies were approaches to art, metaphors lying beyond me waiting to be claimed, named, and mastered" (154). A sport fisherman as well as a furniture salesman, his father employs a catchphrase that David evokes several times in the course of his narrative, and each time it wields a greater metaphoric impact: "'He's taken the hook, let him run with it'" (62). "He" is the manipulated customer who "flounder[s] in his uneasy freedom" (62)—the fish, the audience, the "mark."

But narrator/salesman becomes his own mark; the author becomes his own audience.

In this passage, David is running with the baited hook, with the line of metaphors he has already "sold" us in the first half of his story:

> Those maps were megalomaniacal fantasies, explorations of the unsettled provinces of my own and of others' bodies. ... The mudfish, the worms in my stomach, they were real to me as projections of my body — my wretched, unresponsive body. I didn't take the equations far enough. The mudfish was my [stillborn] sister, and I killed her — yes! But my sister was my penis, and I wanted to chop it off — yes! In drawing maps and creating continents, I was reinventing and renaming myself; devoted, like "Mac" in those Charles Atlas ads, to my own brand of dynamic tension. I looked to those maps for confirmation the way narcissists look into mirrors, the way skinny teen-agers lift weights. (154)

So, spanning a north-central Florida childhood and an adolescence spent in "Palestra" (a fictionalized Pittsburgh), David's eclectic array of interests — map-making, geography, digging in the foul Florida mud (and later archaeology); astronomy, torching anthills, stamp collecting (or gathering, until he learns the difference); baseball, a particular *tableau vivant* or stuffed display at the Palestra museum entitled *Nubian Lion, Attacking Bedouin and Camel* (107); even satiric correspondence with various fringe mail-order societies — are united, equivalent, in that they are all ultimately abortive approaches to fiction. So the attainment of artistic maturity and the acceptance of physical (sexual) maturity are concurrent aspects of a single process: an imaginative castration and a rebirth into a new awareness, the loss of a corrupt innocence. David rapidly exfoliates the metaphor for us; we are deflated, excluded from our role as audience, as active (albeit uneasy) co-creators of the text. All our creative extensions of story events, all our metaphoric connections, are subsumed by his. He has reclaimed the text, refashioning it into a unit of his own self-reflexivity, and nothing is permitted to cloud the reflected image. Any random interpretation is ruled out. David, becoming logical interpreter of the text he is intuitively creating, weaves all disparate narrative strands into a single created object. Nothing is superfluous in this controlled portrait — except the audience.

The central metaphor — *Lunar Attractions* itself as an equivalent of its narrator's artistic coming of age (encompassing his sexual, physical, intellectual, emotional, and political maturation) — is also self-reflexive in that the narrative takes the form of a memoir. Certainly the novel is an autobiography, the narrator's personal memoir in the broad context, the story of the life of its creator. But it is specifically a self-reflexive memoir for another reason. David is compelled to trace the gradual transformation of a single memory, and that transformation reflects the development of his artistic perceptual ability. *Lunar Attractions*, then, on one level, is the artist's investigation of the convoluted processes of his own memory, which somewhere shelters the source of his fiction.

The voice of David's artistry, buried in "the nightsoil of my imagination" (19), in the "purple-black muck" of Florida (19), in the "underground colony," the "anthill" of Palestra (163), will "not surface again for thirty years" (35); by the time it does, it has become *Lunar Attractions*. Take your memories and submerge them, force them from the surface of your consciousness — like early narrators

Normie Dyer in "Grids and Doglegs" ("scream a memory out of existence" [60]) and Sutherland in "Notes Beyond a History" ("Not only has the lake been civilized, but so has my memory" [93]) — and allow them to ferment for three decades until the transformation is complete: this is Blaise's unorthodox recipe for memoir. The idea appears in a piece published three years before *Lunar Attractions*, "The Sense of an Ending," which introduces a number of details the novel later expands upon. In this earlier piece Blaise observes:

> After 30 years of memories things have been buried long enough to be transformed, they've taken root in different soil. Nightsoil. After 30 years your buried selves have mouldered long enough to push to the surface again and confront you like some monstrous mistake of nature, not just dog-eating birds, but armies of snails, say, that you never thought could harm you until they slowly march across you at night, plastering your eyes shut in their wake, and sealing your mouth forever. ("Sense" 65)

The memoir, then, in Blaise's hands, is a kind of self-reflexive late-night horror story. To formulate the memoir is to dig up one's painful past at a precise moment in the development of both the memory and the one who remembers, to confront one's past with language just before it can emerge of its own accord, unexpectedly, devastatingly. To write the memoir is to write against silence, against death by (self-)suffocation.

The way in which the narrator formulates his memoir has everything to do with the conditions of his birth. David is an only child, reminding us frequently and in many ways that he is "a freak" (6): a "thin-fat" (105) "partially right-handed" (6) "wise" idiot (37), and bearer of "the only circumcision" in central Florida (22). He is indelibly stamped with "the comic misprint of my genetic code" (24). He is the incarnation of his parents' contradictions and divergent weaknesses, genetically split and self-reflexive. He is a potential artist. The conditions of his birth provide him with the artistic perspective: he is isolated and divided, pulled furiously between parental poles. The same conditions also provide him with the power source, the drive behind the search for a voice of artistic expression: in the sealed swamp of his personality unspent emotions, like noxious and volatile swamp gases, gain alarming potency. Implosion/explosion is imminent, and there are three possible results: self-destruction, murder, or the violent birth of artistic vision. David describes his conundrum:

> my passion — even my love — had no outlet. It led back to myself, and it still leads me to fall on my knees and shake the crib or the desk, to pound my fist a hundred times a day in a fit of sudden anger, remorse, or embarrassment. The only child is inevitably a monster: all that love dammed up inside him ... with nothing *in his scale* to return it to. ... he possesses some instinct to assure himself, even murderously, of supremacy. He exercises a sterilizing influence, destroying whatever will or potential there had been to create more like him. (49)

His birthright is an unbounded ego. He must sterilize, castrate, murder all that has the power to touch him and evoke his love, and that amounts to worlds ("my compassion, like my fear, was universal. I felt sorry for tires on scalding concrete" [42]). He possesses the instinct to destroy in order to re-create in terms he can understand and control absolutely. A survival principle enacted is an act of love is an act of rage is the act of artistic creation. The narrator's ego fuses love, rage, and art, and that combined force is turned, obsessively, back on its own origins, and on its own progenitor — the narrator himself. The product is a violently self-reflexive memoir, a memoir of its own process of becoming.

David records his earliest memory in the first two pages of his narrative. It is the prototypical experience, the determinant of the meaning embedded in all subsequent experiences, and the basis of his memoir. Father and son embark on a fishing trip to a Florida backwater during which they are nearly thrown from their boat by a giant alligator whose baby is snagged on their fishing line. David's father does not see the creature explode onto the still surface of the water and will never credit David's explanation of the resulting life-threatening upheaval. Though he believes they "were dead anyway," David grabs a knife and slices the line:

> My father was over me in an instant shouting, "Good God, *no, no!*" and beating the metal handle of the now-limp rod against the side of the boat. ... His face was the darkest red I'd ever seen. His anger, for the moment, was directed at the water and sky, but he had seen me cut the line. (4)

This is the first castration, the first assertion of ego, the first act motivated simultaneously by love, rage, and the need for artistic expression, and in the space of a moment the action deeply and inexorably alters David's world. In an instant, and for the first time, the father demonstrates fear, a lapse of control, the fact that he is not invincible. In an instant, and for the first time, the son seizes the knife and the opportunity to assert his own mastery. David's love wields a lethal blade; it packs the force of a blow from an alligator's tail ("a sonic boom" [4]); it is sexually aggressive; it overwhelms and destroys its object. To love, for him, is to subsume, to incorporate love's object into his own ego, to be involved yet alone, to be split and self-reflexive. David enters the realm of obscure isolation, the training ground of art, the interminable lunar night: "the full moon blazed like a spotlight, and I could feel shadows under us as we rowed home in our normal silence. ... The shadow and the silence never lifted" (5). The bond between father and son is severed, and in effecting that severance David has destroyed a part of himself.

A brush, a glimpse of the potent force his as yet unformed persona and his ostensibly serene and orderly world are nurturing, is all a five-year-old David can bear: he buries the memory of the experience deep in imaginative soil. It becomes "the chord my imagination obsessively plays" (3) — compelling and repetitive music. Its volume increases. The memory will not decompose. It will moulder for thirty years, acquiring a monstrous significance. Internalized, it becomes an aspect of his personality, a version of himself. In the meantime, he can *feel* the shadows it casts across his unfolding life. David tries to unearth the subterranean memory monster, the buried self, many times. He is a relentless digger. He makes major digging attempts as a child, as an adolescent, as a young man, and finally as the adult narrator. His efforts span a lifetime — they are one of the memoir's infrastructures — but only in the final attempt is he successful. In the final attempt the recipe is adhered to; memory is at last cooked to the consistency of art.

In the first attempt, little David digs compulsively in the mud behind the family's Florida cottage. He is digging in the imaginative nightsoil: that rich and fetid loam, that welter of birds and maps and foreign words, of constellations and baseball diamonds, of radio broadcasts from shimmering enclaves in distant worlds, like Arthur Godfrey's Miami Beach and the Manhattan Stork Club. He digs "in a dream of escaping this world" (19). He wants to submerge himself in another: "My arms would be black below the elbow, my body gray and crusty.... I wanted to tear away the soil, to have my private peephole.... I wanted to live down there" (19-20). He wants to dig a tunnel to fiction. He wants to retrieve the power contained in his suppressed memory and thereby recover a means of artistic expression. Eventually, he uncovers a mudfish, a "smooth, black, and rubbery" cable, a "fin-headed monster" (45) buried deep in the back yard — deep amid his imaginatively transforming memories. The fish's head is cloven by a fin, as the narrator's psyche is cloven by the sharp edge of his parents' marriage. The original experience has become the metaphoric equivalent of the buried mudfish, which has now become the metaphoric equivalent of the narrator who is obsessed with the memory of the original experience. Metaphor compounds and circles inward, becoming increasingly self-reflexive. David kills his fish, impaling it with the sharp digging trowel in an action as deft as the flicking of a knife through a fishing line. The tool of imaginative investigation, of art, becomes a castration implement and a murder weapon. David is not yet ready for art. His strength — his love and his rage — remains unharnessed, unstructured, unrefined, uncreative. It burrows inward, undermining the imagination. It is self-destructive. The memory must be buried again.

   In his second major attempt at coming to terms with the powerful, submerged memory, a fourteen-year-old David undertakes "that long descent into the pit of Palestra" (164) from the removed, omniscient prospect of his home on Daley Ridge. He crawls into another hole in the back yard and enters a zone where fantasy is realized, and where the gate between dream and reality is flung wide open. This time David's digging tool is instinct, his burgeoning sexual curiosity. He wants to *live* down there. In a littered apartment in a dying neighbourhood, in "the queen's chamber" of "the anthill" (165), David has his first "real" sexual encounter. He is drawn to the apartment and seduced by Laurel Zywotko, the incarnation of every adolescent schoolboy's wet dream, the living monument to fifties America — that schizophrenic decade (the larger context that could breed a David Greenwood) of repression and conformity *and* prosperity and cultural mobility.

   That which is radically divided, forcibly suppressed, and buried deep in the nightsoil must invariably undergo a monstrous transformation. David's first recollection moulders in the shadowed silence. The broken rod becomes the butchered mudfish (alien disembodied genitals) which, mouldering nine years and nourished by sexual confusion, takes on a bizarre new shape. At the point of simultaneous orgasm, David witnesses Laurel vanish from existence, as her "brother" Larry, high-school hood and social outlaw, emerges: "She, in the process of rising, him" (171). Foraging in the pit, David has unearthed Laurel/Larry, a vivid reflection of his own violent duality — the power source of his fiction, his memoir, his quest for self-knowledge. But the mouldering process is not yet complete. David cannot yet synthesize art from raw love and rage, from imagination and experience. He rejects a full understanding of the experience, both "convinced that I'd just been shown the secret parts of Daley Ridge's sexiest girl" (171) and admitting that "I both knew and refused to know" (170).

When the transvestite is murdered a short time later — strangled with the leather thong he uses to tie back his penis, and, of course, castrated — David is held as material witness. David could have enacted the brutal crime: Laurel/Larry is "a bigger dreamer than myself" (170), a more dramatically developed split personality, a more attractive and more sexually powerful sibling, and David is admittedly driven "to assure himself, even murderously, of supremacy" (49). He has already committed ritual acts of fused love and rage against his own family, and thus against himself: castration of the father, mutilation of the mudfish ("my sister ... my penis" [154]). He confesses to fire-bombings ("Hiroshima-like cataclysm[s]" [163]) of anthills in order to confirm his own omnipotence, and his developing sense of metaphor carries him from one kind of anthill to another. He implicates himself within the towering walls of his own imagination, of the lunar night he inhabits, where even pop culture is a hysterical reflection of his all-encompassing ego: "in my dream, wrapped in the silk threads of my cocoon, ... I had walked down the seven hundred and eighty-three steps to Patience Street like Boris Karloff in *The Mummy's Curse*, and, attracted to a fellow mummy, fellow cocoon, I had murdered him" (200).

The police never solve the case: "It was too strange, too aberrational for conventional police methods" (210) — methods that fail to allow for the logic of analogy, of metaphor. But, toward the end of the narrative, it is revealed to David (inadvertently, by Paul Gaylord) that Wesley Duivylbuis is the murderer. Wesley is David's alter ego. He visits a psychoanalyst under David's name, and David wonders if "in some parallel universe [Wesley] just might be David Greenwood" (258). "*Wesley's a psycho*, came a voice that almost whispered. A psycho using my name. A split personality trying to take me over" (259). Wesley is "Wesley" and "David," and David is "a voice" and "David." The two sundered natures merge and identify. David ("on the side of fear, nightmare and of all unanswered things" [210]) *has* committed the crime, then — by association, indirectly, metaphorically. But not actually. He now uses his habitually "unused, braking muscles" (164), so severely strained on the stairs descending to Patience Street. He learns a new strength, a new, structured outlet for the volatile feelings issuing from his divided psyche.

The ostracized and all-knowing material (and immaterial, imaginative) witness, David feels compelled to guide the stumbling detectives to the realization that Laurel does not exist independently of Larry. To that end, he painstakingly composes an anonymous note, his first literary effort, which reveals the extent to which his artistic awareness has developed. David is taken aback; the result is "frightening" (209). In the completed note, "'I' had disappeared. I had become Laurel" (209). David has subsumed Laurel with language, and, recreated in language, Laurel has subsumed David. Language is becoming the fulcrum for David's pain, rage, and love, and that charged, creative language will profoundly alter the dynamics of his enclosed world, will open it wide to new possibility. The voracious ego persists, but now its essence is expressed through creative language. The ego's expression is no longer an unmediated explosion that devastates its object: the object is now endowed with a new, imaginative, and very potent life.

For the actual murderer — with his "Scientific skepticism" (241), his rejection of the "'invalid' and 'inefficient'" (240-41), his "sense of mission" (240) — the victim is an intolerable anomaly, an incomprehensible perversion in a world where there must be a logical, natural, useful place for every possible variation. But David, the junior archaeologist, has learned the value of buried artifacts, of submerged phenomena, of a contiguous collective and personal history: "'Everything is priceless' ... was, in fact, the essence of all I had been believing, in my inarticulate and impure way" (233-34). Everything is the raw substance of art. Everything is acceptable, even anomaly and nightmare, even memory monsters. Blaise has said of his narrators: "Their only triumph is that they have imagination and an ability to accept" (Blaise in Hancock, "An Interview" 57). If these are the criteria, David will triumph. He comes to terms with Laurel (and, ultimately, with his transforming memory) by penetrating her with his imagination instead of a lethal blade. He is learning to transcend his murderous confusion. He is able to justify Laurel by means of a series of metaphoric equivalents, a chain of self-reflexive imagery: she is his moon, his mother, his unborn sister, his own female aspect. But despite their marked development, neither David nor his submerged memory are ready to confront the light of day. The mouldering process continues. David is still "inarticulate and impure," still enveloped in the lunar night of his imagination. His mode of artistic expression is still crude; like the note, it is an irregular, intuitive patchwork of words clipped from a jumbled array of sources. The memory must be buried again until its significance has solidified.

The third major digging attempt occurs in the last pages of the narrative. David is seventeen and still afflicted with artistic and sexual confusion, still compelled to dig for the power deposited in a memory. He then tries to alleviate the oppressive gloom of co-worker Paul Gaylord, who has just suffered a rare sexual rejection: "'Next time she tells you she's got a period,' I told him (not really knowing what it was ...), 'you tell her that's okay—you've got an exclamation point.' He liked it; he said he'd use it" (298). David understands the power of punctuation: he is well-versed in the peripheral, the borderland of the imagination, the unperformed. He is intimate with the fringes, but his understanding is impaired and incomplete. He partakes of the lunar, but the solar continues to elude him; he is able to intuit the sense but not the core substance of things; he is coming to grips with the tools of his art, but its subject remains untenable.

David is increasingly attracted to "the sweaty, sunshiny experience" of others; he longs to mate it with the "long lunar night that I alone inhabited" (55). He is driven by the urgency of his libido, of his sexual and artistic impulse, to be intolerant of exclusion, to encompass *all* dualities within his own experience, his own being. He must be balanced, perfectly split, absolutely self-reflexive. He feels a growing need to shed the cocoon, to access the memory, to crack the code, to embody both sides of knowledge—but it's hard to do:

> I seemed to be facing precisely the wrong way, seeking chastity where there was only smut; imagining love where there was only mockery. ... it wasn't just shabby furniture that had a coded ticket on the back, it wasn't just sofas that had two prices. ...
>
> How much of this was apparent to me then, I'll never know. Sometimes I think I knew from the age of five,

that first intervention [that first castration, the mouldering memory]. I only know that seventeen was a period of passion: unacted, murdered passion in my life
when the school, the store, the houses, the streets were
teeming with bodies, all of them ... writhing with desire, all of them hot and uncomfortable in their clothes,
all of them willing for a price, for a wink, for a crook of
the finger, to take it off, take it all-l-ll off. (298-99)

David (like Frankie Thibidault of "A North American
Education") wants to remain in the audience and to perform the elaborate striptease at the same time. To repeat
an analogy that Blaise uses in "The Sense of an Ending,"
David wants to crawl inside the Grecian Urn while never
losing his perspective on it from the outside ("Sense" 69).
He wants to have the experience and write about it too.
He wants to watch himself live. He wants to be totally
self-reflexive, double-sided. In order to resurrect his
"murdered passion" (299) and to thereby attain the other
side of knowledge crucial to the formulation of his art,
David must engage in an unprecedented act of faith —
an act of love — and there is a mounting (self-generated)
pressure on him to do so.

The only kind of family life the Greenwoods have
unfolds within the context of the furniture business
in which they gradually (completely, by the time David
reaches seventeen) invest all the financial capital and
emotional energy they possess. David, ever craving to
belong, digs in, discovering an apparently safe burrow
for himself in the back room of the store, amongst the
broken and unassembled "home" furnishing. But in the
seamy back room (the underworld, the nightsoil) of cut-
throat small enterprise, he also unearths saleswoman
Sheila Roberts, a ruthless opportunist who, with her

own son in tow, manoeuvres to overthrow David and his mother and to replace them in the family/business hierarchy. Sheila is one of those nightmare snails that Blaise describes as being capable of "plastering your eyes shut ... and sealing your mouth forever" ("Sense" 65), a threat to artistic vision and voice. She is an embodiment of David's "murdered passion" (299), a version of himself buried in the past and mouldered to a sexual grotesque, "overdressed and overmade-up" (300). She incorporates all the castrated selves David has submerged in the nightsoil of memory and imagination (the broken rod, the severed mudfish, the emasculated Larry) in a single ripe and potent manifestation: "It was too monstrous to believe. This *creature* ..." (304).

But David must be ready this time. This transformed memory will not be buried again so easily. He must now demonstrate faith in his arduously developed ability to channel brute rage and love into a controlled artistic strength; he must now confront monstrosity with monstrosity: "It was all I could do to stay put, not to advance like Frankenstein's monster" (304). David has become a match for his own past; he will be able to master memoir. The opponents square off:

Perhaps I expected a gun, something she could hold and point and threaten me with. But of course that wasn't it. The bracelets tinkled violently even before I saw her move, and in an instant I was confronting a lady with her skirt held high and nothing on underneath, and as in a dream I was advancing, my hands open and ice cold, advancing not for the throat but on that vision: oh, I knew so suddenly *everything*, how the parts and the passions fitted and I swear it was a moment of love — unashamed and inviolate and heedless

of consequence. Then my own small pistol went off in
a loud report, doubling me over as she dropped her
skirt the moment my fingers touched her there and she
was gone and the music came back louder than ever
and I found myself clutching the same door frame for
support until the spasms passed and then I ran far
from the parked cars to lie in the grass under the sun
and to wait for the god to invade my blood. (305)

David, encased in his ornately wrought cocoon and
suspended, uncomprehending, in the present, joins with
Sheila, his nightmarishly transformed past ("all affinities
must somehow converge" [134]) for a vivid, compressed
instant. That instant contains a touch, a gunshot, an
ejaculation. David's touch marks the castration of his
buried self; memory is rendered impotent in the sense
that it no longer has the power to hold him in shadow
and silence. The "report" of David's "own small pistol"
(305) marks the violent death of his innocence and in-
articulateness. David's ejaculation marks his abandon-
ment to the hot light and voice on the other side of cold
shadow and silence. Here is David's transcendent act of
faith and love: he surges through the door on a wave of
passion, relinquishing the ordered safety of his lunar en-
closure, the support of the door frame, of all formal con-
straint, of punctuation. The climax (the final sentence)
comes in a breathless uninterrupted unpunctuated flow.

Rooted in imagination, David reaches across to experience and, fusing the two, embraces art. He now
knows "*everything*" (305). His knowledge of "how the
parts and the passions fitted" (305) is absolute (freed
from quotation marks), for they are now all contained
within him. He subsumes all conflicting and interlocking dualities: sun and moon, present and past, light and

dark, chaos and order, voice and silence, rage and love, art and sexuality, aggression and passivity, male and female. He advances on vision and is invaded by voice.

David's monstrous buried selves, as well as his vision, voice, and memory, nurtured over a period of years, reach the peak of their strength and refinement, and, released from the nightsoil, from silence into language, take the form of *Lunar Attractions*. To the adult narrator, the memory he unearths for the last time after thirty years has become himself as a child—a freak and a monster. But gradually, as the narrative unfolds, through the power of a fully developed artistry, the child takes on human dimension. Understood, as the quest for self-knowledge draws (for now) to an end, the monster-child is stripped of his power to suffocate. The price the narrator pays for his creative castration of the threatening memory (employing the tool of his artistic insight) is a life "I've lived through less vividly since" (93). But finally, he is the mature and consummate artist—isolated yet engaged, profoundly split and self-reflexive—who becomes the sole progenitor of the perfectly self-reflexive memoir.

Works Cited

Blaise, Clark. "Grids and Doglegs." *Tribal Justice*. Toronto: Doubleday Canada, 1974. 47-61.

-----. *Lunar Attractions*. Garden City, NY: Doubleday, 1979. Toronto: Doubleday Canada, 1979.

-----. "A North American Education." *A North American Education: A Book of Short Fiction*. Toronto: Doubleday Canada, 1973. 162-84.

-----. "A North American Memoir: Revenge." *The North American Review* Dec. 1984: 56-60.

-----. "Notes Beyond a History." *Tribal Justice*. Toronto: Doubleday Canada, 1974. 91-104.

-----. "The Sense of an Ending." 76: *New Canadian Stories*. Ed. Joan Harcourt and John Metcalf. Ottawa: Oberon, 1976. 63-69.

Hancock, Geoff. "Interview: Clark Blaise on Artful Autobiography: 'I who live in dreams am touched by reality'." *Books in Canada* Mar. 1979: 30-31.

-----. "An Interview with Clark Blaise." *Canadian Fiction Magazine* 34-35 (1980): 46-64. Rpt. as "Clark Blaise" in *Canadian Writers at Work: Interviews by Geoff Hancock*. Toronto: Oxford UP, 1987. 146-63. Rpt. as "Clear Veneer: An Interview with Clark Blaise" in *Clark Blaise: The Interviews*. Ed. J.R. (Tim) Struthers. Toronto: Guernica Editions, 2016. Essential Writers.

Self-Healing through Telling Someone Else's Intimate Story: Clark Blaise's *Lusts*

Sandra Singer

*In a disguised way, it's my story too. I'm writing
my autobiography in a quiet sort of way, through her life.*
— **Rosie Chang, in *Lusts* (5)**

*A major artist with the compulsive theme
of the Holocaust must eventually find
a new language and a new form,
and I don't know if an American
writing in English can hope to do it.*
— **Richard Durgin, in *Lusts* (81)**

The Title Shaping the Novel's Design

Clark Blaise's second novel, *Lusts* (1983), works out the
irrational excesses of mid- to late-twentieth-century life
through the technique of portraying characters who are
marked by historically specific discourses. Blaise's novel
offers both a representation and a critique of Enlighten-
ment models of pleasure and individual autonomy common to American consumer messaging. *Lusts* holds that
no model, perhaps most evidently the Freudian concept of
the autonomous ego that one of the novel's protagonists,

poet Rachel Isaacs, valued and projected as strength of character onto her spouse, fiction writer Richard Durgin, is sufficient on its own for representing the perils of existence. Although widely appreciated and admired, the Freudian valuation of autonomous thought and action is simply not a complex enough construct after the Holocaust for envisaging and informing an ontologically secure and productive role.[1] Nor does any mere attempt to escape, such as took Rachel in her early twenties to Italy, or Richard in his early forties to India some time after Rachel's death by suicide at age twenty-eight, provide a solution. Consequently, if India is to satisfy Richard's desire for "an attempt at salvation" (216), he must alter the way he lives. In the end he chooses to subscribe to a model for healing from personal and historical loss that forms and works intercommunicatively.

Richard Durgin's gradual though unfinished processing over the course of the novel of the events pertaining to his growth — from his childhood in Pittsburgh through each of his three marriages (of which his marriage to Rachel was the first) and the conclusions he draws from this review — serves as a foil for the epistemological approach that the novel's author, Clark Blaise, prescribes. By means of Richard and a scholar, Rosie Chang, examining his wife Rachel's legacy, in particular her experience as a second-generation Holocaust survivor, but also the impact of Rachel's relationship with Richard on both partners and their work, Blaise's novel tests the very forms of knowing (biography, autobiography, epistolary novel, short story, poetry, film, psychoanalytic historiography, and allegory). Richard and Rosie interpret his and Rachel's ways of literary expression, in addition to being self-conscious about their own letter-writing correspondence. Finally, they demonstrate the value of a model of "communicative competence," such as Jürgen Habermas' psychoanalytic historiography describes, which is informed by the problematic past that it probes, but is necessarily not bound to it for envisaging the future (Habermas, "Towards a Theory").

Richard and Rosie's communication strives against and seeks to move beyond the repetitive aspect of traumatic loss. In some respects by retelling the past Richard is engaging in a Freudian psychoanalytic strategy for recovery from the repetitious aspect of trauma that Freud, Habermas, and Freudian trauma scholar Cathy Caruth describe. Trauma results from "the shocking and unexpected occurrence of an accident" (Caruth 6) that would include Richard's finding his unexpectedly deceased wife's body in their apartment bathtub. The plot of *Lusts* demonstrates the repetitive psychological workings of trauma and also the importance, if possible according to Caruth, of working through trauma with another person, preferably someone who was impacted by comparable events (Caruth 8). Traumatic impact is further reflected in Blaise's narrative design of withholding details of Rachel's death from the reader until the end. Reviewing Rachel's experience as a second-generation Holocaust survivor and Richard's loss of Rachel to death prepares the ground for Richard and Rosie's starting afresh, and for Richard's returning perhaps to America, the site of the losses he reveals.

As foregrounded in the novel's title, many related kinds of lust impact the characters' development and well-being. Richard describes himself as "all greed and lust and hunger" and "not confused, ever ... until confusion entered [his] life" by way of Rachel's suicide (209). References to the modernist "industrial lust" of the steel industry during Richard's youth in Pittsburgh (9) are replaced by his sexual lust for third-year sorority girls at

Lovett College (77) and by the "blood-lust" of Richard's sex with Rachel and his hyperbolic, undergraduate existential debates with her (244). Richard's passion includes his "premeditated lust" for Rachel on their first night of love-making (166) becoming — with an appropriate nod to novelist D.H. Lawrence — "Lawrentian love" weeks before their marriage (176, 177), and finally "the fusion of lust, and love, and even tenderness" that ensues (178). In a related, fictional example from Richard's award-winning autobiographical first story, "The Birth of the Blues," "*father and son ... were consumed by lust*" for a woman they encounter during one of his father's maintenance rounds (108; emphasis in orig.). References to lust in the novel develop metonymically as one instance informs the meaning of the next, from "Bruises, bite marks — call it Pittsburgh love" (177), until Richard thwarts lust altogether to foster the "salvation" he seeks (216, 228, 246).

Speaking of *Lusts* in a 1988 interview by J.R. (Tim) Struthers, Blaise equates various kinds of lust with "sin" (Blaise in Struthers). Reflecting on Richard, Blaise says, "while I don't think of him as a moral monster, I do think of him as eventually responsible for the death of his wife. He does need redemption. Lust is a sin and I felt very strongly that he was a sinner, even though it was never clear to him why he was a sinner" (Blaise in Struthers). Much later, traumatized after Rachel's death and with *thanatos* replacing *eros*, Richard explains that the death of a subsequent spouse, Leela Mehta, "made of me a kind of brahmachari, a priest. She has ended my lusts" (240). Thus Richard describes his state from "the celibate sands of Rajasthan" (220) near the conclusion of his correspondence with scholar Rosie Chang as being without lusts, as if he has worked through the drivenness of his past before she arrives to visit him in India.

In the following discussion I analyze *Lusts* first by employing the toolbox of narratology, which I apply for illustrating the protagonists' strategy of seeking understanding. I reflect secondly on the novel as an example of Suzette Henke's notion of "scriptotherapy" in order to unravel its method of recollecting a traumatic event. Finally I conclude by considering the text as a model for the story's protagonists, author, and reader to move onwards from loss by imagining a self-aware and creative future.

Traumatic Loss and Biographical Writing

Richard describes Rachel at the outset of their marriage as "Collaborator in my life's design" (176); design is an important shaping factor in Blaise's novel where architecture (5) and construction and carpentry (10-11, 145, 148-49, 218-19) apply throughout to "writing a biography" (5). Rosie is researching Rachel Isaacs' life-story. Carpentry was Richard's father's work, and its mode of careful planning and execution impacted the son's choice of occupation by leading to his attention to writing craft. Rebelling against the constraints of his father's approach to his trade and his father's dysfunctional union with his mother, Richard describes open design opportunities. Richard seems to appreciate his father's credo, which Richard repeats in his rambling account of family life in Pittsburgh: "measure twice, cut once" (9). However, adolescent protagonist Frank Keeler, from Richard's autobiographical first story circumnavigating the terrain and themes of Richard's youth, lusts after a woman who needs some plumbing done by his father; Keeler has an epiphany impacting his future, in which he reaches an impassioned commitment to openness of form.

Recalling the hand-painted sign "TRADESMEN AND LABORERS" put up by the building superintendent to mark the entry meant for workers, the adolescent protagonist reflects: *"The sign was wondrous to him, a definition of himself he'd never considered. ... Somewhere on that trip a kind of fire rose up in him, and he said in a voice so loud it surprised him, 'I'm going to do things with my life. No one is ever going to tell me where to go. No one but me is going to tell me what to do, ever.'"* (110; emphasis in orig.). The adolescent nature of the protagonist of Richard's story, as revealed by its older narrator in the past tense, includes young Keeler's exaggerated diction. The use of *"wondrous"* and *"ever,"* not to mention the excessive overconfidence of the final declaration by the story's protagonist, as emphasized by the repetition of the word *"me,"* thoroughly undercuts his adolescent self.

Richard's recovery of the past is relayed through Blaise's combination of narrative forms including Richard's first story, "The Birth of the Blues." Disturbing the conventional narrative sequence of beginning, middle, and ending, Blaise's experiment with manipulating time shapes the chronicle of events in ways that impact the reader's experience of Richard's tale of redemption. To produce writing that represents a mode of discovery by author and reader, *Lusts* recommends such a challenge of exploring discourse as that offered up in the aphorism attributed by Blaise to Grace Paley in his essay "Mentors" — "'Write what you don't know about what you know'" (34). The text constantly circles backward as Richard reviews his life for Rosie — the shaping influences of growing up in the American industrial heartland and especially his relationship with Rachel.

Blaise scholar Robert Lecker appreciates the doubleness that manipulation of time — by telling the story of the past while anticipating the future — affords Richard in particular: "Since his narrative is both retrospective and ongoing, Richard is also capable of identifying with two others [Rosie and Rachel] at the same time. Like Rosie, he has become a biographer involved in Rachel's story; like Rachel, he is an author involved in other people's stories and in writing their revenge" (150). Through telling Rachel's story, Richard looks ahead to events that might happen in a future impacted by the past, a future that will follow the presumed eventual meeting of Richard and Rosie, after the novel ends; the inevitability of an intimate relationship between them appears likely when Rosie arrives in India to meet Richard for the first time.[2]

The relationship triangle is reinforced by what Lecker terms "triangular narration" (146), by which the characters write and comment on each other's thoughts and forms of communication. Rosie is writing a book about Rachel, which is the cause of her seeking out Rachel's former spouse, Richard. In their developing connection, Rosie also allows Richard opportunity to process his losses: of Rachel by suicide, and its consequences, as she held an important place in both the successes and the stalling of his writing process. Richard also reveals the death, by disease, of his third wife, research librarian Leela Mehta, whom he met after taking up a writing position at Lovett College, the school where he discovered the relationship between his writing and sexuality.

"[T]riangulat[ing] on Rachel" (*Lusts* 18), Rosie and Richard's letter-writing about Rachel leads to intimacy between them because their insights into Rachel are revealing about her and about each other. After some time, Rosie signs one of her letters "Love" (144), which "stirs" Richard (147), who ends his next letter, "Yours" (147). He describes his expectations of his past relationship with

Rachel in a way that bears on his developing understanding with Rosie: "... I sniffingly insist on being taken
seriously. (I should be using the past tense.)" (196). He
recognizes the way the past shapes the future, and notices in particular through his developing closeness to
Rosie the way the choice of a partner type from his past
has implications for the future. According to Richard, his
third wife, Leela, was "the world's leading authority on
Richard Durgin. ... She was the Rosie Chang of Durgin-
ness" (226-27).

In his "Autobiographical Essay: 1940-1984," Blaise explains that he admires and utilizes "successive layers" of
experience recast through fiction and has learned "how
to frame them" (26). The manipulation of narrative time
for effect (what narratologists call "anachrony")[3] plays
prominently in *Lusts*, and has special importance for the
way it shapes the reader's ranking or balancing of the
significance of events. Discursively announcing an event
before it happens in the real-time of the story world (prolepsis) characterizes Richard's way of telling Rachel's
history and signalling to Rosie, and thus the reader, the
main events of the unfolding plot. His description of
meeting Rachel is therefore both retrospective (that is,
analeptic) and proleptic. Forward-looking prolepsis has
the added effect of creating a sense of the urgency and
inevitability of events relating to Richard's passions for
women and literature.

Concerning the way the line of a person's life impacts
the narrative designs of time and space, Richard draws
out how his and Rachel's personalities were taking form,
which prepared for their inevitable first meeting in the
library of the University of Iowa: "suddenly [in America]
I knew where I was heading, and I knew the shortest way
of getting there. ... Rachel ... was making her own correc-

tion [in Italy] at exactly the same time. All we had to do now was to keep walking straight" (73). Time takes on complex operations in the following huge prolepsis using the future tense, concerning when Richard first met Rachel in Iowa — "And one night about a year and a half from this night I'm describing at Lovett, I too will go to the Iowa Library and spot this girl ... and I'll take a step toward her, and ... as soon as I take that step, I'll be killing her all over again" (120).

Recognizing the power of story itself to prefigure events, using the skills of the storyteller in his letter-exchange with Rosie, Richard grasps the precariousness of Rachel's existence: "So long as we haven't met and married, she's still alive" (120). "We have come to that night" (158), he declares of the time they met in early 1963; "I'm just days now, or maybe hours, from meeting Rachel" (157); then later, he adds, speaking of the events leading to her death, "I'll get to the rampage in a minute" (190). Meta-narratively Blaise, who in his "Autobiographical Essay: 1940-1984," describes himself as "a memorialist" (32) rummaging through his early life experiences for material he repurposes in his writing, seems to be stressing through Richard that the craft of the storyteller is bound to life events which it in turn shapes through sense-making narrative. In Richard's view, the construction metaphor of carpentry developed in the novel draws from life itself. Introducing the notion of "backfilling," he explains to Rosie the way he has regained his own stability following the crisis of Rachel's death: "Let me circle back, Rosie, backfilling as I go, till we come again to that day in January that you want to know so much about. The day that my life balanced on; twenty-nine years of comparative ego buoyancy before it, and these twelve years of dense star-stuff since" (221).

Thus Richard offers Rosie a frame for grasping the pertinent events of Rachel's infamous career (through his early "ego buoyancy") and after her death (engaging with the fallout from her "star-stuff"). Blaise includes a further, self-reflexive layer to the storytelling process. He conveys storytelling or narrative issues through revealing, intratextual remarks by Richard addressed to Rosie and the reader, who assumes a position of informed expectation close to hers in the end. The ironic gap between Richard and the reader grows as we become familiar with his somewhat self-serving accounts of things, some parts of which Rosie outright challenges. He attributes the symbolism of growth to the avocado he first encountered being grown in bohemian Lovett College where "Avocado plants grew on every window ledge" (74). He clarifies the allegory of the avocado, using the parenthetical style Blaise himself also applies in essays; thus, Richard states: "(I can date the birth of my self-consciousness from the growing of my first avocado…. I date my liberation from the time, years later, when I actually cut up an avocado and ate it, and threw away the pit.)" (74-75).[4] Richard's stated "liberation" can be interpreted ironically since the allegory he introduces of growing something, consuming it, and then throwing away its chances of reproduction reflects Richard's destructive behaviour in his marriage and then his abruptly stopping writing after Rachel's death.

Writing and sexuality are related in Richard's life. After violently arguing with Rachel and sleeping with a woman he meets at the cinema, through "a story, fully formed and worked on as [he] walked" (200), Richard imagines a sequel to "The Birth of the Blues." In the sequel, fictional Frank Keeler encounters his five-years-deceased father, who admonishes his son: "*You shouldn't*

*have pulled up the avocado, Frank. I figured you'd protect
the avocado no matter what. ... Consider closely the women
in our lives.'* (201; emphasis in orig.). Evidenced by his
relationship with Rosie evolving through their correspondence, Richard needs writing to process loss in his
life, whether it be, in his early career, the loss of his father
and Pittsburgh or, later, the loss of his first wife, Rachel.

Richard returns to the ambiguous promise of lustful
abandon decades later with Rosie, who insists that his
youthful love with Rachel and others, represented by the
allegorical avocado pit, be recovered — not wasted. Pur-
suing the past is important because Rachel's and Richard's writing needs were so intimately tied to one
another. The text includes fictional peritextual material
in the form of Rachel's poetry, namely her "kaddish" or
Jewish prayer of mourning (211), which is how she describes her never-published poem "The Filmmaker's
Daughter" that she reads to Richard. The poem underscores one of the novel's important themes about the
dangerous nature for Rachel of the forgetfulness of
American culture, represented in her father's film work
and in Richard's previously noncircumspect, inattentive
enjoyment of American entertainment.

Life and Art, Mimesis and Diegesis

Rachel's poem "The Filmmaker's Daughter" (209-11) and
Richard's story "The Birth of the Blues" (97-110) have
intratextual implications for Rosie's and the reader's interpretation of the events Richard reports, as well as for
those familiar with Blaise's *oeuvre* who recognize "The
Birth of the Blues," later placed by Blaise at the opening
of his *Pittsburgh Stories* (2001). The use of "The Birth of

the Blues" in these two contexts — one attributed to the author and another to a fictional character of his — demonstrates the extent to which Blaise's claims in his "Autobiographical Essay: 1940-1984" that "I am an autobiographical writer" (16), that "I loved Pittsburgh, and I hope I have done justice to it in *Lusts* and *Lunar Attractions* and several stories" (20-21), apply to interpreting Blaise's retrospective accounting through fiction. In his autobiographical comments Blaise emphasizes the contrasts in Pittsburgh that were productive for him as a writer: "It is a city of natural confluences, ethnic and establishment, sports and intellect, working-class and upper-management" (20).

The "natural confluences" of Pittsburgh extend to *Lusts*'s design of using a wide and diverse range of cultural comparisons for grasping Richard's and Rachel's literary work. These on-the-surface disparate intercultural references include, amongst others, the 1955 Bengali film directed by Satyajit Ray, *Pather Panchali* (*Lusts* 114, 116), University of Iowa Writers' Workshop instructor and fiction writer Philip Roth (151 ff.), the 1962 French film directed by François Truffaut, *Jules and Jim* (181, 200), Dylan Thomas's poem "A Refusal to Mourn ..." (202), and, importantly for the climax of the plot, the *Hogan's Heroes* television series (242 ff.).[5] It is possible that encountering this American "'stupid comedy show'" (242), as Richard describes it to Rachel (242), drives Rachel over the edge to suicide. On the night before her suicide when the show comes on television, she asks Richard: "'What is this thing?'" — to which he replies, "'It's called *Hogan's Heroes*. I doubt that it rhymes with anything.'" (242). "'Bergen's Belsens,' she mumbled" (242), referring to the Bergen-Belsen Nazi concentration camp. "Then she snapped her fingers in a frenzied little ditty, like a fifties rock song, 'Who put the cream, in the crematorium?'" (242). Arguably, this final verbal exchange between Richard and Rachel accentuates their differences and the incommensurability of her second-generation Holocaust memory to the farcical, bland nostalgia engineered by the American entertainment industry, from which her father sought to shield her.

In his letter-correspondence with Rosie, Richard accounts to himself for Rachel's suicide. "In fairness to myself (that's what this ... is all about, isn't it?)" (182), he concludes in retrospect over a decade after her death: "What can I say, Rosie? I was hurt and I was bitter, and deep down I probably resented her sudden fame, purchased, I thought, in ignorance of America. If she didn't know *Hogan's Heroes*, she didn't know me, either; if she couldn't swallow back that kind of gall, she couldn't cope with the years to come" (242). Richard's grappling with his previous jealousy over Rachel's success contributes to his recovery from her death. Further, recognizing the role of cultural differences that impeded his and Rachel's mutual understanding encourages self-reflexivity as part of his recovery.

Rachel's not comprehending the historical context of *Hogan's Heroes* (1965-71) interpreted as American anti-Vietnam War satire or being able to process the entertainment value of its being set at a safe distance for American viewers in a German Second World War prisoner of war camp is her final breaking point. It also provides an explanation of her failure to accommodate to America, thus possibly reducing Richard's culpability for Rachel's demise by the end of the story when her suicide is described. Caruth characterizes trauma as a "wound of the mind" (4), though at the time of impact one is usually not aware of the extent of psychological injury by a traumatizing event: "the way it was precisely *not known* in the first instance ... returns to haunt the survivor later on" (4; emphasis in orig.). Caruth's description of the double consciousness in trauma stories clarifies Richard's struggle toward recovery after Rachel's death. According to Caruth, there is "a kind of double telling, the oscillation between a *crisis of death* and the correlative *crisis of life*: between the story of the unbearable nature of an event and the story of the unbearable nature of its survival" (7; emphasis in orig.).

How the past is recovered and applied in the present symptomatically affects future survival. Habermas sees danger in "systematically distorted communication," which would include Richard's initial inability to admit responsibility for Rachel's suicide and the entertainment industry's way of preventing engagement with the destructive past, which could then potentially repeat itself in recurrent, damaging ways (Habermas, "On Systematically"). Before meeting Richard, Rachel had attempted to compensate for her lack of rootedness in American popular culture by immersing herself during her early twenties in culturally and socially grounded Italian neorealist film. By comparison, *Lusts* takes account of what popular culture such as an introduction to Hollywood film can and cannot prepare one for. She was "kept ... ignorant of America" (27) by her father's preventing her from seeing Hollywood films to age fifteen. Ben-Zwi Eisachs, Rachel's father, acknowledged by Richard as "a traditional Weimar intellectual" (26), denied her access to the standardization reproduced by American film that he knew well through working in the industry as "a shlock scriptwriter" (26). Perhaps her lacking this standardization that Richard views as offering a "vaccinat[ion] ... against America"

(242) fostered her inability to cope with the entertainment industry's mundane relationship to the Holocaust and thus furthered her demise.

Blaise casts Richard and Rosie as protagonists who correspond through letters, ostensibly about their shared interest in Rachel's life, work, and suicide. Their getting to know one another occurs through a searching letter-writing exchange over many months discussing various issues involving Rachel, including the particular inadaptability of Rachel Isaacs to American culture. *Lusts* utilizes a cluster of narrative components working together — biography, autobiography, epistolary novel, short story, poetry, film, psychoanalytic historiography, and allegory — to demonstrate the complex relationship between fictional forms and life-writing. The characters pursue distinct narrative approaches to life-writing. From Rosie, "In a disguised way, it's my story too. I'm writing my autobiography in a quiet sort of way, through her [Rachel's] life" (5); and, "I am writing a biography of Rachel's life, incorporating your [Richard's] autobiography and a little of my own — and together we might be writing a novel" (50). Richard's text is "a novel-despite-itself" (141) in Rosie's view — notably in form, as he writes in a laconic, storytelling style: for example, from his first words to Rosie, "A long time ago, in a country far, far away, I was married to Rachel Isaacs" (3); to "in the beginning" (33); to "and it will come to pass" (184); and "There comes a time" (196). Retaining the obscuring distinction between autobiography and biography for his and Rosie's letter-writing, Richard describes the resulting epistolary form: "These pages I've been sending you — they aren't a novel, and they're not quite an autobiography either" (217).

Manipulating time, tense, and person adds to *Lusts*'s novelistic aura because it opens up gaps between what is known and what can be known by the narrator, principally Richard, and by his creator Blaise. Similarities between Blaise's and Richard's own formative life stories, including Blaise's actual publication of fictional Richard's award-winning first story, "The Birth of the Blues," as the first story in Blaise's later collection *Pittsburgh Stories* (2001), again accentuate the role of autobiographical experience in his writing. Yet as Blaise remarks in his "Autobiographical Essay: 1940-1984," "You see how dull real autobiography can be. ... My first four books of fiction — the two story collections and the two novels — were scatsongs on a jangling but still intact pool of memories or linked possibilities from the life I had led" (10). By contrast to closer-to-the-facts "real autobiography," the novel's orchestrated, variable time sequence in the fictional account reinforces gaps that reveal unresolved ambiguity and invite interpretation. In terms of Rachel's death, the story is not only being told retrospectively by Richard, but is being composed from a distance of time and place — in Faridpur, Rajasthan, India (in 1982) — for Rosie, "a professor at Berkeley" (*Lusts* 18), who is researching Rachel's life and specifically trying to answer the question, "Why did she kill herself...?" (6).

Blaise, in his "Autobiographical Essay: 1940-1984," says he "escape[d] from all [his] subjectivity" (17) by experiencing India through his wife, the Bengali-born fiction writer Bharati Mukherjee. Similarly, it is from India that Richard slowly confronts the iconic visual traumatic memory of finding Rachel's drowned body in the bathtub of their apartment. The fact that it is Richard's letter-writing that largely permits his psychological recovery can be seen as illustrating Suzette Henke's argument in *Shattered Subjects* for transforming iconic visual and auditory traumatic memories through "scriptotherapy," a method devised to replace Freud's "talking cure" (xi-xii). She defines scriptotherapy as "the process of writing out and writing through traumatic experience in the mode of therapeutic reenactment" (xii). As the novel proceeds, Richard reveals that Rachel drowned herself (*Lusts* 143), "opening her veins" (145), "in January 1968" (208). Delaying the narration of the details of Rachel's death and the presence of Richard in the apartment with her, though unaware at that moment, he says, of her drowning herself, replicates for the reader the effect for Richard of the traumatic moment of discovering her. Yet through Richard and Rosie's taking account of the past, the reader —unlike Richard when he discovered Rachel's drowned body—has been prepared by this point late in the novel to assess the traumatic events of Rachel's death and to probe Richard and Rosie's various conclusions about it.

When Richard addresses his thoughts to Rosie in extended-letter form, she responds based on her inclinations and on her scholarly preparation, including having read some archival material yet inaccessible to Richard. Richard concedes in appropriately Freudian language, "Maybe I'm projecting all this from the perspective of twenty years, and from my own life, deep in the heart of a supreme otherness" (87). And he also uses the word "trauma" to describe being married (after Rachel and before Leela) to drug-addicted Digger (220). The name Digger is a possible allusion to the construction metaphor and the work of "backfilling"—as Richard describes his narrative method (221, 232). Trauma is reflected in his narrative style of layering salient details, but "withholding

... till the end" exactly how Rachel died (250). So the reader discovers in retrospect from a distance in India that, according to Richard, while his father's death from cancer in Pittsburgh allowed Richard to leave the city of his up-bringing and permitted his writing career to begin else-where, Rachel's traumatizing death took his creative outlet through writing away (95). Emphasizing the import-ance of disruptive or traumatic plot events, he underscores for himself and arguably also for Blaise "such a contin-gency" of "sharp, sudden, unforeseen breaks," of "falls, bubbles, and crashes" that brought him to India (145).

By way of answering her question "Why," Rosie de-veloped a "thesis" about the event of Rachel's suicide: the suicide was on account of "the final collision" between Rachel's individual "innocence" and twentieth-century historical "catastrophe" (249-50), and the collision was to a certain extent to be expected as "... Rachel's story is 'the story of a generation'" (Lecker 146, citing *Lusts* 5). But Ri-chard probes further; attempting to reduce his culpabil-ity for her demise, he quips: "Reality confusion is fatal. ... She was a reality junkie, and she died of an overdose" (*Lusts* 28). Put otherwise and offering an explanation of why writing could not save her in this instance, he elabor-ates: "When the past and the future clamp together in one fused moment, they can kill you. When they just graze you like a bat's wing, we can call them poems. They came together one day for Rachel" (45) in a collision watching *Hogan's Heroes* that Richard said to Rachel does not rhyme with anything (242). By suggesting "Bergen's Bel-sens," Rachel was trying to find a rhyme or some similar symmetry in the representation of World History in the American television account of a World War Two pris-oner of war camp. Instead, Richard determines, *Hogan's Heroes* "provided ... proof that the European millions had died in vain, and that her country and her times were incapable of absorbing the lesson" (245).

In art and life, Richard concludes with specific reference to murder like the Holocaust, "we're incapable of stopping it. ... (That's what killed her.)" (125). Richard speaks of "blind, undiminished life" as "the one thing Rachel Isaacs didn't have and couldn't get" (46), through her projections onto him or elsewhere. He declares an identity—"Let's call it Self" (46)—perhaps equatable to the autonomous ego, Freud's post-therapy notion of ontological security in the world.[6] As Rosie observes, using Freudian language, Rachel saw in Richard a form of "the naked ego struggl[ing] in the world"—"an allegory of modern resistance" (143). Part of Richard's guilt that leads him to reflect at length on events of his past with Rachel through exchanging letters with Rosie is his sense that he was not cognizant of his vital role, of the necessity of his supporting Rachel in this allegory of survival through resistance. In an effort to restore his image publicly, if only to Rosie, he reflects: "All those early critics who accused me of crimes I didn't commit—they were right, for all the wrong reasons" (245). Richard finally admits his culpability: "Not for the crimes I committed, but the help I omitted" (245). He failed to meet both her needs, by being unaware of her deeply felt expectations of him and of her suicide attempted while he was in the apartment. Nevertheless, Richard's self-scrutiny is thoroughgoing. Reviewing his much earlier "campus novel," he says, if he were to write it again, he "would concentrate instead on my selfishness, and my innocence" (55). Thus over the course of the novel Richard's growing awareness of the fateful implications of his failings prepares the way for whatever degree of redemption that the reader ultimately imagines for him.

A Model That Works Intercommunicatively

"... I'm looking for ... justice. My interest is redemption" (3), says Richard in a self-depiction at the start of his letter-writing relationship with Rosie Chang, who, by the end of the novel, infers that he achieves "at least partial redemption" for himself (250). Rosie's final conclusions about Richard's actions in relationship to Rachel's combine in the epilogue with the novel's shift: from first-person perspective with alternating focalization between Rosie and Richard, to an omniscient third-person perspective. The change of perspective reinforces the novel's increasing distance from Richard's ambition to tell Rachel's story through his self-narration. He wants forgiveness from guilt by negligence or omission in regard to Rachel's death, but also requires a return to writing, by which he earlier reconciled his relationship to his upbringing specifically in Pittsburgh and generally in America. Any future after the novel depends on his returning home to America from India: "If I am healed, I have to return someday" (219).

Poet Rachel Isaacs needed her spouse, Richard Durgin, who after her death became a college English instructor, then carpenter, to be something more or other than he offered. She was acutely aware of the way culture is bound by expectations and limitations that one is necessarily complicit in through relationships and work. Richard, by a process of narrative recovery through making up her past and his, grasps her second-generation Holocaust trauma and conjectures how he failed to be a sufficient partner to her and thus to prevent her suicide. Discussion of limitations extends also to Rachel's capacity artistically for historical accounting: in Richard's assessment, "A major artist with the compulsive theme of the Holocaust must eventually find a new language and a new form, and I don't know if an American writing in English can hope to do it" (81). Richard continues: "Great fiction, I believe, is healthy and aggressive—it extends reality. A novel should be a living cell of the entire social and individual organism. If we perish and future generations uncover only one artifact, and it is a good novel, they should be able to clone our century from it. ... By those standards, I would except Rachel from greatness; the work is too defensive" (81). Accordingly, he dismisses her "star-stuff" (221) valued through terms of American cultural consumption. A related interpretive question arises as to whether Blaise's American-published novel *Lusts* would satisfy Richard's high goal of finding a new language and form.

Blaise's own narrative style may be equal to the standard Richard set for Rachel of finding a method that is both contemporaneous and historical. *Lusts*'s gathering together in the novel aspects of biography, autobiography, epistolary novel, short story, poetry, film (in the parenthetical "voice-overs"), psychoanalytic historiography, and allegory invites discussion of the significance of merging such a variety of communicative modes, which already reflect expectations of genre, as a means of attempting to "find a new language and a new form," an endeavour that Richard Durgin contends a major American artist embracing historical themes must strive to carry out. The combined effect of Richard's merging forms is a "confluence" that Blaise values from his Pittsburgh upbringing and retains in the design of his fiction writing.

Disparate forms and genres reflect facets of Blaise's personal background and interests. Autobiography accentuates the link between Richard's life and his writing,

and is the vehicle for Richard's self-understanding. Concerning his award-winning story, Richard grasps, "I had
linked up with a past [in Pittsburgh] and I'd cleared out
the future" (96). While Caruth and Henke describe revisiting the past as a mechanism for overcoming personal trauma, Holocaust literary critic Daniel R. Schwarz
would recommend the further ethical promise of Freudian "backfilling" that Richard develops in respect of
Holocaust memory (Schwarz, "The Ethics"). As Dominick LaCapra has noted, in German newspapers in the
1980s Jürgen Habermas debated with Ernst Nolte this
issue of how to incorporate Holocaust memory in the
historical record, Habermas saying that the historical
measure had to be inclusive, not restrictive, in order to
prevent the Nazi fascist past from potentially repeating
itself (LaCapra, "Revisiting"). Bearing guilt for the past,
but on a personal level, Richard is trying to be open in
his account given to Rosie. Consequently *Lusts*, even in
its open-endedness, suggests that Richard's relationship
with Rosie may exceed the scope and possibilities of his
first three failed marriages.

Finding promise in loss, and articulating that potential through a range of on-the-surface discordant forms
and material is part of Blaise's method that Catherine
Sheldrick Ross recognizes in his first two story collections: "The stories are not so much plots as they are ar-
rangements of materials held together by a human voice
or presence. A juxtaposition of details achieves significance in relation to some cataclysmic and transforming
event" (xxii). *Lusts* ends with not all of the irony concerning Richard's self-perception resolved, but nevertheless
on a note of promise that Richard will find in person
with Rosie an opportunity to fulfill his "lusts" for women

and writing, because these have now been redefined by his renewed introspection achieved through letter-writing across distance and time. Blaise's feat in this novel is his use of the plot device of a simple love story between Richard and Rosie as the vehicle for surveying the dependent social and personal layers of Rachel and Richard's twentieth-century failures and achievements, themselves revealed through a range of appropriately integrated narrative forms.

Notes

1. For Freud's scepticism over the limits of psychoanalysis, see *Civilization and Its Discontents*; for criticism of the social application of psychoanalysis, see Jacoby.

2. Lecker concurs with this assumption that is understood, but never stated: in Lecker's words, "The epilogue finds him awaiting Rosie Chang's visit to him in India — a visit that testifies to his willingness to speak of what is past (his story of Rachel), passing (the story of his life in Faridpur), and to come (the anticipation of his future relationship with Rosie, which the narrative foreshadows in terms of rosy change)" (141).

3. For a discussion of anachrony, see Genette 35-47 and Fludernik 34, 43-44.

4. For examples of the parenthetical aside as a layering devise of Blaise's prose, see for example, "[My] third [story], 'Relief'..., concerns the same shanty-settlement on the shores of Lake Harris, this time during the confusion of a hurricane's passing. (Is this the time to acknowledge the bravery of editors who take a chance on beginners? James Boatwright has published five of my stories; I owe

him a lot and have met him, very briefly, only once.)"
(Blaise, "Autobiographical Essay: 1940-1984" 22). And,
emphasizing a future in the retrospective style of story
that we see in *Lusts*, "(It would take five years before I
composed those elements in a story, 'Grids and Doglegs';
if I had tried it as an undergraduate — and probably I did
— it would have come out like warm, flat soda water.)"
(Blaise, "Mentors" 35).

5. Intercultural references in the novel are strikingly varied
    and rich, such as singer Perry Como (13), actor June Ally-
    son (23), George Eliot and Thackeray, Lewis Carroll and
    Raymond Chandler (25), actor Annette Funicello (25),
    Mighty Mouse (26), Thomas Mann (27), John Crowe Ran-
    som (76), Kafka (81), singer Joan Baez (160), Dante and
    Tarzan (161), actor Ernest Borgnine (179), Neil Simon and
    fictional character Humbert Humbert from Nabokov's
    Lolita (229). This list, of course, is meant to be repre-
    sentative, not exhaustive.

    Lecker makes insightful reference to the Dylan Thom-
    as poem "A Refusal to Mourn ..." that represents, for Ri-
    chard, "'a personal code of honor'" so far as Rachel's mem-
    ory is concerned (140-41; Lecker is quoting *Lusts* 202)
    — and the W.B. Yeats poem "Sailing to Byzantium" that
    suggests Richard's position in India involves "creating
    monuments to his own magnificence ... while he sings of
    'what is past, or passing, or to come'" (151; Lecker is here
    quoting Yeats).

6. See *The Ego and the Id* and the chapter on psychoanalytic
    transference in *Introductory Lectures on Psychoanalysis*,
    482-500. In place of psychoanalytic therapy culminating
    in transference, Henke advocates writing: "Might the
    therapeutic power of psychoanalysis reside more in the
    experience of 'rememory' and reenactment than in the
    scene of transference posited by Freud?" (xi).

Works Cited

Blaise, Clark. "Autobiographical Essay: 1940-1984." *Selected Essays.* By Clark Blaise. Ed. John Metcalf and J.R. (Tim) Struthers. Windsor, ON: Biblioasis, 2008. 9-32.

-----. "The Birth of the Blues." *Pittsburgh Stories.* Introd. Robert Boyers. Erin, ON: The Porcupine's Quill, 2001. 15-25. Vol. 2 of *The Selected Stories of Clark Blaise.* 4 vols. 2000-06.

-----. *Lusts.* Garden City, NY: Doubleday, 1983.

-----. "Mentors." *Selected Essays.* By Clark Blaise. Ed. John Metcalf and J.R. (Tim) Struthers. Windsor, ON: Biblioasis, 2008. 33-41.

Caruth, Cathy. *Unclaimed Experience: Trauma, Narrative, and History.* Baltimore: The Johns Hopkins UP, 1996.

Fludernik, Monika. *An Introduction to Narratology.* Trans. Patricia Häusler-Greenfield and Monika Fludernik. London: Routledge, 2009.

Freud, Sigmund. *Civilization and Its Discontents.* Trans. and ed. James Strachey. New York: W.W. Norton, 1962.

-----. *The Ego and the Id.* Trans. Joan Riviere. Rev. James Strachey. London: Hogarth, 1962. The International Psycho-Analytical Library 12.

-----. *Introductory Lectures on Psychoanalysis.* Trans. James Strachey. Harmondsworth, Eng.: Penguin, 1973. Vol. 1 of The Pelican Freud Library. 15 vols.

Genette, Gérard. *Narrative Discourse: An Essay in Method.* Trans. Jane E. Lewin. Ithaca, NY: Cornell UP, 1980.

Habermas, Jürgen. "On Systematically Distorted Communication." *Inquiry* 13 (1970): 205-18.

-----. "Towards a Theory of Communicative Competence." *Inquiry* 13 (1970): 360-75.

Henke, Suzette A. *Shattered Subjects: Trauma and Testimony in Women's Life-Writing.* New York: St. Martin's, 1998.

Jacoby, Russell. *Social Amnesia: A Critique of Conformist*

Psychology from Adler to Laing. Boston: Beacon, 1975.

LaCapra, Dominick. "Revisiting the Historians' Debate: Mourning and Genocide." *History and Memory after Auschwitz.* Ithaca, NY: Cornell UP, 1998. 43-72.

Lecker, Robert. *An Other I: The Fictions of Clark Blaise.* Toronto: ECW, 1988.

Ross, Catherine Sheldrick. "Biocritical Essay." *The Clark Blaise Papers: First Accession and Second Accession: An Inventory of the Archive at The University of Calgary Libraries.* Comp. Marlys Chevrefils. Ed. Jean F. Tener and Apollonia Steele. Calgary: The U of Calgary P, 1991. xiii-xxxi. "Clark Blaise: Biocritical Essay." Special Collections, University of Calgary Libraries and Cultural Resources. 25 Oct. 2006. Web. 15 Dec. 2013. <http://www.asc.ucalgary.ca/ node/826>. Rpt. (rev.) as "Clark Blaise: The First Fifty Years, 1940-1990" in *Clark Blaise: Essays on His Works.* Ed. J.R. (Tim) Struthers. Toronto: Guernica Editions, 2016. Essential Writers.

Schwarz, Daniel R. "The Ethics of Reading Elie Wiesel's *Night.*" *Imagining the Holocaust.* New York: St. Martin's, 1999. 45-73.

Struthers, J.R. (Tim). "Expressions of Your Breath: An Interview with Clark Blaise." Guelph, ON. 12 Nov. 1988. Collection of the interviewer, J.R. (Tim) Struthers. Ts. 28 pp. *Clark Blaise: The Interviews.* Ed. J.R. (Tim) Struthers. Toronto: Guernica Editions, 2016. Essential Writers. Print.

Revisiting Clark Blaise and Bharati Mukherjee's *The Sorrow and the Terror: The Haunting Legacy of the Air India Tragedy*

Dalbir Singh

> *He seeks at least*
> *Upon the last and sharpest height,*
> *Before the spirits fade away,*
> *Some landing place, to clasp and say,*
> *"Farewell! We lose ourselves in light."*
>
> —Alfred, Lord Tennyson, *In Memoriam*, Poem 47

This verse is quoted at the beginning of Clark Blaise and Bharati Mukherjee's fiercely evocative and deeply poignant nonfiction book entitled *The Sorrow and the Terror: The Haunting Legacy of the Air India Tragedy* ([viii]). Previously, the verse was cited with one emendation by two men whose children and wives were lost on the fateful day of June 23, 1985. They changed a line to read, "Our children were lost in light" ([viii]). Blaise and Mukherjee's text delves into what has been termed the worst terrorist atrocity to have occurred during that particular time period. Considered to be Canada's 9/11, the bombing of Air India Flight 182 resulted in the deaths of 329 people, many of whom were women and children. In the

335

present era, we are inundated with reports of the type of terrorism that sprang forth at the beginning of the twenty-first century with the bombing of the World Trade Center towers. However, Canada in the mid-1980s hadn't experienced such a terrorist tragedy (of such large proportions) before and was thoroughly unprepared for the fallout of such an event as evidenced by the immense evidence culled for *The Sorrow and the Terror*. Although I, like other Canadians of my generation, had grown up with the spectre of the Air India bombing looming over my childhood via news reports, there was another reason why I was so intrigued at an early age by the tragedy. I recognized the men that had been charged with conspiracy to bomb the Air India flight, but it wasn't because I knew them on a personal level. As a child who grew up within a Sikh household, for me it was rare to encounter images of my community in the media. I initially remember noticing images of Sikh men in the news reports about the terrorist bombing because they superficially appeared to be like many familiar figures from my own extended family.

It was only sometime later that I recognized that the men were a far cry from my familial connections. Although they appeared to be familiar, their religious fundamentalism set them apart. It's unfortunate that many of my initial memories of Sikhs in the media were produced by this particular tragedy. Owing to the lack of positive portrayals of Sikhs in the media, it was easy for the general public to correlate the Sikh community with issues of barbarism and terrorism—a not completely foreign concept as reflected in the debates concerning Islamophobia and media portrayals. I first encountered Blaise and Mukherjee's book while working on a play I wrote entitled *Your Palace in the Sky: The Bombing of*

Air India Flight 182 for the SummerWorks Performance
Festival in Toronto in 2005, marking the twentieth anniversary of the crash. *The Sorrow and the Terror* was in-
strumental in my conducting research for the play as the
book examined the many issues that surrounded the
tragedy and provided an exact factual account of what
transpired as well as the reverberations it had in general
for the victims' families and the Canadian government.
The authors have provided the general public with an
excellent informed study of a tragedy that still lingers in
the national memory. Part of the nuanced approach to
the subject matter that the authors present is achieved
through the book's economically and intricately presented structure. The structure's form isn't entirely dis-
similar to the collections of short stories for which Blaise
is typically more renowned. In fact, each of the book's
five parts is divided into generally five or six chapters
and feels like an entirely different narrative, with each
part devoted to a separate subject though one connected
to and supporting the enterprise as a whole.

The initial section of *The Sorrow and the Terror* deals
with the events leading up to the crash. The second part
is focussed primarily on the immediate aftermath of the
crash. The third section is devoted to the victims' families and their stories. The eventual salvage operation
and the development of the trial process as well as a description of the terrorists involved form the basis of the
fourth section. The concluding part focusses on the
much larger political context involving the origins of
fundamentalist activity in Punjab, India and the ramifi-
cations of the Air India tragedy for the Canadian government. Each section is so informed with background,
context, insight, and knowledge of the particular subject
matter that it could form an entire book on its own. It is

to the credit of Blaise and Mukherjee that all of these
disparately complex elements are succinctly distilled to
their essences. The effectiveness narratively, indeed dramatically, of their structural configuration of the Air India
story demands attention on its own terms. I will therefore present my thoughts about each part accordingly.

***

The first section appropriately begins with some context. Prior to the bombing of Air India Flight 182, there
were major incidents in India that precipitated the emer-
gence of further atrocities. Blaise and Mukherjee trace
the root of the conflict to the aftermath of Operation
Blue Star, an initiative undertaken by then Prime Minister Indira Gandhi to weed out the Khalistani (Sikh sep-
aratist) leadership that had overtaken and enshrined
themselves within the Golden Temple complex (the most
venerated holy shrine in the Sikh religion). The damage
accrued by the Golden Temple aroused great consternation and anger within the Sikh population, and as a result Gandhi would soon be assassinated by her Sikh
bodyguards. While Blaise and Mukherjee recount the
creation of Operation Blue Star in some detail later in
the book, much attention is given in the first section to
a pogrom that occurred in retaliation for the Prime Minister's assassination. Although the term 'genocide' is never
uttered by the authors, the pogrom was essentially a
genocidal act performed by portions of the predominantly Hindu populace in which "2,700 Sikhs were killed
in the three nights[...]. The brutal tales of stonings, rapes
and torture deaths are as graphic as any in this century's
repertory of horrors" (5).

The authors remark upon this horrific pogrom to highlight how the Air India bombing arose out of a series of tragic events that rocked the Indian communities both at home and within its diaspora. The authors then move on to discuss how the Khalistani terrorists began hatching their plans to exact revenge on an unassuming people; their targeting of the Air India plane served as an extension of targeting a national symbol of the Indian government itself. The reader is then introduced to the facts pertaining to the plane's takeoff and the luggage that carried the fateful bomb. It's important to note that, although Air India Flight 182 suffered the most casualties, another plane was also targeted. CP Air Flight 003 was also carrying a bomb that exploded at Narita Airport in Japan killing two young baggage handlers. The first section concludes by focussing on the immediate pre-crash scene inside the Air India plane: "Breakfast had just been served, and people were moving about in the cabin. One can imagine the commotion. The passengers were mainly women and children. There were eighty-four children aboard, typical of summertime flights to India from North America — particularly this flight, the first after school closing" (34). This is a very effective narrative strategy that the authors deploy here as they do throughout the book. The description includes the facts of what occurred, but collects them together in a way that imparts to the reader what it would have been like aboard this plane at this particular time of year. No embellishment is needed or given. We appreciate and, more importantly, we experience the horror of a plane full of children, excited about the prospects of a summer holiday, away from the confines of school. "[C]ommotion" is all that's said to suggest how the flight most likely was proceeding before the crash. The narrative reads like a Charles Reznikoff poem in which the 'facts' of historical tragedies and traumas are so evocatively framed by the author that the reader recreates them imaginatively.

***

The Sorrow and the Terror's second section highlights the immediate aftermath of the bombing. We are led from the initial realization that the plane disappeared off the coast of Ireland to the recovery and identification of the fallen bodies to the arrival of the victims' families in Cork, Ireland. One of my earliest recollections of the Air India tragedy was as a child watching grainy black-and-white footage shot from inside a rescue helicopter. We see a rescuer hauling up the body of a lifeless young male child. That image has since haunted me — even still as I write this — thirty years after the crash. Perhaps it's because that young child looked just like me at that age, like my younger brother or my cousins. That child could have been any one of us had our parents decided to take a flight to India to visit relatives or go on vacation. But more importantly, it was a reflection of such a young child's life, one of eighty-four whose existences were cut abruptly and wretchedly short as a result of geo-political machinations in which they had had no part.

The authors detail what the recovery process looked like to the young Irish sailors who had never seen such a nightmarish scene as this — an ocean littered with floating and bobbing naked bodies. One particular sailor recalled the victims' faces: "'Sometimes the decompression had flattened the bones. Sometimes you looked into the face and it was only ... like a shell. The eyes were gone, the back of the head was gone. You looked in the face and you saw blue sky behind ..." (49; ellipses in orig.). Besides an onslaught of sharks that had started appearing at the crash site, there were other pressing issues involving the facilitating of victims' families as well as the process of identifying the bodies at Cork Regional Hospital. Blaise and Mukherjee emphasize in exact detail the logistics of a small hospital having to contend suddenly with a major tragedy. What's fascinating about the authors' narrative strategy is that one complication is added on top of another so that by the end of the book we realize just how complex and convoluted the issues surrounding the Air India bombing really are. The identification of the victims' bodies is one example; it wasn't simply a matter of ensuring victims were named.

As the authors point out, the identification process became inundated with questions about the precise cause of death. For instance, it was revealed that a "boy had died of shock and haemorrhage. But the moistness of the lungs [...] suggested [...] the boy might have drowned. [...] If the boy had drowned, he had hit the water alive. He may have been unconscious at that point, but in the context of lawsuits, his being 'alive' brings up the question of possible consciousness, and the chance that he had suffered unimaginable pain during the seconds of descent" (60-61). The question of death, then, becomes the catalyst for additional woes and grievances.

***

The third section delves primarily into the victims' families and their testimonials. As a mid-section of sorts for the whole book, this part represents the heart of the volume. The recurrent description of the book's purpose, reflected in interviews given by the authors, is that the text is, first and foremost, dedicated to the many victims and their families. Particular chapters highlight individual family members like Parkash Bedi or Sam Swaminathan, who lost their entire families in the crash. These few portraits of specific people affected by the tragedy stand for all the families and friends dealing with grief. Bedi's story is doubly heart-breaking on account of its lack of closure. The authors emphasize memorably that Bedi's daughter's body was never found and "[i]n his mind, Anu remains a missing person who might someday be found" (97). It's a poignant reflection that thirty years since the tragedy, the weight of grief would still linger over the lives of all those who have suffered through great loss.

These testimonials also provide glimpses into some of the victims' lives. One such example follows the lives of the Laurence sisters — Shyamala Jean and Krithika Nicola, aged eighteen and sixteen, respectively: "They were honour roll students and tutors at Applewood Heights Secondary School, winners of civic awards and Canada Council grants, holders of the *Natya Visarad* (Great Dancer) title. They were young Canadian high-achievers featured on the CBC program *Going Great*. Over the last four years of their young lives, they gave more than 300 *Bharat Natyam* [classical Indian dance] recitals in school gyms and civic halls and church basements, and through dance brought home to suburban families (in soothing, even flattering, ways) the multicultural reality of the nation" (110). It is here that the authors superimpose their own feelings concerning the intrinsic connection between 'Indianness' and 'Canadianness' and the ability of each to cross-pollinate and affect the other beneficially in a myriad number of ways.

***

We arrive at a consideration of the fourth section, in which Blaise and Mukherjee outline the parameters of bungled RCMP undercover operations, faulty airport X-ray luggage monitors, and the terrorists' own clumsy mistakes conducted in preparation for the mass killing of innocent civilians. What's most surprising about this part of *The Sorrow and the Terror* is that it forms a kind of antithesis to the preceding section. Whereas Part Three provided an empathetic gaze toward those who have enormously suffered, the fourth section analyzes the facts of salvage operations and the aforementioned mechanical and human errors that, compounded, helped to create the tragedy. On numerous occasions the authorities could have done more, the authors contend, to have curtailed the escalation of the terrorists' actions.

In one particular chapter of Part Four, we learn of Blaise and Mukherjee interviewing a man known as 'Sardar' — a completely different portrait than that offered of Parkash Bedi or the Laurence sisters, for example. The authors describe him as "the picture of Canada's 'ideal' immigrant as he strides through the livingroom[...]. Tonight he is a very correct host. In spite of all the rumours of his terrorist involvement, he is also the loving father babysitting his children. His wife is away on business. He's proud of her independence. [...] It is a scene of the starkest, most profound irony. The terrorist as family man. We have spent a winter in Toronto interviewing other family men, now widowed and childless, sitting in their vast, empty houses" (166). The use of contrasts and contradictions between competing narratives and macro vs. micro geo-political contexts supplies the backbone for the text. Nowhere is this more apparent than in the concluding section of the book.

***

Part Five moves past the minor details of the looming court case and individual life stories to a much larger context, examining the root of the Khalistani movement in the Punjab and the Canadian government's role in the aftermath of the Air India tragedy. Repeatedly throughout *The Sorrow and the Terror* the authors admonish the government of then Prime Minister of Canada, Brian Mulroney, for not granting more support to the victims' families. Mulroney placing a call to the Prime Minister of India, to express his condolences for *their* loss, speaks volumes as to the manner in which this tragedy was framed. Even though most of the citizens on board the fateful flight were Canadian citizens, somehow they were still deemed to be 'Indian' and not overtly 'Canadian'. This notion is underlined by the fact that there was a significant delay in sending a Canadian government representative to Ireland to be with the grieving families and to offer support.

***

That slight is still palpably felt by the victims' families to this day. One of the concluding chapters in *The Sorrow and the Terror* explicitly deals with how and why this event should be considered a Canadian tragedy and not a 'foreign affair'. Once "Canadian Secretary of State for External Affairs Joe Clark heard the petitions of bitter relatives in Ireland a week after the Toronto ceremonies [...] he noted [...] that Canada, and not just an obscure appendage called 'Canadians of Indian Origin,' had suffered a terrorist loss" (203). Blaise and Mukherjee are adept at insinuating Canada's much more involved participation in the tragedy but end their narrative with a sobering reflection from Raju Sarangi, one of the bereaved relatives, as he implores, "'Mr. Clark and Mrs. Mukherjee, [...] tell the world how 329 innocent lives were lost and how the rest of us are slowly dying'" (219).

Works Consulted

Alger, Derek. "Clark Blaise." *Pif Magazine*. WordPress, 30 May 2003. Web. 16 Jan. 2015. <http://www.pifmagazine.com/2003/05/clark-blaise/>.

Blaise, Clark, and Bharati Mukherjee. *The Sorrow and the Terror: The Haunting Legacy of the Air India Tragedy*. Markham, ON: Viking-Penguin, 1987. Rpt. with a new introd. by the authors. Markham, ON: Penguin Books Canada, 1988.

Chanda, Tirthankar. "Talking to Bharati Mukherjee." *The Postcolonial Imagination*. Ed. Jean-Pierre Durix. *Commonwealth: Essays & Studies* 18.2 (1996): 56-62.

Lecker, Robert. "Murals Deep in Nature: The Short Fiction of Clark Blaise." *Essays on Canadian Writing* 23 (1982): 26-67. Rpt. in *On the Line: Readings in the Short Fiction of Clark Blaise, John Metcalf and Hugh Hood*. By Robert Lecker. Downsview, ON: ECW, 1982. 17-58.

MacLeod, Alexander. "'Too Canadian for the Americans and too American for the Canadians': An Interview with Clark Blaise." *Essays on Canadian Writing* 79 (2003): 178-90. Rpt. as "Too Canadian for the Americans and Too American for the Canadians: An Interview with Clark Blaise" in *Clark Blaise: The Interviews*. Ed. J.R. (Tim) Struthers. Toronto: Guernica Editions, 2016. Essential Writers.

Moyers, Bill. "Transcript: Bill Moyers Interviews Bharati Mukherjee." *NOW with Bill Moyers*. Public Affairs Television, 20 June 2003. Web. 8 Jan. 2015. <http://www.pbs.org/now/transcript/transcript_mukherjee.html>.

Reznikoff, Charles. *Holocaust*. 1975. Boston: Black Sparrow Books-David R. Godine, 2007.

Wagner, Vit. "Clark Blaise and Bharati Mukherjee." *The Toronto Star*. Toronto Star Newspapers Ltd., 10 June 2011. Web. 15 Jan. 2015. <http://www.thestar.com/entertainment/books/2011/06/10/clark_blaise_and_bharati_mukherjee.html>.

Your Palace in the Sky: The Bombing of Air India Flight 182. By Dalbir Singh. Dir. Chris Dupuis. Palmerston Library Theatre. SummerWorks Performance Festival, Toronto. 5-7, 12-14 Aug. 2005.

Trains and Blaise's *Time Lord*

William Butt

*The release of titanic powers in man through invention
is feared and dreaded at every stage in history....*
— **Northrop Frye, *Words with Power* (295)**

I. Foreword

For a start, consider some texts which document the deep,
persistent fascination of Clark Blaise with trains.

In *I Had a Father: A Post-Modern Autobiography* (1993),
Clark Blaise describes a train that flashed like an appar-
ition through his childhood. The year is 1946, and Clark is
six years old. "Budd Aluminum's 'Train of Tomorrow' came
to Atlanta, and I caught the excitement of streamlined
futurity" (58). He remembers the sleek Art Moderne aero-
dynamic styling, "that straining-at-the-finish-line thrust,
that nose-first lunge" (58). The Train of Tomorrow vision
propelled or compelled him into making art, though not
yet in prose: "I started designing trains on endless sheafs
of my father's letterhead" (58). The elated child became the
adult who in 2000 published the train-infused *Time Lord*.

Later in *I Had a Father*, Blaise tells of researching his
father's family history in Mégantic, Québec. He is reading
a document dated 1898 which marks the change in the
signature of a friend of his father's from 'François' to

'Frank', an anglicizing shift in identity resulting from Québécois emigration to industrial New England — and from the advent of trains. "It was a decade of massive self-transformation after all, the first years of the CPR, the first decade of Mégantic's existence" (136).

Writing of Leon Rooke's stories, Blaise evokes literary history with coinages from three eras of trains and train journeys. First, the civil, decorous, and decorative Victorian: "the old Storyland Limited.... Little stops along the way, quaint stations, scenery like a picture postcard, friendly passengers, velvet banquettes, polished mahogany trim" ("Notes" 157). Then: Modernist. Bleak, stark. The "Twentieth-Century Express" — "They cut the staff, ripped out the upholstery.... Washed-out scenery too — just the backs of tenements" ("Notes" 157). Finally Post-Modern: "the Great Reorganization. Sleek wagons of vinyl and plastic — amazing what they can do with old cattle cars. But confusion reigns. ... No one knows where we are, or the names of towns" ("Notes" 157).

As a writer Blaise melds local rootedness with chronic global travel. Part One of *I Had a Father* he titles "My Life as an Atlas." "I cover the known world" (44), he announces. Trains, like autos and planes, take you places. In Blaise they are a haunting, recurrent, almost obsessive presence. His story "Meditations on Starch" has an enigmatic photo where "A tram snakes off the top of the frame" (124). *Time Lord* is planet-wide in geography, as in time i.e. time zones, because it's a book in large part about trains.

II. Verniers and Collimators

Time Lord is not just about time, though Blaise acknowledges time's theorists from St. Augustine to Stephen Hawking. It is also not just biography of a Lord, Sir Sandford Fleming. Writers from Poe to Pound; movie-makers from Muybridge to Hitchcock; painters from Vermeer to van Gogh to Picasso; instruments technical (theodolite) or theoretical (wrinkle in time); popular culture from Sherlock Holmes to *Star Trek* to the Internet; scientists from Faraday to Heisenberg; the savour of language from Ben Franklin's "'But thou dost love life?'" (42) to nowadays lingo like "multitasker" (61), "networking" (57), "severance package" (125); inventions from reciprocating steam engine to cesium-ion clock; Imperialist history in India, Africa, North and South America; Sandford Fleming's own life amongst a vast gamut of eminent contemporaries; and Blaise's own autobiography, populated by his father and grandfather, and by Jackie Robinson and Martin Luther King—all these and more Blaise lines up in *Time Lord*. (Unless otherwise specified, all citations hereafter of Clark Blaise's work are from *Time Lord*.)

By genre, *Time Lord* is epic. Its purview is the world from creation to conclusion, observed from the point of view of the era of standard time. Blaise's Fleming is anagogic. Blaise might have said, though he doesn't, that Fleming with his railroad vision is like Noah with his ark, Jay MacPherson's "Anagogic Man" in *The Boatman*, who holds "between his nape and crown" "All us and our worlds," "The sun, the stars, the figures of the gods" (56). The entire nameable universe. "We *are* eternal," Blaise proclaims. "Our bodies are the skeletons of dead stars and in the fullness of time we return to our makers" (92).

More than "engineer, visionary, Canadian, Scot, patriot, networker, Empire Loyalist" (49), more than "surveyor, naturalist, scout, meteorologist and geologist" (79), among specialist managers, meteorologists et al. "only Fleming spoke to the world" (105). Blaise quotes Fleming's own proclaiming of his epic-scale ambition: to "'bring the whole worldwide British Empire telegraphic-ally into one neighbourhood'" (137). He writes at length about Fleming's imagined huge chronometer at the centre of the earth: "Standard time is the biggest gauge in the world" (124).

Blaise espies in Fleming's work "the origins of modernism" (176); yet Fleming, time-straddling, also modelled Victorian "vigilant eclecticism" (127), encyclopaedic amateurism at its discerning and synthesizing best. "Call it Victorian modernism" (129). "Breathtaking perspectives ... the result of the new consciousness of time" (157) are what *Time Lord* consists of. Paragraph by wide-flinging paragraph imitates how Fleming's mind worked, "From soaring premise to the rubble of mere detail" (81). Blaise's paragraphs fulfill "The dream of stopping time and shrinking space" (12), "the deliberate restructuring of time and space" (164); they are milestones in a still "unfinished temporal revolution" (165). There is uniform standard time and there is "'natural' thinking" (23), subjective, psychological, cultural time. No scientific theory as yet unites them; but Blaise's paragraphs do. Pages of dignified rational analysis — of Fleming's 1876 paper on "Terrestrial Time" (128-35), Dreiser's *Sister Carrie* (232-37), Gustave Caillebotte's *Paris Street, Rainy Day* (158-64) — plus a modernist "stop-and-go flow of consciousness" (74). "Speed," Blaise says, "eroded traditional morality" (237); in the instance of *Time Lord*, it also has made possible the structure of a new kind of untraditional biography.

Almost any paragraph, page, or chapter of *Time Lord* is a virtuosic scamper, improvisational in texture and feel — zooming through varied spatial settings and fields of human enterprise, forward, back, sidewise in time. The timbre shows up right off in the Foreword, whose first paragraph instances "Naturalists and psychologists" (ix), Daniel J. Boorstin, Robinson Crusoe, and prisoners in the Soviet Gulag. Thereafter, an utterly typical and randomly chosen paragraph plays by association on wrinkles in time, space, and thought (66). Starts with Sandford Fleming in 1872 when appointed CPR Chief Engineer; loops to his 1850 founding of the Canadian Institute; forward to George M. Grant's 1873 book *Ocean to Ocean*; back to Fleming's colleagues J.W. Wood and Thomas D'Arcy McGee and their campaign with Fleming toward Canada's 1867 Confederation; to the 1884 Prime Meridian Conference; to the biography by his friend Lawrence J. Burpee that came out in 1915, the year of Fleming's death.

Besides Fleming himself, Blaise takes for another model "The skinsman in jazz" who, like Blaise on almost every page, "is his own Greenwich, setting the tempo, creating the score freshly with every performance," in an art form where "'time doesn't just pass the way it does as it's defined on a ticking clock or a metronome; it interprets the tempo..., propels you, supports you and it talks to you, ... and you talk with it'" — this last a quotation from Stanley Crouch, the paragraph then surging on to Keats, Whitman, van Gogh and Japanese woodcuts, "Faulkner and Woolf and Proust" (24). Blaise moves as if bopping in air. He quotes E.T.D. Myers on the culture that Fleming lived in and helped create — "'Time was in the air'" — and lets us in on what is no secret, that "Most of *this* book is an application of Myers's ... insight" (104). To Blaise, as to Joyce in *Ulysses*, "Any random day is shown to be, upon close examination, a microcosm of all human history" (*Time Lord* 159). Same for any random sample of Blaise's epic. "[A] brilliant portmanteau" (239).

The Canadian edition of *Time Lord* bears this subtitle:

The Remarkable Canadian Who Missed His Train, and Changed the World. This misfortune happened to Fleming at a railway station in rural Ireland in 1876, consequence of ambiguity that resulted from lack of standardization of time across longitudes. Eight years later, due in part to Fleming's campaigning, worldwide standard time came into effect, and did indeed change the world, in ways that *Time Lord* explores. If rail had not speeded up travel, we wouldn't have needed standard time then; trains made the difference. The vernier, one tool among others for Fleming the engineer, makes visible gradations that are finer than the unaided eye can discern; it can measure at sites and scales where tiny elements may align. The collimator is used to adjust a line of sight, in a telescope say, in order to apply to viewed objects a desired standard, and even in a broad sundry landscape show if they correspond minutely. Blaise cites both instruments in *Time Lord*. He himself applies to his variegated material a sort of imaginative collimator and vernier. Supplemental to *Time Lord*, the rest of this essay applies to the train theme Blaise's engineering method. "When the 'lines of collimation' are connected, uneven surfaces are converted into a precisely rendered grid" (10).

III. Rail Gaze

"As power increases," says Blaise, "so does speed" (17). In Thackeray's *Vanity Fair*, a horse-drawn coach travels "at the rate of four miles an hour" (3). Coaches in Fielding's *Tom Jones*, set a whole century earlier, moved at that same slow pace: "good expedition" by stagecoach was "ninety miles in two days" (531). But trains, Blaise says, ended that natural Tom-Jones-y "easy camaraderie and crude democracy of the stagecoach" (139). Writing *Vanity Fair* in the era of rail, Thackeray with amazement cites "Brighton, which used to be seven hours' distant from London at the time of our story; which is now only a hundred minutes off" (220). George Eliot composing *Middlemarch* in the early 1870s, also well into the rail age, must face life's increased tempo, and adjust her narrative pace: "Fielding lived when ... the clock ticked slowly" (141). A passenger sitting propelled on a train can gaze at an implacably changing vista. Fleming thought the CPR between Calgary and Kamloops "unsurpassed in the variety and magnificence of its scenery" (*England and Canada* 415). He foresaw the setting-up of national parks and camps and tourist infrastructure for visitors thronging to "striking features of natural beauty nowhere else to be seen" (*England and Canada* 416). Elizabeth Waterston calls Sandford Fleming's *England and Canada* a "stirring ... report ... on a life of action and courage, a Hemingway world of 'camping-out'" (351).

To Fleming the locomotive is titanic and sublime. Seated in an engine's cab "I do not think I ever was more conscious of the power of the locomotive.... I felt as if I was borne along on the shoulders of some gigantic winged monster" (*England and Canada* 217-18). This is cinematic. *The Great Train Robbery* (1903) pioneers the railroad-thriller "life of action" — robber gang who skulk aboard when the train stops for water, shoot-out in a baggage car, fist-fight with the fireman behind the unwitting engineer. Back-lit smoke rolls from von Sternberg's *Shanghai Express* to mix with night clouds; winds from the moving train atmospherically ripple the compartment-curtains of gazing passengers and the glistening feathers of Marlene Dietrich's black cape. Once The Beatles in *A Hard Day's Night* hustle on board a train through a crush of fans, rail takes them onward to other glamorously goofy escapades. Blaise sees in films "all the drama, romance, and comedy of America" (145) that trains evoke, in Preston Sturges's *Sullivan's Travels*, Hitchcock's *North by Northwest*, Billy Wilder's *Some Like It Hot* (145-46).

In literature, Clark Blaise's own story "White Children" in *If I Were Me* takes readers to Japan and terrorists on trains, the apocalyptically violent Aum Shinrikyo cult which in 1995 released sarin gas in train-cars, the better to target the maximum number of victims in the smallest enclosed environment. Lander the fictional protagonist narrates: "One morning, my subway train was halted and boarded. Policemen ordered us to abandon everything, and whisked us up staircase[s] and emergency ladders to the street. ... If I'd been on an earlier train, I might be dead. People on that train had been struck by a mysterious illness" (63). From the dawn of rail, writers of adventure yarns exploited trains. Jules Verne's hero Phineas Fogg who raced *Around the World in Eighty Days* (1873) needed rail to cross India and the U.S.A. His friends, aghast, are vicariously thrilled. "'But suppose the Hindoos or Indians pull up the rails.... [S]uppose they stop the trains, pillage the luggage-vans, and scalp the passengers!'" (19). Fogg does face Sioux and murderous Brahmins, and a buffalo herd picturesquely blocks his train for three invaluable hours. Blaise enumerates detective Sherlock Holmes's methodology—"modern science ... magnifying lens ... methods of inquiry ... the technological revolution" (123). Exhaustively, Holmes absorbs railway schedules to help him accurately infer the comings and goings of client or adversary. To Holmes and Moriarty in "The Final Problem," trains are duellers' weapons. Holmes to Watson: "'we must make a cross-country journey to Newhaven, and so over to Dieppe. Moriarty ... will get on to Paris, mark down our luggage, and wait for two days at the depot'" (Doyle 476). Trains made possible legendary real-life exploits too. During Russia's revolution the Canadian entrepreneur/ adventurer Joe Boyle led a foray to rescue the Romanian crown jewels by train from the Kremlin through a gauntlet of Bolshevik zealots. "The train stopped suddenly at a small station. Boyle and Hill slipped out and detected several shadowy figures bent over trying to uncouple 451 from the other cars" (Taylor 224).

Blaise analyzes train mystique and psychology in Dickens' *Dombey and Son* (1848), how Mr. Dombey "made his peace with the sheer brute majesty of the iron rails" (*Time Lord* 144). Again in *Bleak House* (1853), Dickens shows the trauma of transition to a landscape spectacularly marked by rail, looking back twenty years or more to a time when "Railroads shall soon traverse all this country, and with a rattle and a glare the engine and train shall shoot like a meteor over the wide night-landscape, turning the moon paler" (745). Exploring the Canadian Northwest by rail, in 1912 when Fleming still was alive, Rupert Brooke catches the excitement: "Throb, stretch, thrill motion, slide, pull out and sway, / Strain for the far, pause, draw to strength again" ("The Night Journey," Turner 207). Still later, Herzog in Saul Bellow's novel still can find himself inspired by a train's momentum: "Quickly, quickly, more! The train rushed over the landscape. ... Herzog, now barely looking through the tinted, immovable, sealed window felt his eager, flying spirit streaming out, speaking, piercing, making clear judgments, uttering final explanations, necessary words only. He was in a whirling ecstasy" (68).

Like Herzog, poets show more imagination than your average adventurer, and can indeed make of a train-view something rich and strange. Stratford folk in James

Reaney's "The Royal Visit" crave souvenirs less of the
Royals than of the Royal Train: "People put quarters on
the railroad tracks / So as to get squashed by the Royal
Train" (53). Rupert Brooke in his CPR lower berth is near-
ecstatic, by night west of Port Arthur: "as you lie, you can
view the dark procession of woods and hills, and mingle
the broken hours of railway slumber with glimpses of a
wild starlit landscape. The country retains individuality,
and yet puts on romance" (Brooke in Martin and Hall
84). A passenger poet gazes at and enters the scene out her
window, as Margaret Avison in the synaesthetic "Sketch:
From Train Window (Leamington to Windsor) in March":
"Miles of beeswax mist ... // ... visual amplitude so still /
that you can hear the hidden culvert gurgle" (111). The
view may translate her through time as through space,
as in "Perspective" where she starts with the painter An-
drea Mantegna and ends elated in Ottawa:

> ... We swelled and roared
> Mile upon mightier mile, and when we clanged
> Into the vasty station we were indeed
> Brave company for giants. (4)

Dense, relentlessly chugging rhythm in Christopher
Dewdney's "Night Trains" shows how the heft and pulse
of a train can enter and spread in one's imagination:

> A night train is a part of ourselves
> on its way to another part of ourselves
> in the darkside of consciousness. (23)

Blaise's novel-in-stories *If I Were Me* was published
three years before *Time Lord*. A reader can spot continuity
between the two books. Both instance the way rail has

of effecting shifts in human perception. This passage from "White Children" in *If I Were Me*, the protagonist Lander speaking aboard the Bullet train up Japan, could be from *Time Lord*: "Riding the Bullet brings back that pre-Interstate, pre-Jumbojet promise of magneto-trains that were going to take us from New York to Chicago in an hour, with stops. Not so much distance-travel as time-travel, geography as time-lapse photography" (*If I Were Me* 66). The astonishingly rapid Bullet ride north from Tokyo through an "overlay of time and cultures" (*If I Were Me* 67) is as varied and spectacular and richly experienced as any by our train-riding poets above: "Tokyo peels away, the suburbs fall, jewelled gardens glitter like lacquered boxes, ... vegetable patches, greenhouses, and more rice paddies carpet the flatlands, orchards bloom on hillsides, mountains rise, until giant pine forests block the sun. 'Look, a monastery up there,' Kenji would point out with delight" (*If I Were Me* 66-67).

Trains, as Blaise knows well, can emit "a touch of glamour" (145). On pre-rail streets in *Vanity Fair* are nimble curricle, chaise, "Lord Steyne's barouche, blazing with heraldic devices" (699), awed folk "ogling broughams in the Parks" (288). Noble vehicles all, but soon to disappear into storage as their wealthy owners climb aboard Pullmans — "luxury cars, diners and sleepers" (21), says Blaise, admiring. *Vanity Fair* is elegiac. In the rail age, the former mode of travel and self-expression has vanished.

IV. Rail Boom

In his autobiography *I Had a Father*, Blaise evokes Mégantic, the Québécois birth-town of his father and of several prior family generations. In the 1880s when the CPR was being built, the Anglo-Scot élite that Fleming was part of ran Québec's economy from their headquarters in Montreal. Mégantic then was a new stop on the railroad west, where French-Canadian "whiskey-fed railway workers push the CPR tracks across Maine to link Halifax with Montreal and the West. Immigrants get off the train after their sealed transit across Maine, scratch at lice, and cough their lungs out on their two-hour recoaling stop. ... It's the great age of European immigration to North America" (*I Had a Father* 84). Prairie settlement via train still forms part of Canadian lore. It shows up for example in the title poem of Jan Zwicky's *Robinson's Crossing*:

> My great-
> grandmother slept
> in a boxcar on the night
> before she made the crossing. (34-35)

In *Empire and Communications* Harold Adams Innis links two institutions crucial for Canada's east-to-west axis of expansion: "Monopoly of the fur trade held by the Hudson's Bay Company checked expansion north-westward from the St. Lawrence until Confederation was achieved and political organization became sufficiently strong to support construction of a transcontinental railway, the Canadian Pacific, completed in 1885" (4). Northrop Frye's "Conclusion" to the *Literary History of Canada* also puts into focus "that gigantic east-to-west thrust which ... historians regard as the axis of Canadian development" (824). Frye's "Preface to an Uncollected Anthology" shines its light on that same thrust, "the tremendous energy that developed the fur trade routes, the empire of the St. Lawrence, the transcontinental railways, and the northwest police patrols" (168-69). In this grand historical process, few men took a role more prominent and profitable than Fleming. Blaise allows how Fleming "accepted directorships from the CPR and the Hudson's Bay Company" (126).

For Frye this westward push of technology and commerce is "the central comic theme of Canadian life" ("Preface" 169). Comic, and economic. For practically-minded individuals like Fleming the first benefit of a train is commercial: where rail comes the people prosper. To Haliburton's Sam Slick in 1830s Nova Scotia, "this here rail-road ... will beget a spirit of enterprise, that will beget other useful improvements. It will enlarge the sphere and the means of trade, open new sources of traffic and supply — develop resources — and what is of more value perhaps than all — beget motion" (35). The language of the age of steam burbles through Sam Slick's speech — "if you have ... a little safety valve about you, let off a little steam now and then, or you'll go for it" (139). In Ontario, the historian J.M.S. Careless confirms that "no sizeable urban places developed in the interior of the province before railways brought all-weather bulk transport" (66). Margaret Avison's summary in her *History of Ontario* is concrete and succinct: "[The trains] supplied local stores, and made factory goods commoner. Best of all, they offered a farmer hundreds of customers in far-off cities and towns" (91). In the memoir "Working for a Living" Alice Munro quotes a reminiscence of her father's: "'In the evening we went to the station, the old Grand Trunk, or the Butter and Eggs, as it was known in London'" (169). Norman Levine in *Canada Made Me* riding the 1950s butter-and-eggs Algoma Central north from Sault Ste. Marie details its effect on local commerce: "Every fifteen minutes there was a stop. Eton. Frater.

Canyon. Magpie. Cases of milk bottles were taken off from the baggage car for the logging camps deeper in the bush away from the line" (81). Farther west, prairie cities on the rail line amaze Rupert Brooke: they "grow in population with unimaginable velocity" (Brooke in Martin and Hall 97).

Patrician Rupert Brooke may disapprove of the finance frenzy that railroads can bring on, "the national hunger for getting rich quickly," the touts who "prey on the community by their dealings in what is humorously called 'Real Estate'" (Brooke in Martin and Hall 100). Railway-inspired property values obsess indignant fellow-passengers when Carroll's Alice can't produce her ticket for the *Looking-Glass* train. "'I'm afraid I haven't got one,' Alice said in a frightened tone: 'there wasn't a ticket-office where I came from.' And again the chorus of voices went on. 'There wasn't room for one where she came from. The land there is worth a thousand pounds an inch!'" (*Through the Looking-Glass* 217). Stephen Leacock's shyster "Remarkable Uncle" thrives in the thousand-pounds-an-inch milieu, "secretary-treasurer of the Winnipeg Hudson Bay and Arctic Ocean Railway that had a charter authorizing it to build a road to the Arctic Ocean, when it got ready" (6).

Fleming's railroads all did get built. According to Adam Barrows, "All of Fleming's vast global telecommunications and transportation projects were tied up with highly lucrative commercial ventures in which he was personally invested" (49). The writer of a 1978 *Royal Bank of Canada Monthly Letter* entitled "Time and Sandford Fleming" is able to say that Fleming "invested so shrewdly that he was wealthy by his mid-thirties" ([2]). Rail historian Jay Underwood introduces in detail Fleming's self-enriching clique: "the Intercolonial was obliged to take the 'Dorchester Diversion' when it ran through New Brunswick, a fact about which Fleming offers great comment, but little criticism in his history of the line" (109). Underwood indicates that "Fleming and his partners profited by this route, since the Intercolonial took coal from Springhill Junction and delivered it to the wharf at Dorchester ... for shipment to markets in Saint John and Boston" (109). Lorne Green is on the same track: "In all likelihood Fleming did line his own pockets on the Pictou Railway construction" (182). Travelling in a party with Fleming through Canada's Northwest, George M. Grant spots Fleming's opportunism yet again: "We forded the [Athabaska] [R]iver which is about a hundred yards wide, and looking back saw on the east side a seam of coal about ten feet thick.... Pick in hand the Chief [Fleming] made for the coal" (*Ocean to Ocean* 193). Later, shrewdly, Fleming and partners again "made for the coal," investing in Alberta coal and limestone; in time they sold out to Canada Cement. No wonder that when Fleming and his party on their 1884 trip sight a mountain in the Selkirks "rising ... majestically among its fellows" they "name it Syndicate Peak" (*England and Canada* 271).

Since he himself prospered, Fleming imagines train-loads of immigrants will go and do likewise. He has, like the child Clark Blaise in 1946 Atlanta, a train-inspired vision of what Blaise calls "streamlined futurity" (*I Had a Father* 58). But Fleming's vision of prairie settlers is sentimental and rhapsodic: "Their romance lies in the future.... The small wooden house they have put up is one day to give place to a more imposing building of stone or brick, with verandahs and blinds and plenty of room for occasional friends. The piano may come, too, bye and bye, from Moose Jaw or some nearer place" (*England and*

Canada 215). Blaise's maternal grandfather was one who participated in making this domestic vision real. He and his wife were "homesteaders" in Manitoba (*I Had a Father* 41). He became a horticulturalist, helping turn prairie into orchard: "They called him the Luther Burbank of Canada because of his interest in crossbreeding Ontario and Chinese fruit trees and adapting them for growth in western Canada" (*I Had a Father* 41).

Raymond Souster has a train poem, set in Toronto's Sunnyside midway, where a roller-coaster takes riders to a new and jubilant environment. "[A] movieland magic carpet" soaring off its track "swooped slowly above the amusement-park," "heading leisurely out above the blue lake water, / to disappear all too soon behind a low-flying flight of clouds" ("Flight of the Roller-Coaster" 316). But what happens to those riders once they've passed out of sight behind clouds? More movieland magic? Or crash and disaster?

V. Rail Bust

Those like Fleming who help effect a change which they think is for the better probably will not understand all its limits and costly side effects. Trains leave many folk dis-advantaged, un-empowered. Fleming would have told the chorus of locals in *Middlemarch* what Mr. Garth does: "'the railway's a good thing'" (560). But the Middlemarchers won't embark. They live by what Blaise names "'natural' thinking" (4): "'The cows will all cast their calves, Brother,' said Mrs. Waule, in a tone of deep melancholy, 'if the railway comes across the Near Close; and I shouldn't wonder at the mare too, if she was in foal'" (553-54). The chorus suspect who will benefit from railroads: "'Why, they're Lunnon chaps, I reckon,' said Hiram" (555). "'Aw! good for the big folks to make money out on,' said old Timothy Cooper" (560).

For many who do board, the way leads ever on to defeat and disillusion. The hero of Selwyn Dewdney's *Wind Without Rain* arrives by train in a Southwestern Ontario town, resolutely optimistic: "John stood up, a tightening in his throat and chest, the veins tingling in his arms. ... Angus told me I'd like West Kirby, he reminded himself" (3). What ensues is five hundred-some pages of community intolerance, bureaucracy, corruption, disgrace, the death of Angus his mentor, and flight from West Kirby — this time by bus. Or as Harry J. Boyle recalls it in his *Memories of a Catholic Boyhood*, the train may take you to a scary unknown, as when leaving his Southwestern Ontario small-town home for the first time: "'Good-by,' I croaked in the voice of the condemned, and stumbled up the steps. ... The thought of sharpies and gamblers made me feel the wet wad of money pinned to my underwear. ... I was sadder than I had ever been before in my life" (59).

Alice Munro's "Wild Swans" features teenage Rose "going to Toronto on the train for the first time by herself" (57). Her stepmother Flo has warned her: "watch out for White Slavers ... riding beside you on a bus or train" (55). Munro, though probably not Flo, would have read Dreiser's *Sister Carrie*. Carrie is eighteen, on the train alone, to Chicago. "The train was just pulling out of Waukesha. For some time she had been conscious of a man behind. She felt him observing her mass of hair" (5). "Her story," says Blaise, "was a scandal that had to be censored in its day" (233). Since Flo knows of Frances Farmer, her paranoia might also originate in movies: a dark small-town Southwestern Ontario cinema, a woman staring tensely at Fred MacMurray in *Double Indemnity*, Margaret Lockwood in *The Lady Vanishes*, Farley Granger in *Strangers on a Train*. On Rose's train is no White Slaver but a man in the seat beside her, slavering in his fashion, who fondles her beneath his newspaper and her clothes, till her unwilling orgasm spreads and blends with Toronto's gaudy Canadian National Exhibition surging out the window — "The gates and towers of the Exhibition Grounds came to view, the painted domes and pillars floated marvelously against her eyelids' rosy sky" (63). At Union Station, Rose disembarks to what Blaise writing of Sister Carrie calls her rail-induced "endless *becoming*" (233).

In *Words with Power* Northrop Frye writes of "the intertwining of the titanic and the demonic" (295) — the opposite of rail as the great Canadian comic theme that Frye also defined. Even Fleming acknowledged some rail discomfort. "Shortly after leaving Paddington the lady suffered from a spark in her eye, certainly a most painful annoyance. ... I had frequently experienced this unfortunate accident" (*England and Canada* 55). Keaton's *Our Hospitality*, set in the early days of rail, treats train fire comically. The train belching smoke and ash enters a tunnel, and emerges with passengers in sooty blackface. Fleming on the CPR line in 1884: "At some of the stations there are groups of Indians, men and women. We enter into conversation with them through an interpreter on the platform. Pie-à-Pot, the great Indian chief, we are told, has gone on a mission to the Lieutenant-Governor at Regina to complain of the smoke of the locomotive, which he considers to be an evil medicine to ruin the health of his people" (*England and Canada* 210). Fires started by sparks from early trains could indeed "ruin the health." "Fire was the thing that we were most scared of," a prairie woman recalls in Bill McNeil's anthology of oral histories *Voice of the Pioneer* (40). Fleming does not dwell on these conflagrations. But William Morris in his Prologue to *The Earthly Paradise* could have sympathized with McNeil's pioneer and with Pie-à-Pot: "Forget six counties overhung with smoke, / Forget the snorting steam and piston stroke" (3).

Camille Paglia has stared at the conquest of female nature by phallic male technology. "Construction is a sublime male poetry. When I see a giant crane passing on a flatbed truck, I pause in awe and reverence" (38) — as perhaps she might have too if it passed on a flatbed railcar. Surveying, Fleming's forte, is voyeuristic. E.J. Pratt's epic *Towards the Last Spike* uses Pagliatically violent sexual language. The Superior North Shore is femininely pretty,

> ... easy on the eyes
> Stung with the dust of gravel. Cotton grass,
> Its white spires blending with the orchids,
> Peeked through green table-cloths of sphagnum moss.
>
> (379)

With apparent female passivity she lies

> ... presenting but her bulk
> To the invasion. All she had to do
> Was lie there neither yielding nor resisting. (369)

Sadist work-gangs "Surprised her with a sense of violation," "Pouring black powder in her cavities" (370). Fleming and his virile Scot cohort "Take off their plaids and wrap them round the mountains" (348). We know by convention what's exposed when the kilt comes off. Pratt's description of Nature's femme-fatale revenge is almost pornographic:

> ... She took three engines, sank them
> With seven tracks down through the hidden lake
> To the rock bed, then over them she spread
> A counterpane of leather-leaf and slime. (379)

Blaise calls north-of-Superior muskeg "gelatinous" (67).

Though James Reaney has a whimsical poem where "The night-train trails a stream / Of light brown hair" and "Each night she moans by / With her wig of nut-brown curls" ("Night Train" 8), railroads by tradition metaphorically are male. Therefore the damage done is often to females. Examples abound. A different Reaney poem, the "September" eclogue from *A Suit of Nettles*, morphs the iconic CPR Last-Spike photo at Craigellachie into mordant testosterone fancy—"a railway carriage running on a monorail attached to the crotches of a row of bearded gentlemen" (58). Richard B. Wright's eponymous heroine in *Clara Callan* gets raped by two tramps at the railway tracks. "We swayed in the grass by the side of the tracks. 'Now, Missus, now, Missus, you'll like it, you'll see.' ... // Then I fell and he covered me with himself" (57). In Emily Schultz's poem "Down Bear Line" the siding proves a seedy place in all senses:

> Where is the old dirt pull-off by the railroad tracks
> where that hunting boy removed my blouse, left his kiss red,
> welted, on my chest, and an invisible disease inside my
> skin? (34)

In 1893 Fleming met Hawaii's Queen Liliuokalani, deposed that year through the machinations of an American commercial élite led by Sanford Dole, he of the eventual tropical-fruit conglomerate family, named president of the coup's self-declared provisional government. In Honolulu en route to Australia to promote the trans-Pacific pan-Imperial All-Red telegraphic cable, Fleming called on "the deposed Queen" (Fleming in Burpee 252). Here is his bland reminiscence: "'We found her fully as dark as any of the natives, her manners very graceful, natural, and dignified. She talked with each of us for a few minutes. I ventured to say that I had already had the satisfaction of seeing Her Majesty in Westminster Abbey in June 1887, which evidently gave her pleasure'" (Fleming in Burpee 252). That decade, the U.S. annexed Liliuokalani's Pacific realm. From then on, the American plantation owners ruled. Fleming was unperturbed. Paul Gauguin in Tahiti and Robert Louis Stevenson in Samoa in those days witnessed the demise of aboriginal society through European incursion. Unlike Fleming, both became what Blaise calls "avid appreciators of all that the Victorians had dismissed as natural, or primitive" (123). Rosalind Williams describes in detail how "Stevenson became aware of mobility as a collective tragedy" (263).

"All over the world," Alex Soojung-Kim Pang says, "... railroads were more than indirect agents in the ecological transformation of colonial territories" (134). By the late 1880s, John L. Riley notes, "there were fourteen Canadian rail lines delivering wood to ports on Lake Ontario and Lake Erie. Eight rail lines to Lake Huron did the same" (182). One of those, the Northern Railway, ran between Collingwood and Toronto. Fleming had surveyed the stretch north from Barrie to Georgian Bay, an often arduous labour recorded daily in his *Early Diaries 1845-1853*, as seen in the entry for November 1, 1852: "Monday,

1st: Windy morning. Cutting base line along beach. Smith, Markle & Hickley. Gardner & party arrived. Sounding afternoon" (245). Fleming's parents later lived at Craigleith, in a mansion he built for them just west of Collingwood. Fleming lamented "the wholesale destruction of timber, so often the result of carelessness and imprudence" (*England and Canada* 386), but did not grasp how trains contributed to their own decline by making possible resource over-exploitation. Preposterously, he suggested that Indians "be trained to look after forests" (*England and Canada* 385-86). Ron Brown's *Ghost Towns of Ontario* memorializes railroad communities such as Cook Station in Haldimand County that were built and then abandoned (65). Like Thackeray in *Vanity Fair* glancing back at horse-drawn coaches, some Alice Munro stories give elegiac glimpses where railways, no longer economic, are palimpsests. In "Carried Away," "The passenger train from Carstairs to London had stopped running during the Second World War and even the rails were taken up" (41). "Hateship, Friendship, Courtship, Loveship, Marriage" begins in an era "Years ago, before the trains stopped running on so many of the branch lines" (1).

Blaise reminds us (37) of Thoreau's warning: "the railroad … rides upon us" (Thoreau 83). James Reaney hears "faint outcries from the long-distance carters who lose their profession after the Great Western is completed" ("Myths" 255). In the mid-1870s the Donnelly family and others who drove stagecoaches for passengers and freight north from and south to London lost out to the London, Huron and Bruce Railroad when its tracks reached those two counties; they brawled over a shrinking market (Butt, Vol. 1, 76). A few marginalized folk manage to scrape some meagre use from the railroad.

On the prairie, Thomas King's *Truth & Bright Water* has a scene where young aboriginals scavenge. "The cars are unloaded before they get to Truth, but … sometimes you can find a melon that is mostly good, buried among the smashed and rotting pieces" (70). In Lorna Crozier's "Names" from *A Saving Grace*, also set in a prairie town, the speaker tells how

> Yesterday, out with the dog,
> I talked to the woman who lives
> in the cook car abandoned by the CPR
> at the edge of town. (11)

But the note of collective tragedy continues to resound. Miriam Toews wrote a prairie memoir intermittently in the voice of her father, *Swing Low: A Life*, after he availed himself of convenient rail for his suicide. "Some say he knelt on the tracks, facing the little church, with his back to the oncoming train" (190). Mennonite though he was, we cannot know his expectations of the after-life, nor whether this train he took was bound for glory. In any case, a member of a sect that ploughed with horses has been mashed by a train. Blaise has a line to serve as epitaph: "By removing horses from the power equation, steam began the long erasure of stylized nature itself from the countryside" (150).

VI. Rule Britannia

Blaise titles one chapter of *Time Lord* "Britain, 1887." He also details Fleming's 1863 sojourn in "London at its imperial height" (55). He calls Fleming "a strong supporter of Empire loyalty based on common history, culture, and instruments of government" (61). This is understatement; on the subject of Empire, Fleming leans to ecstatic over-stating. Fleming proclaimed how his Intercolonial railway brought "the full consummation of the union of the British Provinces in North America" (*The Intercolonial* 239). To him, rail is the Northwest "'Imperial highway, to convey the products of our illimitable wheatfields to our own seaports for transportation to market'" (Fleming in Burpee 268-69). "By opening up this fertile territory we provide, on British soil, an outlet for the many who are crowded amid a redundant population" (*Report* 15). This was conventional wisdom: "Canadians saw the Canadian Pacific Railway ... as an imperial project" (Fortner 27). With his trains and his telegraphs — which Blaise calls "inseparable" (41) — Fleming's "organicist electric utopianism signalled the dawn of a new internationalism grounded in the technics of electromagnetism" (Thompson 67). Sixty years later, when Newfoundland voted to join Canada, a train in Wayne Johnston's *The Colony of Unrequited Dreams* still functions as apocalyptic symbol of Confederation:

> For a few seconds there was nothing in the world but sound, the continuous blare of the whistle, the chugging of the train. The conductor saw me and waved his hat as he went by, grinning gleefully....
>
> I have often thought of that train hurtling down the Bonavista like the victory express. (562)

Optimists think railways bring order and good government. In Delmer Daves's *3:10 to Yuma* only the title train can get Van Heflin's idealistic frontier-outpost sheriff and his murderous prisoner played by Glenn Ford to justice. Keaton's character in *Our Hospitality* riding in the opposite direction, outward from New York City, heads unknowingly into a backwoods vendetta. Civilization and rule of law end where the track ends, at the barrier of a single felled log. Beyond are lurid, comic feudsters keen to slay our urbanly conventional *naif.* But Frye in *Words with Power* writing of the United States points out the time when "the beckoning call to the horizon, which had expanded the country from one ocean to the other in the nineteenth century, had now settled into a cultural uniformity in which every place was like every other place, and so equally 'here'" (95). Rupert Brooke, who died three years after Frye was born, travelling the prairie by train through rampant 'development', and channelling Kipling, comments wryly how "the floods from Europe pour in" and "the 'Anglo-Saxon' continues to take up his burden" (Brooke in Martin and Hall 90). Drab uniformity results. "Each village — I beg your pardon, 'town' — seems to be exactly like the next" (Brooke in Martin and Hall 95). To Fleming, homogeneity was exactly the point: "'Every improvement in transportation ... is calculated ... to foster friendships among kindred people, and thus to perpetuate their attachment to the cradle of the British race'" (Fleming in Burpee 275). Fleming on Vancouver Island, writing of his 1884 journey from England to Canada's Pacific: "The residents of Victoria speak of the delight which Her Royal Highness the Princess Louise experienced in this healthy locality.... Many anecdotes are still told of Her Royal Highness during her residence, and twelve months have elapsed since she left" (*England and Canada* 350).

From Sea to Sea: Later, on the other coast, Fleming donated Halifax acreage and raised funds throughout the Empire to erect a Memorial Tower "to commemorate the 150th anniversary of the convening on 2 October

1758 of the first legislative assembly in Nova Scotia"
(Cuthbertson et al. 8). Fleming's "Letter to the 150th Anniversary Committee" urged "a historical monument
which would be hailed with a sense of pride by this
young Canadian nation, and regarded with feelings of
genuine satisfaction by the Mother Country and the
whole sisterhood of British nations" (31). *The Stones of
Venice* inspired his design. "If we allow ourselves to be
influenced by Ruskin, on this side of the Atlantic, we may
with advantage ... erect an architectural edifice modelled after St. Mark's at Venice, or some other Italian
tower" ("A Proposed Historical Tower" 13). Fleming saw
Canadian landscape via British-royalist vocabulary. To
his Anglophile eyes, Roche Myette is "That imposing
sphinx-like head with the swelling Elizabethan ruff of
sandstone and shales all around the neck" ("Memories
of the Mountains" 16).

Those not of British descent must be assimilated or
shunted aside. Fleming is rigorously exclusive. "There
are two classes of men to be considered — the investor
and the settler" (*Report* 14). Both classes are of British
descent, or must become essentially so. In the opening
sentences of Adele Wiseman's novel *The Sacrifice* a
Ukrainian Jewish immigrant family, survivors of a 1930s
pogrom, descend from their train at Winnipeg. "Abraham felt strength surge up in him, excitement shaking
the tiredness out of his body" (6). But two decades of
suffering and misunderstanding later, Wiseman's Abraham still cannot adapt to Winnipeg's dominant Anglo-
Saxon culture, and in madness murders a neighbour.
Also not "to be considered" are unnumbered navvies
during CPR construction, many of them immigrant Chinese, many dying from exposure, disease, or errant
dynamite explosions. E.J. Pratt in *Towards the Last Spike*

(where Fleming gets lots of mention) has two twee lines where death will "take its leisurely Pacific time / To tap its fingers on a coolie's door" (375). Pratt's ignoring Oriental workers provoked his poet colleague F.R. Scott to demand, in "All the Spikes but the Last," "Where are the coolies in your poem, Ned?" (194). Fleming had already provided an answer which he felt satisfactory: "I presume the Chinese population will disappear as the railway is completed" (*England and Canada* 316). Thoreau saw the skull beneath the railroad skin. "Did you ever think what those sleepers are that underlie the railroad? Each one is a man" (Thoreau 83).

In Mégantic, Blaise's father's birth-town, back in "the first years of the CPR, the first decade of Mégantic's existence" (*I Had a Father* 136), Blaise imagines unassimilated "Russians, Poles, Italians, Slovaks, Ukrainians, Ruthenians, and Magyars, all passing through a French-Canadian village on their way to Montréal and land out west" (84). None of these will benefit so readily from a railway built as a tool for British Imperial expansion. Nor will Mégantic French Canadians profit much from rail. Blaise tells how his paternal grandfather like many of that generation left for Manchester, New Hampshire, and low-paying "pulp and textile and shoemaking jobs" (89) — jobs made necessary by new railroads, which brought in raw lumber, cotton, leather, and would ship it out to markets as value-added paper, textiles, footwear. In Henry James's *The Ambassadors*, the fictional Woollett is another New England industrial town built on rail, one state south in Massachusetts. There, an Anglo-American élite grew rich from industry. One beneficiary is the novel's protagonist Lambert Strether. "'A Woollett swell'" (50) his European muse Miss Gostrey calls him, teasing. Woollett was no place for fulfilment of any sort, for anyone. Bleakly industrial, its failure is foremost "'[t]he failure to enjoy'" (25), as Miss Gostrey remarks. "'Woollett isn't sure it ought to enjoy'," Strether says. "'If it were it would. But it hasn't, poor thing'" (25). For the wealthy, the reason is the Puritan legacy; for the labouring class, it's poverty. Strether has the means to get to England and France for a finely tuned Jamesian adventure. Most of Blaise's ghettoized French Canadians stay behind. Researching his family history in Manchester parish ledgers, Blaise finds evidence only of "toxic and backward times" (*I Had a Father* 139).

Pang's *Empire and the Sun* has a chapter on the way railroads in colonies worldwide made possible the cultivation and transport of agri-business products to new markets — cotton in India; coffee in Ceylon; beef and wheat in Argentina; coffee, tea, and sugar in Brazil — enriching investors while displacing aboriginal inhabitants. "Technological systems played a critical role in the nineteenth-century Europeanization of colonies, and none was more important than the railroad" (129). In Canada, as trains did elsewhere, the CPR when required brought troops. Jared Diamond, in *Guns, Germs, and Steel*, says that "Technology, in the form of weapons and transport, provides the direct means by which certain peoples have expanded their realms and conquered other peoples" (241). Henry Kreisel saw the phenomenon in Canada's Northwest, and described it in his essay "The Prairie: A State of Mind": "The conquest of territory is by definition a violent process" (261).

In Fleming's time, for a time, imperialism won out almost world-wide. Blaise and Adam Hochschild both notice that the Prime Meridian Conference overlapped with the 1885 Berlin Conference and as Blaise puts it, "agents of the imperial powers carving up, all too literally, the African continent" (13). The Congo River, steamboat route to Congo's rich interior for the agents of Belgium's King Leopold, presented just one fierce unnavigable stretch. Hochschild: "In 1887, a party of surveyors began to chart the route for a railroad to skirt the notorious 220 miles of rapids" (91). Conrad's Marlow watched the next job: "They were building a railway. // ... Six black men advanced in a file toiling up the path. They walked erect and slow, balancing small baskets full of earth on their heads. ... each had an iron collar on his neck and all were connected together with a chain" (19). The whole Congo enterprise caused African fatalities of what Hochschild calls "Holocaust dimensions" (4), not so unlike trains forty years later which brought European Jews to camps like Auschwitz. Also in Africa, Blaise mentions Chinua Achebe's *Arrow of God*—"in temporal terms, a violent, deicidic clash between natural and rational gods, told in terms of colonialism and religion" (Blaise 174). Another instance of the same tragic pattern unfolds in Achebe's first novel *Things Fall Apart*, where a missionary on an "'iron horse'" (80) arrives to the Ibo of Nigeria. Not a railroad; his bicycle. But the same disastrous result: colonial administration, penal laws, and commerce; Ibo deaths.

Fleming's iron horse also meant havoc to an aboriginal animist culture. In 1863, in Britain to promote construction of a railroad to the Selkirk settlement, Fleming speaks for the settler population, "'[e]xclusive of pure Indians'" (Fleming in Burpee 258). Adam Barrows details some of Fleming's later work as "chief engineering consultant and investor in a body called the Para Transportation and Trading Company, which proposed a mammoth opportunity for investors in building a railroad across northern Brazil ... leading to a silver mine in Goyaz" (47). The syndicate looked into the inconvenient "native

populations settled in the region" (Barrows 47). No problem, wrote Fleming's colleagues from the field: "although
'not to be trusted,' [they] were easily manipulated because 'all those [I]ndians have a mortal terror of firearms'"
(Barrows 47).

Fleming himself devotes several glib pages at different points of *England and Canada* to "the fate of the Indian as the plains are filled up" (211); as if they were
empty before. "[T]he Indian territory," he says, "has been
appropriated in the interest of the community" (211); as
if Indians had had no community. "If it be possible the
course to follow is to train the coming generation [of In-
dians] to habits of industry and self-reliance" (211-12); as
if their original habits were indolence and dependency.
The planned residential schools might do, Fleming
thinks. "But the Indians do not willingly see their children separated from them" (387).

Clearing the Plains is James Daschuk's distressingly
detailed study of the national government's systematic
genocidal strategies for Canada's Northwest. Subtitle:
*Disease, Politics of Starvation, and the Loss of Aboriginal
Life.* Daschuk documents grim decades of military brute
force; bureaucratic obstructionism; epidemic tuberculo-
sis, measles, whooping cough, and influenza carried in
large part by the railway vector; deceit in treaty wording
and compliance; measures to reduce and/or eliminate
emergency food rations; missionary collusion or inaction;
and more. "To ensure that the west would be ready for
the Canadian Pacific Railway and settlement, [Prime
Minister] Macdonald himself became superintendent
general of Indian affairs" (Daschuk 108-09). Louise Halfe
in her book-length poem *Blue Marrow* allots to Ohkomipan, the Eternal Grandmother of Cree culture, stark
lines to sum up this holocaust:

The land weeps. I am choking, choking.
The buffalo are a mountain of bones.
My son is shot for killing their cow. (19)

Fleming, incredibly: "Above all things, the Indian is satisfied, for he feels that he is treated with justice" (*England
and Canada* 383-84).

In 1888 Charles Mair, poet promoter of imperialism
on the Northwest plains, published with apparently unconscious irony "The Last Bison," an elegy on the passing
of the bison and the native way of life that bison as the
primary food source no longer made viable. The poem
appeared in the 8 September issue of *The Dominion Illustrated*, six pages after a full-page portrait of Fleming in
academic regalia as Chancellor of Queen's University.
Mair appends to his poem a "Note": "The foregoing poem
was suggested to the author by a personal incident,
near the elbow of the North Saskatchewan, some eight
years ago. Not a buffalo, so far as the author knows, has
been seen on that river since. There are some animals
in private collections ... but the wild bison of the plains
may now be looked upon as extinct" (155). Like Halfe's
Ohkomipan, Mair's Last Bison speaks for the dead:
white hunters are "Strange men who ravaged our domain" (155). George M. Grant tells how littered bison
skulls drew Fleming's interest in 1872 as curiosities for
one of those "private collections": "we passed in the
course of the day more than a score of skulls that were
bleaching on the prairie. All the other bones had been of
course chopped and boiled by the Indian women for the
oil in them. The Chief [Fleming] picked up two or three
of the best skulls to send as specimens to Ottawa" (122).
On the 1884 trip, news of a nearby ravaged bison rem-
nant excited Fleming's band "to the highest pitch, for the

buffalo have not come on this route for many years, and eager hopes were exchanged that we might see and get a shot at them" (Grant 111). To William Storey "the basic underlying structures of the hunt symbolized the triumph of culture over nature and of the colonist over the colonized" (Storey in Pang 133). To Blaise they symbolize "the assertion of human reason over the processes of nature" (69).

On his 1872 trip west, Fleming came across an aboriginal human skull. He scooped it for the Ottawa CPR collection. Another *memento mori*. It appears as an atmospheric engraving in *Ocean to Ocean* (PL. 42). Not long after, Fleming reports, "The long-missing cranium of the headless Indian was accidentally cremated on January 16th, 1874, when the offices of the Canadian Pacific Railway Survey, at the Capital, were unfortunately consumed by fire" ("Memories of the Mountains" 22). That fire image again. The rationalist/industrial complex can destroy not only Nature but itself. No wonder as humans we cannot stop what Blaise calls our urgent "search for refuge in something resembling the sentimental shreds of the 'natural'" (237).

VII. *Afterword*

In the Afterword to *Time Lord*, Blaise remembers his father's 1947 explanation of a parking meter: "'They're renting space. It just comes out time'" (239). In Lorado Taft's *Fountain of Time*, the sculpture which Blaise cites in his Afterword epigraph, time comes out space. By means of a procession of simultaneously present hollow-concrete and reinforced-steel allegorical human figures, this sculpture in a park in Chicago embodies some one hundred years of time: specifically, the century since the 1814 Treaty of Ghent.

The Afterword's title is "The Ghost of Sandford Fleming." In what sense "Ghost"? Well, because Fleming still exists and can interact with us as an immaterial form after his material death: accessible no longer via trains or human legs or other means of transport, but via art, imagination. In *Time Lord*, Fleming lives now in a different sort of time zone. Not what Fleming devised, a spatial zone on planet earth to which a certain hourly time is assigned by convention. Rather, a time zone which, like a space zone, does not disappear as time passes. In "The Paradox of Time," Austin Dobson's poem in the Afterword epigraph, "time stays; we go!" (238): individual creatures go, i.e. die, but time continues — does not go or pass in the sense of come to its end. If time continues, then a creature that has physically died — 'passed' — also continues to exist in that continuing time, that continuum, as what Blaise calls a "Ghost." This indeed is — Blaise's word — "eerie" (238). Blaise is putting into practice the hypothesis at the start of T.S. Eliot's "Burnt Norton": "all time is eternally present" (*Four Quartets* 7). Like *Four Quartets* and like *Time Lord* as a whole, the Afterword is "one mystical moment" (240).

Let us un-pack this Afterword in more detail.

In Taft's *Fountain of Time* and in Blaise's Afterword, many 'time zones' are simultaneously present. Some are where Blaise experienced five of his own chronological ages, "fifty-seven, six, seven, a teenager, and twenty-three" (240), i.e. respectively the years 1997, 1946, 1947, the 1950s, and 1963. He travels explicitly to other 'time zones' too: to the 1930s (when his mother lived in Europe), and to 1884 (the Prime Meridian Conference).

As in time zones, so too in space zones: the Blaise of

this Afterword is well-travelled. "In 1997, according to United Airlines, I circled the globe the equivalent of five times" (238). Here are the space zones that this brief (two-page) Afterword conducts us to: Chicago, Iowa City, Berkeley, India, rural Québec, Manitoba, England, Germany, Montreal, Leesburg (central Florida), Pittsburgh, and Washington, D.C.

Now, let's list the Afterword population in both the time zones and space zones they respectively inhabit: England's late-Victorian and Georgian poet Henry Austin Dobson, American Lorado Taft in Chicago in the 1920s, Blaise himself at five ages and locations between 1946 and 1997, his wife in India and Berkeley in 1997, his Prairie-born mother and his Québécois father in the 1930s, Harry Truman in the late 1940s, 1947 Florida Ku Klux Klan paraders, early-1860s Confederate States President Jefferson Davis, Major League Baseball players on 1997 Iowa TV, Sandford Fleming and Prime Meridian Conference delegates in 1884 Washington, Jackie Robinson and his 1940s/50s Brooklyn Dodgers teammates in various ballparks, 1950s Pittsburgh Pirates at home-games, 1946 Montreal Royals at "old Delormier Downs" (240), Martin Luther King, Jr. and some of the audience (including Blaise and Robinson) of his 1963 "I Have a Dream" oration.

Imagine a certain freight train. Its cargo is not uniform — not all iron ore, autos, liquefied natural gas, or passengers. But the cargo is also not random or miscellaneous. Though each car carries a cargo different from all the others, all cars are related. They cohere. Each car holds one of, say, spruce lumber from British Columbia, plumbing fixtures from the U.S.A., furniture from Denmark, engineered bamboo flooring from Malaysia, Italian marble tiles, electronics from Taiwan, and one car has human passengers. Unpack and then assemble at destination and — "bingo!" as Blaise says (239) — you build and furnish a house. Imagine sentences as pieces of cargo destined for rail transport. You can't just toss cargo aboard, you need first to package it securely according to its nature — a crate of Taiwanese electronics is packaged differently than a crate of, say, Italian marble tiles as the build of every sentence depends on its purpose. Next imagine a paragraph as a laden railroad car: like railway stevedores, the writer has built from sentences each car's load. And then the writer like a yard-crew coupling cars links the diverse paragraphs to form chapters, series of railway cars related by cargo and destination — and thus, finally, a train. The train as book: This is *Time Lord*.

In *Time Lord* Blaise re-fashions the notion of 'time zone' to create "a brilliant portmanteau" (239), two disparate words or word-parts linked to make a joint new meaning. "Time doesn't have zones ... but once we create them, all things are possible" (239). One thing made possible is the book that Blaise in the Afterword sets out to write. *Time Lord*: in words, not in metal, a contemporary Train of Tomorrow.

Works Cited

Achebe, Chinua. *Things Fall Apart: Authoritative Text; Contexts and Criticism*. Ed. Francis Abiola Irele. New York: W.W. Norton, 2009. A Norton Critical Edition.

Avison, Margaret. *History of Ontario*. Toronto: W.J. Gage, 1951.

-----. "Perspective." *Selected Poems*. Toronto: Oxford UP, 1991. 4.

-----. "Sketch: From Train Window (Leamington to Windsor) in March." *Selected Poems*. Toronto: Oxford UP, 1991. 111.

Barrows, Adam. *The Cosmic Time of Empire: Modern Britain*

and World Literature. Berkeley, CA: U of California P, 2011. FlashPoints.

Bellow, Saul. *Herzog.* New York: Viking, 1964.

Blaise, Clark. *I Had a Father: A Post-Modern Autobiography.* Toronto: HarperCollins, 1993.

-----. *If I Were Me: A Novel.* Erin, ON: The Porcupine's Quill, 1997. Rpt. (expanded) in *World Body.* Introd. Michael Augustin. Erin, ON: The Porcupine's Quill, 2006. Vol. 4 of *The Selected Stories of Clark Blaise.* 4 vols. 2000-06.

-----. "Meditations on Starch." *World Body.* Introd. Michael Augustin. Erin, ON: The Porcupine's Quill, 2006. 119-28. Vol. 4 of *The Selected Stories of Clark Blaise.* 4 vols. 2000-06.

-----. "Notes on the 'Canadian' Short Story." *Selected Essays.* By Clark Blaise. Ed. John Metcalf and J.R. (Tim) Struthers. Windsor, ON: Biblioasis, 2008. 157-65.

-----. *Time Lord: The Remarkable Canadian Who Missed His Train, and Changed the World.* Toronto: Alfred A. Knopf Canada, 2000.

Boyle, Harry J. *Memories of a Catholic Boyhood.* Toronto: Doubleday Canada, 1973.

Brown, Ron. *Ghost Towns of Ontario: Volume 1 — Southern Ontario.* Langley, BC: Stagecoach, 1978.

Burpee, Lawrence J. *Sandford Fleming: Empire Builder.* London: Oxford UP, 1915.

Butt, William Davison. *The Donnellys: History, Legend, Literature.* Diss. U of Western Ontario, 1977. 2 vols.

Careless, J.M.S. "Some Aspects of Urbanization in Nineteenth-Century Ontario." *Aspects of Nineteenth-Century Ontario: Essays Presented to James J. Talman.* Ed. F.H. Armstrong, H.A. Stevenson, and J.D. Wilson. Toronto: U of Toronto P, 1974. 65-79.

Carroll, Lewis. *Through the Looking-Glass and What Alice Found There. The Annotated Alice:* Alice's Adventures in Wonderland *and* Through the Looking-Glass. Introd.

and notes by Martin Gardner. Illus. John Tenniel. Rev. ed. Harmondsworth, Eng.: Penguin, 1970. 166-345.

Cole, Jean Murray, ed. *Sir Sandford Fleming: His Early Diaries, 1845-1853*. Toronto: Natural Heritage, 2009.

Conrad, Joseph. *Heart of Darkness: An Authoritative Text; Backgrounds and Sources; Criticism*. Ed. Robert Kimbrough. 3rd ed. New York: W.W. Norton, 1988. A Norton Critical Edition.

Crozier, Lorna. "Names." *A Saving Grace: The Collected Poems of Mrs. Bentley*. Toronto: McClelland & Stewart, 1996. 10-12.

Cuthbertson, Brian, and John Zuck and Associates. *Submission: Historic Sites and Monuments of Canada: Sir Sandford Fleming Park & Memorial Tower: Historical & Cultural Landscape*. Halifax: n.p., 2003. Web. 15 Oct. 2014. <http://www.halifax.ca/district09/documents/Fleming...>.

Daschuk, James. *Clearing the Plains: Disease, Politics of Starvation, and the Loss of Aboriginal Life*. Regina: U of Regina P, 2013.

Dewdney, Christopher. "Night Trains." *The Radiant Inventory*. Toronto: McClelland and Stewart, 1988. 23.

Dewdney, Selwyn. *Wind Without Rain*. Toronto: Copp Clark, 1946.

Diamond, Jared. *Guns, Germs, and Steel: The Fates of Human Societies*. 1997. New York: W.W. Norton, 1999.

Dickens, Charles. *Bleak House*. Introd. Barbara Hardy. New York: Alfred A. Knopf, 1991. Everyman's Library.

-----. *Dombey and Son*. London: Oxford UP, 1950. The Oxford Illustrated Dickens.

Double Indemnity. Dir. Billy Wilder. Paramount Pictures, 1944.

Doyle, Sir Arthur Conan. "The Final Problem." *The Complete Sherlock Holmes*. Pref. Christopher Morley. Vol. 1. New York: Doubleday, n.d. 469-80. 2 vols.

Dreiser, Theodore. *Sister Carrie*. New York: The Modern Library, 1997.

Eliot, George. *Middlemarch*. Ed. Rosemary Ashton. London: Penguin, 1994.

Eliot, T.S. *Four Quartets*. London: Faber and Faber, 1944.

Fielding, Henry. *The History of Tom Jones: A Foundling*. Introd. George Sherburn. New York: The Modern Library, 1950.

Fleming, Sandford. *England and Canada: A Summer Tour between Old and New Westminster with Historical Notes*. London: Sampson Low, Marston, Searle & Rivington, 1884.

-----. *The Intercolonial: A Historical Sketch of the Inception, Location, Construction and Completion of the Line of Railway Uniting the Inland and Atlantic Provinces of the Dominion, with Maps and Numerous Illustrations*. Montreal: Dawson Brothers, 1876.

-----. "Letter to the 150th Anniversary Committee." *Letter to His Honour the Lieut-Governor; Nova Scotia and the Empire; With Other Papers*. Halifax: McAlpine, 1908. 20-31.

-----. "Memories of the Mountains." *Canadian Alpine Journal* 1 (1907): 10-33.

-----. "A Proposed Historical Tower." *Letter to His Honour the Lieut-Governor; Nova Scotia and the Empire; With Other Papers*. Halifax: McAlpine, 1908. 13-14.

-----. *Report in Reference to the Canadian Pacific Railway*. Ottawa: n.p., 1879.

Fortner, Robert. "The Canadian Search for Identity, 1846-1914: Communication in an Imperial Context." *Canadian Journal of Communication* 6.1 (1979): 24-31.

Frye, Northrop. "Conclusion." *Literary History of Canada: Canadian Literature in English*. Gen. ed. Carl F. Klinck. Toronto: U of Toronto P, 1965. 821-49.

-----. "Preface to an Uncollected Anthology." *The Bush Garden: Essays on the Canadian Imagination*. Toronto: Anansi, 1971. 163-79.

-----. *Words with Power: Being a Second Study of the Bible and Literature*. San Diego, CA: Harcourt Brace Jovanovich, 1990.

Grant, George M. *Ocean to Ocean: Sandford Fleming's Expedition Through Canada in 1872*. London: Sampson Low, Marston, Low, & Earle, 1873.

The Great Train Robbery. Dir. Edwin S. Porter. Edison Manufacturing Company, 1903.

Green, Lorne. *Chief Engineer: Life of a Nation Builder — Sandford Fleming*. Toronto: Dundurn, 1993.

Halfe, Louise Bernice. *Blue Marrow*. Toronto: McClelland & Stewart, 1998.

Haliburton, Thomas Chandler. *The Clockmaker: Series One, Two, and Three*. Ed. George L. Parker. Ottawa: Carleton UP, 1995.

A Hard Day's Night. Dir. Richard Lester. United Artists, 1964.

Hochschild, Adam. *King Leopold's Ghost: A Story of Greed, Terror, and Heroism in Colonial Africa*. London: Macmillan, 1999.

Innis, H.A. *Empire and Communications*. Oxford, Eng.: Clarendon, 1950.

James, Henry. *The Ambassadors: An Authoritative Text; The Author on the Novel; Criticism*. Ed. S.P. Rosenbaum. New York: W.W. Norton, 1964. A Norton Critical Edition.

Johnston, Wayne. *The Colony of Unrequited Dreams*. Toronto: Alfred A. Knopf Canada, 1998.

Joyce, James. *Ulysses: Student's Edition*. The Corrected Text. Ed. Hans Walter Gabler with Wolfhard Steppe and Claus Melchior. Pref. Richard Ellmann. Harmondsworth, Eng.: Penguin, 1986.

King, Thomas. *Truth & Bright Water*. Toronto: HarperCollins, 1999.

Kreisel, Henry. "The Prairie: A State of Mind." *Contexts of Canadian Criticism*. Ed. and introd. Eli Mandel. Chicago: U of Chicago P, 1971. 254-66. Patterns of Literary Criticism.

The Lady Vanishes. Dir. Alfred Hitchcock. Gainsborough Pictures, 1938.

Leacock, Stephen. *My Remarkable Uncle and Other Sketches*. Afterword by Barbara Nimmo. Toronto: McClelland & Stewart, 2010. New Canadian Library.

Levine, Norman. *Canada Made Me*. Erin, ON: The Porcupine's Quill, 1993. Sherbrooke Street 5.

MacPherson, Jay. "The Anagogic Man." *The Boatman*. Toronto: Oxford UP, 1957. 56.

Mair, Charles. "The Last Bison." *The Dominion Illustrated* 8 Sept. 1888: 155.

Martin, Sandra, and Roger Hall, eds. *Rupert Brooke in Canada*. Toronto: PMA, 1978.

McNeil, Bill. *Voice of the Pioneer*. Toronto: Macmillan of Canada, 1978.

Morris, William. *The Earthly Paradise: A Poem*. New ed. London: Longmans, Green, 1898.

Munro, Alice. "Carried Away." *Open Secrets*. Toronto: McClelland & Stewart, 1994. 3-51.

-----. "Hateship, Friendship, Courtship, Loveship, Marriage." *Hateship, Friendship, Courtship, Loveship, Marriage*. Toronto: McClelland & Stewart, 2001. 1-52.

-----. "Wild Swans." *Who Do You Think You Are?* Toronto: Macmillan of Canada, 1978. 55-64.

-----. "Working for a Living." *The View from Castle Rock*. Toronto: McClelland & Stewart, 2006. 127-70.

North by Northwest. Dir. Alfred Hitchcock. Metro-Goldwyn-Mayer, 1959.

Our Hospitality. Dir. Jack Blystone and Buster Keaton. Joseph M. Schenck Productions, 1923.

Paglia, Camille. *Sexual Personae: Art and Decadence from Nefertiti to Emily Dickinson*. 1990. New York: Vintage, 1991.

Pang, Alex Soojung-Kim. *Empire and the Sun: Victorian Solar Eclipse Expeditions*. Stanford, CA: Stanford UP, 2002.

Pratt, E.J. *Towards the Last Spike*. 1952. *The Collected Poems of E.J. Pratt*. 2nd ed. Ed. and introd. Northrop Frye. Toronto:

Macmillan of Canada, 1958. 345-88.

Reaney, James. "Myths in Some Nineteenth-Century Ontario Newspapers." *Aspects of Nineteenth-Century Ontario: Essays Presented to James J. Talman.* Ed. F.H. Armstrong, H.A. Stevenson, and J.D. Wilson. Toronto: U of Toronto P, 1974. 253-66.

-----. "Night Train." *Poems.* Ed. Germaine Warkentin. Toronto: new, 1972. 8.

-----. "The Royal Visit." *Poems.* Ed. Germaine Warkentin. Toronto: new, 1972. 53.

-----. *A Suit of Nettles.* 3rd ed. Illus. Jim Westergard. Erin, ON: The Porcupine's Quill, 2010.

Riley, John L. *The Once and Future Great Lakes Country: An Ecological History.* Montreal & Kingston: McGill-Queen's UP, 2013.

Ruskin, John. *The Stones of Venice.* 3 vols. New York: John Wiley & Sons, 1876.

Schultz, Emily. "Down Bear Line." *Detours: An Anthology of Poets from Windsor & Essex County.* Ed. Susan Holbrook and Dawn Marie Kresan. Kingsville, ON: Palimpsest, 2012. 34-35.

Scott, F.R. "All the Spikes but the Last." *The Collected Poems of F.R. Scott.* Toronto: McClelland and Stewart, 1981. 194.

Shanghai Express. Dir. Josef von Sternberg. Paramount Pictures, 1932.

Some Like It Hot. Dir. Billy Wilder. Ashton Productions and the Mirisch Corporation, 1959.

Souster, Raymond. "Flight of the Roller-Coaster." *Collected Poems of Raymond Souster: Volume One 1940-55.* Ottawa: Oberon, 1980. 316.

Stevenson, Robert Louis. *From Scotland to Silverado.* Ed. James D. Hart. Cambridge, MA: Belknap-Harvard UP, 1966.

Strangers on a Train. Dir. Alfred Hitchcock. Warner Brothers, 1951.

Sullivan's Travels. Dir. Preston Sturges. Paramount Pictures, 1941.

Taylor, Leonard W. *The Sourdough and the Queen: The Many Lives of Klondike Joe Boyle*. Agincourt, ON: Methuen, 1983.

Thackeray, W.M. *Vanity Fair: A Novel without a Hero*. Introd. Catherine Peters. New York: Alfred A. Knopf, 1991. Everyman's Library.

Thompson, Graham M. "Sandford Fleming and the Pacific Cable: The Institutional Politics of Nineteenth-Century Imperial Telecommunications." *Canadian Journal of Communication* 15.2 (1990): 64-75.

Thoreau, Henry David. *Walden and Other Writings of Henry David Thoreau*. Ed. Brooks Atkinson. New York: The Modern Library, 1937.

3:10 to Yuma. Dir. Delmer Daves. Columbia Pictures, 1957.

"Time and Sandford Fleming." *The Royal Bank of Canada Monthly Letter* 59.8 (1978): [1-4].

Toews, Miriam. *Swing Low: A Life*. Toronto: Stoddart, 2000.

Turner, John Frayn. *The Life and Selected Works of Rupert Brooke*. Rev. ed. Barnsley, Eng.: Pen & Sword, 2004.

Underwood, Jay. "Fleming and Old 'King' Coal." *Canadian Rail* 506 May-June 2005: 102-12.

Verne, Jules. *Around the World in Eighty Days*. London: Puffin, 2004.

Waterston, Elizabeth. "Travel Books (1880-1920)." *Literary History of Canada: Canadian Literature in English*. Gen. ed. Carl F. Klinck. Toronto: U of Toronto P, 1965. 347-63.

Williams, Rosalind. *The Triumph of Human Empire: Verne, Morris, and Stevenson at the End of the World*. Chicago: U of Chicago P, 2013.

Wiseman, Adele. *The Sacrifice*. New York: Viking, 1956.

Wright, Richard B. *Clara Callan*. Toronto: HarperCollins, 2001.

Zwicky, Jan. "Robinson's Crossing." *Robinson's Crossing*. London, ON: Brick, 2004. 34-41.

A Checklist of Works
by Clark Blaise to 2015

J.R. (Tim) Struthers

1. Nonfiction and Essay Collections

Blaise, Clark, and Bharati Mukherjee. *The Sorrow and the Terror: The Haunting Legacy of the Air India Tragedy.* Markham, ON: Viking-Penguin, 1987. Rpt. with a new introd. by the authors. Markham, ON: Penguin Books Canada, 1988.

Blaise, Clark, and Bharati Mukherjee. *Le chagrin et la terreur.* Trans. Jean Chapdelaine Gagnon. Montreal: Éditions du Roseau, 1988.

Blaise, Clark, and Russell Brown. *The Border as Fiction*; and *Borderlines and Borderlands in English Canada: The Written Line.* By Clark Blaise; and Russell Brown. Orono, ME: Borderlands Project, The Canadian-American Center, U of Maine, 1990. 1-12. Borderlands Monograph Ser. 4.

Here, There and Everywhere. Tokyo: Center for Intl. Programs, Meiji U, 1994. Meiji U Intl. Exchange Programs Guest Lecture Ser. 1.

Time Lord: Sir Sandford Fleming and the Creation of Standard Time. London: Weidenfeld & Nicolson, 2000. New York: Pantheon, 2000. London: Phoenix-Orion Books, 2001. New York: Vintage Books-Random House, 2002.

*Time Lord: The Remarkable Canadian Who Missed His Train,
    and Changed the World.* Toronto: Alfred A. Knopf Canada,
    2000. Toronto: Vintage Canada-Random House of Canada,
    2001.

*Heer van de tijd: Een eenzaam genie en de uitvinding van de
    standaardtijd.* Trans. Patty Adelaar. Amsterdam, Neth.:
    Ambo, 2001.

*Il Signore del Tempo: L'avventurosa storia dell'uomo che ha
    creato una regola per gli orologi di tutto il mondo.* Trans.
    Tilde Riva. Pref. Giulio Giorello. Milan, It.: Bompiani
    Overlook, 2001. Trans. Tilde Riva. Pref. Giulio Giorello.
    Milan, It.: Tascabili Bompiani, 2003.

*Die Zähmung der Zeit: Sir Sandford Fleming und die Erfindung
    der Weltzeit.* Trans. Hans Günter Holl. Frankfurt, Ger.: S.
    Fischer, 2001. Trans. Hans Günter Holl. Frankfurt, Ger.:
    Fischer Taschenbuch-S. Fischer, 2004.

Note: Further translations of *Time Lord*, Blaise advises, include two in Chinese (Mandarin and Simplified) and one in
Korean.

Selected Essays. By Clark Blaise. Ed. John Metcalf and J.R.
    (Tim) Struthers. Windsor, ON: Biblioasis, 2008.

2. New 'Occasional' Critical Writing, Autobiographical Writing, and Nonfiction Writing: 2008-15

Note: For a detailed checklist of Clark Blaise's 'occasional'
critical writing, autobiographical writing, and nonfiction
writing to 2007, see J.R. (Tim) Struthers, "The World of Clark
Blaise: A Bibliography of His 'Occasional' Critical Writing,
Autobiographical Writing, and Nonfiction Writing," in Clark
Blaise, *Selected Essays*, ed. John Metcalf and J.R. (Tim)
Struthers (Windsor, ON: Biblioasis, 2008), 223-80.

Critical Writing

"1850, August 5; A Literary Party Climbs Monument Mountain: Nathaniel Hawthorne and Herman Melville." *A New Literary History of America*. Ed. Greil Marcus and Werner Sollors. Cambridge, MA: The Belknap Press of Harvard UP, 2009. 278-83.

Introduction. [*The Short Story Issue.*] *Canadian Notes & Queries* 79 (2010): 9-10.

"The Muse-C of Metcalf." *Canadian Notes & Queries* 88 (2013): 10-11.

Autobiographical Writing

"Autobiographical Annex: 1985-2006." *Selected Essays*. By Clark Blaise. Ed. John Metcalf and J.R. (Tim) Struthers. Windsor, ON: Biblioasis, 2008. 209-21.

Nonfiction Writing

Mukherjee, Bharati, and Clark Blaise. "She Said, He Said: The Romance of Food in Our Marriage." *World Literature Today* 83.1 (2009): 24-29.

3. Autobiography and Autobiofiction

Blaise, Clark, and Bharati Mukherjee. *Days and Nights in Calcutta*. Garden City, NY: Doubleday, 1977. Rpt. with a new joint epilogue by the authors. Markham, ON: Penguin

Books Canada, 1986. Rpt. with a new prologue by Blaise and a new epilogue by Mukherjee in place of joint epilogue added in 1986. Saint Paul, MN: Hungry Mind, 1995.

Resident Alien. Markham, ON: Penguin Books Canada, 1986.

I Had a Father: A Post-Modern Autobiography. Reading, MA: Addison-Wesley, 1993. Toronto: HarperCollins, 1993.

4. Novels

Lunar Attractions. Garden City, NY: Doubleday, 1979. Toronto: Doubleday Canada, 1979. Toronto: Seal Books-McClelland and Stewart-Bantam, 1980. London: Melbourne, 1981. Toronto: Bantam, 1983. Introd. Clark Blaise. Erin, ON: The Porcupine's Quill, 1990. Sherbrooke Street 3. Windsor, ON: Biblioasis, 2015. ReSet Books.

Lusts. Garden City, NY: Doubleday, 1983. Markham, ON: Penguin Books Canada, 1984.

5. Novels-in-Stories

If I Were Me: A Novel. Erin, ON: The Porcupine's Quill, 1997. Rpt. (expanded) in *World Body.* Introd. Michael Augustin. Erin, ON: The Porcupine's Quill, 2006. 13-117. Vol. 4 of *The Selected Stories of Clark Blaise.* 4 vols. 2000-06.

The Meagre Tarmac: Stories. Windsor, ON: Biblioasis, 2011.

6. Story Collections

"Thibidault et fils." MFA thesis Iowa 1964.

New Canadian Writing, 1968: Stories by David Lewis Stein, Clark Blaise and Dave Godfrey. Toronto: Clarke, Irwin, 1968.

A North American Education: A Book of Short Fiction. Toronto: Doubleday Canada, 1973. Garden City, NY: Doubleday, 1973. Don Mills, ON: PaperJacks, 1974. Toronto: General, 1984. New Press Canadian Classics.

Tribal Justice. Toronto: Doubleday Canada, 1974. Garden City, NY: Doubleday, 1974. Don Mills, ON: PaperJacks, 1975. Toronto: General, 1984. New Press Canadian Classics.
La justice tribale. Trans. Claire Martin. Montreal: Pierre Tisseyre, 1985. Collection des deux solitudes.

Man and His World. Erin, ON: The Porcupine's Quill, 1992.

Southern Stories. Introd. Fenton Johnson. Erin, ON: The Porcupine's Quill, 2000. Vol. 1 of *The Selected Stories of Clark Blaise.* 4 vols. 2000-06.

Pittsburgh Stories. Introd. Robert Boyers. Erin, ON: The Porcupine's Quill, 2001. Vol. 2 of *The Selected Stories of Clark Blaise.* 4 vols. 2000-06.

Montreal Stories. Introd. Peter Behrens. Erin, ON: The Porcupine's Quill, 2003. Vol. 3 of *The Selected Stories of Clark Blaise.* 4 vols. 2000-06.

World Body. Introd. Michael Augustin. Erin, ON: The Porcupine's Quill, 2006. Vol. 4 of *The Selected Stories of Clark Blaise.* 4 vols. 2000-06.

7. Collected Stories

New Canadian Writing, 1968: Stories by David Lewis Stein, Clark Blaise and Dave Godfrey. Toronto: Clarke, Irwin, 1968. "The Fabulous Eddie Brewster." 69-89. "How I Became a Jew." 90-105. "The Examination." 106-20. "Notes Beyond a History." 121-34.

A North American Education: A Book of Short Fiction. Toronto: Doubleday Canada, 1973. Garden City, NY: Doubleday, 1973. "A Class of New Canadians." 3-15. "Eyes." 16-24. "Words for the Winter." 25-37. "Extractions and Contractions." 41-58. "Going to India." 59-83. "Continent of Strangers: A Love Story of the Recent Past." 84-129. "The Bridge." 133-41. "The Salesman's Son Grows Older." 142-61. "A North American Education." 162-84. "Snow People: A Novella." 185-230.

Tribal Justice. Toronto: Doubleday Canada, 1974. Garden City, NY: Doubleday, 1974. "Broward Dowdy." 3-14. "Relief." 15-26. "The Fabulous Eddie Brewster." 27-46. "Grids and Doglegs." 47-61. "I'm Dreaming of Rocket Richard." 63-72. "The Seizure." 75-89. "Notes Beyond a History." 91-104. "How I Became a Jew." 105-19. "The March." 121-95. "At the Lake." 199-208. "He Raises Me Up." 209-15. "Among the Dead." 217-24.

Resident Alien. Markham, ON: Penguin Books Canada, 1986. "South." 47-57. "Identity." 61-75. "North." 79-105. "Translation." 109-59.

Man and His World. Erin, ON: The Porcupine's Quill, 1992. "A Tour around My Father." 9-25. "Meditations on Starch." 27-37. "Did, Had, Was." 39-55. "Dunkelblau." 57-68. "Snake in Flight over Pittsburgh." 69-85. "Man and His World." 87-100. "Partial Renovations." 101-11. "Sweetness and Light." 113-29. "The Love God." 131-43.

If I Were Me: A Novel. Erin, ON: The Porcupine's Quill, 1997. "Prologue: Strangers in the Night." 9-11. "Salad Days." 13-17. "A Saint." 19-22. "Kristallnacht." 23-26. "Drawing Rooms." 27-32. "The Banality of Virtue." 33-44. "White Children." 45-70. "Doggystan." 71-80. "Dark Matter." 81-105. "Epilogue: Yahrzeit." 107-12.

Southern Stories. Introd. Fenton Johnson. Erin, ON: The Porcupine's Quill, 2000. Vol. 1 of *The Selected Stories of Clark Blaise.* 4 vols. 2000-06.
"A Fish Like a Buzzard." 13-24. "Giant Turtles, Gliding in the Dark." 25-39. "Broward Dowdy." 41-50. "The Bridge." 51-56. "A North American Education." 57-71. "The Salesman's Son Grows Older." 73-86. "Relief." 87-96. "Notes Beyond a History." 97-108. "How I Became a Jew." 109-22. "South." 123-30. "The Fabulous Eddie Brewster." 131-48. "Snow People: A Novella." 149-78. "The Love God." 179-90.

Pittsburgh Stories. Introd. Robert Boyers. Erin, ON: The Porcupine's Quill, 2001. Vol. 2 of *The Selected Stories of Clark Blaise.* 4 vols. 2000-06.
"The Birth of the Blues." 15-25. "The Unwanted Attention of Strangers." 27-39. "Identity." 41-50. "Grids and Doglegs." 51-63. "The Seizure." 65-77. "Dunkelblau." 79-90. "Snake in Flight over Pittsburgh." 91-106. "Sitting Shivah with Cousin Bennie." 107-23. "The Waffle Maker." 125-42.

Montreal Stories. Introd. Peter Behrens. Erin, ON: The Porcupine's Quill, 2003. Vol. 3 of *The Selected Stories of Clark Blaise.* 4 vols. 2000-06.

"North." 15-33. "I'm Dreaming of Rocket Richard." 35-43. "Eyes." 45-50. "A Class of New Canadians." 51-59. "Extractions and Contractions." 61-72. "At the Lake." 73-81. "Among the Dead." 83-89. "He Raises Me Up." 91-96. "Words for the Winter." 97-105. "Going to India." 107-22. "Translation." 123-58. "Life Could Be a Dream (Sh-boom, Sh-boom)." 159-68. "The Belle of Shediac." 169-82.

World Body. Introd. Michael Augustin. Erin, ON: The Porcupine's Quill, 2006. Vol. 4 of *The Selected Stories of Clark Blaise.* 4 vols. 2000-06.

"Strangers in the Night." 13-15. "Salad Days." 17-20. "A Saint." 21-24. "Kristallnacht." 25-27. "Drawing Rooms." 29-33. "The Banality of Virtue." 35-45. "White Children." 47-70. "Doggystan." 71-79. "Dark Matter." 81-104. "Migraine Morning." 105-11. "Yahrzeit." 113-17. "Meditations on Starch." 119-28. "Did, Had, Was." 129-43. "Sweetness and Light." 145-59. "Man and His World." 161-73. "Dear Abhi." 175-87. "The Sociology of Love." 189-99. "Partial Renovations." 201-10.

The Meagre Tarmac: Stories. Windsor, ON: Biblioasis, 2011. "The Sociology of Love." 9-23. "In Her Prime." 24-37. "The Dimple Kapadia of Camino Real." 38-48. "Dear Abhi." 49-65. "Brewing Tea in the Dark." 66-77. "The Quality of Life." 78-96. "A Connie da Cunha Book." 97-112. "Waiting for Romesh." 113-24. "Potsy and Pansy." 125-46. "Isfahan." 147-62. "Man and Boy." 163-78.

8. New Stories

"We Are All Illegals." *13: Best Canadian Stories.* Ed. John Metcalf. Ottawa: Oberon, 2013. 152-65.

"The Kerouac Who Never Was." *14: Best Canadian Stories.* Ed. John Metcalf. Ottawa: Oberon, 2014. 70-79.

9. Works Edited

Blaise, Clark, and John Metcalf, eds. *Here & Now: Best Canadian Stories.* Ottawa: Oberon, 1977.

Metcalf, John, and Clark Blaise, eds. *78: Best Canadian Stories.* Ottawa: Oberon, 1978.

Blaise, Clark, and John Metcalf, eds. *79: Best Canadian Stories.* Ottawa: Oberon, 1979.

Blaise, Clark, and John Metcalf, eds. *80: Best Canadian Stories.* Ottawa: Oberon, 1980.

Blaise, Clark, and Sheila Fischman, eds. *Canadian Feature Issue: English Literature and Littérature du Québec. Translation: The Journal of Literary Translation* 20 (1988).

About the Writer

CLARK BLAISE is one of the most accomplished, most exciting, most prophetic writers in North America — the author of some twenty books of fiction, autobiography, and nonfiction beginning with the richly textured and dramatically powerful story cycle *A North American Education* (1973). His considerable qualities as a writer are exhibited supremely in *If I Were Me* (1997), the four-volume *Selected Stories of Clark Blaise* (2000-06), and *The Meagre Tarmac* (2011), in *I Had a Father* (1993), *Time Lord* (2000), and his *Selected Essays* (2008), and in many other titles. Along with his signal achievements as a writer, Clark Blaise has enjoyed a profoundly influential career as a writing and literature teacher in universities throughout the world and as a major arts administrator — Director for nine years of the prestigious International Writing Program at the University of Iowa and, before that, founder of the graduate program in Creative Writing at Concordia University in Montreal. Clark Blaise holds honorary doctorates from Denison University (1979), McGill University (2004), and Concordia University (2013) and was made an Officer of the Order of Canada in 2010. He now lives in New York City with his wife, the writer Bharati Mukherjee.

About the Artist

RON SHUEBROOK is a Canadian artist who is Professor Emeritus at OCAD University in Toronto where he served as President from 2000 to 2005 and as Vice-President, Academic from 1998 to 2002. He has taught and been an administrator at six other Canadian universities and art schools and is a former President of the Royal Canadian Academy of Arts and a former President of the Universities Art Association of Canada. He received an Honorary Doctorate from OCAD in 2005 as well as a Queen Elizabeth II Diamond Jubilee Medal in 2012. He is currently Senior Artist in Residence at Boarding House Arts in Guelph, Ontario. Shuebrook exhibits nationally and internationally and is represented by Olga Korper Gallery as well as other galleries. His work is in more than sixty public and corporate collections, including the National Gallery of Canada and the Art Gallery of Ontario, and in numerous private collections. An image of an untitled painting of his from 1989 (in the Art Gallery of Guelph collection) is reproduced in *Abstract Painting in Canada* by Roald Nasgaard. He lives in Guelph, Ontario and Blandford, Nova Scotia.

About the Editor

Highly respected nationally and internationally by scholars and creative writers for his work as a bibliographer, an interviewer, a literary critic, an editor, and the publisher of Red Kite Press, J.R. (TIM) STRUTHERS has edited some twenty-five volumes of theory, criticism, autobiography, fiction, and poetry—including works in honour of, or by, such important writers as Clark Blaise, George Elliott, Jack Hodgins, Hugh Hood, John Metcalf, and Alice Munro. For over forty years he has been writing about Canadian literature, particularly the short story, including, in 1975, the first two scholarly articles published world-wide on Alice Munro. He has conducted some forty interviews with Canadian writers and has been described by W.J. Keith, FRSC, as "probably the best literary interviewer in Canada." An enthusiastic teacher, he has taught English full-time at the University of Guelph for over thirty years. Tim lives in Guelph with his bride of forty years, poet and scholar Marianne Micros, inspired and delighted by the company of their two daughters, Eleni and Joy, and their four grandchildren, Matteo, Rowan, Asher, and Reed.

Contributor Biographies

MARGARET ATWOOD is the author of more than forty books of fiction, poetry, and critical essays. Her latest book of short stories is *Stone Mattress: Nine Tales* (2014). Her *MaddAddam* trilogy — the Giller- and Booker-Prize-nominated *Oryx and Crake* (2003), *The Year of the Flood* (2009), and *MaddAddam* (2013) — is currently being adapted for HBO. *The Door* (2007) is her latest volume of poetry. Her most recent nonfiction books are *Payback: Debt and the Shadow Side of Wealth* (2008) and *In Other Worlds: SF and the Human Imagination* (2011). Her novels include *The Blind Assassin*, winner of the Booker Prize; *Alias Grace*, which won the Giller Prize in Canada and the Premio Mondello in Italy; and *The Robber Bride*, *Cat's Eye*, and *The Handmaid's Tale*. Her new novel, *The Heart Goes Last*, was published in September 2015. Margaret Atwood lives in Toronto with writer Graeme Gibson.

WILLIAM BUTT has published articles in Canada, the U.S.A., Europe, and Africa. He has written drama scripts for CBC television, and has had six of his theatre scripts produced. He was co-founder and for several years artistic director of a music and video production studio in Mozambique, where he was based as communications consultant for the United Church of Canada. He has published criticism on Canadian writers including Margaret Avison, Clark Blaise, George Elliott, Robert Gourlay, Jack

Hodgins, Eli Mandel, Alice Munro, and P.K. Page as well as *Behind Our Doors: A Memoir of Esther Warmerdam as Told to William Butt* (2011), reminiscences of World War Two in Holland by a woman who was then a teenage girl. He has a Ph.D. in English from Western University, and lives now in Southwestern Ontario.

STEPHEN HENIGHAN is Professor of Hispanic Studies in the School of Languages and Literatures at the University of Guelph. Henighan is the author of more than thirty refereed articles published in international scholarly journals and more than forty-five short stories published in Canadian and international magazines and anthologies. A finalist for the Governor General's Literary Award and the Canada Prize in the Humanities, he is the author of more than a dozen books, including *Sandino's Nation: Ernesto Cardenal and Sergio Ramírez Writing Nicaragua, 1940-2012* (2014) and the novel *The Path of the Jaguar* (forthcoming in 2016).

ROBERT LECKER is Greenshields Professor of English at McGill University, where he specializes in Canadian literature. Lecker was the co-editor of the critical journal *Essays on Canadian Writing* from 1975 to 2004 and the co-publisher at ECW Press from 1977 to 2003. He is the editor of several anthologies, most recently *Open Country: Canadian Literature in English* (2007). Lecker is the author of numerous books and articles, including *On the Line: Readings in the Short Fiction of Clark Blaise, John Metcalf, and Hugh Hood* (1982); *Robert Kroetsch* (1986); *Another I: The Fictions of Clark Blaise* (1988); *Making It*

Real: The Canonization of English-Canadian Literature (1995); *Dr. Delicious: Memoirs of a Life in CanLit* (2006); *The Cadence of* Civil Elegies (2006); and *Keepers of the Code: English-Canadian Literary Anthologies and the Representation of Nation* (2013). His most recent edited volume is *Anthologizing Canadian Literature: Theoretical and Cultural Perspectives* (2015).

ALEXANDER MacLEOD is an Associate Professor of English and Atlantic Canada Studies at Saint Mary's University in Halifax, Nova Scotia. His research is focussed on theories of literary regionalism, social space, and cultural geography. He is the author of the short story collection *Light Lifting* (2010), which was shortlisted for the Scotiabank Giller Prize and The Frank O'Connor International Short Story Award.

ANDREW C. McKAGUE holds an Honours B.A. and M.A. in English from the University of Guelph, an MLIS from Western University, and an LL.B. from the University of Windsor. He practises civil litigation with the law firm Zarek Taylor Grossman Hanrahan LLP in Toronto.

W.H. NEW, OC, FRSC, is University Killam Professor Emeritus at the University of British Columbia. Poet and children's writer, he is the author of fifteen artistic works, including such shortlisted and prize-winning books as *Underwood Log* (2004), *YVR* (2011), and *The Year I Was Grounded* (2008). Editor of the journal *Canadian Literature* for seventeen years (1977-95), he has also edited thirty volumes of prose, verse, criticism, and research aids, including *Encyclopedia of Literature in Canada* (2002) and other works, and has written numerous critical commentaries on the English-language writings of the Commonwealth and the art of the short story. His critical works include *Dreams of Speech and Violence: The Art of the Short Story in Canada and New Zealand* (1987); *A History of Canadian Literature* (1989, 2nd ed., 2003); *Land Sliding: Imagining Space, Presence, and Power in Canadian Writing* (1997); *Borderlands: How We Talk about Canada* (1998); *Reading Mansfield and Metaphors of Form* (1999); *Grandchild of Empire: About Irony, Mainly in the Commonwealth* (2003); and over a hundred essays.

GRAEME NORTHCOTE holds an Honours B.A. and M.A. in English from the University of Guelph and is currently a Ph.D. candidate at the University of Waterloo, teaching courses in English Language and Literature. His studies are focussed on the influential intersections between narrative principles and those of modern sociocultural technostructures and on critical and literary techniques pertaining to the mechanics of the short story.

CATHERINE SHELDRICK ROSS is Professor Emerita at Western University, where she taught in the English Department and in the Faculty of Information and Media Studies (FIMS) and also served in various administrative roles including Acting Dean of Graduate Studies and Dean of FIMS. Interested in texts, authorship, and reading, she has published articles on Canadian writers as well as interviews with Canadian writers, including authors of children's books. Her published books include four information books for children, two books on communication and interviewing written for practising librarians, a biography, *Alice Munro: A Double Life* (1992), and two books on the experience of reading for pleasure: *Reading Matters: What the Research Reveals about Reading, Libraries, and Community* (2006) and most recently *The Pleasures of Reading: A Booklover's Alphabet* (2014).

SANDRA SABATINI is the author of two collections of short stories, *The One with the News* (2000) and *The Dolphins at Sainte-Marie* (2006), one novel, *Dante's War* (2009), and a scholarly study, *Making Babies: Infants in Canadian Fiction* (2003). She lives and works in Guelph, Ontario.

SANDRA SINGER is Associate Professor of English in the School of English and Theatre Studies, University of Guelph, where she has taught since 1995. Her primary scholarship concerns Doris Lessing, in which capacity she has co-edited *Doris Lessing Studies* (2003-14) and two essay collections: *Doris Lessing: Interrogating the Times* (2010; rpt. in pbk., 2015) and *Doris Lessing's* The Golden Notebook *After Fifty* (2015). Her current projects concern fiction, trauma, and terrorism: she has published, in narrative studies, on work by Kate Chopin, Michael Cunningham, and Eden Robinson; in trauma studies, on texts by Wayson Choy, J.J. Steinfeld, Aryeh Lev Stollman, Rebecca Wells, Jonathan Wilson, and Rose Zwi; and in terrorist fiction, on writing by Don DeLillo, Ghassan Kanafani, Colum McCann, Ian McEwan, Claire Messud, Joseph O'Neill, and Bernhard Schlink, amongst others.

DALBIR SINGH is an academic, educator, playwright, editor, and artist. He has edited two books of critical and creative work for Playwrights Canada Press, which include the first anthologies on the topics of South Asian Canadian Theatre and Post-Colonial Canadian Theatre. He has also co-edited a book of critical essays on Tamil culture for TSAR Publications (now Mawenzi House) and currently serves as the Associate Editor of the magazine *Alt.Theatre: Cultural Diversity and the Stage*. His plays include *Your Palace in the Sky: The Bombing of Air India Flight 182*, which was dramaturged by two-time Governor General's award winner Judith Thompson and staged at the SummerWorks Festival in Toronto. He currently is a Ph.D. candidate in the Graduate Department of Drama at the University of Toronto.

RAY SMITH was born in Mabou, Cape Breton, but spent most of his early years in Halifax, where he attended Dalhousie University; he also holds an M.A. in English from Concordia University. From 1971 to 2007 he taught English at Dawson College in Montreal. On retirement he moved to the family home built by his grandfather in Mabou. Described by *The Oxford Companion to Canadian Literature* as "a brilliant stylist," he nonetheless has no single Smith style; each of his seven books of fiction is unique. They include *Cape Breton is the Thought-Control Centre of Canada* (1969), *Lord Nelson Tavern* (1974), *Century* (1986), *A Night at the Opera* (1992), *The Man Who Loved Jane Austen* (1999), *The Man Who Hated Emily Brontë* (2004), and *The Flush of Victory: Jack Bottomly Among the Virgins* (2007). Although usually set in Canada with Canadian characters, the books reflect Smith's extensive travel and international perspective.

J.R. (TIM) STRUTHERS' essay on Clark Blaise's story "A Fish Like a Buzzard" was featured in 2011 as the lead essay in the inaugural issue of the British journal *Short Fiction in Theory and Practice*. In addition to the essay on Clark Blaise's story "The Birth of the Blues" published here, his recent critical writing includes five essays on Alice Munro — among them, a greatly expanded version published in *Short Story Criticism*, Vol. 208 (2015) of the pioneering 1975 essay "Alice Munro and the American South." His extensive bibliographical work includes seminal research on Clark Blaise, Jack Hodgins, Hugh Hood, John Metcalf, Alice Munro, and Leon Rooke. Recently, a bibliography of "Recommended Reading for Appreciating Alice Munro's 'Meneseteung'" appeared in the *Alice Munro: A Souwesto Celebration* issue that Tim co-edited with poet John B. Lee for *Windsor Review* (2014). And as a supplement to "The World of Clark Blaise: A Bibliography of His 'Occasional' Critical Writing, Autobiographical Writing, and Nonfiction Writing" published in Clark Blaise's *Selected Essays* (2008), he has prepared for the present volume "A Checklist of Works by Clark Blaise to 2015."

ALLAN WEISS is Associate Professor of English and Humanities at York University, where he has taught since 1990. His research interests are in Canadian fiction and fantastic literature. He is Chair of the Academic Conference on Canadian Science Fiction and Fantasy and has edited three collections of proceedings from that conference, most recently *The Canadian Fantastic in Focus* (2014). Among his publications are articles on Canadian literature, science fiction and fantasy, and the short story. He is also the author of about two dozen short stories; his story cycle *Living Room* appeared in 2001 and another collection is forthcoming in 2016.

MARY WILLIAMS holds a BFA from the Nova Scotia College of Art and Design and an M.A. in English from McGill University. She lives and works in Montreal.

Acknowledgements

Margaret Atwood's "Ariel or Caliban?" was first published in *The New York Review of Books*. Copyright O.W. Toad Ltd.

Robert Lecker's essay is reproduced from his book *An Other I: The Fictions of Clark Blaise*, published by ECW Press.

An earlier version of Alexander MacLeod's essay was published in *Canadian Notes & Queries*.

An earlier version of Andrew C. McKague's essay was published in *Short Story*.

An earlier version of Catherine Sheldrick Ross's essay was published by The University of Calgary Press in *The Clark Blaise Papers: First Accession and Second Accession: An Inventory of the Archive at The University of Calgary Libraries*, comp. Marlys Chevrefils, ed. Jean F. Tener and Apollonia Steele.

Ray Smith's essay was first published in *Short Story*.

Mary Williams' essay was first published in *Essays on Canadian Writing*.

J.R. (Tim) Struthers wishes to thank Ph.D. candidate Alec Follett and undergraduate students Kelsey McCallum, Will Wellington, and Kelly Wighton at the University of Guelph for their conscientious and very good-humoured service as research assistants at different stages while he prepared the companion volumes *Clark Blaise: Essays on His Works* and *Clark Blaise: The Interviews* for Guernica.

Printed in March 2016
by Gauvin Press,
Gatineau, Québec